Dynamic Systems of Develop

THE DEVELOPING BODY AND MIND

Series Editor:
Professor George Butterworth, *Department of Psychology, University of Sussex*

Designed for a broad readership in the English-speaking world, this major series represents the best of contemporary research and theory in the cognitive, social, abnormal and biological areas of development.

Dynamic Systems of Development

Change between Complexity and Chaos

Paul van Geert

HARVESTER WHEATSHEAF

New York   London   Toronto   Sydney   Tokyo   Singapore

First published 1994 by
Harvester Wheatsheaf
Campus 400, Maylands Avenue
Hemel Hempstead
Hertfordshire, HP2 7EZ
A division of
Simon & Schuster International Group

Typeset in 10/12 pt Ehrhardt
by Vision Typesetting, Manchester

Printed and bound in Great Britain by
T J Press (Padstow) Ltd

British Library Cataloguing in Publication Data

A catalogue record for this book is available from
the British Library

ISBN 0–7450–1136–5

1   2   3   4   5   98   97   96   95   94

Contents

Prologue:
Models, concrete and wooden shoes

In 1918 my grandfather returned from World War I. He had served in the trenches, dug deep into the soil of Flanders' fields, where the poppies grew. Under the blasts of bombs and shellfire, he had lost his hearing, a condition he put to use later when he had to deal with unsatisfied clients or with my grandmother. He started a small contractor firm and he became well known for his technical creativity as well as for his great sense of the absurd. In the years between the wars, it was often difficult to get the right building materials, and sometimes his clients did not have enough money to pay for them. He would then almost invariably come up with the solution to use concrete, instead of the hardwood, marble or grey stone that was required. Concrete was cheap – and my grandfather made concrete out of virtually anything – and could be poured into almost any form and given almost any finish, provided the right sort of technique was used.

His biggest feat – at least one for which he will be remembered forever – came during World War II. Workmen wore wooden shoes in those days. They were cheap, comfortable and warm. Due to the reduction in supplies caused by the war, the limewood out of which the wooden shoes were cut became increasingly difficult to obtain. My grandfather got the brilliant idea to use concrete to make wooden shoes. He experimented with moulds and different sorts of concrete. Meanwhile, about half the neighbourhood, under the guidance no doubt of my grandmother, tried to persuade him that his attempts were futile. Wooden shoes were light, and concrete was heavy; wooden shoes were warm, and concrete was cold; wooden shoes protected the feet from getting wet and concrete would suck up water like a thirsty camel. None of these arguments could change my grandfather's mind. He told them that wooden shoes made out of wood are great, if there is any. But concrete wooden shoes, he said, are better than no wooden shoes at all. He continued to experiment until the war was over and wooden shoes became available again. In the neighbourhood my grandfather was known as Leon Concrete, which in Flemish sounded more poetically, Leon Beton.

What did my grandfather teach me about scientific work? Nothing in particular, I am afraid, but I attribute a particular style of work, model building, to his influence. Scientists are used to make a distinction between the world out there on the one hand, with facts and phenomena to be known and explained and on the other hand, our theories and models. The question to be asked then is: To what extent do the theories and models present a recognizable true picture of the facts and phenomena in the world? The criteria to which the picture is subjected typically involve notions such as isomorphy, similarity, correspondence or likeness. The building metaphor pictures a different approach. Facts and models are not independent of one another; they grow along with the process of model construction. A model is a building, it serves a variety of functions. It protects you against the storms of criticism, it serves as a haven and retreat from the precipitation of unordered knowledge. The question whether a building process has been successful or not is decided on criteria of stability, comfort and aesthetic pleasure. Does your building collapse if left alone, can it withstand an earthquake? How easily can it accommodate visitors, bringing in new facts and unexpected viewpoints? I admit that all this is rather vague, but I never promised I would go beyond the confines of the metaphorical in this prologue.

This book is about a view on development and a technique of model building that only recently began to attract the attention of developmental psychologists. That view and technique are associated with the notion of dynamic systems, of non-linearity, self-organization and of complexity and chaos. All these terms come from mathematical and physical disciplines where they have been defined and studied in rigorous ways. When applied metaphorically to the psychological domain they seem to obtain an almost magical connotation. They open vast new horizons to the imaginative: chaos in personality, self-organization in development, bifurcations in behaviour, strange attractors in thinking. I am afraid, however, that readers of this book will discover that I am only the grandson of Leon Concrete, a man who was never scared of using his imagination, as long as he could pour it in a concrete form.

In this book I have emphasized the constructive or building aspects. I have not really attempted to show that the dynamic portrait is a picture that resembles the face of reality better than all those other portraits that have been painted before. The problem is that we know surprisingly little about that face of reality as far as it relates to the dynamics of development. Certainly, an incredible number of facts about children and age have been collected over the years, but it is remarkable how little these facts tell about dynamics and change.

In this book I construct the rough outlines of a building that is meant to accommodate more children, guests and friends than are currently around. If they do not show up in the future, the place will remain depressingly empty. That is to say, I develop a model that is currently only very moderately supported by available facts and data. A lot more research is needed of a rather different kind than is generally available.

The constructive or building aspect also shows in a second way. Throughout the book I describe the process of model construction explicitly. Especially in the second part of the book, starting with Chapter 4, the chapters contain a lot of 'tutorial' boxes (models) explaining in as much detail as possible how simple dynamic models can be built and tested. Instead of presenting a model of development, I present a way of building models, models of a particular kind, for sure. In accordance with my own view on the function of building however, I believe, or at least I hope, that presenting a construction procedure will at the same time present a new sort of model and approach to development.

There is a third sense in which the author of these pages sees himself as the grandson of Leon Concrete. My grandfather used concrete just about everywhere in his buildings, where others would have used wood, marble or steel. By doing this, he could build for almost everybody, where others had to wait and sometimes wait very long, for the few clients who could afford the expensive materials. My concrete is the spreadsheet and the type of models that are easily built in the form of spreadsheets. Spreadsheets are relatively cheap computer programs that will do computations over columns and rows of cells. Almost everybody has one and in most cases people use them to calculate their income taxes, or to enter data from an experiment and draw a diagram. It is amazing, though, how versatile they are, and how much they can teach you about unexpected aspects of developmental models. No doubt a variety of techniques and computer programs exist that are better suited for particular model-building tasks. For those who have the time, the money and the talent, the alternative and better-suited models are certainly worthwhile. But my grandfather would have heartily agreed that for those who are used to carrying the burden on their shoulders, the use of a wheelbarrow is already a major improvement. On the other hand, every now and then everyone is likely to run into a problem that even my grandfather could not solve, namely how to make wooden shoes out of concrete.

The book contains nine major chapters, divided in two parts. Chapters 1 to 3 explain the notion of dynamic systems as applied to developmental processes. Chapter 1 discusses the concept of development in general and some interesting problems and insights that are rarely taken into account in developmental theories. It introduces the notion of an iterative process, which is central to the dynamic system approach described in this book. The chapter also discusses the notion of an abstract space of properties and defines development as a particular trajectory through such an abstract space. Chapter 2 presents various types of trajectories or developmental paths. Its starting point lies in a generalized notion of a dynamic system and prototypical paths of change that such systems follow. It deals with the different ways in which a dynamic system, including developmental theories, can be represented. It shows how radically those representations differ from the common view on what a developmental theory or model describes and how. Chapter 3 presents a general approach to problems of measurement and empirical methods of investigation. It focuses on the problem of measurement error and tries to answer some of the problems raised in Chapter 2 by conceiving psychological measurement as a dynamic process in itself. The chapter is not aiming at describing and explaining specific statistical methods for checking dynamic models against available data. The discussion is rather philosophical and I am afraid not very practical and probably disappointing to those readers who expected to find something about research methods and statistical techniques.

The second part of the book discusses the dynamic models and the procedures for building them. Chapter 4 introduces the fundamental notion of growth as a dynamic process and applies this general model to psychological development. Chapter 5 discusses a second type of change, namely sudden qualitative transitions, and presents a model that puts the gradual and transitional change under a general framework of change and growth. It addresses, among other topics, the eventual fractal nature of development. Chapter 6 deals with a third type of change, namely one that amounts to oscillations or cycles. Development is usually seen as a trajectory towards a higher stable level. Many processes of change, however, amount to cycles visiting similar sequences of states over and over again. Chapter 7 explains the ecology of development in terms of connections among 'growers'. Connection patterns account for qualitatively different macroscopic forms of development. The chapter also discusses basic connections in simple systems consisting of only two growers, such as two positively interacting skills. Chapter 8 presents a case history of actual model building. It describes the attempt of Kurt Fischer and myself to build a dynamic growth model of Fischer's developmental model and data. I have chosen a case history instead of a systematic account of model-building techniques, in the hope that a case history manages to give a better idea of how model building actually works. Chapter 9 deals with social developmental dynamics and invokes the various relationships between a 'tutor' and a 'tutee' involved in a process of co–constructing the tutee's knowledge and skills.

The tutorials present a detailed account of model-building procedures. Readers who are not familiar with spreadsheets should first become acquainted with the elementary spreadsheet techniques. The fastest and easiest way is to ask a more experienced user to assist in building some of the simple models. I have chosen to explain the models with one particular spreadsheet program, Lotus 1-2-3 for Windows. Lotus 1-2-3 is probably the most widespread program of this kind. It is also available for Apple Macintosh computers. The non-windows and windows versions are highly similar. Other spreadsheet programs, such as Quattro Pro and Excel differ only in the way the menus and instructions work. They are similar, however, as far as the form of the equations is concerned. With a little help from the manuals, it should not be too difficult to translate the Lotus 1-2-3 into Quattro Pro and Excel procedures. Recently, Lotus has released a spreadsheet with a radically different setup, called Lotus Improv. Improv users who have never used the classic version will have to invest more translation efforts, given the form of the equations and models in the book. During the year we worked on Kurt Fischer's model, Kurt changed from Lotus 1-2-3 to Improv. Improv proved a real improvement as far as the transparency of the equations was concerned. It was considerably less time consuming than 1-2-3 to write down the equations and models, but proved to be rather cumbersome and inflexible in its graphics. Newer releases will no doubt improve that. Readers who are used to a programming language such as BASIC or C can easily build the models in their favourite language. The spreadsheets compute iterative loops of simple equations and do so for a fixed number of repetitions. Loops of this kind are easily modelled in standard programming languages. Nevertheless, I would recommend absolute novices to study the spreadsheet program approach.

Let me also say a few words about the style of the book. Maybe it is not a very good example of what a scientific book should look like. I introduce many of the problems and models with little personal stories. For some unexplained reason, these stories and memories came to my mind more or less accidentally when I was preparing the chapters and sections. Maybe they can serve as anchor points for the many abstract principles presented in this book. Maybe they make it more easy to swallow the rows of equations that make so many chapters less agreeable to read. And maybe some readers will be rather irritated by these little confessions and reminiscences of my past, but I hope they are prepared to excuse me for such idiosyncrasies as my grandfather's wooden shoes and my first visits to the local café. On the other hand, I felt that presenting the content matter of this book in the usual rather formal manner would not have corresponded with the status of the ideas presented here. They are still in the process of making, often more intuitively than systematically justified. They present a way of viewing rather than a view itself. I wanted to share the process of thinking and model building with the reader and hoped that the somewhat impressionist style of many chapters would enable me to better communicate that intention.

This book is the product of a sabbatical year that I spent at the Center for Advanced Study in the Behavioral Sciences at Stanford, California, which was made possible by a grant from the John D. and Catherine T. MacArthur Foundation, and by the support from the Center and the University of Groningen, The Netherlands. I am grateful to my Groningen colleagues for giving me the opportunity to take leave for a year and for taking care of the domestic things.

The Center for Advanced Study is a great place to be. It is based on a sort of mixed concept of an Italian monastery and a Club Méditerranée vacation resort, and a Fellow's only obligation is to be present at lunch. Paraphrasing Thorstein Veblen's classic, some have called it 'the leisure of the theory class', which, of course, is only based on envy and chagrin. I am grateful to the friendly and helpful staff and to my fellow Fellows for this great year of scientific productivity and human interest. A special word of gratitude goes to Kathleen Much for her invaluable editorial help.

A great deal of the work I present in this book grew to its actual form in the context of a working group called *Modeling and Measuring Development*, initiated by my distinguished colleague and friend Kurt Fischer from Harvard University. The group was very small – it consisted of Kurt and myself – but we had several regular visitors: Robbie Case, who was actively involved in the model-building endeavour, Kathryn Nelson, Abe Tesser and Paul Harris. We had regular visitors and consultants, such as Nira Granott, Bob Thatcher, Peter Molenaar, Han van der Maas and John Willet. Working with all these people was a great honour and a source of joy (that is, we had a lot of unprofessional fun together). But most important of all is that I learned so much from them. I am especially grateful to Kurt Fischer, for the stimulating meetings we had and for his interest, effort and friendship. Besides the working group, I had a second opportunity to meet colleagues interested in the problems of mankind. That group usually met after lunch. While performing some light physical exercises such as running after balls that would inevitably get stuck under somebody's car, the members discussed the most complicated problems in the most lighthearted way possible. Many people contributed, and I mention only the most faithful visitors and scholars: Bob Scott, Lynn Gale, Marlene Scardamalia, Carl Bereiter, Marcello Suarez-Orozco, Susan Cotts Watkins and Susana Larosa. Although the products of our collaboration never lasted longer than the duration of the meetings, they helped me make a lot of progress.

People from the (very informal) Groningen Dynamic Systems Group read the manuscript and made a number of valuable editorial suggestions. I am grateful to Martin Cats and especially to Saskia Kunnen who was very near the edge of a nervous breakdown when she found out she could not perform a number of model-building exercises, due to the present writer's negligence and his inability to spot typing errors in his own equations. Very useful editorial comments also came from Alan Fogel (University of Utah at Salt Lake City) and Kurt Fischer (Harvard University).

Finally, a word of gratitude to my family, who supported me so much in their own particular ways: Liesbet, by choosing the arts, the dog, Nathan and the Dutch weather; David, for a terrific year at Foothill and for his decision to keep out of the back of pick-up trucks; and Leen, for so many things that I do not know which ones I shall mention first.

Paul van Geert

The forms of change

Thinking about change and development

What makes a cat look like a cat?

In the 1920s, Piaget investigated the child's conception of the world and found that young children see the world in an artificialist way (Piaget, 1929). Everything has been made by man, on purpose, with a specific goal in mind. Artificialism, however, is not a mere transient phenomenon typical of children, but deliberately abandoned in adult thinking. On the contrary, in a new disguise artificialism appears to permeate much of our adult conceptualization of the world. Of course, adults know the distinction between man–made objects and nature. But, if we are asked why the things of nature are as they are, and especially why they come into being with their proper and particular form, it is difficult to avoid a style of thinking that is highly reminiscent of the young child's artificialist explanations. Take for instance the animal kingdom. What makes a cat look like a cat (or a Dutchman like a minister[1])? Educated adults know about biological conception and about genes containing the information that makes cats cats. But in what way are genes responsible for the bodily form and behaviour we think typical of the feline genus? This is where we have difficulty avoiding a form of artificialism, we are inclined to see genes as building plans. The genome looks like an agenda, a sequence of instructions describing step by step what the contractor firm Biology Inc. should do. It starts with an instruction for cell multiplication, for instance, and it even continues during the cat's adolescence, when it turns on the gonadal hormones to prepare the animal for the (partially) pleasant task of procreating new cats.

Do genes really act like a building plan or agenda? Do feline genes contain a blueprint for a tail or whiskers and human genes one for a Habsburg chin or an IQ of 110? Genes contain large amounts of information, but all this information is aimed at the synthesis of proteins, not of large bodily structures. In a sense, genes contain a building plan, but it relates only to the first step, the building of proteins. The properties of these proteins lead them to cluster in specific structures. But there is no

overall building plan that a general supervisor takes care of (Oyama, 1989). Each step in
the process of bodily growth creates conditions that specify and constrain the next step.

The idea that a complicated structure such as an organism's body can come about
without an explicit building plan and without a controlling instance external to the
building activities is difficult to accept. What steers the process? The answer that each
step constrains and specifies the next step is hardly acceptable as an explanation. And
we find such an explanation unacceptable because of our deeply rooted artificialist
tendencies, which make us insensitive to explanations that rely on the intrinsic
ordering activities of time. Oyama (1989) calls this belief in a genetic building plan the
'central dogma' of evolutionary thinking. Developmental psychology offers many
comparable examples. In the sections that follow, I shall discuss a few examples from
other disciplines devoted to the study of change and illustrate the point that structure
over time does not require the working of a master builder or the following of a plan. In
the second part of this chapter, I first introduce a basic notion, *iteration*, which lies at
the heart of the dynamic approach presented in this book. I shall show how iterative
processes describe development in the form of trajectories through abstract spaces.

Structured pictures and random scribbles

Biological evolution is a prime example of a process of long-term change that has led to
a complicated and orderly structure, namely the world of biological species and
ecosystems. We may safely say that Darwin's legacy has become an intrinsic part of our
world view. There are circles in which creationism rules, but the inspiration behind
that is a religious belief, not a deep belief in artificialism *per se*.

In biology class, students are taught that biological evolution is not a matter of a
pre-existing building plan. Species change and turn into new species because the fittest
survive and the less fit die before they have been able to transmit their genes –
containing less favourable properties – to new generations. Unexpected random
mutations create new genetic opportunities, which can be tested against the difficulties
of survival. Evolution is a very gradual process of both pruning and forming and it
depends on purely coincidental factors; randomness rules, but order enters because the
pruning is based on fitness and selective survival.

Darwin's principal accomplishment is that he has eradicated all traces of
artificialism in our scientific thinking about biological origins. It is interesting to see,
however, that so many of Darwin's interpreters have not been able to appreciate this
point. The principle of survival of the fittest founded the belief that evolution heads
towards increasing adaptation, complexity or quality of organisms. Evolution is going
somewhere; it has a goal and endpoint. This belief is evident in widely different
interpretations, such as Teilhard de Chardin's or social Darwinism's. In the late
nineteenth century, the survival principle underscored the idea that the adult
European male was the ultimate crown on Mother Nature's head. This notion of
finalism or teleology is related to an artificialist stand: things evolve because there is a
purpose or a goal involved. Nature, on the other hand – and this is clearly stated and
repeated time and again in *Origin of Species* – has no intrinsic goal, it does not care and

it floats on the stream of randomness and mere coincidence. The fact that even man, the jewel in the crown of creation, was a mere coincidence has always been difficult to accept (Gould, 1992).

This difficulty is not only observed in our thinking about evolution. If we reflect on our personal lives or the lives of others, we find it difficult not to see the actual outcome as something that was there from the very start. You become a professor of psychology because you are born with a sufficient amount of intelligence (though not enough to become a professor in a more advanced science, it seems), because you have a natural interest in the minds of other people, and so forth. The 'child is father to the man'; there must be potentialities in us that become actual and mature. What we finally become cannot be a matter of mere coincidence, of mere random drift. Random factors, we are taught in our first statistics class, will compensate for each other's effects. Because they occur in such large numbers, random effects will actually average out. But is this really so? A simple example will show that this conclusion is wrong, at least as a general rule. The example is based on a simple mathematical model and it will be the first example in a long list of models and tutorial boxes that will illustrate and I hope support the major point of this book. (I know that Shortman Webstar English College Dictionary defines 'tutorial boxes' as 'parts of textbooks marked by a box or horizontal lines, that are mostly skipped and at best only superficially glanced at'; in this book, however, those boxes are essential parts of the text, if not the most important parts of the text and, moreover, if you skip them you will miss a lot of fun). So take your favourite spreadsheet or programming language, or if you do not have or use one, just follow me.

Model 1.1 Random walks and random order

The Great Marketplace of the Belgian city of Sint Niklaas is world famous, because it is said to be the biggest marketplace in the entire universe (well to be honest, it is world famous only in Belgium . . .). Not only is it very big, it is also surrounded by a really impressive number of cafés and pubs. On a cold autumn day, one of the local beer specialists, obviously in a state of moderate drunkenness, leaves a pub at the west side of the Market and heads for one of the pubs on the east side. The gusty winds blow fiercely over there, and they change direction almost every second. So our poor walker is now pushed to the right, then to the left and because of the darkness and his bodily instability, he becomes the subject of the blind forces of the autumn weather. Where will his random path lead?

The wind acts like a truly random force, with regard both to its northwest direction and to its force. Since the Marketplace is so big, we may expect that the average effect resembles a straight line. But will this really be the case?

Open a spreadsheet and type the title "Random Walks" in the upper left corner. You can type any further information you consider necessary in the adjacent cells. Go to cell A10 and type the following equation specifying a random number varying between $+1$ and -1:

@rand $-$ @rand (1.1)

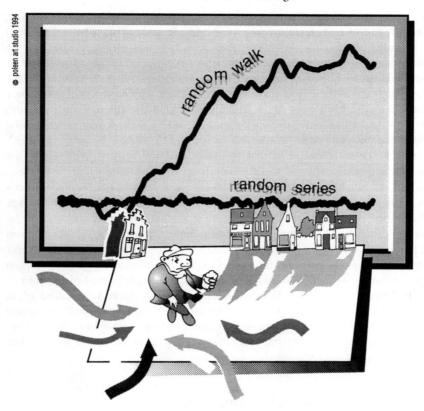

Figure 1.1 The drunkard's path depends on random forces (the gusty winds of Sint Niklaas) that come from all possible sides. The series of random numbers simulating those forces is represented at the bottom of the diagram; the random walk resulting from those numbers has a definite overall structure which deviates markedly from a straight line.

(note that most spreadsheets will not allow you to type spaces in the equation; I have just added them for the sake of clarity).

Copy this equation to the cell range A11..A2000 (if you are completely unfamiliar with spreadsheets, consult your manual. Copying is usually very easy. If you use a Windows-based version of Lotus 1-2-3, I suggest you use the 'Lotus-classic' way of copying, especially if it requires copying over such large ranges as with the present model; note that some spreadsheets use a different cell range notation, namely A11:A2000, I use the Lotus and Quattro Pro notation throughout the whole book). Go to cell B10 and enter the initial value for the random walk, 0 (zero). In cell B11 type the equation that defines the random walk:

$$+ B10 + A11 \tag{1.2}$$

Copy B11 to B12..B2000. This equation adds the value of the random number in the adjoining A cell to the sum of all the preceding random values. In order to obtain a smoothed representation of the random walk path, go to cell C10 and enter the equation for a moving average of fifty consecutive points:

@avg(B10..B59) (1.3)

and copy this to the range C11..C1950.

To see the result of the computations, define a line graph that depicts the range C10..C1950 (the manual will explain how to do this if you are not familiar with this procedure). I suggest you show two patterns in this graph, one of the random walk (C10..C1950) and one for the series of random numbers upon which the walk was based (A10..A1950).

Figure 1.1 represents the smoothed paths of the A and C ranges, respectively. Whereas the random numbers on average resemble the effect of a straight line, the random walk goes in a specific direction. Of course, each time a random walk is run on the computer, a different overall pattern will come out. But each of these patterns will have a definite macrostructure that differs qualitatively from the smoothed random line.

What can we learn from the first model? We might have expected that the net result of added random factors would boil down to something that wiggles around a straight line. After all, the mean value of the numbers is always very close to zero. The line of random numbers actually fulfils our expectation. But the essential difference between the random line and the random walk is that the latter consists of conditionally coupled random points. That is, each point in the random walk is the result of all the preceding randomly driven points. In the true random series of points, each random point is independent of all the others. Conditionally coupled randomness leads to an overall macrostructure, and this, dependence of each later stage on the previous stages, is basic to development.

Assume that the random walks represent 'lifelines' of individual human beings, represented in a two-dimensional framework. Figure 1.2 for instance contains imaginary curves of changing school achievements of four subjects, which in reality are random walks based on Model 1.1. Although each of them begins at about the same point, they very soon diverge and lead to characteristic individual patterns with a definite overall macrostructure. If they represented real school achievement curves, we would probably tend to explain the macrostructure as the result of major qualitative changes (e.g. a major change in direction). If one goes up and another down, we might assume that there is some underlying property, some hidden difference in the initial state or in the individuals' abilities or innate competences, that drives them in clearly different directions. A change of direction, for instance, might be attributed to some underlying change in motivation or interest. Of course, real lifelines are almost certainly determined by differences in genetic endowment, in educational opportunities and so forth. But the point of the present illustration is that random microvariations (random factors varying at each point in time) produce a macrostructure if conditionally coupled, for instance in the form of a random walk. Conditional coupling is an elementary principle of development and it is capable of producing macrostructure out of nothing more than mere random variation.

I am certainly not suggesting that all major changes over time are just coincidental,

Figure 1.2 Two curves representing imaginary scholarly achievement. Although they are based on the drunkard's random walk, their overall structure is such that a casual observer would be inclined to explain them on the grounds of major life-events or comparable influences, instead of the small continuous random events.

random-driven events. Maybe none of them are and to decide upon that is a matter of empirical research. The point is, however, that major event patterns over time do not necessarily invoke underlying tendencies of change in this or that direction, or major effects called into existence before a basic change in the nature or direction of a process. Random variations, if conditionally coupled, can create a form of long-term order. Observing such order may lead us to believe that it should be the product of some underlying order. That is true, perhaps, in that the underlying order may be as simple as a conditionally coupled sequence of random variations.

Smooth causes, abrupt effects

Introductory textbooks on developmental psychology usually describe developmental stages such as Piaget's four stages of cognitive development. They paint a picture of relative stability punctuated by sudden qualitative jumps. Many current researchers, however, see development as more gradual than the great masters of developmental psychology made us believe and, in a sense, quite similar to the form of biological evolution. Biological evolution is the accumulation of many small changes and is basically gradual and smooth. Selection against the odds of a dangerous world and random mutations goes on with any individual organism and at any time. There are no moments in history where survival pressures are relaxed, or where adaptation is less important. Nevertheless, the gradualist stance has recently been challenged (e.g. Eldredge and Gould, 1972; Eldredge and Tattersall, 1982). Evolution is not gradual at all, but occurs in the form of rapid changes, spurts in speciation that connect relatively long periods of species stability. This is the so-called punctuated equilibrium view of evolution. Evolution is a stair rather than a slide. This view is highly reminiscent of the stage theory view in psychological development.

If the viewpoint is correct – and it is highly likely to be so in many cases – then the question is how the punctuations of an equilibrium can be explained. Surely the Darwinian principle of selective mechanisms that act on a continuous and gradual scale is not at stake. Better survival chances of better adapted individuals are still the motor behind evolution. But how can a gradual mechanism that never ceases to operate explain a long-term process of stability penetrated by sudden changes?

The difficulty is that there is a qualitative distinction between the cause, the gradual, continuous mechanism of selective survival, and the effect, non-gradual, discontinuous change. We seem to have conceptual problems dealing with this kind of asymmetry. It is usually solved by postulating an external contingent factor: species remain stable as long as the environment remains stable. But if a large comet hits the surface of the earth and changes the climate for the next thousands of years, it probably sets the process of rapid change in motion. As far as the vanishing of dinosaurs is concerned, it appears almost certain that such an external force has had a major impact. But even in this case, the comet was only a deadly stab to a group of species that was already in decline.

But the point is that sudden changes are not necessarily explained by external forces. Some, though not many, of the punctuations may result from the internal dynamics of the processes at issue. Again, this is something that we find difficult to reconcile with our common notions of cause and effect. Let us proceed to Model 1.2 to see how a continuous cause can produce discontinuous effects, and how our notions of continuity and discontinuity depend on the time scales we actually contemplate.

Model 1.2 Time frames and explosions

There is a well-known tale of an Indian king who played chess with a servant. What I remember is that the king lost, and he seemed so impressed by the victory of his servant, and by the sheer talent this victory testified to, that he promised to give the servant whatever he wanted. The servant asked for one grain of wheat on the first checker, two on the second, four on the third and so forth. The servant was applying the so-called doubling scenario. The process, doubling the preceding number of grains, is isochronic, which means that it is similar over the consecutive points in the sequence (there is no point where it turns into tripling, for instance).

Open your spreadsheet program, type whatever titles and information you need in the upper left corner and go to cell A10 where you enter the digit 1. Go to cell A11 and type:

+ A10*2   (1.4)

Copy the content of cell A11 to the range A12..A210. This will result in an iterative process, where each consecutive cell takes the value of the preceding cell, multiplies it by two and returns that value to its successor.

What would the curve representing the sequence of numbers look like? Since the process is isochronic – that is, similar over each point – we may expect a steep but gradual increase. Define five different line graphs: one for the range A10..A12 (a very small time window indeed), and the others for the ranges A10..A35, A10..A60, A10..A110 and A10..A210. Look at the first graph, for A10..A12 (see Figure 1.3). The increase looks quite linear, although there is a mild, expected increase in its speed. So it seems that we might extrapolate this form to time windows of any arbitrary size and we would expect to find the same smooth increase.

Compare this with the other graphs; what they show is very different from the small time window of only three points. Qualitatively, the doubling scenario results in a long period with, relatively speaking, no change at all, followed by a sudden explosion at the end of the time window. There is nothing in particular that actually ignites the explosion at the end, other than the continuous doubling process applied to each time point. The small window suggested a smooth increase, but this did not extrapolate to larger windows, i.e. windows beyond a given scale (in the case of the doubling scenario, the scale threshold is as low as twenty steps). In all cases there is a sudden jump, which becomes more pronounced as more points are taken into consideration.

We may argue that a doubling of the preceding magnitude naturally leads to an explosive increase, but that an increase with a much smaller rate will present a gradually increasing curve, as expected. So, instead of multiplying by 2, try 0.01. And indeed, 200 consecutive points show a smooth and calm increase. But take 2000 points, and the seemingly qualitative jump occurs again.

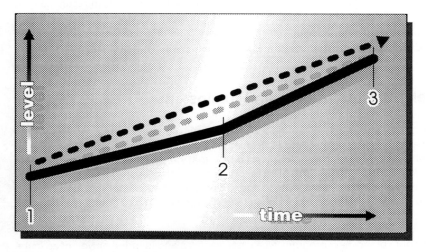

Figure 1.3 A very small time window, consisting of three consecutive points, suggests a gradual, almost linear, increase; a large time window, however, will reveal the explosive nature of this kind of increase (see Figure 1.4).

What can we conclude from this simple model, as far as our intuitions on the causes of sudden changes are concerned? The process we applied was *isochronic*,[2] that is, it was similar for all points along the time axis (or similar for each step in the iterative process). If we took a small window, we observed a seemingly gradual process. But if we watched through a sufficiently large window, we saw a process remaining almost the same for a long time, and then suddenly changing its direction, almost as if it had exploded.

We may draw two conclusions. The first is that sudden changes are not necessarily caused by external factors appearing just before the change sets in. Of course, many sudden changes are caused by external factors, or a *deus ex machina*, such as a comet or a winning lottery ticket. But conditionally coupled events such as the doubling scenario naturally show sudden changes just by the way they behave over time.

The second conclusion is that such conditionally coupled processes have a quality that we call *non-linearity*. Non-linearity has a technical, mathematical meaning, but I shall use and define it in an intuitive manner. It means that a linear increase in one variable corresponds with a non-linear change in another. Take for instance Figure 1.4, based on the doubling of grains at each checker. The number of iterations (i.e. applications of the same doubling principle) increases with time along a straight line. The corresponding number of grains, however, explodes at the end (at this scale of representation, that is). If the relationship had been linear, we would have expected to see an increase in the number of grains along another straight line.[3] The doubling scenario is a very simple example of non-linearity. Further in this book I shall give examples of non- linearity that relate much closer to the process of development (in the

Figure 1.4 Although the number of doublings changes linearly (one at a time), the number of grains shows an explosive increase (white arrow). This is a simple form of non-linearity. The curve in the back is based on a non-linear growth model of a type that will be explained later; the non-linearities are complex.

background of Figure 1.4, you will see a complicated curve, based on a simple model of interacting growers explained in Chapter 7, foreshadowing the interesting patterns our models will generate).

Isochrony and (non-)linearity are important aspects of developmental processes and difficult to deal with. We are used to making linear extrapolations and to acting as if isochrony necessarily means linearity. This habit of thought makes it very difficult to appreciate the nature and effects of developmental processes, where each new step builds onto the results of the previous ones.

Meno's problem

Visiting Athens on the First of May, one will find the Parthenon closed for Labour Day. The Greeks who used that place more than two thousand years ago did not have to worry too much about manual labour – their slaves took care of that – so they could enjoy the works of the mind. Slaves could even be the subject of experiments in educational psychology; Plato, for instance, tells of one in one of his Dialogues (Hamilton and Cairns, 1963). The story describes a discussion between Socrates and Meno (and it also features a slave boy and a fourth person called Anytus) taking place, probably at the Parthenon, but anyway a long time before Labour Day was invented. The issue is whether virtue can be taught, but the underlying problem is whether something can be put into the mind if it was not already there. Socrates shows that you can teach new knowledge. He demonstrates by teaching the slave boy a geometric principle, in his characteristic Socratic way, namely by letting the boy find out the principle by himself. But the new knowledge, Socrates concludes, is nothing but a recollection of knowledge that was already there. Whatever looks like new knowledge in the mind is nothing but a reordering of existing knowledge.

Meno's problem is still among us. For instance, is adult thinking qualitatively different and thus structurally new, in comparison with the infant's or the child's thinking? Or is it the result of a gradual quantitative change of a structure present at birth?

Piaget for instance considered the age of 6 or 7 a major qualitative turning point. If you ask a 4-year-old whether the amount of water in a jar, after having been poured from a container with a different shape, is still the same, the child will most probably say no and will support this answer, perhaps by referring to the fact that the water is higher than before. Six-year-olds will say that there is the same amount, for instance because although the water is higher, it is also 'thinner' (or whatever form of compensation they will apply). The answers reflect fundamentally different principles of cognitive organization. Whereas the younger child still dwells in the realm of action, the older child has entered the kingdom of operations, which are mental actions that are reversible.

It remains difficult to imagine, however, how a fundamentally new mental organization can come about. The difficulty is actually based on a 'Socratic' argument. How could a structure create a more complicated structure if the more complicated aspects are not already present, in some form or other? I can teach somebody the meaning of *poodle* by saying, 'Look, that's a poodle', if a poodle happens to pass by. But that person must by necessity already have the meaning of poodle, since, if that is not the case, my saying 'that is a poodle' will have no meaning at all, except for the trivial meaning that 'that dark hairy thing over there is a something I don't know'. This is, approximately, Fodor's argument on the impossibility of a learning theory of meaning development and it is very close to Socrates' one.

It is probably out of intuitive uneasiness with having to accept that something really new can come out of something old, that many investigators have been trying to show that Piaget's view was incorrect. The argument is that what he saw as qualitative shifts can be explained by quantitative changes in some underlying variable. For instance, if the child's working memory is too small to contain more than one chunk of information, the child will not understand problems that need two chunks to be solved correctly. Once the quantitative growth of working memory has widened its scope to two chunks, the child will actually understand. This is far from a major qualitative restructuring in the child's cognitive principles, however, although the quantitative change might have very considerable consequences for a large domain of problems.

What are the major conceptual components or aspects of Meno's problem? The first is concerned with the fact that our ideas on the nature and content of the mind are still strongly idealistically coloured. Socrates concluded that the boy, to whom he taught a geometric rule, could come up with the right answer only if the required knowledge was already present and installed in his mind during a former life. We may see this as an antique view involving reincarnation, but Socrates' conclusion is closer to modern thought than it looks at first glance. Modern innatist views would not speak about the boy's former life, but about his biological ancestors in whom the knowledge has become installed and transmitted, not in the form of a memory but in the form of genetic information. But this is basically the same as the Greek argument. Socrates' conclusion is based on the assumption that the mind cannot create something that it cannot entertain. Thus, in order to produce a developmentally advanced more complicated thought or thinking structure, the mind must assemble that thought or structure and therefore it must be capable of harbouring or containing that structure. But this is an impossible achievement, for how can you assemble a box that is bigger than the hall in which the assembly takes place? Consequently, all structures that the mind can create must be present before that creation occurs, which, therefore, is not a genuine creation but a form of retrieval.

The problem with this Socratic contention is that it reduces the mind and the meaning of whatever is in there to the mind's own confinements and enclosures. This viewpoint is not in itself old-fashioned or obsolete, as Fodor (1980) showed. But the question is whether it is wise to take it as an axiom for further understanding (since it is an axiom, preceding the status of a contention with an empirical truth status). We could as well opt for another axiom, that seems more appropriate, namely that the mind's contents have meaning not in themselves, but in the interplay with their environment. Thus, to construct a box bigger than the assembling hall, you construct the part, which must fit into the hall, and assemble them outside. Similarly, a child may come up with a solution to a problem that the child does not see as qualitatively distinct from what it usually does. The way in which such a solution works out with the problems presented in the outside world, however, may turn out to be qualitatively different from what the child used to do. For instance, for the child, the application of the reversibility principle – thinking a problem backwards – may seem similar in nature to and only superficially different from employing the familiar forward strategy. But, the new strategy may open up a whole new world of problems and problem-solving opportunities that mark a qualitative shift in the child's thinking. The qualitative difference, then, did not reside in the child's representation of the reversibility strategy, but in the fact that there is a large class of problems in the world for which such a strategy is necessary, and that is qualitatively different from the problems accessible with the old strategy. The contents of the mind could be like keys suited for opening different doors, giving access to domains that are qualitatively different. But the material out of which the new key is made need not be qualitatively different from the old one.

A second conceptual aspect of Meno's problem is that there seem to be difficulties with accepting the possibility of sudden qualitative shifts. Mechanisms that act gradually and isochronically cannot bring about effects that are non-gradual and heterochronic, it seems. But this conclusion is based on the false premise that short-term changes extrapolate linearly over long-term changes. Model 1.2 illustrated clearly that this is not always the case. Where does this false premise come from? Maybe it comes from the fact that humans, as biological beings, are built to make short-term decisions. For this type of decision, anything that approximates a linear extrapolation gives the best solution. But in order to see long-term consequences, we need mathematics or electronic artifacts such as computers and it appears that their way of reasoning has not yet entered our human intuitions as to what constitutes an 'acceptable' model of change.

The world is full of events that boil down to sudden qualitative shifts. For instance, if walkers increase their speed of walking, they will come to a speed where the walking pattern suddenly changes into a qualitatively different pattern, that of running. We call the patterns qualitatively different because the components of both patterns, such as the typical movement of the legs, trunk and arms, cannot be mixed freely in intermediate motion patterns. The motion components in each pattern are positively coupled; once one component occurs it will trigger all the others. But why would a component of running interfere with a walking pattern? Probably because of a mere coincidence, a 'random perturbation' of the walking pattern. Because of the physics of walking, the chance of such perturbations occurring increases exponentially with walking speed. For instance, at high speed the walker risks stumbling or losing balance and the onset of a running pattern will actually restore balance.

In Chapter 5, I shall describe a model of transitions, that is, sudden shifts in a process, based on interactions between variables that are similar for all the points on the time-scale. Nevertheless, these interactions produce a sudden shift at one particular point in time. Figure 1.5 shows a mathematical simulation of growth in three different cognitive dimensions: conservation, decentration and reversibility. In the mathematical model, these three dimensions are loosely positively coupled. The child described in the model would be in a state of non-conservation, perceptual centration

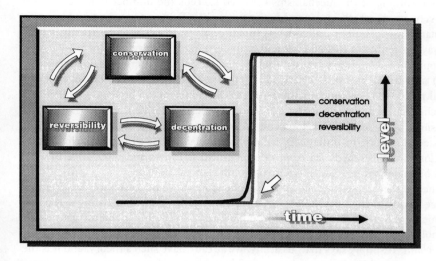

Figure 1.5 Three cognitive skills – decentration, conservation and reversibility – have been modelled in the form of a loosely coupled group of variables that positively affect one another. Their growth curves take the form of a coordinated, sudden jump towards a stable level.

and non-reversibility for quite a long time. The curves actually represent the probability that the child would answer a question invoking any of these three variables. Then a sudden change occurred in which the three cognitive properties involved jumped to a maximal level. That is, the probability of a child giving a correct answer to a variety of standard questions, such as the standard conservation question, is almost 1. This then is the final state, which will remain fixed. Although the jump is based on an isochronic principle, growth that acts similarly on all points of the curves, the effect is strongly heterochronic: the jump occurs at one specific moment. It is difficult to believe that the jump is not caused by some external factor and that the causes that act upon the system of three variables are similar for the whole time range.

Understanding development

Meno's problem is of course not solved by these models and examples. What they demonstrate, however, is that part of the problem rests on our inability to understand why and how qualitative shifts may come about if the nature of the developmental mechanism is gradual and quantitative (more of the same). Most of our developmental models are quite complicated, and involve many variables that are related in all sorts of ways. But we have no other means of inferring longitudinal processes of change than simple linear extrapolations which are valid and useful for small time frames. Linear extrapolation turns inadequate as soon as the number of repeated interactions or repeated working of the mechanisms involved exceeds the number that we can still intuitively grasp, which in general is not more than four or five.

Dynamic model building offers a way (not the only way, maybe and certainly not the final way) to get out of this impasse and to understand why development is what it is. Development is not always gradual (but it is not always a matter of qualitative shifts, either) and development is clearly different between individuals, but also shows general patterns or prototypical trajectories. Development is not always aiming at a hierarchically higher steady state, but shows cyclical patterns, transient and lasting regressions and decay. Development is sometimes highly dependent on small coincidental factors, or differences among individuals as far as their developmental conditions are concerned; sometimes development is robust and insensitive to what would be major threats under different circumstances.

A theory that could explain all these phenomena would certainly considerably advance developmental psychology. If dynamic systems modelling claims that it can offer such a theory, it sets itself the formidable task of rebuilding and reconstructing the whole discipline. But the point is that dynamic systems modelling does not make such a claim. It simply says that, basically, we already have such a theory, and it is the good old theory of development that we find in a variety of forms, ranging from Piaget to Vygotsky, and from information processing to skill theory. These models contain a limited set of simple, basic explanatory models and those suffice to explain all the phenomena mentioned before. But so far they have not really explained these phenomena, because they suffered from the major problem discussed in this chapter, namely the impossibility of extending the effect of those simple mechanisms to more than a few points in time. What dynamic systems theory offers is a technique or an approach, to study what these models do if we let them do their work for more than just a trivial period.

Iterates in space

What is an iteration?

I have always been a great admirer of the Muppets and I especially liked the *Pigs in Space* part, featuring, among others, the dazzling beauty Miss Piggy, who would never become tired of demonstrating that true love reaches even beyond the boundaries of biological species. For completely trivial and unscientific reasons, the *Pigs in Space* thing went through my mind when I was trying to find a short description of a fundamental formal property of development that I could use as a title for this section. I only had to replace the pigs by iterates.

If anything like a basic developmental mechanism exists, it must be an iteration. An iteration is a process that takes its output as its new input, produces new output, which it takes as input, and so on, *ad infinitum*. Originally, the notion of iteration came from mathematics, where it denoted functions like:

$$x_{i+1} = f(x_i) \tag{1.5}$$

and an example of such a function would be:

$$
\begin{aligned}
x_0 &= a \\
x_1 &= 2x_0 = 2a \\
x_2 &= 2x_1 = 4a \\
x_3 &= 2x_2 = 8a \\
&\cdots
\end{aligned}
\tag{1.6}
$$

which we recognize as the doubling scenario from Model 1.2. It starts with an initial value of a (e.g. 1), doubles it, then doubles this number and so forth. The function taking its output as its new input is the function 'times 2'.

Here is a geometric example. Take a straight line of any arbitrary length. Divide it in three equal parts and delete the middle part. Bridge the open part by two lines whose length is one-third of the original line. This will produce a geometric form consisting of four straight lines. Apply the function (dividing, deleting, bridging, etc.) to each straight line. This will result in a new geometric structure consisting of straight lines. It is remarkable how fast the complexity of the forms increases with the number of iterative applications.

Apply the principle once to a straight line and you will obtain a pattern as in Figure 1.6 (left side). Apply it five times to the resulting straight lines and a pattern results as complex as Figure 1.6 (right side). It is impossible to carry out such iterations merely by using visual imagery. A computer (or lots of patience if you want to draw it by hand) is needed to reveal the complexity and form of the pattern.

These kinds of designs are often described as fractals, and nowadays they occur in a variety of popular books that show what amazing structures such simple iterations produce. Benoit Mandelbrot, a mathematician who cooperated with Piaget for a while, can be considered the modern founding father of the science of fractals. In the beautiful book *The Fractal Geometry of Nature* (Mandelbrot, 1982), he shows how natural forms such as coastlines, clouds, cauliflowers and brains reduce to simple spatial iterations. Biological processes too can be considered iterations. Take for instance sexual reproduction. Sexual reproduction is a biological process that takes two individuals, a male and a female, as its input, and, on average, produces individuals of opposite sex as its output. The individuals of opposite sex enter the sexual reproduction operation again, produce new individuals of opposite sex, and so on, *ad infinitum*.

Iterations in mental and behavioural development

Whereas the iterations of evolutionary biology take place at the time-scale of successive generations, those of developmental psychology require a time frame ranging from seconds to several years, but all within a single life span. Let me begin by telling a short story about a developmental process at work and see how the notion of iterative functions can be applied to it.

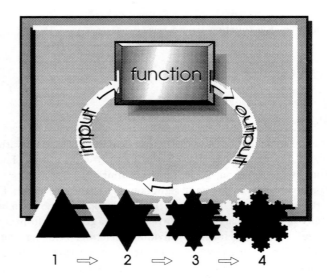

Figure 1.6 An iterative procedure takes its own output as its next input. Applying simple iterative geometric procedures to an initial form (the triangle) produces a complex pattern after only five iterations (the snow crystal at the right).

Many children are very interested in computers and some have learned a lot about how to use them without any formal training. Here is a 10-year-old boy who is playing with a graphics program that his mother got with a new mouse. He clicks on the pencil icon and draws the rough outline of a house. He then clicks on the brush icon, goes to the outline, clicks again, and the house turns yellow, as he expected. He then draws a window, clicks on the brush, chooses red, clicks on the window. But instead of nicely filling the polygon, the colour spreads all over the screen. The boy is very puzzled. He asks his mother what he can do, and she advises him to click on the 'undo' icon. He then goes to yellow, since the explanation of the disaster may of course be the red colour. But the result is a yellow screen. He clicks on the pencil, draws a new window, tries to colour it again; now it is perfect: a bright red window. Is it a testimony to his competence, or just to his good fortune? He asks his mother why the colour leaks. 'You've probably not closed the line', she says from behind her book. The boy is puzzled: not closed? What could that mean? 'You should close it, like a fence', his mother goes on. If you do not close the fence the animals will run away. It is just the same with the colour. Then the boy looks back at the first window. The beginning and ending of the line in the second one cross one another, but the first window shows some open space between the end points. That should be the explanation: forms must be closed, otherwise the colour will leak out. He then draws a third and fourth window, and both can be coloured as expected.

The story can be interpreted in various ways, dependent on your theoretical background. Let us begin with a Piagetian one (Piaget, 1975). Piaget would view the scene as an example of the *adaptation principle*, as it operates in the spontaneous activities of children. The boy has an impressive, yet still limited knowledge of the graphics program. One could say that in his view the whole program boils down to a few functions, such as the 'draw' and 'colour'. The child's interpretation (actually his reduction) of the program with all its different possibilities to a limited number of known functions is what Piaget calls *assimilation*. But the child encounters difficulties, such as the leaking of the colour from the first window. The child's experiencing this as a difficulty depends on his knowledge that the program should be able to fill forms selectively. The knowledge-dependent nature of this so-called *cognitive conflict* shows that it is an example of assimilation. Then his mother tells him about open and closed forms. Because he knows the difference between them and understands the metaphor of the animals and the fence, his mother's advice makes sense to him. He then looks more closely at the difference between the two windows. One is a closed form the other an open one and he can actually see the colour flow through the little hole and fill the whole screen. It becomes clear to him, then, that drawing and colouring is not just a matter of creating a form. It should be a closed form. In the future, he will have to reckon with that particular property of forms if he wishes to colour his drawings properly. This adaptation of the child's knowledge to the properties of experienced reality, experienced though in the form of a conflict, and mediated by his mother's verbal information, is called *accommodation*. Assimilation and accommodation are the polar constituents of *adaptation*.

After his experience with the open and closed forms, the boy has learned about the difference between them and about their function in the graphics program. Next time he might encounter a form that seems to be closed, but still leaks colour. That would produce a conflict between his expectation and his actual experience, and lead him to understanding the magnification button on the screen menu. Sometimes holes are so small you can hardly see them on the screen, and then you have to magnify the picture. Thus the understanding of why the magnification icon is necessary is a function of his previous discovery that forms should be closed, and of the resulting experienced conflict that a form seems closed, but is not, since it leaks colour.

It is clear that the Piagetian adaptation function (let us call it PA) is an iterative function. It takes current knowledge and an experience whose meaning is based on that knowledge as its input. As its output, it produces new knowledge and new experiences that are a function of the altered knowledge state. The production of new experiences and not just new knowledge is essential; adaptation takes place in the form of action. Action entails personal knowledge and experiences that form the interface between the person's knowledge and the reality touched upon in that action. It may take a while, of course, before a current experience, such as a cognitive conflict, is transformed into new consolidated knowledge. This is the amount of time expressed as the parameter 'i' in the subscript:[4]

$$(\text{knowledge}_{t+i}, \text{experience}_{t+i}) = PA(\text{knowledge}_t, \text{experience}_t) \tag{1.7}$$

The equation says that later knowledge and experience (at time $t + i$) is a Piagetian adaption function of current knowledge and experience (at time t).

In his book on the mechanisms of development, Piaget (1975) formalized the activity of assimilation and accommodation in a form very similar to the iterative function presented here. Piaget could not explore the most important property of iterative functions, namely the possibility of deductive experimentation. That is, once a computable form has been given to the iterations, we can study the effect of different values of the parameters involved, we can investigate whether or not iterations ever stop producing new outcomes and so forth. By doing so we are performing theoretical, not empirical research; we investigate the potential developmental trajectories that lie hidden beneath the seemingly trivial form of the iterative equation. So far, developmental psychologists, or psychologists in general, for that matter, have not been used to carrying out this kind of deductive investigation of their models, because the verbal form itself prevented them from doing so. Only if our models are transformed into a calculus, however simple its form, will deductive inferences become possible. Since the nature of the developmental mechanism is iterative and since iterative mechanisms produce results that are in general not conceivable by linear extrapolation, a deductive investigation of the possibilities of a model is far from trivial.

The information processing model (e.g. Siegler, 1983) would have interpreted the scenario differently. Under this model, the child is employing a rule that a class of computer figures – some broad class of polygons – can be filled and coloured with the brush icon. Then he encounters an event where the rule does not hold. He comes up with a hypothesis – with a little help from his mother, to be sure – which he then tests, and either refutes or accepts, dependent on the empirical outcome of the test. Accepted hypotheses form new rules, and they are given actual truth values (true or false) in each experience where they are put to the test. If a rule leads to a negative truth value (it is false, as in the case above), then the mechanism of hypothesis testing sees to it that a new rule is suggested and tested and that the old rule is replaced by the new one. If the truth value is positive (the rule is true), the mechanism takes care of a further consolidation of the rule. The iterative function of hypothesis testing (HT) is very similar to the one proposed for the Piagetian model, if 'knowledge' is interpreted as hypotheses and 'experiences' as 'truth values':

$$(\text{hypothesis}_{t+i}, \text{ truth value}_{t+i}) = HT(\text{hypothesis}_t, \text{ truth value}_t) \qquad (1.8)$$

(which says that later hypotheses and truth values are a hypothesis- testing function of earlier ones).

The reader will probably notice that the form of this equation is similar to that of equation 1.7; at this level of mathematical abstraction, the Piagetian and the information processing model are indeed similar. Differences occur at the level of the mechanisms that each theory invokes to explain the working of adaptation and hypothesis testing.

Let us finally try a Vygotskyan perspective to the drawing story. Vygotsky (1978) distinguished two major mechanisms of transition at the time level of ontogenesis. The first is the mechanism of *interiorization*. It explains how activities that take place at the interindividual plane, that is, in cooperation with other people, shift to the intraindividual realm of mental capacities. The second mechanism is contained in the concept of the *zone of proximal development*. This is the domain between the child's actual developmental level and the developmental level represented by those activities the child can carry out with the help of more competent others. If this help is adequately adapted to the child's actual level, it will be interiorized and will lead to a higher level of development, enabling the child to do by himself what he could do earlier with help. By making his computer drawing of the house and colouring it, the child shows his actual developmental level. The boy's mother can then build on this level, by telling him to test whether his figures are closed or not. He will then interiorize this advice and test the closure of figures without being explicitly told to do so. With this particular boy, the simple verbal advice represented adequate help. His mother could also have told him to try again, or to read the manual. With adults, the suggestion 'read the manual' could be very helpful, but with 10-year-olds it is probably a wasted effort. On the other hand, the boy's mother could have inspected the drawing of the window herself and told him what to do step by step, without giving much of an explanation. Then the boy would not have learned very much. Now imagine what would happen next time the boy drew a polygon and the colour leaked out to the entire screen. His mother could again suggest to him to control for the closure of the figure, but that would not be of help, since the boy already knows that. Consequently, in order to promote the boy's further learning, his mother should adapt her help to the higher level of competence her son has reached, thanks to her previous help. It is clear that this mechanism is again an iteration, that could be written in a form similar to the Piagetian form, with 'developmental level' standing for 'knowledge' and 'help' for 'experience'. It is also possible to write the mechanism in the form of a set of coupled equations, however, which are not iterations themselves, but which as a couple form an iterative process.

Let us distinguish the 'tutoring' function T from the interiorization function I. Tutoring takes as its input the child's actual developmental level, as expressed in the child's problem-solving actions. As its output, it produces help adapted to the child's actual developmental level. Interiorization takes help as input and produces a new developmental level as output:

$$\text{help}_{t+1} = T(\text{developmental level}_t)$$
$$\text{developmental level}_{t+2} = I(\text{help}_{t+1}) \tag{1.9}$$

(help is a tutoring function of developmental level; developmental level is an interiorization function of help).

This set of coupled equations can also be written in a singular form, namely:

$$\text{developmental level}_{t+1} = I(T(\text{developmental level}_t)) \tag{1.10}$$

The mere fact of concocting these formal expressions is not quite a major contribution to developmental theory, since they add hardly anything to what we already know about Vygotsky's model. But, once they are put in a form that enables us to compute a sequence of developmental and help levels, they will reveal a number of developmental

possibilities that would have remained unknown if only the verbal form of the model
had been taken into account. How such computations can be carried out will be
explained in later chapters.

The elementary iterative form of developmental processes

Although the nature of the concepts involved differs over different developmental
theories, they all basically agree on an elementary iterative form. It is so elementary
that it appears almost trivial; it states that the next developmental state (ds) is a
developmental function (DF) of the previous developmental state:

$$ds_{t+i} = DF(ds_t) \tag{1.11}$$

'State' does not mean the same thing as 'stage' or 'phase' (see van Geert, 1986). It is a
very general term used to denote whatever developmental level concept you wish to
employ. For instance, for a continuous developmental function such as a continuous
increase in the mastery of a skill, the developmental state could be any point on the
continuous curve that models this increase. In a Piagetian model, 'state' could refer to
one of the four major stages, or to a substage.

How trivial is it to say that a developmental state is a function of its predecessor?
Probably less trivial than it seems at first sight. Imagine a sequence of developmental
states behaving exactly like a sequence of heads and tails resulting from tossing a coin.
Each toss is completely independent of each preceding one. Many people have
difficulty appreciating this principle of independence, however, since it is an essential
aspect of common sense that the future is at least to some extent determined by the
past. For instance, in the unlikely but possible event that you threw 100 heads in a row,
many people would believe that the probability of getting another head for every
further toss would significantly decrease, but that probability is actually always 50 per
cent.

If we were to endorse a strictly maturational theory, the developmental states would
arise independent of one another. Their real dependence would be on the underlying
genetic program. Assume that the genetic program would trigger formal thinking, for
instance, at the age of 11. The previous stage of concrete thinking would not relate in
any sense to the emergence of this new form of thinking, except for the fact that during
a short transition period, thinking might show some mixture of formal and concrete
elements. Similarly, a theory describing developmental states as mere environmentally
driven functions, determined by the developmental or learning tasks set by the
environment, would not subscribe to the iterative model either. For instance, a specific
educational environment may decide to teach Latin to 10-year-olds, and analytic
geometry to 12-year-olds. In this case there is nothing like an obvious developmental
logic behind this sequence of knowledge acquisition. Nevertheless, we may question
whether it is possible to avoid a later stage being determined, in a non-trivial sense, by
the previous stages. Even if we must learn a completely new skill, such as an exotic
language having nothing in common with our mother tongue, the initial states of

learning will differ from person to person and depend on each person's general learning skills, semantic knowledge and so forth. As soon as the learning process has started, however, each new step in the learning will have to rely on the previous steps. Now, imagine we have to learn a list of unrelated nonsense words. Each word is a learning task of itself and the learning of one word would not contribute to the learning of others. But learning new words may become increasingly demanding as the list of words to be remembered grows longer, as the person becomes more fatigued or bored. We may conclude, therefore, that the iterative function expressing each state as being determined by a preceding state is an almost universal, inescapable property of change. In developmental processes, the iterative principle probably applies in the most explicit way possible.

Time series, trajectories and the concept of a developmental space

Development trivially implies change over time. How will the change be represented? In dynamics, changes are depicted in spaces of various kinds, time being reduced to one of the spatial variables employed in a model. For instance, a simple population dynamics model might specify a space consisting of the time dimension and a dimension for the number of individuals in a population, of foxes for instance. A more complicated model might add the number of rabbits as a third dimension. At each moment in time, there is a specific number of rabbits and a specific number of foxes. That is, the state of the system is represented by a single point in the time-fox-rabbit space. Since the numbers of foxes and rabbits change, the process of population growth and decline of rabbits and foxes is represented by a single line in the three-dimensional space. This line is the *population trajectory* for the fox and rabbit system.

Let us apply this notion of a descriptive space to development. My current social knowledge, for instance, differs quite drastically from the social knowledge I had when I was only 2 years old (well, I sincerely hope it does). It is possible to describe the distinction between my knowledge now and my knowledge then by using a finite number of descriptive terms. One of the descriptive terms could refer to my cognitive representation level, which is now formal operational and used to be sensorimotor when I was 2 years old. Another descriptive term specifies the number of social roles I am able to distinguish. A third refers to my egocentricity in social matters, and so on. Each descriptive term functions as a dimension in a space that covers all possible states of social knowledge. I can employ whatever collection of descriptive terms I consider necessary for the task of distinguishing any two developmental states.

The standard way of specifying my development in this descriptive space would consist of taking a test that covers a specific descriptive dimension. By repeatedly applying that test, with an interval of, say, a year, a so-called *time series* of measurements would be obtained for that dimension. The time series is easily represented in the form of a curve. To obtain a complete image of the developmental process, time series for each of the descriptive dimensions should be collected. A collection of time series is far from a coherent image of the overall development, however. One way of achieving a simple overall picture in the form of a time series works as follows. I can connect any two points in my multidimensional descriptive space by a straight line of definite length. Figure 1.7 shows how this is done in a space with no more than three dimensions. The initial state with coordinates (0,0,0) is connected by a diagonal line with the final state (1,1,1). If the length of each of the dimensions (or sides of the cube) is set to the unit length 1, the length of the diagonal is equal to the square root of *n*, the number of dimensions. The simplest possible way to phrase the question of developmental dynamics is this: How is the distance bridged between initial and final state and does the speed and direction eventually change over time? Put differently, the multidimensional space of descriptive dimensions has now been reduced to a two-dimensional space consisting of a distance and a time dimension.

It goes without saying that the transformation of an *n*-dimensional distinction between developmental states to a one-dimensional, unspecified distance is a formidable reduction, and we might worry that it is too drastic. But although it is a severe reduction indeed, it is not irrelevant. The point is that the general dynamics, that is, the basic characteristics of the way in which the initial state transforms into the final state, can be specified by using the single distance line.

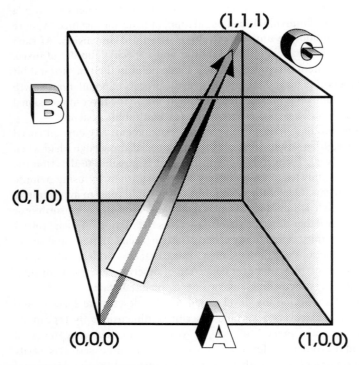

Figure 1.7 A three-dimensional space consisting of three distinctive features *A*, *B*, and *C* represents the set of possible paths in a developmental model. The paths are lines connecting the vertices of the space. The diagonal line represents the distance between the initial and the final state.

Figure 1.8 depicts a possible, characteristic trajectory between an initial and a final state, in the form of a stepwise growth process. Such a representation is called a *time series representation*, because it displays a series of data points over time. The data points must be at intervals small enough to capture the basic dynamics of the process at issue. Of course, what is considered basic depends on the scale on which we choose to study a particular phenomenon. Note again that the present way of representing development does not boil down to assuming that the development of social knowledge, or any other form of development for that matter, is a one-dimensional issue. The single dimension is an abstract entity drawn from a descriptive space in which each dimension has a particular meaning. The obvious question that arises as we specify development in such terms is what this abstract dimension means empirically. We would certainly have to look for 'local' empirical correlates of this abstract dimension.

Let us return to the imaginary multidimensional space that represented the distinctive properties of social knowledge. We do not have to know all these dimensions, it suffices that we know they constitute a space in which distances can be measured and axes drawn. Instead of graphing the change in only one dimension at a time, I now combine the measurement of a dimension or property A with that of a property B. The developmental state is a point with an A coordinate and a B coordinate value. When I connect the A–B points in the right temporal order, I obtain a line in the A–B plane which is called the *trajectory* of the developmental system (which is my social knowledge in this particular example). The trajectory runs through a space, the A–B plane, and connects successive developmental states. The A–B plane is called the

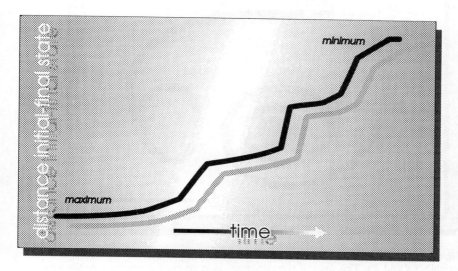

Figure 1.8 If a developmental process takes place in a space of variables as in Figure 1.7, the resulting developmental process may follow a trajectory of step-wise growth.

state space and the trajectory through the space the *state space representation*. Note that, unlike the previous pictures, there is no time axis in the state space representation. Time can be added by imagining the trajectories are paths, or bike tracks, for instance: the biker needs a certain amount of time to go from the start to the point where the ride ends (which in path 2 is probably somewhere along the cyclical part of the path).

State spaces can contain any number of descriptive dimensions, but they are usually confined to only two, for reasons of clarity. Any choice of two dimensions will greatly reduce the level of detail and specificity of the resulting developmental picture. I can try to overcome this by selecting any two axes through the multidimensional space that yield the most characteristic picture. Even if I do not know the meaning of those two abstract axes, they may be helpful in that they allow me to see the characteristic developmental trajectory.

Figure 1.9 shows an imaginary state space representation of the development of social knowledge in two subjects. Each subject is represented by a single line. Their starting points are very close to one another, but the way they grow towards their final state point differs. Path 1 shows more progress over the B variable at the beginning, while path 2 starts to progress over the A variable. The endpoints are different in that path 1 spirals towards a point attractor, whereas path 2 keeps spiralling over a cyclical path in the A–B space. Path 2 represents a developmental path which never ends.

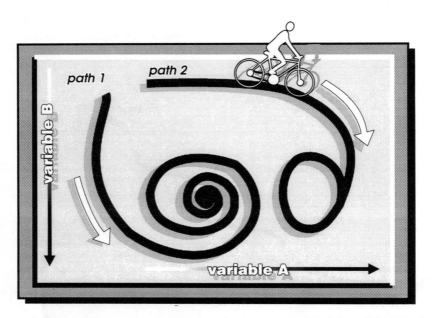

Figure 1.9 A state space representation of a developmental model consisting of only two variables (*A* and *B*). This kind of representation lacks an explicit reference to the time dimension; developmental trajectories are like bike paths on the plane formed by the variables *A* and *B*; path 1 evolves towards an endpoint, path 2 towards a repetitive cycle.

From time series to trajectories

Students of dynamic systems like to look at things from a variety of different angles. When they see a process they want to know not only its time series representation, but also its state space trajectories. Whether you prefer to show the properties of a process either in a time series or in a trajectory form is a matter of taste, of convenience, but often also of clarity. Some processes show their properties better in the form of a trajectory. We have seen that a state space representation requires at least two dimensions. But what if a process changes over only one dimension? Is it possible to transform a time series into a trajectory representation? How do we carry out that transformation?

Model 1.3 Economic interest cycles: transforming representations

David, who is 19, has decided to take a course in macro-economics. You might say that David is very interested in macro-economics – he has actually thought of taking it as his major. Neverthless, if we say that David is very interested in macro-economics, we do not mean that he is equally interested all the time. Sometimes he is more interested in maths, in playing soccer or in finding the cutest girl at the Halloween party. We could say that his interest in macro-economics is oscillating with a period equal to a day. His economic interest is expressed in his doing his economics problems for homework every day without being pressed to do so, his willingness to start a discussion on economics and so forth. A fugitive thing such as a student's oscillating interest in a subject is probably very difficult to measure. But, we can just pretend we know the function, and can pretend that we have a mathematical model generating it. This mathematical model is a model for a so-called exhaustible resource, which will be explained later.

The equation is very simple. It is actually based on the logistic growth equation that will be explained later, but applies a delay to the resource level. I suggest you define a set of range names that will enter as parameters in your equations. The spreadsheet manual will explain how to do this in your particular spreadsheet. Basically, however, it goes like this. Go to a cell, for instance C100 and type the name of a parameter, r. In the adjacent cell, D100, enter the value of the parameter r, 0.1. In cell C101 specify the name for the second parameter, e and in D101 its value, 0.2. Via the command Range Names you can specify the name, r for instance, and the corresponding range, D100 (the cell where you can find the value of r). After defining the range names, go to cell A100 and enter the initial value 0.01. In cell A101, type the equation:

$$+ \text{A100}*(1 + \$r - \$e*\text{A70}) \tag{1.12}$$

In cell B101, type a very simple version of the first derivative of the process described in the A range:

$$+ \text{A101} - \text{A100} \tag{1.13}$$

Copy range A101..B101 to range A102..B500 (or a bigger range if necessary). Define three graphs: one is a line graph of the range A100..A500 (or whatever A range you have specified), the second is an xy graph, with the A range associated with the y-axis, and the B range with the x-axis. The third graph is again an xy graph. It takes the range A100..A500 as its y-axis and the range A108..A500 as its x-axis (note that the x-axis contains the same data as the y-axis, with a shift of eight cells).

Let us assume that we have been able to measure the oscillatory movement of the student's interest and that it looks like the time series in Figure 1.10 (bottom); the student's interest oscillates over time (time is the horizontal axis). The time series can be transformed into a trajectory representation in two different ways. First, take the sequence of successive levels of the interest variable and put this on the x-axis. Then take the first derivative of each point in the sequence. In Figure 1.10, I have feigned the first derivative by the difference between two consecutive cells. These values are then put on the y-axis, so that for every value of the interest level there is a value of its first derivative:

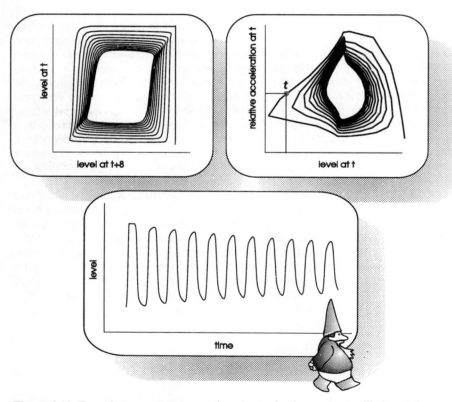

Figure 1.10 Two phase space representations (top) of a time series (oscillation at the bottom). The phase space at the left is based on the time–delay procedure, the one at the right depicts the relationship between the local level of the process and the acceleration at that level.

$$(x,y) = (L_t, \Delta L_t), (L_{t+1}, \Delta L_{t+1}), \ldots \qquad (1.14)$$

This set of x–y points yields a representation of the oscillation function known as the *phase space* representation. It is a classical representation in physical and technical sciences where many processes amount to oscillations of a variable. The phase portrait of the imaginary student's 'interest in economics' level is depicted in Figure 1.10 (top right). Note that the time axis has been removed from the picture; the x-axis represents the student's interest levels, the y-axis the corresponding changes in that interest level. The grey dot marked 't' represents the student's interest level at time t and the amount of change in that level at time t. Although the oscillation itself looks quite regular, the phase space shows characteristic increases and decreases in the speed with which the interest changes and this is the kind of information that is much harder to infer from mere inspection of the time series. The phase space representation shows a line spiralling inwards, which normally refers to an oscillating process that aims towards a steady (that is, stable) state. The phase portrait of a regular sine wave, on the other hand, would be a perfect cycle. Many statements about the form of a process, such as its being cyclical, its aiming towards a steady state or 'point attractor' and so forth, are based on a phase portrait representation. It is a natural way of representing processes and it is an intrinsic component of dynamics studies.

There is a second way of representing a phase portrait of a process, one that does not require computing the first derivative. The x-axis is the set of points occupied successively by the variable whose change we want to represent (such as the student's alleged interest in economics function). The second axis, however, portrays the same sequence of points, starting not with the first but with a later point. For instance, if the first point of the series is taken at time t, begin the sequence at the y-axis at time $t + n$ (Figure 1.10, top left). Thus each point in the sequence is coupled with a later point, for instance eight points later:

$$(x,y) = (L_t, L_{t+8}), (L_{t+1}, L_{t+9}), (L_{t+2}, L_{t+10}), \ldots \qquad (1.15)$$

This set of points yields a function that is quite similar to the classical phase representation and provides roughly the same information (Figure 1.10, top left). The choice of an optimal delay (for instance, the eight time points employed here) depends critically on the phase with which the process cycles. With some trial and error, it is in general possible to find the optimal distance fairly easily.

The many faces of a process

Let us apply the strategy of multiple representations to an empirical example. Kurt Fischer, whose work will be discussed further in this book, has measured the development of skills, such as arithmetic problem-solving skills, under different testing conditions (Fischer and Pipp, 1984). If the testing implies feedback from the tester to the child and information and support given in the testing situation, the curve representing the skill growth (in terms of the percentage of correct answers to a test) shows a characteristic shift: a sudden considerable increase around the age of 15.

Without practice and support, the curve shows a pattern of smooth, constant increase (see Figure 1.11a). Fischer's point is not that practice and support measurement captures the 'real' level, whereas the other is 'false' or a measurement error. His point is that there is no such thing as a real competence level. A skill is actually a bimodal or bidimensional object and those dimensions can be captured by measuring the skill under two different conditions.

This particular view on the nature of a skill fits naturally with the notion of multidimensional representation described in this chapter, except that 'multi' means no more than two in this case. Let us explore the different ways in which the development of a skill can be represented. It should be noted, however, that the empirical curves used in this example are not longitudinal time series of a single subject. They are based on cross-sectional research. Since the focus of the present demonstration is on different representations of processes, I shall pretend that the curves are indeed individual and longitudinal and therefore real time series.

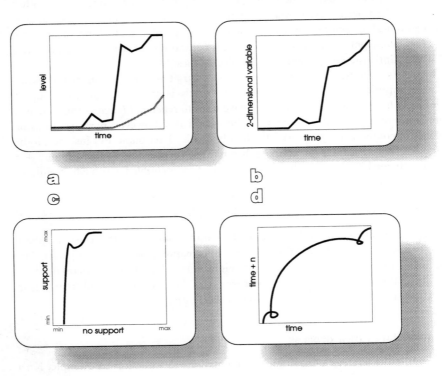

Figure 1.11 A time series representation of two developmental processes (growth of arithmetic understanding with and without support during the testing condition, figure a) can be caught in the form of a combined dimension (figure b), in a state space representation consisting of the variables 'testing with' and 'testing without support' (c), and, finally, in the form of a time-delay phase space (figure d). Each form of representation has its particular advantages and disadvantages.

Model 1.4 Mathematical problem solving in two dimensions

Open a spreadsheet and type the following numbers in column A, beginning with A1: 1,1,1,1,15,7,9,90,83,87,100,100. These numbers are percentages correct on a practice and support test of arithmetic thinking. Each number is the mean score at an age level expressed in years. In column B, type the numbers corresponding with the scores on a non-supported arithmetic thinking test: 1,1,1,1,1,1,1,5,10,16,21,35.

Let us first define a simple time series representation. Define a graph which has as its A range the numbers A1..A12, and as its B range B1..B12. Define it as a simple line graph. The result will look like Figure 1.11a. The curves show how the distance between a 1 per cent correct and a 100 per cent correct score is bridged over a period of twelve years.

Next, define a different type of curve, an xy curve, that you can choose from the graph menu in your spreadsheet. As x-axis, take the range B1..B12, and take A1..A12 for the A range. The result will be as in Figure 1.11c. It is a state space representation of the development of arithmetic thinking in a state space consisting of the dimensions 'practice and support testing' and 'unsupported' testing. The state space representation specifies development as a journey in a space of two measurement dimensions.

The third form of representation reduces the two-dimensional state space again to one single dimension, namely the distance between an initial state and a final state (which correspond with the initial and final test scores on both tests). In the spreadsheet, cell A12 contains the last score of the practice and support condition, whereas the last score of the unsupported condition can be found in cell B12. Go to cell C1 and type the following equation:

$$@\text{sqrt}((\$A\$12 - A1)\ \hat{}\ 2 + (\$B\$12 - A1)\ \hat{}\ 2) \tag{1.16}$$

The function of this equation is to compute the distance between any point in the state space and the endpoint of the growth process of the skill, as measured under two conditions.

Copy this equation to C2..C12. Define a line graph that takes C1..C12 as its A range. The result will be as in Figure 1.11b. It is the one-dimensional distance representation of the trajectory over the two measurement dimensions.

The fourth representation requires a smoothing technique that I will explain later. For the moment suffice it to say that it is based on the numbers from column C, the one-dimensional representation. It is an xy representation and it takes the value of the C column at time t as its x-axis and the value at some later time as its y-axis. The result is a time-delay phase space representation.

The four representation forms describe the same data series, one from practice and support and one from unsupported testing. They are four different ways to look at the dynamics of change in arithmetic problem-solving. Developmental psychologists are not really used to working with state and phase space representations, or with abstract representations such as the one-dimensional distance representation. Their data usually consist of simple time series representations for separate dimensions. Some properties, such as cyclical and quasi-cyclical developments, require different representation forms, such as the state space. In the case of models with many variables and dimensions, a distance dimension representation might reveal underlying characteristics that cannot be seen in the separate curves. One of the advantages of a dynamic systems approach is that it offers a variety of different representational formats and a very liberal approach to how they should be used.

Notes

1. Before any misunderstanding arises, what makes Belgians look like Belgians is their country, and moreover, they do not belong to the animal but to the Belgian kingdom.
2. A *heterochronic* process would be one in which the nature of the mechanisms involved changed over time, or is time-dependent. For instance, if the process started with a tripling scenario, then changed to a doubling and ended with a quadrupling, the process would be termed heterochronic.
3. Strictly speaking, however, the relationship is not non-linear but it is not linear in the straightforward sense either. It is *log-linear*, that is, if you plot the logarithm, you find a straight line again.
4. Later we shall call this the *feedback delay* and argue that it is of considerable importance in development.

2

Developmental paths and systems

The paths of change

Uniform change

In the previous chapter we saw that developmental mechanisms are iterations, doing their repetitive labour in spaces consisting of the properties we consider important in a specific developmental field. Iterations produce paths or trajectories in these abstract spaces. What are the characteristic trajectories, or 'paths of change' in developmental processes? In this chapter, I shall first discuss a variety of developmental paths that can be generated by non-linear dynamic models. I shall then proceed with a second, theoretical question: What kind of developmental theory is a non-linear dynamics model? We shall see that the way such models conceptualize and describe development is very different from standard models of development. Let me begin with an overview of prototypical ways of bridging the gap between initial and final states.

The simplest possibility is that the bridging of the gap amounts to a gradual and uniform reduction of the distance. That is, the distance reduction is a linear function of time. If it takes a week to learn twenty new words, then the child will know forty words after two weeks, sixty after three and so forth. If the child no longer encounters new words (which is highly improbable in a culture like ours where the vocabulary fills literally thousands of dictionary pages), the learning stops.

The iterative function that goes with this sort of change is a simple additive operation:

$$x_{t+1} = x_t + a \tag{2.1}$$

for a an increase (or decrease) parameter. The dependence on time is expressed by the function:

$$t \cdot a \tag{2.2}$$

In Chapter 1, however, we encountered another type of simple linear increase, namely the doubling scenario. It amounts to the iterative function:

$$x_{t+1} = x_t + a \cdot x_t \qquad\qquad (2.3)$$

for a a rate of increase. The change is again a function of time, namely:

$$a^t \qquad\qquad (2.4)$$

In Chapter 1, we have seen that it leads to a 'sudden' explosion, however. If I plot the *logarithm* of the change, the logplot follows a straight line (see Figure 2.1; a spreadsheet program usually has an inbuilt facility for logplots).

Stated in the jargon of dynamic systems, these processes have a *point attractor*. That is, the process is attracted toward a single point in the state space, namely the point whose coordinates are the final state values of all the variables that form this state space. What is the point attractor of the gradual change represented by the 'plus a' and 'times a' scenarios? It is the mathematical point infinity. Real processes of this particular kind will never reach infinity (whatever concrete meaning that point might have, if any exists); they will be stopped by some external factor, such as death.

The simple additive or logarithmic increase serves as a powerful prototype for short-term change in many developmental investigations. If a researcher repeatedly tests a child for the same developing variable (such as writing skill or moral judgement) and finds an irregular, oscillatory or downward path, it is usually assumed that this must reflect random fluctuations or measurement errors and that the true variable follows a path of linear or log-linear increase.

Steady-state 'paths'

A second possible path is one in which nothing happens at all. The development

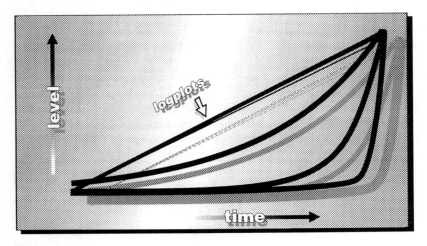

Figure 2.1 The fact that the $x + ax$ scenario is called 'linear' follows from the straight logarithmic plots of the curves based on that scenario. The plots of the actual levels are curvilinear.

achieved in some variable stays at the same level. The iterative developmental function produces a stable state, that is, its inputs are identical to its outputs. It may seem strange to call this a path, but that name is well chosen since path technically means nothing more than a sequence of states over time. Whether the states differ or remain the same does not matter. The point attractor of the process is the steady state itself and the attraction is no change at all as far as that state position is concerned.

The steady-state path occurs, for instance, when the child has reached the level of linguistic maturity and has appropriated the mother tongue's grammar, or when an adolescent has reached the level of formal operational thinking.

The steady-state path is very important in classical models of development. Models such as Piaget's on cognitive development, Erikson's on identity and Kohlberg's on moral development describe final states or stages, such as the stage of formal operational thinking (Piaget). As soon as such a state is reached, development takes the form of a zero transformation; the iterative function that made the process evolve towards the final state is now continuously producing outputs similar to its inputs.

Of course we could claim that with the advent of the final state, development ceases to exist, or that the engine that made the process move has come to a standstill. But this is probably not so. A standstill in nature means death. The mature body, for instance, renews itself continuously in a metabolic process very similar to growth. But whereas growth produces change (in length, for instance), the steady state merely maintains the system. It is highly likely that behavioural development obeys the same law; the mechanisms that accounted for growth and development during the early years probably continue to operate to maintain the system and prevent it from deterioration.

Deceleration paths

The third characteristic path form is based on the idea that retrieval from an exhaustible resource produces a combination of gradual increase ending in a steady state. As a developmental path, it reduces development to a process of appropriation or learning. Examples of exhaustible resources are the limited vocabulary of a language, the limited range of social rules and habits and the current state of accepted knowledge in a scientific discipline. The iterative function modelling this path is similar to picking candies from a box. Each time you take some candy out of the box, the amount of available candy decreases and this decreased supply is then the input for the next candy-picking operation, until the box is empty (there is one biblical example – with a different type of supply – in which this general rule did not hold, of course, but for the rest of history it has remained an iron law of nature that candy boxes, or baskets with loaves and fishes, for that matter, get empty after a finite amount of time).

There is, however, a much more interesting iterative function than the candy box scenario, namely:

$$n_{t+1} = n_t + a(S - n_t) \tag{2.5}$$

The point attractor of this process is S (for instance, knowledge of all the words in the vocabulary). Given this particular form of the equation, n will never reach S; it will only asymptotically approach S. If S is a discrete number (such as the number of words), there will be a final state for which $n = S$. The path produced by this equation is one of continuous deceleration; its rate is maximal at the beginning, and it decreases as it approaches its asymptote. Note that the iteration keeps working forever, but that it will produce outputs approximately similar to its inputs if n approximates S closely enough.

It may come as a surprise that a simple iteration like equation 2.5 produces the curves typical of classical learning theory, which thrived in psychology roughly until the early 1960s. An example of such a curve is Figure 2.2. The logarithmic plot is not a straight line, but a line similar to the curve itself. The nature of the change is therefore different from the 'times a' scenario, although the resulting curves are superficially similar and look like each other's inverse.

These curves occurred in classic learning experiments, where subjects had to learn lists of nonsense words or paired associations. In 'natural' learning processes, however, taking place over a longer time and involving meaningful and relevant material, we will very probably find curves that deviate a good bit from the ideal. But again, if confronted with irregular repeated measurements of a learning function, many students of development would still be inclined to say that the irregularities are random errors and that the real underlying learning curve has the ideal form of Figure 2.2.

Rise and decay paths

A very old conception of human life sees it as a process of rise and decay. At birth we are taken out of the cosmic void, we develop and prosper and finally we experience our final

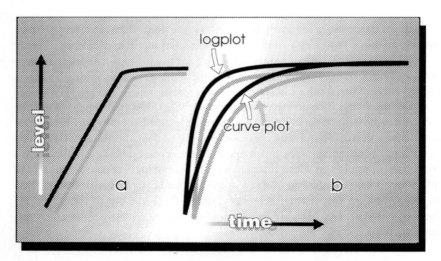

Figure 2.2 Paths towards a steady state: (a) the 'candy'-scenario; (b) the learning scenario. Note that the logarithmic plot of the learning scenario is curved, and not straight as in the case described in Figure 2.1.

decline and return into the same eternal void at death. Of course, this rise and fall notion is also applicable to much less romantic phenomena. Take for instance the use of so-called two-word sentences. In general, children younger than 18 months will stick to one-word sentences and show a growth spurt in the number of words they understand and use. Then they discover that combining two words in a single utterance greatly enhances their communicative ability. Some children show a two-word boom. As they discover the possibility of combining three or more words, and the use of syntactic and morphological rules, the frequency of genuine two-word utterances drops again to about zero. So the developmental variable 'two-word grammar' shows a characteristic rise and fall sequence.

Comparable examples hold for any transient developmental phenomenon, such as for instance the temporary use of pre-operational logic by children younger than 6, which emerges, grows and blooms, then disappears with the rise of operational thinking. In its ideal form this type of developmental path follows a bell shape (Figure 2.3). This path again has a point attractor, namely the zero state.

Partial decay forms are also possible, for instance when pre-operational thinking is overtaken by operational thinking, but continues to be used in a small domain of problems. In this case, the point attractor is the constant, low level of use that this form of thinking retains.

Paths with changing growth rates

The rise and fall scenario and the preceding asymptotic growth scenario are both examples of processes where the rate of change differs over the process. In the

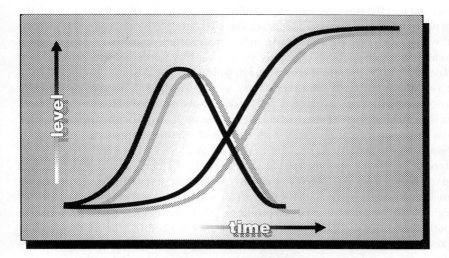

Figure 2.3 A typical 'rise-and-fall' path of a linguistic strategy (two-word combinations) whose decay is caused by competition with another, more complex strategy (syntactic structures).

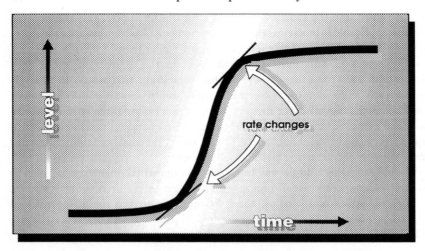

Figure 2.4 Variations in the rate of change can take the form of a spurt, characterized by an increase and a decrease in the rate.

asymptotic case, the rate of growth decreases towards the end. In the rise and fall case, the rate turns into a negative value (decay, loss) at the summit. In fact, the majority of developmental paths, as we intuitively understand them, show some sort of combination of changing rates of growth.

A classic example of a process that shows a definite acceleration followed by a deceleration is the so-called naming explosion that normally takes place between the ages of 18 and 22 months (see Figure 2.4). It is characterized by a considerable increase in the rate with which the child learns new words. After a preparatory stage in which the child builds up a lexicon of, for instance, about fifty words, a lexical growth spurt will occur. Finally, the rate of lexical growth will level off by the time the child starts to use two and more word sentences. Every parent will be able to give examples of development that seems to proceed slowly for quite a time, then suddenly explode and later slow down again. For instance, there are peaks in children's stubbornness over the years, or in how easy it is to deal with them in disciplinary situations.

Sometimes temporary regressions may occur, in which children seem to get worse instead of improving on some specific skill (Figure 2.5). Very often this announces a leap to a higher level of mastery. For instance, young children use a limited number of spatial prepositions in a grammatically correct way. Then, as they try to discover the rules behind the use of the prepositions, they sometimes overgeneralize the hypothesized rules and make more errors than they did before. For instance, a child speaks about 'in the bed' and 'in the table', although it formerly distinguished both verbal contexts and correctly used 'on' in the context of tables. But such a regression often heralds a spurt in the correct use of a larger variety of prepositions (van Geert, 1983).

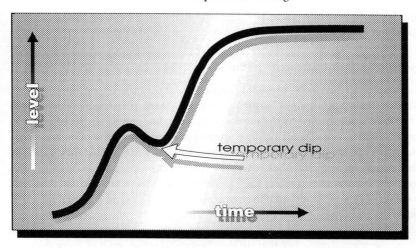

Figure 2.5 A transient regression or dip may precede a growth spurt.

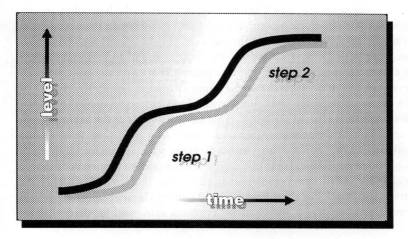

Figure 2.6 A step-wise increase in the initial–final state distance is characteristic of stage theories.

Finally, the classic stage theories can best be represented as a stepwise increase (Figure 2.6). For instance, each Piagetian stage is a single step of a stair with four steps in all. This type of curve amounts to several asymptotic growth curves superimposed on one another. We may of course object that Piaget, and most other structural theorists, for that matter, have described the stages as qualitative changes, and that a one-dimensional representation is unsuitable. This is correct, but as the reader will probably remember, the line represents a distance in the multidimensional space specifying the qualitative differences in Piaget's model. It specifies how this distance is bridged without referring to the qualitative nature of the transition.

Non-linearity in point-attractor paths

The trajectories described in the preceding section are of the classic type: development aims towards a final state (a state of maturity), and stays there. The final state is a single point in the state space formed by the variables that together specify the set of possible developmental states. So, classically, development is a process with a point attractor. The paths, however, are not characteristic in the empirical sense, in that they have not really been found in empirical data, except in very confined situations such as the classic learning experiment. Rather, they are widely seen as prototypes of development, as curves that we should find if measurement problems would stop playing their dirty tricks on us. Onto a few elementary paths, such as the increase and the steady-state path, we may build more complicated paths, such as the stepwise path behind stage theories. Remember that, in the theoretical sense, each of these paths is not just a line in space, but the product of an iterator. For some elementary paths, the iterators are simple. For others, such as the stepwise growth or the transient regression, they are more complicated and we shall postpone discussion of them to Chapters 7 and 8. The iterator generates paths: give it any point of a curve – at the beginning, the end or somewhere in the middle, at a summit or a dip – and it will return the next point of that curve, no matter how complicated the curve is.

The more complicated curves differ from the simple ones in an important aspect. The simple curves obeyed a monotonic increase pattern. Start with any arbitrary point on the curve and the iterator produces the same change, a uniform increase, for instance. In the more complex ones, such as the transient regression, the form of change differs over the length of the curve. That is, take a point at the beginning and look at its successor. It shows a slow increase. Take a later pair; they show a faster increase. Still further the increase turns into a decrease, which turns into an increase again. This phenomenon is called non-linearity. It is an important property of dynamic systems, which are called *non-linear dynamic systems* in that case. I shall discuss non-linearity in Chapter 3. For the moment, suffice it to say that non-linearity involves non-uniformity, or diversity, of the relation between a cause and its effect.

Cyclical transitory paths

Cycles in classical theories

The previous paths are typical of development in that they generally aim towards a higher level, a single point in the state space. Many developmental theories, though, explicitly reckon with cyclical patterns of change. Although such theories clearly distinguish an overall process towards a higher, stable state, they often conceptualize each step as a cyclical process. Piaget, for instance, sees in every major stage an underlying process of equilibration. Equilibration means that the components of a structure compensate for one another so as to form a coherent and functional whole. In what sense is development cyclical, according to Piaget? When the child discovers a new structural level of thought, such as concrete operational thinking, the cognitive system starts with a state of disequilibrium. For instance, the child tends to apply the concrete operational logic to all kinds of problems, whether it actually fits or not. The adaptation mechanism, however, will gradually lead to equilibrating the system, in that the child learns to use the concrete operational logic to compensate for different kinds of disturbances, such as misleading counter-suggestions. Arriving at the summit of the concrete operational competence with its full equilibration of the logical means that go with it, the child discovers a new and higher level, namely formal operational thinking. With the discovery of this new level, the original equilibrium reached with the previous form of thinking is set to zero again and the child has to repeat the cycle of finding a new equilibrium. The process takes the form of an S-shaped curve that jumps to a higher level of functioning as it approaches its maximum. But this higher level of functioning (a higher stage) is automatically the lowest level of equilibrium. If we project such a process on a single plane, abstracting from the shifts in cognitive level, we find a sawtooth curve, projected on different levels of cognitive functioning (Figure 2.7).

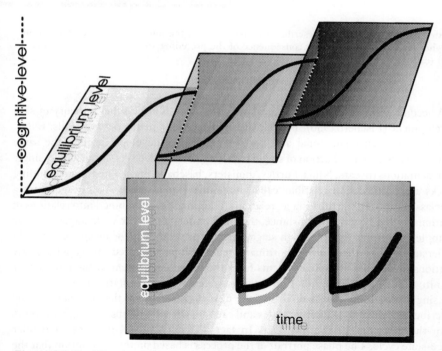

Figure 2.7 Equilibration follows a rise-and-sudden-fall scenario in three dimensions. Each new cognitive level (e.g. Piagetian stages) shows a new equilibration process, resulting in the emergence of another level. The three-dimensional process reduces to a sawtooth pattern if represented in two dimensions.

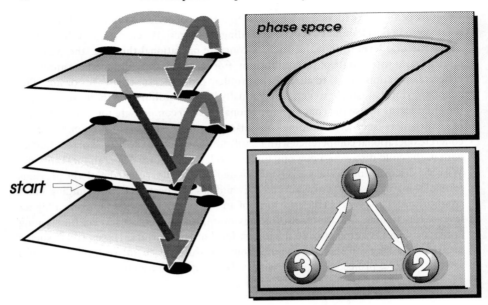

Figure 2.8 Fischer's theory describes a four-step cycle: the fourth step is the first step on a higher level that emerges as a consequence of the preceding steps. Each developmental level (called a *tier*) consists of three sublevels (1, 2, 3).

A second example of a cyclical pattern comes from Kurt Fischer's theory of skill development (Fischer, 1980). Fischer distinguishes four major tiers of skills: reflex, sensorimotor, representational and abstract. Each tier develops through the same cycle. It starts with a collection of single building blocks called sets, for instance, single representations (of cars, Ninja Turtles, monsters, baseballs, etc.). Then single building blocks are coupled into relations called mappings (for instance, Volkswagens are a subclass of cars). In the third stage, relations (mappings) are combined into relations of relations, called systems (for instance, the child understands that Volkswagen is to car as apple is to fruit). In the fourth stage, systems are coupled (for instance, the child understands that there are subordinate relationships mirrored by superordinate relationships). These coupled systems form the initial component of the next higher cognitive level (see Figure 2.8). For instance, systems of representational systems form the singular building blocks or sets of the next higher abstract tier. Fischer's model describes a cycle of four discrete states and each fourth state jumps to a higher level to form the first state of the next tier. In fact, Fischer's model describes a regular three-state cycle. The phase portrait of the process is based on the assumption that the distance between any two consecutive stages has the unit length 1. After smoothing, the trajectory takes the form of a circle flattened into a bean-like shape. It is a characteristic cyclical trajectory.

Quasi-cycles in actual development

In Chapter 1, I explained the notions of phase space and state space and gave the example of an oscillating resource, such as a person's interest or effort spent in a specific subject. Comparable oscillations can be observed in language development. In Roger Brown's classic study on first-language development (Brown, 1973), we can find curves showing the development of syntactic rules such as the present progressive in individual children. The curves of the average percentages of correct use per month show a far from steady rise, but go up and down quite considerably. The underlying trend, however, is a continuous increase towards (almost) 100 per cent correct. Figure 2.9 renders a smoothed version of the monthly averages, clearly showing the curve's oscillation around the rising average. Similar patterns can be observed in the learning of new words. It is not so much the number of words that oscillates – there is hardly any evidence for children's large-scale word forgetting over short periods – but the rate with which new words are learned. We might expect this rate to be stable; it depends on cognitive abilities that do not seem to fluctuate widely, or that are supposed to improve,

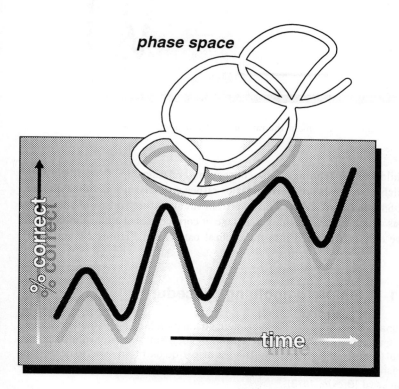

Figure 2.9 The steadily increasing oscillatory pattern of acquiring the correct use of the present progressive has a semi–cyclical phase portrait.

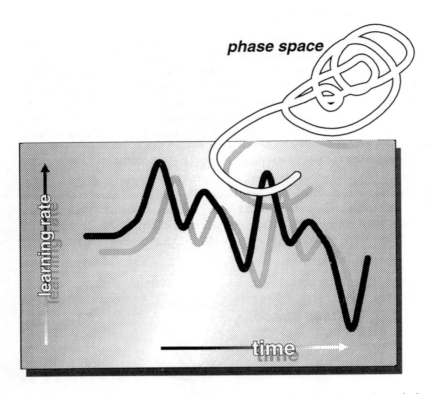

Figure 2.10 Irregular oscillations in the rate of word learning: time series and phase portrait.

such as the child's understanding of new concepts and relationships. Nevertheless, the rate with which new words are learned varies rather strongly in individual children (Corrigan, 1983; see Figure 2.10). The data from the literature consist of single data points, such as a monthly average of percentage of correct uses of a morpho–syntactic rule. How are they transformed into the cyclical patterns of Figures 2.9 and 2.10?

Model 2.1 A simple smoothing procedure

Drawing the phase space involves filling in intermediate data points and then smoothing the curve. It is a technique called 'splines', and various statistics software packages contain several techniques for doing this. There is also a 'quick 'n' dirty' way to do the trick with a spreadsheet. Let us apply this to Roger Brown's data on the acquisition of the present progressive (Brown, 1973).

Open a spreadsheet file and type the following series of numbers, beginning with cell A1: 0.12, 0.7, 0.2, 0.6, 0.78, 0.43, 0.9 , 0.7, 0.98, 0.9, 0.82, 0.97. Represent these data points in a line graph; they form a sawtooth-like pattern. Try a time-delay phase diagram: define an xy graph with range A1..A12 as its x-axis and range A2..A12 as y-axis. The result is very different from the nice and smooth phase portraits of Figures 2.9 and 2.10. The process for making a smooth diagram is a bit tedious, unfortunately.

Go to cell B1 and type + A1. Then go to cell B21 and type + A2, to cell B41 and type + A3 and so on. Go to cell B2 and write the following equation:

$$+ B1 + (\$B\$21 - \$B\$1) / 20 \tag{2.6}$$

Copy it to the range B2..B20. Go to cell B22 and type:

$$+ B1 + (\$B\$41 - \$B\$21) / 20 \tag{2.7}$$

Copy it to range B22..B40. Go on until all the empty spaces between the data cells have been filled (do not forget to adapt the numbers).

Next, go to cell C1 and type:

$$@avg(b1..b10) \tag{2.8}$$

and copy this to the range C2..C240. This range will contain a moving average over the cell ranges B1..B10, B2..B11, B3..B12 and so on.

Define a line graph for the range C1..C150: it will show the smoothed form of the line graph based on the original numbers in range A1..A12. To arrive at a time-delay phase space diagram, define an xy graph with as x-axis range B1..B240, and as y-axis B10..B240. The result should be the moving, cyclical path shown in Figure 2.9. You can also try a different phase space version, based on the combination of the level and of the change in the level. In cell D2, type:

$$+ C2 - C1 \tag{2.9}$$

and copy this to cell range D2..D240. Define an xy graph with range C2..C240 as its x-axis and D2..D240 as its y-axis. The result should be very similar to the time-delay phase space.

I have placed the current set of trajectories under the heading 'cycles', and from the viewpoint of a mathematical model this is not correct. All paths described here actually grow towards a stable state. That is, they have a point attractor, not a cyclical one. The cycles are like intermediate paths between an initial state and a point attractor at the final state. We could also say that they are cycles that move over an oblique axis, as in Figure 2.9.

Paths to chaos

The cycles described in the previous section are all transitory, that is, cyclical paths that lead to a point attractor that is the final state of development. In principle, this final state is not expected to change or oscillate over the life span anymore. For instance, once a child has acquired mastery of a specific grammatical rule, it will not forget the rule or show noticeable oscillations in the grammatical errors made (real errors, that is, based on lack of mastery or understanding).

But, should we expect that all final states of development are stable in the sense of a point attractor? Take intelligence, which might be considered a prime example of a stable property of intellectual functioning. Whether a person's real intelligence fluctuates, we do not know, but whatever an IQ test actually measures, its scores are not stable throughout life. Instead, individual scores fluctuate quite considerably (McCall, Appelbaum and Hogarty, 1973). You could object, saying that the fluctuations are error variations and the real score is stable. This objection, however, is based on the assumption that something exists which we call intelligence and that it must be a stable attribute of any single person. But of course we do not know whether this assumption holds. The only measures that we have are IQ scores and they seem to fluctuate. The limited evidence that we have suggests that these fluctuations are far from regular and that they certainly do not resemble the neat sinusoidal fluctuations produced by cyclical processes.

Similar irregular oscillations apply to many other non-cognitive functions. Take for instance self-esteem. Almost nobody feels the same about themselves all the time; the level of self-esteem fluctuates. It is codetermined by experiences and a bad experience, such as failing an important exam, will have a degrading effect on almost anybody. But the effect of an experience on your self-esteem is most probably mediated by the level of self-esteem during the experience.

In summary, we may expect many cognitive and non-cognitive properties of individuals to change in a more or less irregular fashion over the life span. Overall trends exist, such as major cognitive acquisitions between infancy and adolescence, but they are not neat and smooth increases. Steady states are less steady than they should be, according to theoretical expectations.

The stability of a person's characteristics over the life span has been investigated in several longitudinal studies, such as the California Longitudinal Study (Eichorn et al., 1981), the Fels Longitudinal Study (Kagan and Moss, 1962) and the New York Longitudinal Study (Thomas and Chess, 1986), and in longitudinal studies of personality development in adulthood, such as the Kansas City Study (Neugarten, 1964) and the Boston Study (Costa and McCrae, 1976; 1980). As could be expected, these studies reveal a mixture of stabilities and instabilities, dependent on the individual person, the property at issue and the age of measurement. As far as the longitudinal studies allow us to draw conclusions on fluctuations of properties in individuals, they show that such fluctuations are considerable and also quite irregular.

The classic response to observation of irregularity is to deny it, by reducing it to 'error', 'coincidence', 'randomness' or whatever other denigrating concept you can come up with. Irregularity is polished away by taking population means, averages, prototypical patterns and so forth as images of the hypothesized simplicity underneath. Whatever the background philosophical inspiration of this epistemological reflex, it denies the simple fact that irregularity, diversity and randomness are very general and stable properties of all life. The irregular fluctuations of a person's properties over the life span are of course constrained and run within specific boundaries, but that makes the changes no more regular.

States and transitions

States and stages

Any recent overview of development begins with classical theories, such as Piaget's or Erikson's and describes the main stages that these theories discerned. It then usually explains that there is currently much doubt about the existence of such broad stages and that developmental trajectories are confined to task-specific domains. Within domains, however, a problem would arise: Is there stagewise development or not? For instance, is there a stagewise increase (in the form of steps) in a person's arithmetical problem-solving skill between elementary school age and late adolescence? Some authors, such as Kurt Fischer, claim there is, but others would probably favour a more gradual, eventually oscillating path. Anyway, the problem of stages – whether broad or content-specific – is an important issue in developmental psychology.

Instead of using the notion of stage, I shall employ the neutral term 'state'. Recall that I chose to describe development in terms of a multidimensional descriptive space. At any time, a person is characterized by some value on each of these dimensions, and the values change with development. A person's developmental state is simply defined as that person's position in the multidimensional space. Stage theories are characterized by spaces which consist of only a few descriptive, basic dimensions. The dimensions are often dichotomous. For instance, a child's thinking is either operational or it is not, internally represented or not (for further discussion of this view, see van Geert, 1986; 1987a,b,c; 1988). In this case, the number of possible states a person can occupy is highly limited. The states often last for a considerable length of time. We may call such states 'stages'.

Where states and stages exist, there must be transitions between stages, and therefore transitions are characteristic forms of change wherever development occurs. What is a transition and what are its characteristics?

Weak transitions and accelerations

First, a transition is an event that is qualitatively different from the states it connects. Second, it connects prolonged system states that differ in one respect but are similar in another and, finally, the transition duration should be significantly less than that of the states it connects. I admit that this description does not appeal to intuition very much, so let me give an example: conservation acquisition. The two prolonged states are the *not knowing* and the *knowing* of the conservation principle. They are similar in that they both represent a single knowledge state that lasts for several years. They are different in that the knowledge is different. The intermediate phase of switching answers lasts for a relatively short time and it is different in quality from the states it connects in that it is not stable at all, but shows unpredictable alternations. Put differently, the states show a low to non-existent rate of change, but the event that we call the transition shows a marked growth acceleration.

How should we proceed to find out whether there are transitions in a developmental

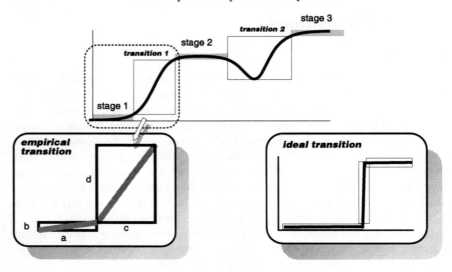

Figure 2.11 Weak transition criterion applied to a developmental curve based on a mathematical simulation. The developmental curve shows a step-wise increase and a pre-transitory dip. The transition value is given by the relationship between the lengths of *a*, *b*, *c* and *d*. The figure at the right shows an 'ideal' transition in the form of a sudden jump.

phenomenon? The first thing we need is a good, sufficiently long time series of data from one or more individuals. The data represent the change in a variable, such as conservation knowledge or in a space of variables, such as the space consisting of conservation, classification and seriation knowledge in a child. We begin by trying to identify a prolonged state of any sort, starting with the initial value of the developmental curve.

Take Figure 2.11 as an example. It shows a simulated developmental curve, for instance of a child's progress in solving fraction problems. Intuitively, there are three stages in the curve, corresponding with the more or less flat regions at the beginning, the middle and the end of the curve. They are our prolonged states.

Second, we should agree on a limited 'bandwidth' for defining a state. If the developmental curve were really flat, the bandwidth could correspond with the single value of the variable in that flat region. But values will always fluctuate a little bit, or rise slowly, as in Figure 2.11. The chosen bandwidth should therefore be a small domain of scores, for instance 2 per cent of the maximum score. Any sequence of successive values that stays within that band belongs to the first prolonged state or stage. In Figure 2.11, the band has width *b* and length *a*.

Third, once we have found the first stage, we look for the second by shifting the band with width *b* over the curve in an upward movement. This will lead us to the intermediate plane, where the values of the measured variable tend to change only a little. By definition, the width of the state band is b. Its length is most probably different from the first stage, say a'.

Fourth, we want to know whether the values of the measured variable between stage 1 and stage 2 constitute a real transition. These values can be covered by a rectangle with dimensions c and d. Given the intuitive criterion for a transition – a sharp rise between two more or less stable states – it will be clear that the ideal transition is one for which the value of the fraction:

$$(b \cdot c)/(a \cdot d) = T \tag{2.10}$$

is as small as possible. The point, then, is to define a value T of the fraction so that it corresponds with intuitive decisions about what would still be a transition and what would not. Say that we set the boundary value at 0.2. The values of the transitions in Figure 2.11 would be 0.11 and 0.15, respectively. That is, both are transitions according to the criterion that T should be smaller than 0.2.

Let us have a closer look at the second transition. It contains a slight regression before the leap to the higher (and final) level. Such regressions, announcing a marked leap, occur quite often in cognitive development. The geometric effect of such a regression is that it enlarges the size of d and therefore decreases the value of the fraction described above. Put differently, geometrically as well as intuitively, the existence of a temporary regression just before a considerable leap amplifies the transitional character of the event.

In reality, however, our longitudinal data will never look like the neat and smooth curve from Figure 2.11. They will, rather, look like the scatter of data shown in Figure 2.12. The figure simulates a set of measurements of a child's skill in solving fraction problems. The points could be the scores on tasks administered every two days.

First, we smooth the raw data by applying a method of moving average scores, as explained earlier. The figure shows three such curves, based on increasing domains over which the average has been taken.

Second, we take a smoothed data curve and apply exactly the same steps as before. We notice, however, that the bandwidth we have to choose to obtain a reasonably long steady state or stage is significantly larger than in the first example, which was based on an ideal curve, not disturbed by random variation. As a consequence, the height d of the rectangle covering the score domain between two consecutive stages will become smaller as b grows larger.

Third, we try to find a bandwidth b such that the resulting values for a, c and d lead to a transition fraction with minimal value. In Figure 2.12, this leads to values of 0.29 for the first transition and 0.19 for the second (which showed a transient regression that is now concealed by the randomness of the data).

Finally, why is this form of transition called 'weak'? It is weak because it depends on a conventional decision about how big T can be. No natural value for T emerges as a result of empirical or theoretical investigations. Second, it is weak because the states between which the eventual transitions occur can lie anywhere in the plane formed by the variable and time. For instance, there is no intrinsic reason why a child's mastery in solving fraction problems would level off at a score of 10, 20, 30, etc. per cent of a

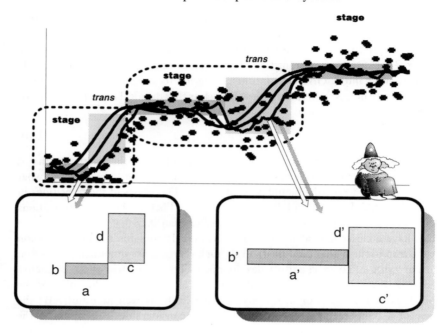

Figure 2.12 A simulation of a scatter of measurement points shows that the stages and transitions become more difficult to observe, but do not disappear. The 'measurement' is based on a random transformation of the developmental curve in Figure 2.11.

fractions test and not at any other level. If we administered the test on fractions to the whole adult population, we would probably find a distribution of stable scores covering all possible values.

If weak transitions exist, we may assume there are also strong transitions. Do they occur and, if so, what are their properties?

Strong transitions and catastrophes

A weak transition connects two semistable states by travelling through all the intermediate states. A growth spurt, for instance, connects a height of 80 cm to a height of 90 cm, but the person will of course at one time be 81 cm, then 82 cm and so on.

A large variety of systems exists where such intermediate states do not really occur, or are even difficult to conceive. An example is the aggregation state of matter: it is either gaseous, liquid or solid. Whatever exists between any two of those states is something highly transient. Does anything like this exist in development? Piaget, for one, claimed that the major stages of development represent mutually exclusive forms of organization; there is no conceivable intermediate state between pre-operational and operational thinking, for instance. A child is either in a pre-operational or in an operational state of mind. That state of mind can be highly context- and problem-dependent (although Piaget would rather see it as a general property of cognition as a whole).

Recently, van der Maas and Molenaar (1992) claimed that the development of conservation is a good example of a bimodal developmental state: the child either understands the principle or does not. Sudden switches of a system state into an entirely different one have remarkably similar properties over a wide variety of systems. They are studied mathematically in catastrophe theory. I shall call a developmental transition a strong transition if it amounts to a sudden shift from one state to another and if it has a number of properties characteristic of a catastrophe (in the mathematical sense of the word). Strong transitions and catastrophes will be discussed in Chapter 5.

In the preceding section, we saw that there is a large variety in the paths taken by development, ranging from growth towards a stable state to chaotic oscillations and from uniform increase to sudden transitions in the form of catastrophes. This variety is the essence of development and it should not be seen as a superficial disguise of the real, underlying simple Platonic forms, whatever they may be. Put differently, the often unpredictable oscillations of a process of cognitive learning, for instance, are not a matter of appearance, or of a random variation that actually conceals the real underlying smooth increase. The irregularity can (but should not necessarily) be a fundamental property of this form of learning.

Does this mean then that there is no underlying regularity in development? Far from it. The underlying regularity lies not in prototypical forms of development, such as uniform or S-shaped growth, but in the simplicity of the dynamics that generates the incredible variety of surface phenomena we observe in reality and in our dynamic models. So far, however, I have not yet answered a fundamental question: What is a dynamic system and how does it relate to a theory of development?

The many faces of dynamic systems

Systems and dynamic systems

In the late 1960s and early 1970s, the children of academia were interested either in Marxism–Leninism or in Eastern philosophy and religions and some (I almost hesitate to confess I was among this crowd) managed to be interested in both. In our rooms and dorms, we had little brass statues of Vishnu standing next to very incomplete complete editions of Marx and Engels. The smell of incense blended with the remarkable odour of socialist printing ink in irregular swirls that prefigured the later interest in chaos and the baker's transformation (a very colloquial name for a class of topological operations that describe kneading and mixing and loss of information typical of dynamic systems).

Both great groups of doctrines had some interesting commonalities. They both saw the world as a place of becoming, of change, acted on by hidden underlying mechanisms that revealed themselves in many different forms. But Marxism, like many other Western philosophies, discerned a basic essence, whereas eastern religions such as Buddhism saw the world as nothing but appearances that one could take but also leave.

Dynamic systems have a little bit of all these different flavours and it is probably not too coincidental that California, one of the main seats of the former hippie kingdom, was the stage for many basic discoveries in this field. So what is a (dynamic) system?

A system is a set of variables to which an observer relates. Take any object or part of the world. How does an observer relate to it? Many different viewpoints can be taken, but there is no privileged access to the essence of that piece of the world, no Camino Real to reach its heart (as Freud thought the dream was the Royal Highway to the unconscious). What the world is, is a function of how it is observed and perceived, its nature a matter of the channels opened to communicate with it. In this sense, all our scientific encounters with the world we want to study and understand are by necessity *reductionistic*, but calling them this does not entail a form of criticism. In fact, we necessarily reduce the world that we encounter to our own interests and possibilities of understanding and by doing so we create the possibility of changing that interest and understanding, reducing our egocentricity. This is the major lesson that the pipe-smoking Genevan private investigator of the child's mind has taught us and that we tend to forget as soon as it applies to us academic adults.

A system, however, is more than just a collection of variables or observables we have isolated from the rest of the world. It is a *system* because the variables mutually interact. That is, each variable affects all the other variables, but also affects itself. This is a property we may call *complete connectedness* and it is the default property of any system. The principal distinctive property of a variable is that it changes over time. Consequently, mutual interaction among variables implies that they influence and codetermine each other's changes over time. In this sense, a system is, by definition, a dynamic system and so we define a *dynamic system* as a set of variables that mutually affect each other's changes over time.

Let a, b, c, etc., be variables describing a child's cognitive system. For instance, a could be its logico-mathematical knowledge, b its knowledge of social relations, c its linguistic knowledge and so forth. If the cognitive system is a dynamic system – and it is very likely that it is – its time evolution is described by the set of coupled equations:

$$a_t = f(a_{t-i}, b_{t-j}, c_{t-k}, \ldots)$$
$$b_t = f'(a_{t-l}, b_{t-m}, c_{t-n}, \ldots) \tag{2.11}$$
$$c_t = f''(a_{t-o}, b_{t-p}, c_{t-q}, \ldots)$$

which means that the present state of the a, b, c, etc., system is based on the state of each of its separately distinguished variables. The state of a variable at time t is a function of the state of all the variables at an earlier time ($t - i$, $t - j$, etc.). In general, i, j, k, etc., are equal, but systems may differ in the delay between causes and effects. Each of the state equations is an iteration and together they form a system of coupled iterations.

This brings us back to the point of the iterative function mentioned earlier; the system evolves because, formally speaking, each system state is the input to an iterative function that produces the next state (or *a* next state) as its output. What is this function? It is the way in which each of the variables involved affects the others. The best way to explain what a dynamic system of development is, is to construct one. In the following example, we will travel to the friendly but unfortunately non-existent Siberian city of Yeltsingrad and follow the musical development of its juvenile inhabitants.

Singing in Yeltsingrad

The people of the city of Yeltsingrad are modest and hardworking folk with one great passion, singing. They love to sing at work, at home, while taking a cold shower; they sing all the time and everywhere. As you may imagine, becoming a good singer is an important achievement over there, not only for economic reasons – you can make a lot of money performing in the opera house or in the local pubs – but even more for the psychological gratification. More precisely, the self-esteem of the Yeltsingradians depends heavily on the quality of their singing performances and psychotherapists are usually more concerned with their patients' timbre than with their mental problems. Almost all children go to the Academy of Music to enjoy the lessons given by great musical performers. But deep underneath there is something tragic in this happy community. We know that self-esteem depends on the approval obtained from other people, especially when self-esteem is highly dependent on the quality as a performer. Almost all the Yeltsingrad children are so busy getting enough approval from others in an attempt to increase their self-esteem that their quest actually interferes negatively with their learning to sing and slows their progress. Besides, some children who are very uncritical about themselves adapt their self-esteem too quickly to changes in their singing competence. For instance, with any applause they get, they become increasingly certain they are Siberian Pavarottis, ready to conquer the world. Empirical research carried out by the School for Education of the local university has shown that there is considerable individual variety among the children, although the teaching is of uniformly high quality. Could the cause be talent, or some innate predisposition? Let us try to explain the possible developmental trajectories by building a dynamic systems model and see if there is an ideal combination between learning to sing properly and acquiring a reasonably fulfilling level of self-esteem (see Figures 2.13 and 2.14).

Our first assumption is that performance quality improves as a consequence of teaching and the children's efforts and that it continues to do so until a limit is reached, dependent on the child's talent. As we shall see later, this type of performance growth can be modelled by the logistic growth equation. But, we have seen that the growth of the child's self-esteem, based on the child's improving singing performance, requires a lot of extra-curricular effort and this interferes negatively with learning to sing. So we actually decrease the performance growth by a factor dependent on the level of self-esteem. Second, we know that the child's self-esteem depends on the quality of the singing performance. Without singing, the self-esteem would shrink and lead the child into a deplorable state of inferiority feelings. In fact, it requires a lot of public performance to at least maintain a level of self-esteem, let alone to increase it. This

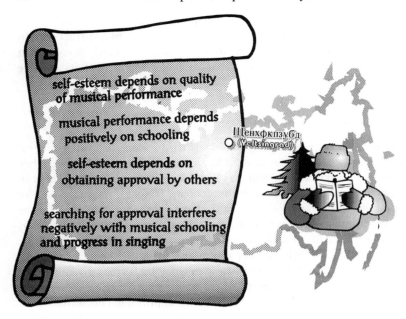

Figure 2.13 The 'psychological model' of singing development in the imaginary city of Yeltsingrad, Siberia.

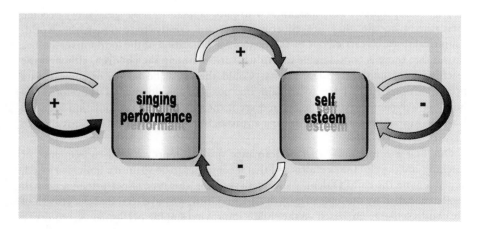

Figure 2.14 A standard graphic representation of the dynamic relations between the model components. Arrows between the variables (self-esteem and singing performance) represent supportive or competitive relationships. The arrows entering from and returning to the same variable represent growth relations within the variable at issue: singing performance increases (plus sign) by itself, but self-esteem decreases (minus sign) if it is not supported by singing performance.

particular relationship between singing performance level P and self-esteem level S can be expressed in the form of the following set of coupled equations:

$$P_{t+1} = P_t(1 + r - rP_t/L - cS_t)$$
$$S_{t+1} = S_t(1 - s + dP_t) \tag{2.12}$$

The parameters have the following meaning: r is the rate with which the singing performance improves, given the particular teaching and the child's effort; L is the performance limit determined by the child's natural talent (it has 1 as default value); c is the factor that determines how much the performance improvement suffers from the child's being absorbed in getting the approval of others to increase self-esteem; s is the factor by which self-esteem would decrease if the child were not allowed to sing and show personal qualities to others; d is the factor specifying how much self-esteem increases as a consequence of an improved singing performance.

Time series and state space representation

The state space consists of the dimensions 'singing performance' and 'self-esteem'. It might be very difficult to measure these variables empirically in a reliable and valid way, but for the purpose of model building we have to pretend that we simply know a child's real performance and self-esteem level (the town, the children, and the developmental process are imaginary anyway, so there are no objections to pretending we have direct knowledge of what goes on in the children's minds). Each child enters the singing class with an initial performance quality (some are quite good at the beginning, others still need much improvement) and an initial self-esteem level (some think very highly of themselves, others feel quite inferior). That is, for each child there is a single point in the state space (P, S) that corresponds with his or her *initial state*. Let us compute a single time series for a changing performance and self-esteem level, by taking the following parameters: $r = 0.03$, $L = 1$, $c = 0.03$, $s = 0.03$, $d = 0.1$, $P_{init} = 0.1$ and $S_{init} = 0.4$. We start with the initial values as mentioned above and apply the set of equations over and over, until we reach a time series of 1000 data points for each variable. The result can be seen in Figure 2.15.

We observe that both the singing performance and the self-esteem oscillate until they finally settle into an equilibrium state. We can run this little simulation with different initial states and with different parameter values. We will find the same overall pattern in the form of oscillations, but with a different amplitude and frequency and a different final point.

Instead of the time series, we can make a state space representation, plotting each point of a performance growth sequence against the corresponding point of the self-esteem sequence and do this for a few different time series, for instance based on different initial states and different parameters (e.g. the d parameter). The result is depicted in Figure 2.16. It shows semicircular trajectories, aiming inwards towards a stable point (which corresponds with a stable value on the P and on the S variable). What we can tell from this state space representation is that the initial state of the performance variable does not seem to matter too much; different initial states will end

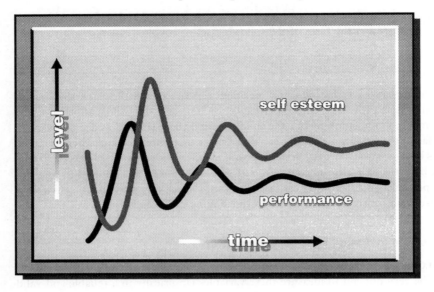

Figure 2.15 A time series representation of the growth of singing performance and self-esteem in a single Yeltsingradian child.

in the same final state (f2 and f3, for instance, which have very different initial states i2 and i3). If one of the parameters differs, however, then trajectories starting from the same initial state end up in very different final states (f1 and f2, for i1 and i2 equal).

Let us now do some further experiments with different initial state values. Suppose we had picked a group of children whose initial state of self-esteem and of performance are perfectly positively correlated. These are the children with realistic judgement of themselves. Of course they will differ with regard to the level of this state and in the group we study it will range from low (both low self-esteem and performance) to high.

Let us pretend we have a group of fifty children whose scores neatly divide the initial state variable into fifty consecutive points and run the dynamics equation for each initial state point. This gives us fifty final state points (by convention, I take the five hundredth step in the computation as the final state, which is a reasonable approximation in this particular system). These fifty points are drawn in the state space, which means that we exclude the fifty trajectories from being represented in the state space, and confine ourselves to the endpoints. This results in a curved line as in Figure 2.17, showing that the relationship between initial and final states is far from linear.

In the dynamic model discussed earlier, we hypothesized that self-esteem increases with improving singing performance. Children will differ as to how much their self-esteem will rise as a consequence of a socially approved rise (or fall) in their performance. Let us repeat the experiment with the same fifty initial states, but with a

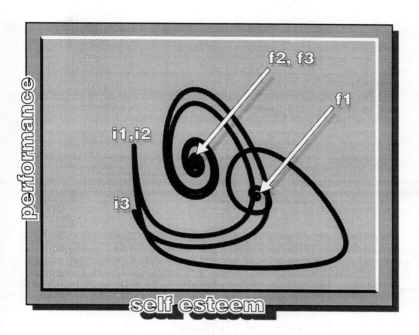

Figure 2.16 A state space representation with different trajectories for different initial states and parameters. Trajectories with different initial states (*i2* and *i3*) lead to similar final states (*f2* and *f3*), whereas similar initial states lead to different final states (*i1* and *i2*). These differences are explained by different parameter values underlying the growth processes.

different self-esteem increase parameter. We use in total five different parameter values, in increasing order. The effect may seem paradoxical, in that the final level of self-esteem drops as it adapts more strongly to increases or decreases in performance. This can be seen in Figure 2.18. The lines representing the final states are projected in lower regions of the state space as the esteem parameter increases. Since the vertical axis is the self-esteem axis, this lowering actually means a lowering in final self-esteem, although there remains a considerable variation, which is represented by the fact that the lines are curved, not straight.

In reality, Figure 2.18 is a three-dimensional representation, with the x-axis equal to the performance level, the y-axis the self-esteem level, and the z-axis (perpendicular to the pages in this book) corresponding to the self-esteem increase parameter.

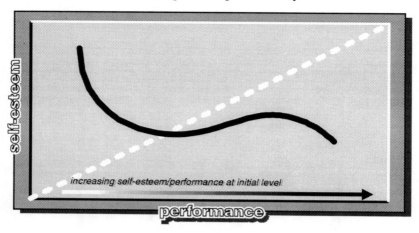

Figure 2.17 The diagonal, white line represents 50 initial states, consisting of maximally positively correlated initial values for the variables self-esteem and singing performance. The black, curved line represents the 50 end states that result from the initial states on the white line. The initial–final state relationship consists of a topological transformation of a straight into a curved line.

The topological forms of dynamic systems

Our voyage to the imaginary town of Yeltsingrad and the study of the musical development of its equally imaginary children has, I hope, brought us a bit closer to a more direct understanding of what a dynamic system is. The whole dynamic system explaining and describing the potential musical development of all Yeltsingradian children is represented by the coupled equations, the two simple lines stating how self-esteem and singing performance affect one another over time. In order for the equation to produce time series describing possible developmental paths, a number of variables (parameters and initial state values) have to be specified. These variables form a multidimensional state space.

The specification of the state space together with the dynamic equation constitutes the formal definition of the dynamic system. Such a definition, however, is hardly informative about the possible paths and trajectories it contains. Instead of just presenting the equation, we can also specify the basic state space – self-esteem and performance – and draw a representative collection of possible trajectories in this space.

The dynamic system represented by its state or phase portrait

The basic state space with some prototypical trajectories is what we call the *topological representation* of the dynamic system. There are different ways of presenting such a

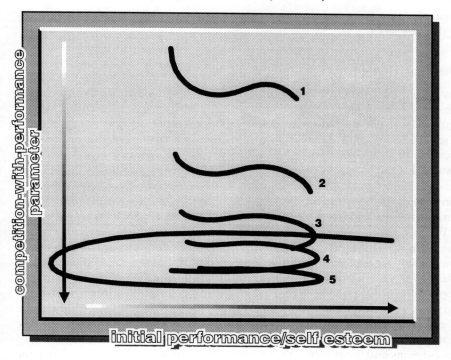

Figure 2.18 A representation of five sets of 50 final states each. The sets have the same initial state values as the set represented in Figure 2.17, but differ in the value of the competition parameter (the competition parameter value increases from top to bottom).

topological representation. One is the space and some of its representative trajectories, as in Figure 2.16. We call this the *state portrait* or *phase portrait* of the dynamic model. It is truly a portrait in that we give a visual impression of the dynamics and do so by confining ourselves to some characteristic lines, as with a drawing or caricature of a person's face.

The model of the development of singing in Yeltsingrad, which is after all an imaginary town on the Siberian steppes, is not a serious developmental model, but let us pretend it is, just for the sake of showing how models are represented in dynamic systems theory, as opposed to more conventional developmental model building. Figure 2.16 is the phase portrait of the model. It is very different from the way in which models are usually presented in developmental psychology. For instance, it does not describe a 'typical' developmental trajectory, since there is no such thing, but specifies the set of possible trajectories. By doing so, it explicitly reckons with the fact that considerable individual differences exist between subjects. Each possible trajectory on the plane is a potential individual developmental path. In the actual picture, such as

Figure 2.18, we represent only a few trajectories to serve as examples of what is possible in the state space.

The dynamic system as a topological landscape

Instead of conceiving the state space as a straight plane with trajectories, you could also see it as a folded object, or a landscape with a specific elevation. Imagine a satellite equipped with nothing but a water detector; it flies over the earth and collects pictures of streams and rivers. We could in fact reconstruct a reasonably adequate relief map of the earth by just looking at the lines of the water. Water goes down and we simply assume that the bigger the rivers, the lower the position as measured with regard to sea-level. Lakes mark the presence of confined valleys, straight narrow river lines correspond with steep flanks and so on. Put differently, the observed dynamics of the water is transformed into a statics of the earth surface, namely its relief.

We can do a similar thing for the state space. Take Figure 2.17. It represents a curved line consisting of final states. The initial states actually lay on a straight line, which was considerably longer than the curve of the final states. From each point on this long straight line we let a ball roll, simulating a specific trajectory. We observe that the ball stops at a particular position on the final state curve (Figure 2.19a). Just as we did with the water, we could imagine the dynamics of the balls specifying the relief of the surface. They leave at some higher point, roll down and come to rest in the valley specified by the final state line. This valley is also called a *basin of attraction*. Figure 2.19b provides a three-dimensional impression of the basin of attraction; the line on the valley floor is the set of potential final states of the trajectory followed by the rolling ball.

The topological transformation of a process into a landscape of imaginary hills and valleys is not just for fun. The landscape types to which many dynamic equations can be reduced, constitute to a small set of topological forms, such as basins and saddles, each characterized by a specific pattern of the trajectories involved. Such basic topological forms are well-studied mathematical objects and allow us to generalize over superficially different dynamics models and trajectories.

The landscape form is actually quite familiar in developmental psychology, where it is used as a metaphor. The origin of this way of representing developmental tracks lies in the work of the geneticist Waddington, who coined the term *epigenetic landscape* (Waddington, 1957). The hills and valleys of the imaginary landscape confine the possible paths of a ball that represents a single developmental trajectory.

The dynamic system as a folding procedure

In addition to the phase portrait and the landscape form of topological representation, there is a third way of representing a dynamic system. Take Figure 2.18, which represents five different sets of final states in the form of curved lines. The sets come from the same collection of initial states, but differ in one parameter, namely the parameter specifying how much self-esteem progresses as singing improves. The parameter values differ quite considerably, but imagine that we let the parameter

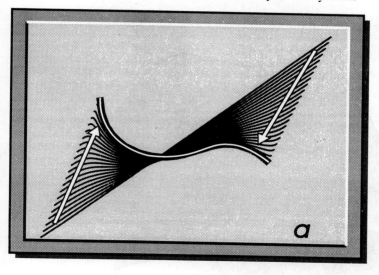

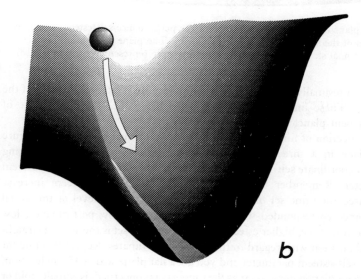

Figure 2.19 The transformation of a set of initial into a set of final states can be modelled in the form of a folded surface with a valley or basin. Figure (a) represents the transformation in the form of a line bending and stretching procedure. Figure (b) provides an alternative image, based on the notion of an epigenetic landscape.

Figure 2.20 The plane of all possible end states of the performance/self-esteem dynamics, for different values of the self-esteem increase parameter. The plane is a continuous collection of sets of final states values (five separate sets were represented in Figure 2.18).

increase by an infinitesimally small step, then compute a final state line for each of the parameter values. These lines form a plane; not a flat plane, such as a piece of cardboard, but a bent plane, such as a sheet of paper.

The infinite collection of final state lines would have formed a plane as in Figure 2.20. It is a plane in a three-dimensional space, with as x coordinate singing performance, as y coordinate self-esteem and as z (or depth) coordinate the self-esteem increase parameter. Remember that for each value of the self-esteem increase parameter, we used the same set of initial states, one where the level of the initial singing performance corresponded with that of self-esteem (low performance, low esteem, higher performance, higher esteem). The initial state set is therefore a straight line in a diagonal position with regard to the x and y coordinates. Repeat this line for each value of the self-esteem parameter and you get a flat plane with a 45° inclination. What the dynamics equation does, as far as the topology is concerned, is actually fold or bend the flat plane of the initial states into the curved one of the final states; the dynamics is a prescription for surface bending and folding (see Figure 2.21).

It should be noted that the present flat plane of initial states, mapping upon the bent plane, is just one set of initial states, namely the set defined by equal values of the singing performance and self-esteem variables. In theory, however, the whole space of potential initial states can be filled with such sheets (for instance, a parallel sheet lying a tiny distance below the sheet considered here). The initial state space looks like a ream of paper, with each sheet lying in a specific position. Each of these potential sheets

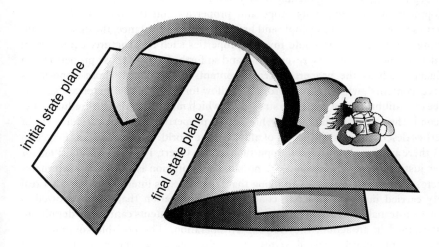

Figure 2.21 The dynamics equation of the Yeltsingrad model implicitly describes a procedure for surface bending and folding: the straight plane of initial states (left) is bent into the curved plane of final states (right).

would map onto a bent final state sheet. These final state sheets are wrapped into one another, in a way specific to each of the separate initial state sheets. The whole process is similar to taking a newspaper, with all the pages neatly ordered and wrapping it all up in some complicated pattern. The original newspaper is the initial state space; the wrapped paper is the final state space.

The dynamics model is represented as a particular procedure for folding an initial into a final state space. How does this all relate to the good old, simple developmental theories we find in our textbooks, theories that are not used to seeing themselves compared to a ragged old newspaper?

Developmental theories and dynamic systems

The bare necessities of developmental theory building

It took me years to realize that the song of Baloo, the bear in Walt Disney's *Jungle Book*, summing up the bare necessities for living in the jungle, contained a pun. This fact nicely illustrates that the delay between a developmental cause and its actual effect is sometimes rather considerable, an observation that will play an important role in the building of dynamic growth models later in this book. It also took me quite a while to realize that all developmental theories require the same bare necessities to do their theorizing, irrespective of what comes out of it. What are those necessities?

To begin with, a developmental theory should specify a domain of change and development, by describing its range and properties and the way in which such properties may vary between people and between ages. For instance, the domain could be acting and thinking and could involve properties such as structure, equilibrium, formal and concrete contents, reversibility and so forth. Some of those properties can be binary, such as the property 'formal contents of thinking' whose opposite is 'concrete contents', whereas other properties allow for continuous differences, such as 'degree of equilibration of cognitive structure', which may differ along a gradual scale.

Second, the theory should specify how those properties combine into clusters of properties describing possible states of affairs in the world. For instance, in Piagetian theory there are three basic binary properties (see van Geert, 1986b, 1987a and 1988 for further justifications of this claim). A possible combination is 'actional – internal – concrete'. It describes a form of thinking that takes place as internal imagery of a real activity carried out with concrete contents. A combination that is not allowed is 'actional – internal – formal'. The reason is that formal contents cannot, by definition, be entertained in an action; they require an operation. The possible combinations specify possible developmental states. Note that state has the neutral meaning described earlier, that is, a combination of values of variables in a specific theory. If states last for a sufficiently long time, if there are only a few of them and if they are irreversible, we may decide to call them 'stages'.

Third, a theory should specify how the potential states can be ordered in potential developmental sequences. In earlier publications (van Geert, 1986a,b; 1987a,b,c; 1988; 1990; 1991), I have made a distinction between two procedures. One takes the final state as a conceptual point of departure and views all the other states in light of the final one. It can be shown that this particular procedure, which I called 'retrospective', provides a fixed number and order of preceding stages. Piaget's stage theory can be reconstructed by employing this retrospective procedure. The other procedure takes the class of potential initial states and tries to infer the set of states potentially following the initial one. This 'prospective' procedure is not just a logical opposite of the previous one. It produces developmental sequence descriptions of an open type. Werner's theory is an example.

In fact, the second and third property coincide: a sufficiently extensive definition of the predicates or properties employed to distinguish potential developmental states implicitly specifies the way in which these predicates or properties can be combined into potential developmental sequences. For instance, it follows from the Piagetian definition of the properties of advanced logical thinking that the set of properties actional – external – concrete must be the initial state of development (if any such state exists in reality, which is a different question). This set of properties specifies the stage known as 'sensorimotor thinking', which is Piaget's initial stage.

Fourth, a theory should specify a set of mechanisms explaining why the developing system changes from one state into the other. Piaget, for instance, has used the general mechanism of adaptation and divided it into the opposite mechanisms of assimilation and accommodation. The mechanism explains developmental change on all levels. It explains, for instance, why a baby acquires a coordinated schema of looking and grasping, but it also explains why a child progresses from a concrete to a formal operational mode of cognitive functioning.

Stage theories often rely on a mechanism of conflict or incompatibility to explain why a stage transforms itself into a different stage. Piaget has spoken about cognitive conflict as a motor behind cognitive restructuring, but it is not the major mechanism in his theory. Erikson has laid considerable emphasis on the notion of 'crisis', which is a combination of internal and external conflicts, forcing the subject to make a new commitment or a choice for a new way of functioning.

Finally, a theory should specify how the concepts it employs to distinguish among developing people, developmental states and mechanisms are mapped onto reality. For instance, a theory such as Piaget's allows for the possibility of a set of logical groupings describing potential forms of cognitive organization in the concrete operational child. Those groupings need not necessarily occur in real children, in that some are actually found empirically, whereas others are just theoretical possibilities. Of course, the theory should be able to explain why some theoretically possible states occur and others do not. This may seem like a suspect form of tolerance; should not theories be faithful to reality, describe what really is and therefore preclude everything that is not present in the world outside?

But, the decision as to which empirical possibilities a theory should allow for is not and should not be decided entirely on the grounds of empirical actualities. Imagine a meteor striking the earth, and killing all people, except a small family of mentally retarded Belgians who have never reached the level of operational thinking. Would the meteorite have blown Piaget's theory into oblivion? It is no longer true, after all, in the sense that there is no longer any living being capable of operational thought. But the theory has not lost its validity (provided it was valid before the meteorite struck). For instance, it can predict that the family, given such-and-such cultural and biological conditions, will finally grow out into a larger population that will develop the art of operational thought within a specified number of centuries. Put differently, for a theory it is as important to describe the real state of affairs in the world as it is to describe a relevant set of potential states that follow logically from its basic assumptions.

Developmental theories as dynamic systems models

The bare necessities of a developmental theory fall into three classes. One could be called the *statics*, and refers to the potential states and sequences of states that a developmental system can be in. Another should of course be called the *dynamics* of the theory and specifies why a system moves from one state to another. There is no obvious candidate term for the third aspect, except for a rather funny neologism. You might call it the *empirics* of the theory, and it describes the mapping of the statics and dynamics onto circumscribed empirical domains. The right word should of course be 'methodology' or something of that kind, but that does not rhyme with dynamics and statics and that is, of course, a major scientific objection. Moreover, methodology also refers to the method of theoretical or deductive inference of hypotheses, which is not in itself an empirical issue but part of the dynamics.

The statics aspect of the theory corresponds with the dynamic state space in a dynamic model. It is formed by the properties and parameters the dynamic model employs to distinguish between potentially different states. The relationship between the statics of a developmental model and the state space of a dynamic model is not always one to one. The dynamic model requires its own specific parameters and those are not necessarily distinguished by the developmental model.

The dynamics of a developmental model are of course directly related to the heart of a dynamic model, the dynamics equations. Again, the relationship is not always simple and straightforward. The growth models in this book basically work with simple increments and decrements of the variables discerned, whereas developmental models describe all sorts of mental processes and intentional activities that do not map onto the simple pluses and minuses of the dynamic model. The connection between a developmental model and a dynamic model is usually a matter of a rather complicated mapping of groups of concepts in one model to groups of concepts in another.

The dynamics is an intrinsic part of any developmental theory. So are not all developmental theories about dynamics? What is the difference between a dynamics theory and any other developmental theory?

Actual theories emphasize a particular aspect of the entire developmental process. This is so because actual theories are limited versions of ideal theories and they are limited for trivial reasons, such as the lack of time to develop all the aspects of the theory, the lack of researchers who want to spend their time in elaborating a specific aspect or the untimely death of a major founder, such as was the case with Vygotsky's model. As I have noted before, some theories pay considerable attention to the stages or statics, such as the textbook versions of the classic developmental theories. Other theories are particularly interested in describing the mechanisms that make development work. Werner's classic book on development provides lengthy descriptions of how the processes of differentiation and integration work in different fields and time scales (Werner, 1948).

A dynamics theory of the kind explained in the present book is basically interested in the dynamics, the general forms of change over developmental time. We have seen that such changes are expressed as coupled increments and decrements in the variables the theory deals with. A dynamics theory tries to account for the general patterns of change by providing rather simple interaction models stated in the form of difference or differential equations. The Yeltsingrad model provided a good example.

Consequently, a dynamics theory pays less attention to the actual psychological mechanisms that underlie the dynamic relations between the variables involved. This is not because those mechanisms are considered less important. It is a mere matter of division of labour. A dynamics theory tries to capture the laws and forms of change over time, whereas a psychological mechanisms-oriented theory tries to find out the proximal mechanisms that make an individual change. By 'proximal' I mean the mechanisms that take place in the form of consciously entertained activities of developing subjects, such as teaching, guiding a child, learning or trying to solve a cognitive conflict.

The split between these styles of theorizing is far from absolute, however. After all, the theory styles result from rather trivial limitations on the human endeavour of theory building and do not reflect deep empirical and theoretical issues. A theory emphasizing its own particular aspect should therefore try to justify its claims by making a link with other styles of explanation. A dynamics theory should explain which psychological mechanisms could actually account for the general dynamic interactions it postulates. It need not do so in very much detail, but at least part of the justification of the theory should lie in its linking with a model of the underlying mechanisms.

Finally, the third aspect, the empirics, poses entirely different problems. Dynamic models produce time series, state spaces and other particular representations of processes. Testing them against the available data requires an approach that differs considerably from the one we are used to in developmental psychology. Ordinary developmental models usually confine to differences between age groups and to time series based on those groups and, therefore, are not really dynamic in the true sense of the word. Let us first see whether the dynamics approach implies any particular message about the empirics, the methods and assumptions involved in empirically testing such models.

3

Observing and measuring dynamic processes

Errors, mistakes and failures of observation

The most aggressive boy at the volleyball court

Human knowledge is, almost by necessity, very incomplete. One of the reasons is that our access to the world we would like to know and understand is limited. For instance, if we want to understand a particular child's development, we can observe the child only for a limited time, and we may see overt behaviour but will never get direct access to thoughts and covert intentions.

Take for instance John Cooper. He is known to be a very aggressive boy. On the volleyball court he swears like a retired sailor and kicks the other kids if they try to catch a ball he thinks was meant for him. The other day he got into a serious fight with a boy who claimed John had touched the net, which John fiercely denied. That John is aggressive is beyond doubt, but how do we know it? We simply see it: he swears, fights and kicks other players. John's aggressiveness *is* simply his tendency to swear, fight and kick in situations where other children would probably react more mildly. That it is a 'tendency' or 'trait' of John's is clear from the fact that it is predictable; we are very often correct when we expect John to act in this way. Of course, John's actual kicking and swearing is only a subset and by definition a limited subset of all the swearing and kicking that John could do, if he had more time and more occasions. This is an ontological limitation on our observations. Second, our actual observation of John's aggressive behaviour covers just a subset of all the aggressive behaviour that John displays somewhere or sometimes. This is an observational limitation.

These two limitations – ontological and observational – are a characteristic feature of aggressiveness, or any other personality trait for that matter. One could claim that our actual observations of John's aggressiveness produce a distorted image. Since most of John's current fellow players are peaceful and contemplative, the likelihood that John will act aggressively is considerably lower than if he were surrounded by equally aggressive players. But the fact that John will tend to act less aggressively if surrounded by his current friends is a property typical of his aggressiveness, and not a matter of distorted observation. Of course, if we want to predict how John will react with a different team, we should take into account the fact that his present team significantly mutes his aggressive outbursts.

Some psychologists may think that our occasional observations of John present an unreliable image of John's real aggressiveness. His real aggressiveness is conceived of as a personality trait and we should have a reliable and objective measurement of it if we are going to use it in psychological theory building. A good psychological test of aggressiveness should do the job. Why? If it is a good test, it will not show the contextual dependence that our casual observations do. That is, as observers we may be fooled by the fact that John plays on a very peaceful team now, which definitely lowers his aggressive outbursts. A good aggressiveness test is standardized, presenting the same context to all subjects on all occasions.

Second, walking along the volleyball court and watching John play, we sometimes witness real fights, leading to black eyes and swollen noses, whereas the next day we will spot a completely changed John Cooper, a boy who is only mildly aggressive and not very different from the other boys. Thus our casual observations reveal a highly fluctuating aggressiveness, whereas the test is supposed to show a similar picture over repeated test sessions.

Again, the point is that these observations are limited, and thus give a distorted image of John's aggressiveness. The test, however, allegedly succeeds in overcoming these distortions and presents a more faithful image of John's real aggressiveness. But does it really? We know that a characteristic feature of aggressiveness is that it is context-dependent. We know that another characteristic feature is that people are not always equally aggressive; they have their good days and their bad days. Thus aggressiveness is a fluctuating rather than a stable trait. These two characteristic features are exactly what the test conceals; it acts as if a trait like aggressiveness is something that is deep inside the person, that it is context-independent and stable (over a sufficiently short time, that is). It is at least remarkable that in a world of continuous dynamic fluctuation, a test that produces a static image is believed to be more 'true' than an observation that reveals the continuous change.

At this point we could make the inference that, if all the previous points are true, then the whole idea of tests as ways of observing people's traits should be abandoned. This is not what I intend to defend. What I contest is the idea that casual observations give only distorted images, and that a technical form of observation, such as a test, is required to reach the heart of the matter. My point is that the reality of a phenomenon is revealed by the multitude of observations it allows and not by some 'essential' observations in particular. Casual psychological observations are important, because psychological reality reveals itself in casual encounters between people. They allow the observer to see how context-dependent, fluctuating and 'fuzzy' a trait such as aggressiveness actually is. Technical observation tools, such as tests, serve different purposes. For instance, they allow us to predict average levels of aggressive encounters in a tested population, even if they do not allow us to predict which individuals will act aggressively or when they will do so. If administered repeatedly, however, most if not all tests will show the same fluctuation over time and the same context dependence as casual observations do. As most textbooks on psychological tests explain, it is the stability of repeated scores that counts as a measure of the test's reliability, so fluctuations are interpreted as an indication that the test shows a certain amount of failure in measuring the real, underlying personality trait.

The topic of this chapter is the relationship between our deeply rooted views on the nature of change and development and how that view relates to our assumptions about the meaning and truth of our methical observations of phenomena that change and develop. In the first part of this chapter I will argue that our standard ways of correcting for observation error are based on a model of a basically static or smoothly and gradually changing reality. The second part of the chapter begins with a discussion of the historical roots of our scientific and statistical methods and argues that our emphasis on group comparisons and statistical independence stands in the way of a thorough understanding of developmental processes. The third part of the chapter discusses the problem of observation, measurement and error in a somewhat non-conformist way by assuming that an observer has a completely transparent, almost divine knowledge of the contents of a child's mind. I shall then invoke the devil – but rest assured, it is a very friendly devil – to argue that the true, basic pattern of change and development is irregular, context-dependent, event-based and discrete and far from smooth, continuous and gradual. Let me begin, however, with the problem of measurement error and stability of observations over time.

'Erarre hummanum est'

A great part of scientific methodology deals with the error-prone nature of all human activity, and the Latin proverb in the heading assures us that making errors is human. In fact, there are also some errors in the heading, and they are examples of what I could call the class of *simple errors*. For instance, the correct spelling is not 'hummanum', but 'humanum'. The error is simple in that the conventionally agreed Latin spelling is 'humanum', so any deviation from it, such as 'hummanum', is an error. The example is clear because the thing itself, the spelling of the word as agreed on in a linguistic community and its representation, such as its actual appearance in this book, are of the same kind. Now, let us take a second example. Suppose Abe's IQ is 168, but his score on the Wechsler Intelligence Scale is 179. In what sense is the score incorrect, or an error?

Let us first try to find out what I mean by 'error' if the measurement tool is isomorphic with the measured dimension. A good example is a person's height. The yardstick shares an important aspect with the human body, a real physical extension (just as the correct spelling was of the same kind as the wrong one, namely a series of letters that can be compared one to one). But even in this very simple case we have to agree on a number of restrictions. For instance, height is measured with the person standing upright, shoes and baseball cap off. The point is that even a straightforward and simple looking property such as height is in fact fuzzy. Is a boy's hair a part of his height? Does his height begin at the sole of his foot, or at the tip of his big toe? But even if we come to a full agreement on what it is that we measure, however, we may still make measurement errors. For instance, the boy is not always standing fully upright, we sometimes err in reading off the digits on the yardstick and so on.

Various techniques have been developed to deal with this sort of error and they have been adopted in psychology too. In essence, they amount to making a number of repeated measurements over a short time period. It is assumed that since errors are randomly distributed, such measurements will cluster into a normal distribution. The average value, the top of the hill, has the greatest probability of representing the 'real' value of the measured attribute, such as height. Provided it is at all possible to make enough repeated measurements, the eventual finding of a normal distribution of measurements is not in itself a proof of the fact that there is measurement error around the mean value. If there is measurement error, the measurements cluster in the form of a normal distribution. But, if there is a normal distribution, it may have been caused by error as well as by any sort of systematic change in the real scores. But since we assume that the measured property is stable over the course of the repeated measurements, we interpret the normal distribution of the measurements as an indication of error.

After Arthur C. Clarke's *2001: A Space Odyssey*, most readers will be perfectly willing to accept the idea of huge black monoliths coming from outer space, sending signals to their creators. So imagine that a Foreign Legion trooper who got separated from the rest of his pack finds a grey monolith in the heart of the Sahara. The monolith sends a continuous stream of sounds, and the legionary, not having completely forgotten his scientific training, sets out to measure the monolith's dimensions, equipped only with the most primitive means to carry out the job. Repeated measures of the size of the monolith, using his gun as a yardstick, clearly vary. The variations are perceived as measurement errors, due to the very poor conditions under which measuring must take place, since the legionary assumes that the physical size of the monolith must remain constant.

Measuring the sound level emitted by the monolith is a bit more difficult, though. Fortunately the legionary plays the bugle in his military band, and so he is capable of estimating the pitch. Repeated measures will again produce fluctuations, but here the legionary assumes that, although contaminated by errors, the fluctuations are real, since he expects the monolith to send some sort of auditory signal that is assumed to fluctuate. Moreover, the monolith's whistle is probably not just a single frequency, but a band of frequencies, whose composition probably changes over time.

The message behind this rather silly example is that the concept of measurement error depends on the assumptions we make about the nature of the measured dimensions. Are they stable attributes with single values on a well-defined scale, or do they fluctuate? Since there is clearly more fluctuation than stability in the world, we should expect many properties to be of the latter kind. Are psychological variables stable over (sufficiently short) time periods? If they are not, measured instability over time is not a sign of measurement error, but of real fluctuations (or, of course, of a combination of both).

Errors in psychological measurement

In the previous section, I mentioned the example of an error in establishing a person's IQ; we gave Abe 179, whereas he has only 168. What is the nature of our error? We could of course have made all kinds of trivial mistakes, such as errors in adding the subscores; we could have made a typing error in our report and so on. A well-defined procedure exists for administering the test, scoring the items, computing the total score and so on. If we deviate from that procedure, we make an error of the simple kind, comparable to a writing error. But this is not the kind of error we refer to in the case of Abe's IQ. If you consult a handbook on psychological measurement and methodology, such as Nunnally's classic *Introduction to Psychological Measurement* (Nunnally, 1970), you will find a different interpretation of a measurement error. It is assumed that no obvious procedural errors have been made and that Abe actually has an IQ of 168. The fact that we have scored 179 instead of 168 is a consequence of the fallible nature of the test, more precisely of the fact that the test gives a distorted view of the measured IQ. The central issue here is the assumption that Abe actually has an IQ of 168. What could be intended by that statement?

Let me first say that I understand by *measurement* the association of a number to an empirical attribute. Unfortunately, reality is not always separated into nicely distinguishable attributes. Measurement is a procedure for making it isomorphic to the measure. For instance, if we measure a boy's height, we do not look at how fat he is, or whether he has blue or brown eyes. We do ask the person to stand upright, to stretch and press his back against the wall. By so doing we make the body isomorphic to the vertical, stiff yardstick. The resulting specific match between the body and the yardstick is the boy's height.

In a similar vein, the measurement of a boy's IQ requires a specific procedure. Just as there is a widely varying vertical stretch of the human body, dependent on the boy's posture, there is a widely varying display of intelligence, dependent on the actual problems a boy has to solve, his current motivation and so forth. An intelligence test is a procedure for establishing an isomorphism between this highly variable domain of human conduct on the one hand, and an intelligence measure on the other. The intelligence measure is based on the paradigm of one-dimensional numerical distance. Whereas the measurement of height requires the boy to stand upright and stretch, the measurement of intelligence requires the boy to solve a predefined and ordered set of problems, often within a limited time span. Just as the boy's height is, by definition, the match between the body and the yardstick, provided the isomorphic procedure has been followed correctly, the boy's IQ is by definition the match between his intellectual activity on the one hand and the intelligence test on the other, again provided the isomorphic procedure has been carried out properly.

Since IQ is entirely defined by a particular testing procedure, it is meaningless to claim that a boy has a real IQ outside any testing procedure and that a test error consists of the deviation between the test score and the real score. In my view, test errors are errors of procedure and are not related to some sort of ontological question. Of course, it remains an important issue which test (of IQ, for instance) is best suited for which sort of goals, such as the prediction of scholarly achievement. Another problem that remains to be solved is whether the IQ test overlaps sufficiently with other situations that are assumed to be indicative of a boy's intelligence. Should the validity of a test not be determined by the amount it overlaps with the normal manifestations of the trait it pretends to measure? The answer of classic test theory is yes. A test is valid insofar as it reveals the same information as the totality of natural manifestations of the measured trait would do. Consequently, a test makes a measurement error to the extent that it deviates from the collection of natural manifestations. The reason we use tests is that the natural manifestations are sometimes difficult to observe, because they occur only infrequently or are expected to take place only in the future.

Just assume, however, that a specific trait like aggressiveness or intelligence is manifested in a way that is far from consistent over time and that this lack of consistency is a major, intrinsic property of the trait. There is absolutely no reason why traits should be consistent over time and contexts. If we think about traits, we see them as we see the size of the legionary's monolith. Why should traits not behave like the monolith's whistle, instead, as something that, by its very nature, changes over time?

There is evidence that a property such as intelligence may show a dramatic change over time. The Berkeley Longitudinal Study (Honzik, MacFarlane and Allen, 1948) showed that the IQs of about half of the children in the sample fluctuated over time, sometimes up to thirty IQ points. IQ fluctuates in response to environmental events. For instance, when a child is born in a family, the siblings often show a regress in IQ, lasting for several years. Scores then recover and rise even higher than in siblings who did not have a younger brother or sister (McCall, 1983; Zajonc and Markus, 1975).

Some mental properties not only change over time, but also are multidimensional. Intelligence is the classic example, with components such as social or verbal intelligence. We could argue that they are just different forms of intelligence, not dimensions of a single trait. But then consider the example of skills discussed previously (Fischer and Pipp, 1984). A skill is two-dimensional in the sense that it is characterized by two different types of measurement (one supportive, the other 'neutral'). These two forms of measurement cannot be considered different forms of skill. They are different sides of the same thing.

But if human traits are fluctuating, inconsistent over time and context and multidimensional, there is no ground for claiming that a test measures a trait reliably and validly insofar as the measurement is consistent with the natural manifestation of that trait. How could a single measurement be consistent with something that has different levels dependent on time and context? Let us dig somewhat deeper in the theory of measurement error in an attempt to answer the question of what such psychological measurement errors really are.

Samples and signals

There are two classical sources of measurement errors. One is concerned with the relationship between a sample and the population from which it has been drawn, the other with a signal and superimposed noise. Questions about properties of a population, would ideally require that each member of the population be studied. This is impossible for merely practical reasons, such as limited research time and resources. Instead, the investigator takes a subset of the population (a sample), studies its properties with all its individuals and then generalizes to the entire population. For instance, during the 1992 election day a sample of the American voters were asked whom they had voted for, in order to make a prognosis of the final results before the votes were officially counted. The potential measurement errors are obvious; only rarely is the distribution of properties over the sample identical to that of the population.

The second type of error is concerned with a signal and the superimposed noise. Take for instance a noisy family. The television is playing and Dad, preparing a cup of coffee in the kitchen, wants to hear the weather forecast for next weekend. But his children, wife and neighbours, all gathered in the living room, make so much noise that he can hardly understand whether it will rain or shine. The sources of error are obvious in this case too. There is a circumscribed signal – the weather forecast – and a specific procedure for receiving it: to listen and watch in a quiet room. The nature of the problem is almost the reverse of the sampling problem. In sampling we have to expand incomplete information; the signal problem involves the reduction of too much information.

An impressive length of bookshelves can be filled with publications on these issues and a considerable number of problems in the social sciences involve either the sampling or the signal question. It is less fortunate, however, that the signals and the sample models have proliferated far beyond their adequate applications. Let us return to our aggressive young friend John Cooper to illustrate this point.

Our occasional observations of John's aggressive outbursts are only a subset of all his acts of aggression and they in turn are just a small sample of what could happen. It is easy to make the comparison with the sampling problem, therefore. The few observations are a sample drawn from the set of observations that would give a complete and true image of John's aggressiveness. But the comparison is flawed. Whereas a population of real subjects has an objective extension (there are that many persons at this time, and they have specific properties), the set of potential behaviours has no boundaries whatsoever. Aggressive behaviour is context-dependent (in addition to being person-dependent, of course) and whether and how a person's aggressiveness is manifested depends on a multitude of mere coincidences.

There is no direct relationship, therefore, between the person's attribute aggressiveness and a circumscribed set of manifestations of it. Any reasonable subset of observations is as good as any other one and as complete as the total set of actual aggressive outbursts of the person. The sample model becomes relevant only if we wish to generalize from a set of actual observations to a set of missed observations. For instance, John plays volleyball every school-day, but since we watch him only on Wednesday afternoon, we want to generalize those observations to Monday or Tuesday.

Instead of following the sampling model, we could have employed the signal and noise paradigm. The idea is that John has a fixed attribute, a level of aggressiveness. His behaviour is a signal of that aggressiveness, but the pure signal – which would tell us exactly how aggressive John is – is covered up by 'noise'. The noise is the effect of coincidental factors, that is, events independent of the signal. For instance, if John plays with placid, peaceful and highly tolerant boys, the aggressiveness signal is lower than it should be, given John's 'real' aggressiveness. If John plays with an aggressive team, it is likely that he will show more aggressive behaviour than he would normally. The teammates are of course not causally or logically related to John's aggressiveness, so they may be considered 'noise', deforming the pure signal. Statistical filtering techniques should help us to get at the undeformed signal, that is, at a reasonable estimation of John's real aggressiveness.

The assumption underlying the model is that there exists a single source emitting a signal independent of the factors that influence our perception of it. Aggressiveness, however, is clearly a property not of the person alone, but of the combination of a person and a specific context. The noise is not independent of the 'signal'. In fact, if we observe John's aggressive behaviour, we are receiving a pretty clear signal, as far as that is concerned. But it is a signal about an interaction, not about a pure attribute of a single person. There is hardly any attribute of a person that is not interactional, that is, independent of the context in which the attribute is expressed. Moreover, attributes are not only interactional or contextual, but also time-dependent and variable. How are we going to characterize a psychological property of a person that does not seem to be a property of that person at all?

Competence and performance

A classic attempt at solving many of the problems above consists of making a distinction between a person's competence and his or her performance. It is especially relevant in areas such as cognition and language. Let me tell you a story about the learned Dr Kurt Harris from the University of Harford who has spent a lifetime doing research in conservation, but has, unfortunately, never managed to publish anything. His characteristic experimental set-up goes like this. Once he has found a child, 5-year-old Susan, for instance, who appears to understand the principle of conservation, he presents her with the standard conservation problem, with the beakers and the water. In this particular experiment, Susan answers correctly that there is the same amount after pouring the water into the thinner and higher container. But then Dr Harris tells her that Roger, whom she greatly admires as a very smart boy, has been asked the same question just before she came in. Roger, he says, just explained there is more water after pouring, instead of the equal amount she thinks there is. Dr Harris then shows her the experiment again, now pouring the water back into the broader, lower container and repeats the question. After ample reflection, Susan tells him there is less water than before. Asked why, she says that the water is lower now than it was before, so there is less.

A week later Dr Harris reports this little experiment in a class on cognitive development. He explains to his students that it shows the distinction between Susan's competence and her performance. Let me give you another example of the distinction between competence and performance, he says. He first explains the Chomskyan notion of competence and performance, then claims that every mature language user has the competence to understand sentences with an arbitrary and (in principle) infinite amount of embedding. For instance, you have the competence to understand the sentence 'The mug that the psychologist who the teacher who the headmaster hired introduced used broke', but you would never use the sentence, or you would understand it incorrectly, because your language performance is hampered by your limited memory. The students agree, write down the sentence and note that it is an example of competence and performance, similar to the conservation example under different testing conditions.

The question is whether the conservation competence and the linguistic competence are of the same kind. What the learned doctor means by Susan's conservation competence is the 'real' level of her understanding of conservation, or her purely cognitive representation of the conservation principle. It is assumed that her actual answers do not necessarily reflect this real level of purely cognitive understanding. They are contaminated by contingent and non–cognitive factors, such as memory limitations, social contagion and so forth. The competence, in this case, is an individual attribute, whereas the performance is context-dependent and interactional.

It will probably have become clear from the previous sections that I think the concept of a pure personal attribute is untenable. The child's conservation under-standing is an interactive and not an individual property; it is a property of a particular child in a particular situation. It is characteristic of 5-year-olds that their conservation understanding depends on social information and agreement, whereas 7-year-olds' conservation understanding is insensitive to such factors. Put differently, there is no empirically and theoretically meaningful notion of a competence *qua* psychological property of an individual person.

What does competence mean in the case of language as opposed to Susan's conservation knowledge? The doctor was probably not entirely on the right track when he told his students that they are the same. Linguistic competence is not a psychological attribute of an individual person in the same sense that conservation competence is. If the doctor explains that linguistic competence implies that a sentence can have an arbitrarily large number of embeddings, he actually makes a claim about the possibilities of sentence formation that follow from the formal properties of the grammar. That is, the claim is about the language, not about a language user and his or her psychological properties. Language and cognition are entities with a specific formal structure. Similarly numbers and arithmetic operations obey a structure of formal rules. Under the arithmetic rules, it does not matter whether we add numbers of billions of digits or numbers of just two. It does matter for our actual addition operations, however, whether the numbers are extremely long or reasonably manageable. How is the step made from formal properties of a structure to a statement about a competence *qua* psychological attribute?

If we observe a speaker producing and understanding sentences, making errors, asking for clarification, etc., we can conclude that his/her language use (or 'performance') conforms to the use of a grammar, with specific rules of sentence formation, irrespective of the errors he/she makes (which are recognized as errors because we recognize the regularity). That is, what the English speaker's speech defines and distinguishes from others speaking Danish or Flemish is the grammar of the English language. It is only in this sense that we can claim that the use of English grammar is a competence of the English speaker. Because English grammar, or any other natural grammar for that matter, formally allows the formation of infinitely embedded sentences, we conclude that it is within the competence of any English speaker to formulate infinitely embedded sentences. But 'competence' is not synonymous with 'ability'; that is, the conclusion says nothing about what the actual speaker can do; it tells only what the speaker's *language* can do. There is no transitivity here. It is true that the speaker possesses the grammar. It is also true that one of the formal possibilities of the grammar is that it allows infinitely embedded sentences. But this does not imply that the speaker is capable of forming or understanding such sentences and that it is only by intervention of non-linguistic forces, such as memory limitations, that the speaker is cut off from the actual possibility of exercising this competence.

In summary, a *competence* is the formal definition of what a person is doing when he or she is exercising that competence. It is not a programme of what goes on in the head of the person, or a set of rules that generate the behaviour. For instance, when a child is adding and subtracting numbers, he/she is exercising his/her competence of elementary numerical arithmetic. That is, what he/she does is not just mere drawing of lines on paper, or the performance of a trick. What he/she does is calculation and that is defined by a set of formal rules. They specify the child's action as an instance of a competence.

As far as measurement is concerned, the notion of competence is an essential descriptive device, necessary to specify what it is that humans are doing when they are calculating, thinking logically or forming grammatical sentences. But it does not present a measurement problem in the sense that the actual observable behaviour gives a distorted image of that competence, because it is contaminated by contingent phenomena such as memory limitations.

The problem at stake here could better be described by a metaphor than by a lengthy philosophical discussion. When the beautiful Narcissus looked into the water of the pond, he saw a distorted image of his face, caused by the ripples on the water surface. He had to reconstruct the real image of his face by compensating for the distorting effects of the ripples. In the standard psychological view, this is about what happens with the measurement of competence. There is a competence – as there is a face belonging to Narcissus – and we have no direct access to it, like Narcissus, who has to look into the water of the pond. The access we have – via behavioural observation – distorts the image of the underlying competence and so we have to do tricks to reconstruct the real image. But I do not believe there is anything like a competence in this sense, that is, an individual psychological property that we see only through the distorting reflections of transient performances.

Let us consider a different view. What if Narcissus's brother looks at Narcissus's face? He sees a face whose actual form is context-dependent; Narcissus laughs or Narcissus cries. The face changes over time. It changes over a short time, for instance when Narcissus talks, and over a long time span, for instance between Narcissus as a baby and as an adult. What his brother sees is not a distorted image of Narcissus's real face, which he has to subtract from the contingent movements and emotions on it. Whenever his brother looks, he sees the real face of Narcissus, but it is a face that changes constantly, though it nevertheless remains the face of Narcissus. The wrinkles around Narcissus's laughing eyes are real, dynamic, temporally changing features of the face. They are fundamentally different from the wrinkles in the reflected face produced by the ripples in the water. In a similar vein, the changes and fluctuations in what we call a person's competence are real aspects of that person's competence (not of the competence *qua* formal rule structure), and not distortions we would have to look through in order to see the real thing. Competence, defined in the abstract formal sense, reveals itself as a dynamic, ever-changing phenomenon as soon as it takes the form of activities and behaviour of a real person.

Investigation as communication

Divine observation

From my Roman Catholic boyhood a number of vivid images remain. The teacher in the first class of my primary school, a placid man with a stocky figure who probably did not realize what damage he did to the unspoiled souls sitting in front of him in uncomfortable wooden desks, had just finished a drawing on the blackboard that, in all its simplicity, was a masterpiece of horror. In chalky but terrifying colours, it displayed a high mountain with a steep and narrow road leading to Heaven, and a broad and easy road going straight down to Hell. The choice to be made as well as the difference in efforts to be spent to reach the heavenly goal were obvious. The teacher then explained that in trying to reach for the heavenly goal we should not think we could hide anything from the good Lord, since He was omnipresent and constantly observing not only what we did but also what we thought and wanted. Needless to say, we boys were quite impressed by that message. Until then I had neither felt nor realized that somebody was watching me, that all my deeds and thoughts were observed and remembered, or that my most personal phone line was constantly tapped. It was actually pretty stupid of the good Lord to allow this teacher of ours to reveal the terrifying secret, because as soon as we knew that He was watching we started to try to fool Him, since none of us wanted to be on the fast lane to Hell. If He wanted to know what we did, He should have kept to His unobtrusive, unnoticed and non-influencing style of divine contemplation, and never have allowed our teacher to reveal the dreadful secret.

The ideal of an unobtrusive, undisturbed and direct observation reigns widely in science, and there are many fields of investigation in which it has been approached pretty closely. When Tycho Brahe watched the planets moving, through his primitive telescope, his observation did not prevent the planets from continuing their eternal ellipses. But, as the nature of the measurement or observation on the one hand, and the nature of the observed process on the other, come closer to one another – that is, if they tend to be of the same kind and magnitude – observation becomes a form of communication. Observation on the level of quantum physical processes is no longer unobtrusive, but of the same kind as the observed process and affects it in particular ways.

In psychological observation, or measurement for that matter, the observer and observed are very much of the same kind. They differ in that one is a psychologist and the other a child, or a student in a social psychology experiment with a stooge; they are similar in that they both belong to the human community. The fact that psychological investigation is almost always communication has been observed many times and has given rise to different conclusions.

The position I would take in the debate is that psychological research is an act of communication between psychologist and subject and that communication is a very general, powerful form of event dynamics. The concept of communication involves a notion of 'communing', that is, of exchange or interchange. Whereas the original divine observation of our boys' souls was unobtrusive and did not imply an interchange, all this changed when the teacher told us He was watching and that we had better watch out if we wanted our final destination not to be the hot furnace of Hell. In psychology, unobtrusive observation is almost impossible. If a psychologist administers a test to a child, there is explicit or implicit information that the psychologist wants the child to do its best, that this is an important issue, that he/she wants to learn something important about the child and so forth. In return, most children will do their best, or maybe feel very nervous about it and spoil the results. When studying a child's language development, we cannot abstain from communicating with and guiding the child's ongoing linguistic acquisition process. Of course, you can simply videotape an interaction between a child and a caregiver, but the principle remains the same, in that the caregiver plays his or her normal role and interacts with the child in an educational way.

Another example of the communing aspect is the notorious training effect that accompanies repeated testing. If you want to know how a child learns about the nature of objects, you should ideally administer the same object concept test with the same child on numerous repeated occasions. But the child will of course become used to the test and learn how to do it. This changes the nature of the test, in that it no longer measures the intended variable, such as object understanding, but also 'measures' the increasing familiarity with the test procedure. This is generally seen as a disadvantage, but it is simply an illustration of a basic fact about human beings: they learn. To find out how they learn, for instance about object properties, is the very aim of administering the object concept test that I gave as an example. Instead of trying to make tests where no training effect will take place, the investigator should try to develop a logic of testing and data processing that explicitly takes the training effect of test repetition into account. But, as long as the basic models about observation and measurement come from the classic physical sciences, where repeated measurement is not supposed to 'teach' the observed event, investigators in the social sciences will have great difficulty establishing a proper way of dealing with the nature of their phenomena.

The conclusion that should be drawn here is simple. Psychological research is an example of the same dynamic principles that govern the phenomena it studies. I defined a dynamic system as a system of interacting components, changing each other in the course of the process, based on an idea of mutual causality. In psychological research, and developmental research in general, there is a mutuality between researcher and subject. It lies, for instance, in the training effect of repeated testing, or in attempts by the subjects to comply with the demands they assume in the psychologist's research activity. It has been common practice to get rid of this dynamic interaction by avoiding all situations in which it could come about. In the next section, I shall look into the historical roots of this avoidance and try to make clear how it affected our standard research methodology.

The science of change and difference

Quetelet and the science of human differences

When I defended my PhD thesis in 1975 at the University of Ghent, I was not aware that I was continuing the tradition that had begun with Lambert Adolphe Jacques Quetelet, who presented the first dissertation at the University in 1819. I was not exactly standing where he must have stood so many years ago, since somebody had made an error in booking the Aula, and my company and I were referred to a storage room for old chairs. There I stood, behind a reading desk that bore the very unacademic inscription 'Good Night, Chérie', nervous but ready to defend a very unQueteletian study on the language development of a single child.

Quetelet can be considered the founding father of the statistical study of human properties, and it is remarkable how many of his original ideas are still alive in the current methodology of the social sciences. Quetelet based his statistical method on two general principles. The first is that causes are proportional to the effects they produce. The second is that large numbers are necessary in order to reach valid and reliable conclusions. Quetelet wanted to know the general laws of the social, and assumed that statistical measures (the mean, in the first place) could be used to overcome trivial differences between people and reveal the typical or common aspect. The mean of a property, as distributed in a large population, was believed to show the working of the 'constant causes', that is, essential causal influences that shaped the real underlying properties of humans. Individual differences, fluctuations around the mean, were caused by 'accidental causes'. Accidental causes must, by natural law, fluctuate symmetrically around the mean. The essence of humans was revealed by the means of the distributions of many properties in large populations and the construct to which these average properties were attached was called *l'homme moyen*, the 'average man'.

Quetelet also applied these principles to what he called moral traits and what we would now call 'psychological' traits. What a person actually does is caused by his/her real propensity (such as the propensity to do scientific work) and a variety of accidental factors. In his younger years, Quetelet was a gifted painter and poet, and he worked as an apprentice in a painter's studio. He might have stayed there and then someone else would have had to become the founder of statistics in the social sciences, but it seemed that for Quetelet the 'accidental' painting did not stand in the way of his real propensity. The use of large populations and the computation of the mean, Quetelet believed, can uncover the real propensities of people. Such propensities are related to the essential causes, which lie in a person's sex, age or social background.

It is indeed remarkable how much of our current research methodology is still explicitly or just tacitly following these principles. No one would endorse them in the naked forceful form that Quetelet moulded them into, but they seem to be part of our methodological intuition to more than an insignificant extent.

For accidental reasons, for which I should not be credited, my PhD thesis was very different from the methodological pattern that started with Quetelet. It was a study of the language development of one child, my son; it consisted of daily observations of a constantly changing knowledge and contained no statistics at all. The committee of highly learned ladies and gentlemen was eager to know how I thought I was going to generalize my findings, since one child was indeed a very small sample. I think I then tried to explain that I was trying to generalize about how a mechanism of language development worked, and that information about language acquisition in groups is a sociological and not a psychological issue. I am pretty sure the committee was not impressed, but since my supervisor had, somewhat reluctantly, agreed to my topic and method, my torture ended in an academic grumble.

The longitudinal study of a single child taught me more lessons than I could fully appreciate at the time. For instance, it demonstrated that in a developmental process causes are not proportional to their effects; the effect is dependent on the context and time in which the cause occurs. Sometimes you correct a child over and over again, and he will simply not hear it. And suddenly, at an unexpected moment, after he himself has found out there might be something wrong with *foots*, he understands and never makes the mistake again. Second, the use of great numbers as a way to grasp an underlying principle is of no use if that principle keeps changing all the time, as happens with the developing linguistic skills of children between the ages of 1 and 3. Third, accidental causes often do not average out. The language heard by the child contains a considerable amount of errors, repairs, incomplete sentences, etc., but they do not result in some average error level in the child's grammar. He picks up the correct grammar despite the lousy evidence and it is still not completely understood how children manage to do that. Fourth, I saw that I myself was not only an observer but also a coproducer of the phenomena I studied, although I had no idea at all about how I contributed to that process. Finally, I learned that the study of a single case can teach you more about a population than the actual study of the population would do. The single case brings you to the mechanism – an example of the mechanism – whereas the study of the population would conceal the way in which the mechanism works, because it would require averaging over many individually different forms in which that mechanism works.

It is true that many children who have provided the material for language studies are unrepresentative and precocious. But once an understanding of the longitudinal, dynamic mechanism is achieved, the population distribution can be reconstructed by varying the parameters the individual study has revealed.

In fact, many principles of change and development (discussed in Chapter 1) do not match Quetelet's principles. That would hardly be a serious matter if it were not for the fact that Quetelet's principles still underlie much of the methodology that we use to study and understand processes of change and development.

Whereas Quetelet was interested in finding the average man, his heirs, such as Galton, Pearson and Cattell, undertook another quest, aimed at the study of individual differences. Much of the statistics widely used in psychology today has been developed to support the study and description of individual variation in and between groups. Many problems in psychology deal with such individual variation in groups, but an equally important group of problems addresses the entirely different problem of processes. Developmental psychology is a case in point. Its objectives are the study and understanding of developmental processes and mechanisms; it tries to discover what causes individual subjects to acquire a language, to develop a specific personality, to solve identity crises and so forth. Let us try to find out how the study of groups is different from that of processes.

Groups and processes

Whereas the study of groups rejoices in the possession of long-standing, firmly established statistical techniques, the study of psychological processes has a far poorer historical background. The great founding fathers of the discipline, such as Freud and Piaget, put considerable effort into working out a methodology for the study of processes. Unfortunately, their approaches are entombed in the category of clinical – read 'unscientific' – methods.

Nowadays it is common practice to consider a developmental problem as a problem of groups and individual differences within the group. The central criterion for distinguishing groups is age. Instead of using a group of criminals or French army conscripts, as Quetelet did, we form groups of 4-year-olds, 5-year-olds and so forth. We then study means and standard deviations of some property in each group, and finally tie them all together to form a wreath of years and developmental differences. Put differently, our empirical model of development is a collection of groups and group properties, ordered in increasing years, not a model of developmental processes and mechanisms.

It is interesting to note that the adoption of the Piagetian universe by North American psychological research in the early 1960s actually consisted of applying these and comparable group methods to Piagetian stage criteria. The study of developmental mechanisms is pushed into the same shackles. An example is the investigation of whether cooperation among children is an important cognitive development. Lots of studies have been carried out. In general, the differences between groups in such experiments are quite small, but doubt is washed away by assuring the reader that the differences are significant.

I am not condemning this research practice and there are no doubt numerous problems in which it is a suitable strategy. For instance, if the Dutch Minister of Education wants to know whether it is wise to invest a considerable sum in a programme of cooperation at the elementary school level, he had better ask somebody to carry out a preliminary study on how much improvement in cognitive skill you can expect after a year or two of cooperation teaching. He may then decide whether an eventual improvement of, say, 3 per cent on a scholastic achievement test is worth the taxpayers' money.

But it remains to be seen whether this method is suitable for discovering how cooperation works in cognitive development. We want to know, for instance, under which circumstances cooperation works and whether it works as a strategy in some children, or for some forms of cognitive learning or just during specific learning episodes. We would like to know whether the effect of cooperative learning is delayed or not – that is, whether the effects can be seen immediately or require a considerable 'incubation time'. We would like to know whether cooperation causes a temporary regression or fallback in the child's understanding, followed by a large leap, or whether it works continually and similarly over time. All this (and probably much more) we would want to learn about cooperation if our question is cooperation as a developmental mechanism. But the nature of our experimental set-up prevents us from drawing conclusions on these matters. A chief obstacle here is a notion that is fundamental to group-based statistics: independence.

Vive l'Indépendance

In 1960, the former Belgian Congo became independent. As a 10-year-old I was intrigued by the meaning of the word 'independence', which, in the colonial French, sounded a lot more impressive than in Flemish. It turned out that the independent Congo, although no longer ruled by the Belgians (who had done rather well, measured by the standards of those times; see Gann and Duignan, 1979), was far from independent of various international influences and pressures, ranging from the USA to the USSR, that were imposed on her juvenile freedom.

In the statistics that we use currently in our developmental research, a comparable emphasis is put on the importance of independence and similar doubts can be raised as to what this actually means as far as the mutuality of influences in a developmental system is concerned. Let us first try to figure out what independence means in common statistical practice.

Assume that we take a sample of individuals from a population and study their personalities. The personality characteristics of each individual are independent from those of each other individual in the sample. This means that there is no relation of conditionality or selectivity between any two people. Next assume that we do not take a sample, but just pick out a single person and ask him or her to ask friends or relatives to become members of the sample. In this case, the personalities in the sample are likely to depend on one another, since we may expect the person to select others on the basis of certain compatibilities of personality. Here is another example. If I measure a characteristic such as a person's intelligence, I am likely to make a measurement error. The error I make is believed to be independent of what I measure, or who or when. But just assume that I am more sensitive to lower intelligences, because I understand them better. In that case, I will probably make fewer measurement errors than with people who have higher IQs. From early in the development of statistics, the threats of dependence have been noticed and attempts have been undertaken to counter them. Test situations became standardized, testers were thoroughly trained and techniques were developed to bypass dependence in those cases where it was unavoidable. If the experimenter expects a learning effect of one item on another, he or she will counterbalance the order of the test items over the group of subjects, so as to make an estimation of order-independent scores possible.

The idea buried deep under all these assumptions and methods is that the world is made by the collision of forces that are truly independent of one another. This metaphor is adequate for a variety of phenomena, and the study of individual differences over groups has proven to be a good example. But for each phenomenon where the assumption of independence holds, there is one for which it is joltingly incorrect. One such phenomenon is development.

Take for instance the development of social-role understanding in a child. The development follows a sequence of knowledge states (not necessarily stages), which are clearly linked. Later knowledge states are a developmental function of earlier ones; that is what development is all about. Genetic dependence is far from the statistical independence of the standard paradigm. It is true that later states depend on earlier states, but do they not depend also on environmental influences? Are these influences not dependent on the developmental state? It is obvious they are. The way in which an environment reacts to a child depends very much on the child's actual developmental level. Moreover, children tend to select information on the basis of developmentally determined sensitivities. The environment's dependence on the developmental state does not imply, however, that it is determined by that state. There may be fluctuations in the mutual dependence between child and environment, but as a rule, dependence and not independence is the default condition. When you engage in a psychological measurement procedure, you enter into a process of communication, that is, a process of mutual dynamic dependence.

Independence over time: expecting smooth changes

Scarcely any country in the world has as many political parties for its population size as The Netherlands. When I moved to Groningen, I learned about the existence of a – relatively speaking – not so small party that called itself the Anti-Revolutionary Party. Its members had a very outspoken fear of revolutionary changes, sudden slides in the social landscape, and irregularity in general. A regulated, smooth transition to a higher state of well-being was what they were after. Their political ideal came very close to an assumption that reigns widely in developmental psychology, namely that developmental change must be smooth and continuous. More precisely, the underlying, 'real' developmental curve is assumed to be continuous and smooth in the mathematical sense, which implies, among other things, that even stepwise changes grow smoothly out of a stable level. Nevertheless, there is hardly any longitudinal study that does not show irregular fluctuation over time. Take for instance the longitudinal data on the increase of the number of meaningful units per utterance in the children investigated in Roger Brown's classic study. On average, the length of the sentences increases, but there is a

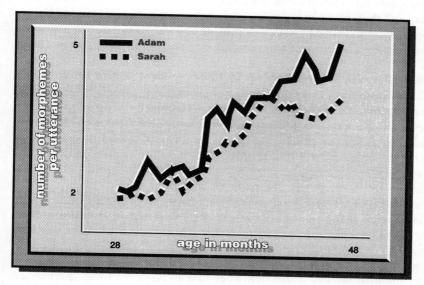

Figure 3.1 Empirical growth data mostly show irregularities superimposed on an overall increase, as with these data on mean number of morphemes per utterance (Brown, 1973).

chaos-like fluctuation imposed on that increase. The same is true for other language data, or language data from other studies (see Figure 3.1). The standard assumption most likely to be put forward, then, would be that the real growth of sentence length is a linear increase, or at any rate a smooth one and that the fluctuations either are caused by accidental factors independent of the growth of sentence length, or represent errors of observation. In this double sense, the fluctuations are considered independent of the growth of sentence length and, therefore, not a real property of that growth process.

You could object, however, that current developmental thinking no longer falls prey of the independence assumption. It is accepted, almost by definition, that consecutive points in a developmental series are dependent of one another, in that later states depend on former ones. That is, each next point of the curve represents a slight increase or decrease in comparison with the former point. The increases or decreases may alternate and thus produce curves that show increases and temporary dips, but the changes remain smooth.

Against the background of the smoothness assumption, the independence adage takes a different form. It now entails the belief that whatever deviates from the smooth pattern must be something that is independent of the developmental process that produces this smooth pattern. But where does our firm belief in the intrinsic smoothness of processes come from? Most probably, it comes from the way in which physics and mathematics have historically understood change in general. This is the way of differential calculus. Its basic idea is that you can take a difference between two states of a process, say the temperature of a steam engine, over two different periods in time. You can then decrease the time difference over which the two temperature probes are taken, until the time difference approaches the zero limit. At this point, the change in the process is represented by a linear sloped line, the first derivative. The notion of a derivative requires a process that is intrinsically smooth and does not show any abrupt changes.

The idea that such infinitesimally small changes produce smooth processes over time is deeply rooted in our scientific intuition about change in general. Put differently, there is a deep, historically founded belief that the inherent dynamics of any process whatsoever are of a kind that produces smooth change. It follows then that, if the observed changes are not smooth, the causes for this lack of smoothness must lie outside the dynamics inherent to that process and therefore be independent of that dynamics.

In the age before computers, the formulae of calculus were meant to solve the problem of computing a state of a process without having to go through each separate step. For instance, in the growth equations of calculus, growth is a function of time, and you do not need to compute every preceding step to know what the growth level will be after a time t has elapsed. The point is, however, that not all differential equations are analytically solvable. That is, many differential equations cannot be solved by inserting the time parameter. They have to be solved by an approximate calculation of each step in the process, and if the processes cover very small steps over long time periods, the calculation becomes laborious. As a result, there has been a historical emphasis on differentiable, that is, smooth and analytically solvable equations. They have become the standard images of physical or biological processes.

With the advent of computers, it became relatively simple to experiment numerically with differential equations that were not analytically solvable; the computer would simply go through thousands or millions of successive steps and plot the graph of the equation without any human interference. The computer would go through these differential equations by estimating their successive values and by using algorithms that were basically iterative. Not only differential equations, but also difference equations could be tried out, that is, equations that are intrinsically stepwise. As a result of all this numerical experimentation – most of which can be done on a personal computer – we have come to a much better understanding of the nature of processes. We have discovered, for instance, that deterministic processes can look pretty random, as is the case with the logistic difference equation (see Chapter 4). We have learned about non-monotonic and non-linear processes, that is, processes that can show sudden regressions, fallbacks or jumps to different states as a result of their inherent dynamics and not of some sort of external influence independent of that process. We have learned that coupled equations, each describing a simple change can lead to very unpredictable behaviour over time, if by 'predictable' we mean that they can be linearly extrapolated. More precisely, we have learned that simple models do not necessarily produce simple, smooth processes over time. Sudden changes and even chaotic irregularity may occur, not as the consequence of external, independent factors, but as a deep intrinsic property of the processes themselves.

Model and reality

Developmental curves from a divine viewpoint

In the previous sections I have argued that there is no such thing as a psychological attribute in the form of a competence that is a stable trait of a person and expressed only in a distorted way due to accidental factors affecting but independent of the actual performance. I claimed that competences are context-dependent and person-dependent at the same time, that they fluctuate over time, that there are several different ways of measuring them and that different measurements point to their multidimensionality. I suggested that irregularity and even chaos can be an intrinsic property of a process and not something imposed on that process by independent, coincidental factors.

On the other hand, I presented a number of developmental growth curves, for instance of the singing performance of the Yeltsinogradian children. They were singular curves and often quite smooth and regular. How can the notion of a growth or developmental curve be reconciled with the previous notion of a rather fuzzy competence (or skill or knowledge, for that matter)? The mathematically derived developmental curve ascribes a single point on a single dimension to a specific age and not a fuzzy cloud of points on a variety of dimensions.

Since the good Lord, as I explained earlier, spiced my boyhood with a considerable number of nightmares and anxieties, I could ask Him a favour now, namely to lend me some of His unobtrusive and undisturbed observation of the human soul. And imagine that my wish comes true. He gives me one of His supernatural videotapes of a boy's soul covering the age range between 4 and 12 years. Well, actually it is only one track of the tape, covering everything that relates to the child's acquisition of a mathematical skill, addition. Not only can I look right into the soul of this child solving addition problems, I can also replay the child's whole development of the ability to add. Since I can look into this child's mind and mental capacities, I can directly see whether or not he really understands a particular problem, how much memory he uses, how interested he is, whether the correct answer he eventually gives is just sheer luck and so forth.

While my imaginary subject is solving several addition problems, I observe that his actual difficulty with those problems is caused by a variety of factors. One concerns how many numbers there are in the addition (two, three or more), another the size of the numbers. Those are problem-specific factors. If I observe what happens when the child is given a problem that lies pretty close to his most advanced level, I see that when he really concentrates on the problem, and spends a sufficient amount of effort, he has no difficulty dealing with it, but if he is distracted, bored or tired, he is likely to make a mistake. Effort, attention, fatigue and so forth are person-specific factors, but they are clearly transient and fluctuating. I also observe that part of his early difficulty with addition problems is due to the relatively inefficient way in which he deals with his memory limitations. This is a person-specific factor of a more stable, slowly changing sort. Finally, a number of environmental aspects influence his problem-solving. For instance, with some problems he was given feedback and support and other problems were just part of a test.

The factors that influence the degree of difficulty of an actual addition are called *control variables*. Each of the control variables can be thought of as a single control dimension. An addition problem actually administered to the boy can then be conceived of as a single point in the multidimensional space of control variables. This is so because each particular problem has a specific problem property (e.g. three numbers of four digits have to be added), but also hits on specific child- and environment-dependent control variables (e.g. with this particular problem the child was highly motivated but was not given any support or feedback at all). Put differently, each point in the control space represents a potential problem context, e.g. a problem involving six digits solved by a very distracted but bright child in a quiet and familiar environment. Note that by *problem context* I do not mean the question *per se*, but the act of problem solving by a particular child at a particular place and time.

In order for me to construct a growth curve of the addition skill in the child, I have to map the multidimensional control space onto a single variable that I shall identify as the growth level of addition in this particular child. How do I do that (remembering that I still have this divine observation power)? At each moment the child is in a particular state of attention, effort retrieval, fatigue and so forth.

Assume that there are n manipulable control dimensions and that each dimension is transformed into a scale with m different levels. For instance, the dimension 'problem complexity' is turned into a ten-point scale. This means that my control space now contains a total of m to the power n different problem contexts (different combinations of control variable levels). The child, in his present state, will be able to solve a certain percentage of this total amount of problems. Given my divine observation powers, I can determine that percentage exactly. To put it differently, the child passes a specific percentage of the total number of possible problem contexts. This total number is, of course, a single dimension (the product of all control variables). I shall call this dimension the *concatenated dimension of problem difficulty*, because it is a concatenation of all the points on all control variables. The percentage problem contexts the child is able to solve at any given moment in time is called the *pass level*. It applies to a specific type of problem – addition – and to a specific subject – my nameless imaginary victim of observation.

Now that I have this purely abstract dimension ordering all possible problem constellations for the addition problem in my subject, it should be easy for me to discover the growth of the addition skill in the child, as measured against this concatenated dimension. I can do this by taking time as my second (horizontal) dimension. For each point in time, my divine observation powers allow me to determine the child's exact pass level. In the short run, this pass level will go up and down, since the control variables will fluctuate. For instance, the child will go through cycles of activity and rest, of interest and boredom, or varying degrees of effort and so on. In the long run, the growth curve will go up, but it may show transient dips or stationary states. That is, if I enlarge my time window from a few days to a few years, I will lose the fine-grained details of the first observation window and find a curve that probably looks more like the curves from the mathematical models.

If one is granted such mighty powers as I am at this moment, the Devil is never far away. "If you can indeed directly observe anything that is of relevance to the child's answering a specific addition problem," the Devil asks, "why do you bother to look to such transient control variables as effort or interest? Why don't you take a direct look at the essential control variable, the child's knowledge of addition? You are not going to tell me that the child has no knowledge of addition," the Devil whispers in my ear. The child has a knowledge of addition, of course, but that knowledge is the result of the current state of all the control variables, and not a separate control variable. "But then," the Devil goes on, "it shouldn't be too difficult to subtract the variation in the separate control variables from the continuously sampled pass signal. For instance, why don't you subtract the fluctuating effort level from the pass signal? That would give you a signal that is independent of the transient effort factor."

I hesitate a little, because the thought is really tempting. My reply is that since knowledge is not independent of effort, it would be unwise to subtract effort from the pass signal. For instance, if the child has just mastered adding three numbers in a row, it takes him a lot of effort to solve such a problem, whereas if the problem is of a very familiar sort, the child comes to a correct answer with almost no effort at all. So the relationship between effort and solving the problem says something about the nature of the child's knowledge at that particular time. If I subtracted the effort signal from the pass signal, I would lose the information about a distinctive property of the child's current knowledge, namely its strong context dependency. At this point the Devil seems satisfied with my answers and decides it is time for him to go, promising me, however, that he will return.

Back to earth, and a long conversation with the Devil

At this point the good Lord decides that I have had time enough to fiddle around with a propensity that should be His and His alone, namely pure, unobtrusive and complete observation of the human mind. He takes the divine eye away from me and reinstalls me in my poor old human condition. To what extent do my conditions of earthly observation present me with a wrong, error-laden, incorrect or distorted image of the curve that I saw during the happy moments I had this divine insight? What I saw at that time was a fluctuating and context-dependent growth trajectory, and what I see now is also very clearly fluctuating and context-dependent. But is the 'earthly' curve the same as (or sufficiently similar to) the one that I saw earlier? Just look at the possibilities now. I can manipulate the problem variables, but not the person variables that actually codetermine how difficult a particular problem situation is. In order to estimate where this pass level actually lies for a given child on a given occasion, I would have to present the child with lots of problems. I cannot do that in general without driving the child, myself or the mother mad. I can only give the child a few addition problems once in a while and observe what answer he is giving. What I observe is only a rough estimate of the child's pass level. The fact that I have to estimate the real pass level on the basis of a limited number of problems, test items or whatever, is a main source of error, which accounts for the mismatch between the curve I observed when I was endowed with divine observation powers and the curve I observe back on earth.

I should have foreseen that the Devil would be back at the most inconvenient time, and indeed, there he is, eager to sow the seeds of doubt in my mind. "Have you ever realized," he asks me, "that those divine observation powers that you borrowed a while ago, and that made you see the real underlying growth curve have actually fooled you? The signal of pass levels you observed is a continuous signal," he says. "It is based on your knowledge of what the child would do if you gave him an addition problem, isn't it? But in reality you didn't give him such a problem, since, after all, you didn't have to because you had this divine insight. But then you made a lot of fuss of knowledge being context-dependent, didn't you? But what is the problem context if the child did not really solve the problem? Of course, you could have seen what the child would have done if you gave him a particular problem, but you could have given him any particular problem with any particular level of distraction or support from your side. But then the knowledge level is indeterminate, since you did not give the child any actual problem to solve. So, what is the child's level of problem- or context-dependent ability when there is no context or when he doesn't solve a problem?"

I must admit that for a while I was quite disconcerted, but then I realized that this objection is exactly what the notion of pass level accounts for. The pass level – this one-dimensional representation of the control space – divides the domain of possible problems into a subset the child would pass, that is, understand and solve, and a subset the child would fail. The subset of pass problems contains a variety of problem situations, for instance, difficult problems with support given by an adult, or less difficult ones the child has to solve alone. In this way, it does not matter which problem you present to the child; any problem belongs either to the pass or fail class, and a subset of these problems lies exactly along the boundary between passing and failing and is therefore particularly suited for diagnosis of the child's knowledge or skill level.

The Devil scratches his forehead and stares me in the eyes. "This seems like an acceptable reply, young man," the Devil says, "but you make the mistake of invoking what could have been the case in explaining what really happens. Especially if you study development, it is not always possible to generalize from the potential to the actual, unless you like being immersed in logical entanglements and paradoxes. Let's recapitulate," he says. "You have been asking about the relationship between the observed growth curve and the real one. You argued, probably on good grounds, that the real curve is fluctuating and context-dependent. Then you invented the notion of a concatenated dimension of control variables which enabled you to compress all those control variables into one single dimension. Next, you invoked those divine observation powers so that you could see a real growth curve. For any possible moment you could see what the pass level would be if an actual problem had been administered and the trajectory of successive virtual pass levels yielded the real growth curve, is that right?" I reply that I myself could not have given a better summary.

"But now we have a difficulty," the Devil says. "I don't need to tell you that your basic idea is that of an iteration, a developmental event that repeats itself and that takes its previous output as its new input. Let me avoid the jargon and just say that an iterative process is one in which each earlier state is the cause of each later one, do you agree?" I nod approbation not expecting the Devil coming with his major point. "But the points on your allegedly real growth curve are potential points," he says. "How can a potential point be a cause for another potential point; there is no causal relationship between potential points. The point is," he goes on, "that any actual working on a problem has an effect on the growth of the problem solving capacity. That is what you mortals call learning, isn't it? Sometimes the effect is almost nil, but sometimes it is quite dramatic. Many of your theories account for that fact. If a child is creating a state of cognitive conflict right at the moment you make him solve a problem, that problem might very much affect the growth of his insight. Or, to mention a different theoretical angle, if the child has just created a hypothesis on how a specific form of addition should be carried out, and you give him support while solving that problem, he might make a real cognitive discovery. The diabolic point is, then, that the actual solving of a problem that you use as a diagnostic measure is also a potential causal factor in the further growth of that which you measure. I admit," the Devil goes on, "that the effect is very often small, but it is big enough for you methodologists to apply the principle of random order of problems if you administer a test in a population, since you fear the order and learning effects that the first problem might have on the second, don't you?"

"Have you ever heard about the butterfly effect, the Devil asks?" I say that everybody who has read Gleick's *Chaos* – and that is almost anybody – has heard of that effect. "Well, it was a rhetorical question anyway," the Devil goes on. "Just imagine what it could mean for learning and development, where one particular problem situation at the right time and place could have an enormous effect on the later development of that problem domain. I am not saying that this happens often, but it can happen, and it probably happens a number of times in everybody's life."

"And now finally for my conclusion, young man," the Devil says. "What I intended to show you is that a real cognitive growth curve is a succession of real discrete events, namely the set of actual expressions of the cognitive aspect it represents. The growth curve of addition in a particular child is the set of actual additions made by the child, some of which were in the form of a real educational interaction, some in the form of a test, others in the form of a spontaneous use of addition in real-life situations. It is a discrete signal, and probably a rather scattered signal. And it also does not map neatly onto a pure problem-defined succession of growth levels, since a problem is always defined by the person- and environment-determined context in which it is asked. Fortunately, the mathematical curves that your models produce are not real ones, but sequences of discrete points; each point is a single iterative step. But then you made a mistake to think that between each two successive points a sheer infinite number of potential intermediary points exist, points that you thought you could see when you borrowed the divine observation power. But you fell into a Faustian trap, my friend," says the Devil, "since all that was only illusion. All there is in the real curve is the sequence of real events and in that sense it is not a curve but a succession of discrete points. Instead of having a time series of pass levels, you have an *event series*, for instance, a series of actual manipulations of numbers or arithmetic problem-solving. Needless to say, these event series are far less regular and smooth than the mathematical curves of your growth models. You were tempted to see your curves as representations of an underlying continuous psychological variable, such as a child's addition competence, but there is no such thing. There's only a series of conditionally coupled actual events. I wish you good luck in your attempt to reconcile your mathematical curves with the vagaries and discontinuities of life," the Devil concludes. He disappears in a cloud of fuzzy numbers, and, as a tribute to Lewis Carroll's Cheshire Cat, only his grin remains.

Real curves and measurements: the principle of qualitative invariance and resemblance

Let me try to recapitulate the discussion so far. I started with the idea of a continuous growth curve. In order to account for the context- and problem-dependency of that curve, I invoked the notion of a pass level, which was a concatenation of all the control variables that interfere in a particular problem context. I endowed myself with divine observation powers in order to see the real growth curve of pass levels of, for instance, addition skills. I then noticed that my limited human observation powers constituted a source of error in that the empirically estimated pass level curve would deviate from the real one. Then I introduced my personal Devil who argued that the divine curve was an illusion, exactly the sort of Faustian thing I, a mortal, get when I think I can act beyond my power. The real developmental curve of a skill, for instance the child's ability to solve addition problems, is a sequence of discrete and to a considerable extent also completely coincidental events relating to how and when that skill has been exercised in real situations. But if this is what a real developmental curve is supposed to be, the notion of developmental curves acquires a coincidental character, at least to a certain extent. It is coincidental in that the occurrence of the events that constitute the curve – actual addition problems worked on – is not legitimately related to the developmental mechanism. Whether or not a child is given a specific problem at a specific moment is to a certain extent determined by mere chance. The classic reply to this observation would be to filter away the chance elements in the event sequence in order to arrive at the real underlying growth curve. In the preceding sections I called upon not only my own meagre authority but also that of the good Lord and the Devil to lend more substance to the idea that there is no such thing as a real underlying competence resulting from sieving out the vagaries and unpredictabilities of context and person. The real curve *is* the coincidental, contingent, discrete sequence of events. The task of a model builder is to try to capture characteristic properties of such real curves, for instance their fluctuating nature, eventual regressions, the general shape of the increase or decrease and so on.

The starting point of model building is a sequence of empirical measurements, for instance, a longitudinal measurement of a child's addition skill, measured with a standard test. Each test session is, by definition, an event in the sequence of events that forms the real growth curve of addition skill in the child. Since the child has done a lot more addition problems than the ones administered during the test sessions, the measurement set is a small subset of the overall sequence of addition skill events. In general, we may assume that repeated tests or measurements of a skill are only a small subset of the events that constitute the growth pattern of that skill. How can we generalize or extrapolate from the limited set of measurement points to the often extensive set of measurable growth levels that correspond with the child's actual involvement in addition problems? This question relates to the problem of eventual scale invariance of growth curves.

The set of points that I achieve with a repeated measurement of a skill or competence is, most probably, randomly dispersed. Moreover, the intervals between measurements will be quite long, for instance a school semester. If I could observe a group of subjects every day or every week, as is often done in early language studies, I would have an ideal, dense and regular time series. But ideal cases are rarely observed, as they have the disadvantage of being costly and time consuming. How can one generalize from a sparse to a dense set of data points?

Let us work the other way around. Assume that I have a very regularly filled curve, for instance one with daily measurement points, for a child's score on daily arithmetic work. The score shows a typical fluctuation. I then take measurements at an interval of a week (note that those measurements are not averages of weekly scores; they are measures of a single arithmetic work session, but separated by a week). The kind of fluctuation I observe is probably qualitatively similar to the fluctuation I saw over days. On average, I see a tendency towards increasing scores,[1] on which fluctuations of different magnitude are superposed. If I measure at monthly intervals, the pattern will probably be quite similar. Of course, it is a qualitative and not a quantitative similarity, in that, for instance, the absolute increase over months is in general higher than over weeks or days. Qualitative similarity means that if someone shows me a 'blind' curve based on scores obtained at weekly intervals and one with an interval of three months, I will probably not be able to see a qualitative difference between the two curves. That is, if the absolute scores are not given, I will not be able to tell which curve is the weekly set and which the bimonthly.

The fact that a pattern of change and fluctuation is qualitatively invariant of the measurement scale – days, weeks, months, years – is highly characteristic of a great variety of natural and social phenomena. It is called *scale invariance* and refers to the possible *fractal* nature of phenomena. By fractal I mean that the same principles are operating irrespective of the time-scale or level of aggregation of the problem (see Chapter 5). So far it is only an assumption that scale invariance applies to the growth of a skill like addition. But since it is such a general phenomenon in nature, it is safe to assume that it also occurs in development and it is at least as plausible as the assumption that development is a gradual and smooth process.

I started the discussion by asking how we were going to extrapolate intermediate measurement points, if only points at long intervals are actually known. This led us to the assumption that a process such as the growth of addition competence was scale invariant. Now, scale invariance is the key to intrapolation. Assume we had only five measurements A, B, C, D and E separated by eight-month intervals (Figure 3.2). The fluctuation can be circumscribed in a parallelogram along the axis A–E. In order to find extrapolated points between A and E, we assume that the points will fluctuate over the A–B axis in the same way as they do over the A–D axis. The parallelogram can be

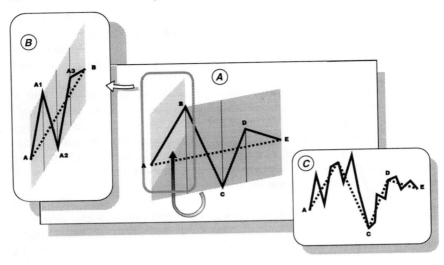

Figure 3.2 A set of five repeated measurements of a variable consists of values A, B, C, D and E (figure a). Values for the time interval between measurements A and B are intrapolated by projecting the variation over the interval A to E onto the interval A to B (figure b). Further intrapolations can be made by projecting any series of measurements onto any interval (figure c).

mapped onto a smaller one covering A–B, retaining the distribution of the points B, C and D. This breaks the line A–B into four lines, defining the extrapolated measurements A_1, A_2 and A_3, which are separated by intervals of two months. Since the scale invariance is qualitative, any five consecutive measurement points can be taken and extrapolated onto any interval between two existing points. You can repeat this process over and over, until the original eight-month intervals are reduced to intervals of days or weeks.

The extrapolated curve will, of course, not be identical to the real curve based on real daily measurements. The chance that extrapolated points will coincide with real points is small. But if scale invariance applies, as we assumed, the qualitative similarity between the extrapolated and the real curve will be very high. That is, the dynamics of change of the real curve, the nature of its fluctuations, its general outlook and so forth, will be captured quite reliably by the intrapolation. The real curve and the constructed, extrapolated curve will be like children from the same parents. They differ in a number of superficial characteristics, but on the other hand they show a lot of genetic similarity. You could object, however, that qualitative similarity or family resemblance is a meagre result; you want to see a reliable image of the real curve. The real curve, however, with all its peculiarities, is a contingent and coincidental structure, in that it depends very much on a variety of coincidences, such as the actual doing of the homework or taking the test, holidays and unexpected sickness. What is important in the real curve, therefore, is the qualitative properties it shares with the extrapolated curve, such as the nature of its normal fluctuation, the probability of infrequent high fluctuations, the existence of general trends upwards or downwards and so on. The intrapolation has its time limits, however. For instance, when I continue decreasing the time interval between any two consecutive additions, I will reach a point where the effects of boredom and fatigue will become noticeable. Put differently, the intrapolation procedure works only within limited ranges.

Between theoretical idealization and empirical test

The great Spanish painter Velázquez owes part of his fame to the psychological and physical realism of his many portraits. His portraits of King Philip IV of Spain, however, are strongly idealized, and far from realistic in the sense that his other portraits were. They are idealizations in that they hide certain properties of the thing they represent, while making others more salient, all in an effort to communicate a property they consider essential or typical of the represented subject. Neither Velázquez nor his public ever assumed that the rather ugly and morose face of the King was actually not his 'real' face and that the face Velázquez painted captured the real face lying 'underneath' the ugly one. The function of the idealized portraits was to show a likeness of Philip, but at the same time to show that he was the King and therefore noble in every respect. Velázquez' first portrait of Philip IV, in the Prado Museum in Madrid, is highly idealized. But the X-ray image shows that under the idealization there lies a very realistic portrait, one that his commissioners did not seem to have liked. The painters of modern nobility have found a different form of idealization in caricatures. Good caricatures are very realistic in the sense that one can immediately recognize whom they represent, but on that likeness they impose another message: criticism or mockery.

The theoretical and mathematical curves based on dynamic systems models function in ways quite similar to idealized portraits or caricatures. First, they should show a good likeness with the empirical curves they depict. The models should try to paint a portrait – or draw a caricature – of the real empirical data. If the portrait or caricature is adequate, we should be able to recognize the data through the picture, even if the picture and what it depicts do not overlap in the trivial sense.

Second, in the particular way that curves approach a resemblance to empirical data they emphasize important qualitative properties of those data. For instance, it is likely that the error of fit between a smooth curve and a set of mildly irregular data is smaller than that between the empirical curve and a theoretically inferred irregular curve based on the principle of scale invariance. The reason is that the average deviation between a smooth and an irregularly oscillating curve is often smaller than between two irregularly oscillating curves. If the fluctuations are a distinctive characteristic of the empirical phenomenon at issue, however, the less well-fitting irregular curve should be preferred over the better-fitting regular one. The model is a bit like a caricature: by exaggerating characteristic traits, it may gain in recognition and 'realism' at the cost of decreasing the literal match between the model and the mere physical appearance of what the model depicts.

The assumption of context-dependence and intrinsic fluctuation in developmental and growth curves might pose a serious threat to model building, even to models of the non-linear and dynamic type. As can be observed in the examples discussed so far, many (but not all) of the dynamic models yield smooth curves (and many more will be seen in Chapters 4 to 9). Are such models, therefore, not missing an important dynamic aspect of real change? They are, but in the meantime they capture other dynamic properties of growth and development that many classical models did not capture. For instance, they show temporary fallbacks, preceding sudden leaps to higher levels, or they produce qualitatively different patterns based on quantitative changes in the parameters only. Their eventually smooth and regular nature is a consequence of their simplicity and typical of the way such theoretically inferred curves idealize that reality. For instance, the logistic growth and transition model that will be the topic of Chapter 4 produces regular curves (as long as the major parameter stays beneath a bifurcation value, that is). The model is therefore unrealistic in the smoothness it produces, but what it loses on this side of the comparison is gained by its emphasis on the S-shaped form of growth.

In summary, what mathematical curves often do is to abstract from the real short-term fluctuations and concentrate on an aspect of the growth and developmental processes considered typical or essential. In general, it should not be assumed that it is the smoothness and regularity that represents the 'real' underlying growth process and that the process we actually observe is messed up by contingent factors and errors that prevent us from seeing it. The fluctuations in the real data are as essential as their overall shape (although part of the fluctuation could very well be measurement error). The fact that our models in general capture only the overall shape is a problem of the models, not of the data. Maybe a different type of model succeeds in explaining the irregularities, but we may encounter difficulties in constructing models that explain both the overall, long-term developmental shapes and the short-term turbulences and fluctuations.

Note

1. It is assumed that I use an absolute scoring system, that is, one that reflects the increasing complexity of the arithmetic operations the child is able to perform, increasing mastery and so forth. Normal school marks are relative; an A in the third grade refers to a level of understanding and mastery of arithmetics that is far below a B in the seventh grade.

4

The dynamic growth model

The growth metaphor

California Spring

In an attempt to find inspiration for this chapter, I was looking through my office window. The Center for Advanced Study in the Behavioral Sciences where this book was written lies on a hill and my window overlooks the Stanford University campus. Among the views that should be intellectually inspiring, no doubt this one ranks among the highest. But it was not this great place of scholarship that struck my attention, but the trees and bushes on the hill slope. It was early February and that seems to mean Spring in this part of California. The buds were swelling and little green leaves appeared everywhere. This year seemed to be the end of a long drought and there was abundant growth wherever I looked.

The growth I observed on a sunny February morning carried an old and powerful metaphor of development. Growth happens all by itself, nourished by environmental conditions such as sunshine and rain. It has a quiet, almost hesitant beginning, as when the first green tint covers the trees, or a seedling shows its first tiny leaves. But then it explodes in a rapid deployment of its inherent forces and the hills and gardens change almost overnight. Finally, growth settles down into maturity. Growth also bears an aspect of unfolding. The green bud contains the little leaf tightly folded and wrapped in its protective cover and as the growth season starts, the leaf literally unfolds. In its original Old French form, the word 'development' itself meant nothing but 'unfolding' or 'unwrapping'.

Powerful as the growth metaphor is, it does not account for all the phenomena of development. But it does cover a lot not only in the intuitive, casual use of the concept, but also in many classic theories of development (Nagel, 1957). The unfolding aspect relates especially to theories such as Piaget's, or more precisely to the popular interpretation of his theory. The course of developmental stages seems prefigured in their earliest forms, and the stages unfold according to an assumed programme.[1]

This chapter discusses several basic aspects of the growth model of development:

the conceptual components of the model; the simple non-linear model for growth
contained in the logistic growth equation; the relationship between actual, developmental processes and this simple growth model; and, finally, the modelling of empirical
data on the basis of this extremely simple but powerful growth equation.

A definition of growth

The growth metaphor applies to poetic subjects such as Spring leaves and mimosa
blossoms, but how does it apply to psychological development, for instance to
cognitive development? The definition of (for instance, cognitive) growth I shall
present here is an extension of one given in an earlier paper (van Geert, 1991):

> Growth is an autocatalytic quantitative increase in a growth variable, involving
> the consumption of resources and following the emergence of a specific
> structural possibility in the cognitive system.

Examples are the growth of the lexicon in a child, but also the growth of the child's
understanding of another person's point of view, the growth of skills such as solving
addition problems and so on. The definition implies a number of specifications.

The first is that growth applies to a quantifiable variable and expresses a quantitative
change. For instance, the lexicon counts an increasing number of words, or the child's
social understanding contains an increasing number of elements he/she can simultaneously relate to one another. The variable (number of words, elements considered in a
thought process, etc.) must be quantitative in the sense of natural numbers and this
requirement might cause problems with a lot of psychological phenomena.

The second property of growth is that it is *autocatalytic*. By that I mean it is a process
that sets itself in motion and whose own products keep the process going. Whatever
boils down to a mere addition of elements or magnitude by some external agent cannot
be considered a genuine growth process. If, for instance, we call the child's increasing
understanding of social roles a growth process, the product of that process – a specific
level of understanding – must by itself trigger the further discovery and elaboration of
more complicated social role understanding. The plant metaphor makes this aspect
particularly clear. When a seedling grows, it is not because water and nutrients are
pumped into the plant, as if it were a balloon that enlarges because air is blown into it.
The plant grows because its cells are dividing and multiplying, as a result of internal
mechanisms of cell growth.

The third property is that growth, even if it is internally driven, needs and consumes
resources. In plants, the resources are obvious: sunlight, nutrients, space, etc. In what
sense does an apparently ethereal thing like the learning of new words or the discovery
of a rule of social relationships consume resources? That does not seem to involve a big
physical effort. Cognitive (behavioural, mental, etc.) growth, however, relies on more
or different resources than physical effort alone. I shall explain this in a later section.

Fourth and finally, growth follows a *structural property* of the cognitive system (or of
whatever developmental system it applies to). With the metaphor of plant growth, the
structural possibility is the presence of a seed, for instance. There is growth only if

there is something that can grow – that is, increase its size, number or magnitude. The growth of the lexicon implies the presence of a minimal lexicon of at least one word. This requirement seems to disable the possibility for the construction of something new during development. If the growth principle explains development and growth requires the presence of the grower in at least some minimal form, then everything that grows must be present at the beginning. Growth, however, is not the only explanatory mechanism in development. Growth is what happens after the construction of a new, germinal form. The construction of such forms out of existing material involves its own particular dynamic principles that will be discussed later in this chapter.

First steps towards a mathematical model of growth

The definition provided us with basic constituents and relationships that may lead towards a mathematical formulation of the growth principle. The first constituent was the growth variable, which at any moment in time has a specific level or magnitude, L_t, L_{t+m}, L_{t+n}, etc. For instance, the levels refer to a child's understanding of emotions at the age of 1, 2 and 3 years. It is understood that this level of understanding can be expressed in the form of a true quantitative variable.

Since I have assumed that growth is autocatalytic and not forced upon the grower by some external agent, we may take the relationship between the successive points in the row of growth levels as a constitutive or characteristic property of the growth process at issue. The relationship between successive points is expressed in the form of a ratio:

$$L_t/L_{t+m} = R_{t+m}; \; L_{t+m}/L_{t+n} = R_{t+n}; \; \ldots \tag{4.1}$$

The ratio R is an important parameter of the growth process, since it expresses its internal dynamics or autocatalysis.

Next, we know that growth consumes resources. I assume that, all other circumstances being equal, the same amount of available resources leads to the same growth level and that the more resources available, the higher the growth level. We may therefore equate the growth level to a function of the resources consumed to reach that level:

$$L_t = f(C_t) \tag{4.2}$$

I shall use C as a symbol for resources because it refers to the idea of consumption and to avoid confusion with the R of growth rate. If the resources are infinite, we have no reason to introduce the resource variable into the growth model, since the specification of the resources consumed will make no difference. But if the resources are limited, which is most likely the case, each step in the growth process will be affected by the amount of resources consumed in the previous steps:

$$R_t = f(C_t/C_{max}) \tag{4.3}$$

Since the growth rate is supposed to express the intrinsic productivity of the grower (that is, the autocatalytic process), R cannot be a function of the limited resources alone, but must also depend on an intrinsic productivity factor (learning or acquisition factor in the case of cognitive development). Thus we change the previous expression into the following:

$$R_t = f(C_t/C_{max}, r)$$ (4.4)

for r the learning, acquisition or growth factor.

If we combine the equations described so far, we obtain the following expression:

$$L_{t+\Delta t} = L_t + \Delta t \cdot L_t \cdot R = L_t \cdot (1 + \Delta t \cdot f(C_t/C_{max}, r))$$ (4.5)

If we can solve the function $f(Ct/C, r)$ to a computable expression, we have found our mathematical model of growth. Note that equation 4.5 states that the growth level at a later level $t + \Delta t$ is caused by a growth level at an earlier time t. Cause and consequence are separated by a time interval Δt.

The basic growth model

Watership Down on reclaimed land

Richard Adams' famous novel *Watership Down* describes a bunch of heroic rabbits in search of a new colony. Let me transfer their story to The Netherlands. The Dutch are world famous for such cultural contributions as postcards of windmills and tulip fields and the invention of the wooden shoe, but also for the land they reclaim from the sea. In my story, they have just created a new island in the IJselmeer. It is still a barren place, covered mainly with the colonizing vegetation that likes a salt soil, with no animals to populate it except the seagulls, whose far cries intensify the loneliness of the place. Our heroic rabbits, in search of a new colony, jump onto the local ferry, and, after a short trip, find themselves on the shore of the island. It is not a very hospitable place, but there is enough grass, other edible plants and plenty of space and they soon start to reproduce. The rabbit population thrives, increasing year after year. As long as there are not too many rabbits, there are enough edible plants to sustain them. Rabbits reproduce quickly, but they have their natural enemies to keep their numbers within bounds. Hawks and other predatory birds will occasionally catch a rabbit. The migrating geese from the North forage on the same grasslands and they compete with the rabbits for the scarce resources. A few years after the founders have migrated to the island, the colony has reached a more or less stable population size. Births and deaths are clearly in equilibrium, because of the limited food resources available, the predation and the competition with the geese. But sometimes, if Spring is nice and warm and diseases are less likely to affect the litters, many more rabbits survive than in an average year. They survive only to discover that there is not enough food to sustain them all and that their abundant numbers attract predator birds from all over the place. What began as a year of prosperity ends in the disaster of a devastating death and at the end of the year the surviving population is much smaller than it was before. But it will slowly regenerate to its original level, if circumstances remain within the normal limits.

The story is unrealistic, I must admit, especially the part where the rabbits take the ferry.[2] But it is realistic enough to allow for some important generalizations. First, it shows that the resources are of various kinds: grass, other edible plants, space to dig holes, warmth and so on. These are positive resources in the sense that they sustain the population and contribute to its increase or maintenance. But there are also negative resources, in the form of the predators that reduce the population and the geese, which by competing for the grass have the same effect on the population as actual predation. Technically we have a multidimensional resource space, some of whose dimensions are positive, others negative. The resource dimensions are to a certain extent interchangeable or compensatory. An increase in the amount of grass might be compensated by more geese foraging on it, or by more predators attracted by the increased number of rabbits. But the compensatory relations are not systematic, in that more grass will not by definition attract more geese or more predators. Sometimes the positive resources are more abundant than the negative ones, or vice versa.

Second, we see that although the resources are multiple and various in nature and they cannot be covered under a single measure, they do correspond with a single indicator. The population reaches a maximum level, at which births and deaths are in equilibrium. This is the number of rabbits the available resources can sustain. There are no resources left for more rabbits and if more rabbits are born than can be sustained by the available resources, the surplus of rabbits will die and the equilibrium population will be restored. This equilibrium is the result of all the resources, positive as well as negative. Put differently, the multidimensional space of resources corresponds with a one-dimensional value, the maximal number of rabbits the resources can sustain. This population size is called the population's *equilibrium density*. The structure of dynamically related resources that sustains this equilibrium population is called the *carrying capacity of the environment*. If the population is below the equilibrium density level, a fraction of the available resources is still free. This fraction is the *unused capacity for growth*.

Third, the growth of the population is a *delayed function* of the available resources. During a good year, many more young rabbits survive. They will not only contribute to a population increase because they mate and have their own litters, but they will also increase the consumption of the available food resources. By the time the surplus of young rabbits is born, the surplus of parent rabbits has eaten more than the normal portion. The young rabbits will be born in a world that has far fewer resources to offer than necessary to sustain their increased numbers and mass starvation will be the result.

The formal growth model

In a previous section, I developed a series of equations aimed at specifying growth mathematically. I ended with an equation containing a function that still had to be solved, namely the contribution of the remaining resources. In the preceding section, I explained how the multidimensional resource space corresponded with a one-dimensional variable, the equilibrium density, the stable population the resources can sustain. Thus instead of having undefined multidimensional parameters C_{max} and C_t

referring to the resource space, we can now use a one-dimensional parameter, the carrying capacity or equilibrium density of the population. In accordance with the usage in ecology, we call this parameter K. This parameter is of the same order as the growth level L (in fact it is the growth level at the point of stability). Let us go back to equation 4.5:

$$L_{t+\Delta t} = L_t \cdot (1 + \Delta t \cdot R) \tag{4.6}$$

It is a logical step to make the growth rate R proportional to the remaining resources, that is, the unutilized capacity for growth. The utilized capacity is the ratio between the current population size and the equilibrium density, that is the size at the carrying capacity of the environment:

$$L_t/K \tag{4.7}$$

The unutilized capacity, therefore, is what remains:

$$(K - L_t)/K \tag{4.8}$$

This equation is the solution for the undefined function of remaining resources from equation 4.5. Making R proportional to this function means that the growth level increase over a time period Δt equals:

$$L_{t+\Delta t} = L_t(1 + \Delta t \cdot r \cdot (K - L_t)/K) \tag{4.9}$$

If we assume that Δt equals a time unit 1, the equation can be simplified as follows:

$$L_{t+1} = L_t(1 + r - r \cdot L_t/K) \tag{4.10}$$

Equation 4.10 is the basic equation for logistic growth. It describes how a later growth level, at time $t + 1$, is caused by an earlier growth level, at time t, and by two additional parameters r and K. Since t is undefined, it describes how any later growth level depends on an earlier one. If applied iteratively, starting with t, proceeding to $t + 1$, $t + 2$, $t + 3$, etc., the equation generates a sequence of growth levels that follow one another and form a growth curve. The numbers 1, 2, 3, etc., added to t can have different meanings. They refer either to a fixed time unit (a day, for instance) or to a mere ordinal position. In the latter case, t would mark the first event, $t + 1$ the second, $t + 2$ the third and so forth, without specifying the length of the time interval that separates any two events.

A second way to infer this same equation exists and it shows how the notion of an equilibrium density follows naturally from the concept of limited resources. The reasoning goes as follows. Growth is not only the result of a positive term, the growth rate, but also of a negative term. In the case of biological populations, the positive term is birth, the negative term is death. If growth applies to psychological phenomena, the positive term could be learning, the negative one forgetting. If growth is concerned with the actual behavioural expression of a skill, the positive term enhances the use of the skill in a problem situation, whereas the negative term suppresses it. Growth is resource–dependent and the resources are limited. We do not know, however, where this limitation lies in terms of an equilibrium density or carrying capacity. The only thing we can say is that the negative term increases as the population or growth level increases, because the bigger the population or growth level, the more resources it has consumed to build itself up, or the more resources it needs to maintain itself. Let r be the positive and a the negative term and Δt again be equal to 1. Our equation would then be:

$$L_{t+1} = L_t(1 + r - a \cdot L_t) \tag{4.11}$$

Under what conditions will this equation lead to an equilibrium density, that is, to a stable population or growth level? It will be when each successive population or growth level is equal to the preceding level, when:

$$L_{t+1} = L_t; \text{ or } (L_{t+1} - L_t) = 0;$$
$$\text{or } L_t(1 + r - a \cdot L_t) - L_t = 0 \tag{4.12}$$

This condition is fulfilled when:

$$r \cdot L_t - a \cdot L_t^2 = 0 \text{ or when } L_t = r/a \tag{4.13}$$

By convention, this is the equilibrium density level or carrying capacity and it is represented by K. It follows therefore that:

$$r/a = K \text{ or } a = r/K \tag{4.14}$$

Now substitute a for r/K in equation 4.11 and the result is equation 4.10, the equation that started with the assumption of an upper growth level.

The growth equation has a long history. It was developed by the Belgian mathematician Pierre François Verhulst,[3] who published his original studies in 1844 and 1847. Verhulst tried to understand the problem of population growth in the spirit of the Malthusian view on limited resources. Malthus foresaw doomsday, but Verhulst showed that a population would settle around an equilibrium determined by the resources available. The Verhulst model is called the logistic growth model and the equation is known as the logistic growth equation. The term refers to the military term 'logistics', originating from the French word 'logis', which means lodging. Logistics are the means and infrastructure necessary to sustain the troops. The equation is traditionally known under its *differential* form, that is, the mathematical form that solves the equation for the time step approaching the zero limit (DeSapio, 1978). The differential equation is:

$$N_t = \frac{K}{(1 + c \cdot e^{(-Kkt)})} \tag{4.15}$$

for K the carrying capacity, k the growth rate, t time and c a constant that is equal to:

$$c = \frac{K}{N_0} - 1 \tag{4.16}$$

for N_0 the starting value of the growth level N, and k the growth rate (called r in the previous equations).

In 1976 Robert May published a paper in *Nature* in which he explained the *difference form* of the equation (May, 1976). Whereas the differential equation involves the time variable, the difference equation simply works with discrete steps (as in equations 4.10 and 4.11). It is a good example of the type of iterative equations and processes introduced in Chapter 1. What might sound like a mere technical issue – differential or difference – turned out to mark a fundamental distinction between two classes of solutions. Whereas the differential form always evolves towards an equilibrium state (the carrying capacity), the difference form showed a rich spectrum of solutions, ranging from the simple equilibrium state to chaos. Model 4.1 explains how the difference form of the logistic growth equation can be implemented in the form of a spreadsheet. The logistic equation is not only a source of great fun (for whoever thinks equations can be funny), but in all its simplicity also reveals interesting and deep properties of natural processes.

Properties of the logistic growth equation

One model, four types of change

'I would therefore urge that people be introduced to the logistic equation early in their mathematical education', said Robert May in his *Nature* paper of 1976. 'Such study would greatly enrich the student's intuition about non-linear systems. Not only in research but also in the everyday world of politics and economics, we would all be better off if more people realized that simple non-linear systems do not necessarily possess simple dynamical properties' (May, 1976). What are the properties that make a distinguished scholar think it could teach all of us something essential about life? Decide for yourself with the following tutorial.

Model 4.1 The logistic equation: a source of qualitative variety and complexity

Type the name of the program in cell A1, for instance 'Model 4.1: Logistic growth equation'.

Use cells D1..D3 to specify the values of the main parameters and cells E1..E3 to write down their names. In D1, type '0.1' and in E1 'r (growth rate)'; in D2 type '1' and in E2, 'K (carrying capacity)'. Finally, D3 takes the initial state value '0.01' and E3 'in (initial state)'. Define the range names for each of the parameter cells D1 to D3. If you use Lotus 1-2-3 for Windows, the command will be Range Name Create.[4] Other spreadsheets will have comparable commands. The name for D1 is 'r', for D2 it is 'K' and for D3 'in'. Now your spreadsheet knows what values to insert when you use those names in your formula.

I suggest you use the cell range A10..A110 to specify the logistic equation. Go to cell A10, the starting cell, and type 'in'. The program knows that 'in' refers to the value of the initial state, entered in cell D3. You will see that the number 0.01 appears in A10. Cell A11 contains the first logistic equation. In cell A11 type:

$$+ A10*(1 + \$r - \$r*A10/\$K) \tag{4.17}$$

Note that the formula should be typed without spaces! Compare this with equation 4.10.

Instead of L_t the equation contains a reference to the previous cell, A10. The $ sign preceding the parameter names is necessary to let the program know that it should keep the reference to r and K constant. Copy the content of cell A11 to the range A12..A110. If you use Lotus 1-2-3 for Windows, I suggest you use the Lotus Classic Menu to do this kind of copying (it is fast and simple, especially if you have to copy to big ranges). You will notice that each cell contains a number, which is the value of the equation in that cell. To see the equation, for instance, in cell A20, put the cursor on A20 and look at the editing window below the Menu bar. Another way to see the equation is to double-click on the cell content. This will bring you into the editing mode, and you can edit the equation if you want to. You will notice that the equation in cell A20 contains a reference to cell A19. Cell A20 represents the state of the growth level after ten iterative applications of the equation.

So far you have seen only a range of numbers. Go to the Chart menu and define a line graph for the data range A10..A110 (different spreadsheets use their own ways to define graphs; if you are not familiar with making charts, consult your manual). Go back to the computing window, change the value of the parameters and watch the different graphs. Try any growth rate value between 0 and 3 (e.g. 0.1, 0.5, 1, 1.9, 2.4, 2.7). Pay special attention to the threshold values described further in the text.

If you actually performed the exercise above, you have just witnessed the remarkable non-linear behaviour of an equation whose simplicity is in no way related to the incredible complexity of its potential outcomes.

For $r < 1$, the resulting curve has a characteristic S-shape. Its asymptote, the point it touches at infinity, is the carrying capacity level (equal to 1). It is called *asymptotic growth*. Put differently, the value of the equation, or more precisely the growth level, is attracted towards a single point, the carrying capacity value. That is why the process is said to have a point attractor for values of r smaller than 1. This is the scenario for a rabbit population that is constant from year to year.

For r larger than 1 but smaller than 2, the curve shoots above its carrying capacity, then drops, increases again, drops, in a decreasing vibration. The larger r, the longer it takes for the process to approach the carrying capacity. This type of growth can be called *approximate growth*. It oscillates until it finally hits its point attractor, the carrying capacity again. If the growth rate r is between 2 and 2.57, a new pattern emerges. The growth level fluctuates between a series of states lying above and below the carrying capacity, but never reaches that carrying capacity. For instance, with $r = 2.2$ there are two such states and with $r = 2.5$ there are four. As r approaches nearer and nearer 2.57, the number of states visited by the curve doubles more and more rapidly. Because the curve cycles between 2, 4, 8, etc., states, we call this growth *oscillatory*. Its attractor is not a single point, but a cycle, so it has a cyclical attractor. Both approximate and oscillatory growth correspond with the scenario in which the rabbit populations fluctuate between a too small population one year and a too large population the next.

Above the rate value of 2.57, the process loses its periodicity and moves into chaos. It is now *chaotic growth* and has a chaotic attractor. The word 'chaos' is actually quite misleading. The chaos reigns only at the surface, so to speak, in that the succession of growth levels seems truly random. In fact, this equation is sometimes used as a random

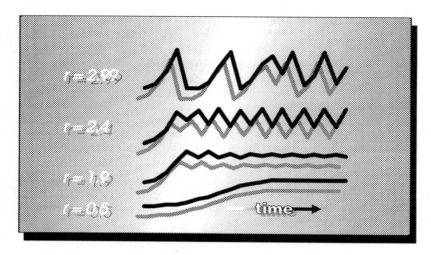

Figure 4.1 Four qualitatively different types of growth based on different growth rates *r* (corresponding values to the left).

number generator. On the other hand, this apparent chaos is caused by a simple and perfectly deterministic equation. Why do we call this chaotic succession 'growth'? Because it is a succession produced by a model we agreed to call a growth model, and which effectively produced canonical growth for most of the growth rate values (see Figure 4.1).

Above a growth rate of 3, the equation produces negative values. That is the point where the practical application of the model ends, since there are no negative numbers of subjects, or negative levels of a skill or ability.

Non-linearity in logistic growth

A major property of the equation is its non-linearity. By this I mean that effects do not simply add up. For instance, if I increase a growth rate of 0.1 by 0.5, and obtain a growth rate of 0.6, the result is a marked increase in the speed with which the S-shaped curve reaches its upper level, but the end result is similar; a process approaching its asymptote. If I add 0.5 to a growth rate of 1.8, I cross a qualitative boundary, between approximate growth with a point attractor, and cyclical growth with a cyclical attractor. Non-linearity thus refers to the fact that the result of an operation (adding the value of 0.5) critically depends on where along a linear variable (growth rate) it has been applied. The non-linearity of the equation is most explicitly expressed in the fact that it yields four qualitatively different types of growth. This brings us to a further property of the growth equation, its bifurcation behaviour.

By *bifurcation* I mean a sudden shift in the nature of the outcome of the equation as a quantitative threshold is crossed. We have seen that if the growth rate crosses the magnitude of 2, it suddenly jumps from approximate to cyclical growth. In the case of the logistic growth equation, the bifurcation is literal. It is usually shown in the form of a bifurcation diagram and Model 4.2 will show how such a diagram can be constructed.

Model 4.2 The bifurcation diagram

Start with your first model, but change the title to 'Model 4.2; Bifurcation diagram'. Add a parameter called 'r_max' to the list: type its name 'r_max (maximal r)' in cell E4, and its value, '3' in cell D4. Define the range name 'r_max' for cell D4. Before continuing, set the method of recalculation to 'manual' (consult your spreadsheet manual if you don't know how to do this).

In Model 4.1, you defined a column between A10 and A110, which contains a row of equations, starting at A10 with the initial value. Recall that you referred to the growth rate as '$r'. In this model we shall define 150 growth curves, with different growth rates. The growth rate of each column of equations will be put in cell 9 (for instance, the growth rate of the column H10..H110 is in cell H9). Go to cell A9 and type '$r'. Go to cell A11 and change the contents of the formula as follows:

$$+ A10*(1 + A\$9 - A\$9*A10) \qquad (4.18)$$

You will notice that the divider '$K' has been omitted; this is the same as setting it to the default value 1, which simplifies the equation. Go to Edit/ClearSpecial (or any comparable command in your spreadsheet) and clear the range A12..A110. Next copy the equation occurring in cell A11 to cells A12..A50. Copy the column from A10 to A50 to the range B10..EU50. This will result in 150 columns that take column cell number 9 as their growth rate. If you run out of memory, try a smaller number of columns.

What we shall do now is give each of the 150 columns of equations a different growth rate. The growth rate of each column should be a little bit bigger than the rate of its predecessor (the column to its left). To obtain this result, go to cell B9 (where the growth rate of the B column is). Type:

$$+ A9 + (\$r\_max - \$r)/150 \qquad (4.19)$$

(the divisor should be equal to the number of columns you have defined).

Next copy cell B9 to cell range C9..EU9. This will cause the next growth rate to be a bit higher than its left neighbour and at the end of the row of columns it will have reached the value 'maximal growth rate' (never make it higher than 3). Set the level of the initial state high enough, say 0.9.

What you have now are 150 series of growth levels (or less). Their initial state is similar, namely 0.9. Their growth rate, however, increases from left to right. Set the value of r (the growth rate) to 1.8, and the maximal growth rate to 3. Then press the button for Recalculation (which is F9 in Lotus).

In designing a bifurcation diagram, we are interested only in the later part of each growth curve, after the curve has found its steady state, if one exists. The bifurcation graph is created as follows. Make a new graph, call it 'bifurcation', and define its A

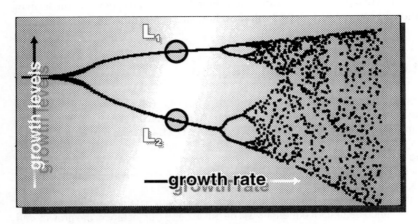

Figure 4.2 A bifurcation diagram for growth rate values ranging from 2.8 to 2.9. The growth rates are projected onto the horizontal axis. The vertical axis specifies the values of the growth levels corresponding with the growth rates on the horizontal axis; a growth rate of 2.83, for instance, produces a growth pattern consisting of two alternating levels $L1$ and $L2$.

datarange as 'A30..EU50'. Thus the range covers the 150 growth curves, excluding the first 20 or so steps and presenting only the steady-state outcomes. Make the graph an ordinary line graph, and set the method of display to symbols only (not to connectors or to connectors and symbols). Along the x-axis you will find the series of increasing growth rates, while the y- axis will display the steady-state values corresponding with each growth rate. The result is a beautiful tree structure known as the bifurcation diagram (your screen should look like that of Figure 4.2; lines and rectangles have been added afterwards).

The bifurcations are literal, in that the process has a single end state until the growth rate value crosses the boundary value of 2. The single branch of end states splits into a fork, which again splits at the value 2.57. The higher the growth rate, the more rapidly the branches bifurcate. A linear increase in growth rate thus leads to a non-linear jump in the number of end states. It is not entirely true, however, that an increasing growth rate corresponds with an increasing number of end states. In the chaos of end states, islands of simplicity occur, as for instance around the growth rate value 2.83. If you set the growth rate to 2.8 and the maximal growth rate to 2.9, your bifurcation diagram shows a magnification of the window confined by the values 2.8 and 2.9. The increasing chaos of end states suddenly switches to a simple three-state cycle, which then bifurcates again and flows into chaos. In fact, the bifurcation diagram is self-similar, or scale-invariant, because copies of the diagram reappear at smaller and smaller scales. For more details (on a reasonably accessible level), see Peitgen, Jürgens and Saupe, 1992 (Part II).

The bifurcation diagram provides a particularly good illustration of the principle of non-linearity that governs an equation as simple as the logistic one. It makes clear how a linear increase in a control parameter (the growth rate) corresponds with sudden shifts in the qualitative outcome of the process (number of end states). Another aspect of the non-linearity of the growth equation is its sensitivity to small initial state differences. It is an illustration of the fact that small causes can have big consequences, in that small differences at the beginning can be magnified afterwards. The non-linearity extends even to the domain of applicability of this principle, however, since it holds within the range of chaotic growth, but not within the range of growth towards a point attractor. In the latter case, even major differences lead to similar outcomes. The next tutorial gives an example of how the sensitivity can be tested.

Model 4.3 Sensitivity to small initial state differences

Start with your original model (Model 4.1) and copy the range A10..A110 to the range B10..B110. Define the B datarange in your graph as B10..B110. Set the value of *r* to 2.7. In cell B10, type 'in + 0.0001'. This means that the initial state of the B column is only a tiny fraction bigger than that of the A column. Make a line graph for two data ranges, namely A10..A110 and B10..B110. Watch the graph. What you observe is that the two graphs stay virtually similar for the first thirty-two points of the iteration. But then the small initial state difference gets magnified into a major difference in outcomes (see Figure 7.5).

What you witness here is the butterfly effect in action; a tiny difference does not show up until it suddenly gets magnified and leads to a pattern entirely different from the original one.

Properties of growth in mental and behavioural development

Limited resources for mental growth

Mental growth (cognitive, behavioural, etc.) is as dependent on resources as biological or bodily growth. For the sake of arranging an overview of the different resources, it could be convenient to make a distinction between two descriptive dimensions. The first concerns the *origin* of resources and distinguishes between internal (within the subject) and external (outside the subject) ones; the second dimension deals with the *nature* of the resources, namely spatio-temporal, informational, energetic–motivational and material resources.

The concept of internal spatial resources refers to the limited amount of information we can deal with simultaneously. What has been called our working memory has a limited extension, estimated, since Miller's famous paper, to be around 7 units (whatever 'units' may mean, however; Baddeley, 1983; Kahneman, 1973; Miller, 1956). The size of this mental capacity increases with age, either in the form of a literal increase, or in the form of increasing efficiency of information processing (Case, 1992a;

Case *et al.*, 1986; Globerson, 1983; Pascual Leone, 1970). It is interesting to note that the growth of memory span itself follows a pattern that can probably be modelled by the logistic growth equation (Case, 1992a). Internal temporal resources refer to the time on task we are able or willing to invest in a specific cognitive activity, relative to the number of different cognitive activities carried out during a specific period. Internal informational resources consist of the knowledge and skills already present in the subject, which act as the internal learning or acquisition context for new skills and knowledge and which may either ease or impede the acquisition of specific new knowledge or skills. Internal motivational/energetic resources consist of the amount of energy, arousal, effort and activation invested in specific acquisition activities (e.g. Sanders, 1983). Fischer and Lazerson (1984) argue that some significant changes in IQ over the life span may well be explained by changes in motivational structure, resulting in a different allocation of resources. If energetic investment is defined as a content-specific variable, we may call it motivation (see for instance Leontew's theory in which motivation plays an important developmental role; Leontew, 1973). Internal material resources amount to the bodily outfit of a developing subject, for instance the availability of correctly working sensory and nervous systems. A very important material resource for mental growth is of course the brain. Ample evidence now shows that brain development occurs in stages (Thatcher, Walker and Giudice, 1987). Spurts in brain development correlate with behavioural and developmental transitions (Fischer and Rose, 1993).

External spatio-temporal resources are the spatial and temporal degrees of freedom given to developing or learning subjects by their controlling environment. Caretakers and educators explicitly restrict the free-moving space/time of children, with the often implicit intention to structure this limited space in an optimally profitable way for the child. This principle is also inspired by the educator's need for resource economy in the environment. Valsiner (1987) has described this principle as the 'Zone of Free Movement'.

External informational resources primarily amount to the number, availability and form of the items that could be assimilated by the developing and learning subject (e.g. the lexicon presented by the speaking environment, or the specific ways in which the teaching environment makes information available to the learner). The third form of external resources is the energetic/motivational, for instance, task-specific 'pay offs', such as the reinforcement provided by the environment for specific activities of the learner. External material resources are things like food and shelter, or objects such as books and writing paper.

The availability, nature and relationships of all these resources differ greatly among individuals and groups and also within individuals (e.g. temporal variations in the information given to a child, or in the nature and amount of the energetic resources invested).

However variable the resources may be, they are always limited, although this may not seem true on so local a scale. For instance, if a child is really interested in some subject – such as dinosaurs – he or she may easily increase the time and effort spent in reading or watching television programmes on dinosaurs, go to the library and so forth.

But this is basically a reallocation of resources, since the time and effort spent on dinosaurs cannot be spent on other learning activities, notwithstanding the fact that in learning about dinosaurs the child may also improve his or her reading skill or scientific thinking in general.

Continuous *versus* discrete growth and the principle of feedback delay

Intuitively, growth seems to be a continuous process. In Chapter 3, however, I argued that growth curves are not continuous, but discrete. They follow the discreteness of the events and contexts to which their expression is confined. The fact that the probability of occurrence of a specific action or behaviour – such as a correct answer to a problem – has increased from one act of problem-solving to the next, does not necessarily imply that the line connecting these occurrence probabilities represents an intermediate continuous growth process. The growth process that gave rise to the increased probability of giving a correct answer, for instance, could as well have taken place during the problem-solving activities only, or during actual practice.

Moreover, the actual processes of information exchange or problem-solving that act as triggers or causes of growth by nature are discrete. A child formulates a hypothesis, tests it, observes its effect and draws a conclusion to either change or consolidate that hypothesis. Each part of the process takes its own time and even if some parts may overlap, they are not really taking place continuously.

The discrete nature of these psychological processes goes hand in hand with a certain inertia in the emergence of effects relative to the occurrence of the cause. There seems to be a delay between a causal factor or event and the expression of its effects in actual behaviour. For instance, if we change a condition of learning, such as the teaching method in a class, its effects may be delayed for quite some time. The reason is that the individual pupils need some time to adapt to the new approach, because they have formed their learning habits with the old one. The process of adaptation requires some time and thereby delays the effect of the environmental change.

In other cases, the delay is caused by the time required for the system to prepare an adequate response or reaction to a perceived problem or opportunity. For instance, if a group of children loses its 'natural' leader, for instance because he/she moves to another town, it may require some time before one of the other children has taken that place. Time is needed to build a coalition that supports the new leadership.

Delay may occur because the circumstances under which a new skill or behaviour can be displayed take place much later than the actual learning condition. For instance, in social imitation learning from watching sex-stereotypic models on television or in movies, the opportunity for showing the imitated behaviour may have to wait for a social context in which the imitated behaviour may actually be shown. In some cases the delay may be extreme, as with parents who once suffered from child abuse. Having children themselves, they may rely on the abusive behaviours they once witnessed in their parents, since they have had very little opportunity to learn how to deal with anger more constructively.

In summary, there are various reasons to believe that the effect of an event on a skill, knowledge or behaviour is delayed. I have chosen the term *feedback delay* to refer to this characteristic inertia in processes of mental and behavioural change. Feedback delay adds a certain degree of coarseness or lack of precision to a process. During the time a response is prepared, the actual conditions making that response adequate may have changed. The result can be a continuous mismatch between goal state and actual state. A good example is the behaviour of the logistic growth equation in the chaotic domain.

How can the discreteness of mental and behavioural phenomena on the one hand, and feedback delay on the other, be reconciled? Before answering that question, I have to go a little deeper into the differences between modelling discrete and continuous processes. Continuous processes are the traditional domain of calculus. A process is continuous if it changes at any time-scale, however small that scale is. A continuous process has a derivative, that is, a parameter of change that applies to an infinitely small time period. Such a process is described by a differential equation. A good example of a continuous process is the flow of water through a tap or heat conducting through a metal object. Discrete processes, on the other hand, jump from value to value. An example is the increase or decrease of a group of people when a person enters or leaves a room. If a process is clearly discrete, it can best be modelled by a difference equation, that is, an equation working with discrete steps. The logistic growth equation in our spreadsheet is a good example of such an equation.

Feedback delay applies to continuous as well as discrete processes, but the difference is that it applies optionally to continuous events and obligatorily to discrete ones. For instance, the movement of my arm towards a target is a continuous process, but it suffers from feedback delay. The actual hitting of the object takes place after the onset of the movement, and after receipt of the information that has triggered the movement (that is why we make anticipatory movements: we aim towards the place where the target will be after the movement time has elapsed). In a discrete process, there is always feedback delay, in that a time lag exists between any pair of successive states.

Computers can solve differential as well as difference equations, but the way in which they do so is basically the same in both cases. That is, even differential equations describing continuous processes are modelled in successive, iterative steps. Various numerical algorithms simulate the effect of continuity while using discrete steps. Difference equations are just straightforwardly iterative processes. The big question now concerns the type of equation that should be used to model developmental growth: difference or differential? The answer depends on the specific nature of the processes at issue. If their discreteness tends to continuity, if the time lag between successive points of change is very small, then a differential equation should be used. Feedback delay can then be added to the differential equation by making some of its components depend on some past state of the process. If the real process tends to a level of discreteness of the same order as the expected or average feedback delay, then a difference equation type should be used.

I have chosen a difference model throughout this book for several reasons. First, given the results obtained with the model, in curve fitting and general model building,

I believe the difference model has proven to be a good choice. Second, it is a very simple model and can be applied easily in the form of spreadsheets or simple computer programs. Third, psychological processes of change suffer from a certain coarseness and randomness of input. In general, the intrinsic coarseness of the difference equation is as good an approximation of the natural coarseness as a differential model with a random factor added.

Minimal structural growth level, growth onset time and the origin of growers

If the initial state in the column of iterative growth equations that you have tried to build is equal to zero, no growth will occur. Put differently, there must be something that can grow in order for growth to occur. Since the initial state of growth is in principle the lowest possible growth level and since this lowest possible level cannot be zero, it should be some arbitrarily small number (e.g. one word, in the case of lexical growth). This arbitrarily small number is the *minimal structural growth level* of a developmental variable, such as a skill or a particular knowledge domain.

In many cases, a variable such as pre-operational thinking, shows negative growth after a period of increase. That is, it tends to fade after it blooms. It will rarely disappear completely, however, in that it will always retain a minimal structural growth level. For instance, although the thinking style of adults, we may hope, is basically rational and logical, some remains of a pre-operational thought form that is magical and egocentric survive. Another example is a skill learned at school, such as speaking French. If it is not practised, it will fade away. Although almost completely invisible, it may survive at a minimal level that could form the basis for the rebirth of that skill if need be.

The *growth onset time* is the moment at which a structurally minimal expression of a cognitive element emerges. For instance, the growth onset time of a child's lexicon is theoretically the age at which the child has acquired the first real word. The minimal extension is not only hard to ascertain empirically, however, it is also likely that the minimal set is actually a few items.

If we do not assume that everything that can grow in mental and behavioural development is innately present in some minimal, or germinal form, we have to explain how the step from a nil-state (growth level is zero, i.e. the variable is non-existent) to a germinal state (growth level is an arbitrarily small positive number) can be made. This step cannot itself be a growth process. Three possibilities can be discerned. First, the germinal state is innately given. Second, the germinal state has been inseminated from outside the developing subject; it has been taught or imitated. Third, the germinal state has been constructed by the developing individual. Perhaps these logical possibilities also constitute psychologically relevant distinctions.

With regard to the first possibility, presence in a germinal state actually refers to the innate nature of the concepts and strategies in question. Basic concepts in particular have an important genetic component. In a recent paper, Jean Mandler has explained how many basic concepts, such as object or causality, have a basis in innate mechanisms of perceptual analysis (Mandler, 1992). The actual onset of growth of these innate germinal states is probably timed by the growth of conditional or control variables. These variables could be neurological, environmental, cognitive or a combination of them all.

The second possibility for making the step from a nil-state to a germinal state is by assimilating an externally presented model, through imitation and demonstration or teaching. This process refers to the main source of intellectual growth as far as the transmission and appropriation of culture by every new generation is concerned. In teaching, the germinal form of a new grower is inseminated from outside and its growth is carefully supported and controlled in a process that is now often termed 'co-construction' (Rogoff, 1990).

The third way in which a new grower can be initiated amounts to an autonomous construction by the subject. That is, since there is neither an example that can be imitated, nor any innate inclination, the subject discovers a new cognitive possibility. This is what probably occurs in true creativity.

The construction of new germinal forms is a major problem of development, and in Chapter 1, I referred to the original version of this discussion in Plato's *Menon*. It is likely that at least some of the processes that lead to new forms in psychological development are formally similar to those that lead to new species in biological evolution. Given a specific cognitive (or biological) structure, a limited domain of degrees of freedom exists for constructing new forms (see Ho and Saunders, 1984; Saunders, 1984, for examples from biology). The construction of new forms is an intrinsic possibility of a developing system, in that its reproduction over time and its maintenance are vulnerable to random perturbation (mutation) and to imported models (imitation) (Fogel and Thelen, 1987; Siegler, 1984). In some cases, these unintended mutations of some existing capacity are selected and supported by the external environment. A good example is the early growth of words, based on meanings given by the adults to proto-meaningful acoustic productions in a baby (see for instance Jakobson, 1959, on the growth of 'mommy–daddy' words).

In general, however, newly emerging forms will have to compete with ones that already exist and although in the long run the new forms will turn out to be more powerful than existing ones (e.g. operational as opposed to pre-operational thinking), they are definitely much less powerful at the time they emerge in a germinal form. In evolutionary biology, a comparable problem occurs in explaining the emergence of new species: the problem of cladogenesis (Gottlieb, 1984). It is often solved by using the concept of *allopatric growth* or allopatric speciation (Mayr, 1976; Simpson, 1983). Allopatric speciation is rapid evolutionary change in a geographically separated (i.e. frontier) part of the original species population. Because the separated part occupies its own small habitat, relatively isolated from the 'mainland', it can change under relatively safe circumstances with little or no competition from the main species. Later, the altered species form, if better adapted to circumstances that might have changed in the meantime, may take over the habitat of the original main population.

If applied to development, allopatric growth means that a new capacity or skill may be constructed by random variation, selection or imitation. This may occur in a relatively isolated and uncompetitive subfield of the field of application of an already established capacity or skill. At least in the cognitive domain, allopatric growth is a natural phenomenon, since almost all fields of application of a rule or production system break down into subfields. These subfields are characterized by differences in cognitive complexity, difficulty, specific domain of application and so on.

A particularly clear example is offered in Klausmeier and Allen's (1978) longitudinal study of concept development during the school years. The authors distinguish four different conceptual rule systems that form a developmental sequence, namely concrete, identity, classificatory and formal levels. They have observed that conceptual development is not equal for all concepts at all levels. For instance, there is a natural delay – or *décalage* as Piaget calls it – between object, geometric and abstract concepts and between concepts within each domain, as far as speed and ease of development is concerned. It would be very difficult to construct a new conceptual rule system (e.g. a classificatory level) for the whole domain of concepts at once, but it is relatively easy to do so for limited domains, such as a particular concept from a particular class (e.g. the concept of 'cutting tool' from the object class). By the time a conceptual strategy in a more difficult concept domain has reached the limit set by its carrying capacity, a more advanced strategy is likely to be ready in a relatively isolated easier subdomain (e.g. a specific concept). The latter may then be adapted to the requirements of the more complex conceptual domain with relative ease. Décalages, as they have been called by Piaget, are the key to development, in that they create opportunities for allopatric growth of new developmental forms.

The ecology of the mind

So far my examples have been mostly biological; I told an apocryphal version of *Watership Down*, for instance, and compared the emergence of new forms to the process of speciation. But in the biological example we work with real units, that is, species, which are separated from other species by reproductive isolation (a hummingbird cannot and will not mate with a sparrow or a titmouse, for instance, nor even with related species of hummingbirds).

If we think about a child's mind (the system of skills and knowledge, abilities and so on), we may metaphorically describe the structural elements that we can discern here, such as skills, concepts and rules, as *species in a mental ecology*. Each species occurs with a specific population (growth level) and relates to other species, that is other structural elements (Boulding, 1978). For instance, it is likely that fast growth of the species 'words' in a child will affect, positively or negatively, the growth in the species 'grammatical knowledge'. This is so because one growth process may feed on the other. The onset of grammatical growth may depend on the acquisition of some threshold number of words, in that skills necessary to learn new words contribute to the learning of grammatical rules. On the other hand, rapid increases in grammatical knowledge consume part of the time and effort that might be employed in building up the initial vocabulary (Dromi, 1986). I shall therefore compare the mental and behavioural system of a developing person with an evolving ecological system, which is not an ecosystem of animals and plants, but an ecosystem of mental species that take the form of rules, concepts, skills, abilities, beliefs, activity patterns and so on.[5]

You may object that the units in the mental ecology are not naturally separated in the same way as biological species. Why consider 'words' as species, and not the whole of language? Why not consider abstract words as separate species next to concrete words? It is indeed true that there is no natural compartmentalization in the mental ecology, in that the units are not separated by real boundaries. Nevertheless, once we agree on some level of analysis, that is, on taking either broad categories such as language, or smaller categories such as abstract words, it is not difficult to reach a working consensus as to what the units are at that level. For instance, if language is considered a 'species' in the mind, then we will probably see it next to another broad category such as 'social knowledge'. If we take 'abstract words' as a 'species' level, we will see 'language' as its overarching family and 'concrete words' as its fellow species. There is no reason, therefore, to discard the mental ecology and species metaphor only because there are no such things as real mental species.

The ecological metaphor is very convenient in that it specifies several powerful heuristic principles (van Geert, 1991, p. 5):

1. Given a specific structural model, the human cognitive system can be described as an ecosystem of species (i.e., structural elements such as vocabulary, grammatical rules, problem solving skills, concepts, etc.) that entertain growth relationships with specific fields of application.
2. The elements engage in various types of functional relationships, which are either supportive (the growth in one supports the growth in another), competitive (the growth in one relates to the decline in another), (virtually) neutral, or conditional (the presence of one is necessary for the emergence of another).
3. The elements show strongly dissimilar growth rates and growth–onset times.
4. The components compete for limited spatio-temporal, informational, energetic, and material resources.
5. a. There exist more cognitive "species" (skills, knowledge items, rules, etc.) that can in principle be appropriated than actually will be appropriated by any particular person. b. In principle, any cognitive "species" may occur with any possible growth level. c. The set of cognitive species and respective growth levels characteristic of a person's cognitive system is the dynamic product of cognitive growth under limited resources.

These heuristic principles are reminiscent of those for biological ecological systems in general, and evolutionary systems in particular. For instance, the fifth principle is reminiscent of a principle in Darwinian theory, that the number of offspring exceeds the number of organisms an environment is able to support, long enough for each organism to reproduce. From this it follows that the adaptation of organisms to their environment increases over generations. Likewise, we may heuristically claim that learning under competition for limited resources favours 'more learnable' more than 'less learnable' mental species. Since 'learnability' is dependent on the set of supporting cognitive resources that together form a person's cognitive system, more easily learnable cognitive species (rules, skills, concepts, etc., that are more easily learnable in the person's current cognitive system) tend over time to become more frequently represented in such a system than do less learnable ones (see for instance Newport, 1982, for an application to language; van Geert, 1985).

In the framework of this ecological metaphor, we may speak about a 'cognitive grower' and its 'environment'. A cognitive grower[6] can be any of the species in the mental ecology, any structural element or component of a cognitive system to which the growth relation applies; by 'grower' I do not mean an individual child, but rather the child's lexicon, or the child's use of the inversion rule in questions, or any other mental species. Trivially, a grower is a cognitive species that grows. The environment is the totality of supporting or competing resources upon which the grower 'feeds'. Thus as far as the nature of the cause or the magnitude and time of the effect is concerned, I make no a priori distinction between subject-dependent and external resources, such as the number of available models or tutorial support (see also Fogel and Thelen, 1987; Thelen, 1989). A child's mental ecology, therefore, consists of the contents of his or her own mind in addition to the accessible environment.

Modelling real growth

Keren's early lexicon

In principle, a growth equation models a process of growth in an individual child. The growth rate and carrying capacity parameters are specific to an individual, in that it is highly unlikely that they will be similar for all subjects in a population. Even if the growth rate were biologically determined, which is very improbable, the carrying capacity would at least in part depend on the input from the environment, which differs between children. In order to test whether the growth equation provides a good explanation for a growth process, we need to look for good individual data based on a longitudinal study with dense measurement points. This type of data can be found particularly in the field of early language studies, where a majority of researchers have followed a single-subject design.

In a fascinating study of the early language development of her daughter Keren, Dromi (1986) presents a number of growth curves, one of which covers the growth of Keren's lexicon between the ages of 10 and 17 months. Keren was indeed a linguistically creative and precocious girl, and data from other studies reveal a slower growth rate (e.g. Nelson, 1985) in other children. Nevertheless, the point is not whether the data are characteristic of the whole population of early language learners; they need not be, since there are considerable individual differences in the rate of almost any developmental process, but rather whether the process can be explained or modelled by applying the logistic growth equation.

Dromi's study covers the time of one-word sentences, that is, before the onset of true syntax learning. Syntax is an important resource factor in the development of language, since it definitely changes the need for specified words (such as words belonging to different syntactic classes) but also allows for the expression of meaningful content in the form of word combinations instead of single words. Let us therefore assume that the one-word stage is a period where no significant changes occur in the carrying capacity for new words and that this capacity will change as soon as syntax starts to develop. This is of course a rather crude assumption, since we may expect the carrying capacity to fluctuate. It is assumed only that there will be no major, systematic change that is comparable to the emergence of syntax. Since Keren's lexicon counted approximately 350 words by the time she started to use multiword sentences, the one-word stage carrying capacity can be set to 350.

Because we have no idea how long the assumed feedback delay is in the case of early word learning, I shall set it to one week, which corresponds with Dromi's sampling points. That is, the iterations of our equations are conventionally set to one week. This estimation is as good as any other, since the exact length of the feedback delay is not really important at this level of modelling.

By applying the equation to any pair of successive sampling points, we arrive at an estimation of the growth rate r (which is approximately the average of the rs resulting from comparing each consecutive pair of points). The following tutorial shows how the data can be transformed into a logistic growth model.

Model 4.4 A logistic model for Keren's data

I reconstructed the data from Keren's cumulative lexicon for successive weeks of observation by measuring the points in Dromi's diagram, which is probably not the most reliable method for obtaining somebody's data, but it certainly suffices for the present model.

Put the data in successive cells in your spreadsheet, for instance in the range B1..B32 and fill a column A1..A32 with the number series 1 to 32, for the weeks of observation. The number of words in the lexicon are 2, 2, 2, 2, 3, 5, 5, 7, 10, 15, 23, 31, 34, 35, 40, 43, 52, 55, 63, 68, 88, 104, 118, 140, 184, 220, 250, 272, 293, 319, 333, 340.

Given the equation for logistic growth (4.10), it follows that the growth rate r can be computed for any two successive data points in the following way:

$$(L_{t+1}/L_t - 1)/(1 - L_t/K) \tag{4.20}$$

In cell C2, adjacent to cell B2, you write the spreadsheet equation computing the growth rate for points B1 and B2 as follows:

$$+(B3/B2 - 1)/(1 - B2/350) \tag{4.21}$$

and copy this to cells C3..C33.

Compute the average growth rate in cell D1, for instance, by inserting the expression:

$$@avg(C3..C33) \tag{4.22}$$

The result is 0.31.

Next go to cell G1, and write 'growth rate r'. Enter the value of the average in cell F1, and define the range name 'r' for that cell. Enter the following equation in cell C2 and copy it to the range C3..C32:

$$+ C1*(1 + \$r - \$r*C1/350) \qquad (4.23)$$

Write the value of the first data point (2, for two words) in cell C1. Go to cell D1, and enter the equation:

$$@round(C1,0) \qquad (4.24)$$

which means that you want to see the value of C1 rounded off to the integer level. The reason is that you will never observe 3.2 words, for instance, but either 3 or 4. Copy this equation to D2..D32. Define a graph 'Timeseries' with A1..A32 as A range, and D1..D32 as B range. The A range holds the data; the B range is your model outcome. Look at the result. The similarity between data and model is not very convincing.

How can it be improved? Try several possibilities, for instance, start with a significantly lower initial state. The value 0.66 for instance will result in a very good fit with the data. But this value makes no empirical sense, since the child has either 1 or 0 words. Try different growth rates. Lower growth rates result in a reasonable fit, but this method has two disadvantages. First, the computed growth rate was 0.31, not a lower value. Second, the state at iteration point 32 is significantly lower than the empirical data point. The best solution can be obtained by applying the following assumption. First, assume that the initial state, the minimal structural growth level, is 1, and not 2 as in the data. Second, assume that the growth onset time is somewhat later than the onset of the observations. That is, copy the number 1 to cells C1..C3, thus making the growth onset time equal to observation week 3. The resulting model curve shows a very good fit with the data, except for the first few weeks (Figure 4.3).

Finally, write the data series in range AA1..AA16, but skip one data point each time (thus, use the observation weeks 1, 3, 5, 7, etc.). Compute the growth rate as described in this tutorial. Since the interval between data points is two weeks, the growth rate is computed for a corresponding feedback delay (two weeks). Try a growth rate of 0.71 for the reduced set of 16 data points (Figure 4.4).

The fit between the mathematical curve and the data is very good and it is quite remarkable that a seemingly uncontrolled and random-based process such as early word learning follows a mathematical curve so closely. We have seen; however, that the curve is critically dependent on the initial state value. A change of only one word at the beginning made a considerable difference in the form of the curve. This seems to lead to a rather serious objection to the mathematical model: Could a small, probably purely random-driven difference in a single word at the beginning of the growth process really be so important that it determines major differences in growth trajectory? This is a very unlikely assumption. The point is, however, that the initial state (of the lexicon, for instance) is a lot more 'fuzzy' than later states. Are the two or three things that we call 'words' at the very beginning words in the fundamental sense of that concept? This question is very difficult to answer. The child's first utterances are seen as words because the investigator decides they sound sufficiently similar to real words from the adult lexicon, but what are they from the child's point of view? Are they really functional in the same way as the later words are? It is clear that this fuzzy beginning

The dynamic growth model

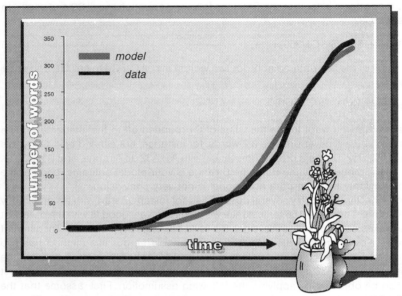

Figure 4.3 A comparison between empirical data on lexical growth in a child (after Dromi, 1986) and the logistic model with parameters fitted onto those data.

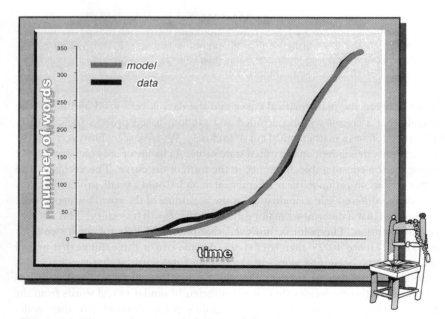

Figure 4.4 Theoretical curve of lexical growth based on a feedback delay of two weeks.

carries the roots of the whole lexical growth process, but it is unclear to what extent the numerical properties of that fuzzy state should be taken in an absolute sense. The solution I prefer is to manipulate the data from the initial state somewhat and to try to find a good theoretical fit with minimal manipulation.

Instead of actually manipulating the data at the initial state level, we may conceive of the whole range of data as affected by some random influence. That is, the number of observed words is probably not exactly the same as the number of actual words Keren knows (although it is probably pretty close, in view of the high observation density). Moreover, the growth process itself may not be as deterministic as the mathematical model suggests. It might be more realistic to see each step in the lexical growth as a randomized function of the previous step, instead of an absolutely deterministic one. Nevertheless, the basic belief in the dynamic systems model is that simple equations faithfully model real processes. So, although some randomness may be tolerated, it should not be too much. Put differently, if I need a high degree of random influences to explain my data, the model has little to contribute.

Let us try a small random factor, therefore, and investigate what happens if it is imposed on the theoretical model. One way of studying the effect of random noise is to multiply the growth level by a random number bigger or smaller than 1. The growth equation then becomes:

$$L_{t+f} = L_t \cdot (1 + r - r \cdot L_t/K) \cdot (1 + (\text{rand} - \text{rand})/d) \tag{4.25}$$

for rand a random number between 0 and 1 and d a divider. It should not be too difficult by now to build a spreadsheet model with this equation. Figure 4.5 shows the result of applying a maximal $+/-5$ per cent random fluctuation to the growth process (with $d = 20$). The initial state is set to 1 word, K to 350 words and r to 0.29.

So far I have manipulated the initial state level in order to obtain a better fit with the data. I have also tried a model with a small random fluctuation imposed on each computed growth level point. The feedback delay, however, has not been changed. In view of the arbitrary setting of that delay (equal to the sampling points), we might as well try to change it and see how it affects the theoretical curve. By taking a feedback delay of two weeks (simply double the sampling time), you find a growth rate r of 0.71, resulting in an even better fit (see Figure 4.4).

On closer inspection, however, Keren's lexical growth curve during the one-word stage seems to consist of two substages. The first is a stage of growth that seems to level off during weeks 16–19, at a growth level of about 50 words. It is immediately succeeded by a second substage of almost explosive growth, leading to the temporary ceiling level of around 350 words. The bend in the growth curve actually corresponds with a change in semantic strategy. This shows that our original assumption, that the carrying capacity does not change significantly during the one-word stage, was probably incorrect. In order to model this change more adequately, we should employ a model of connected growers, for instance a model specifying the relation between lexical growth and the growth of a new semantic strategy. A connected growers model can solve the problem of a less than optimal fit with the lexical growth data (see van Geert, 1994).

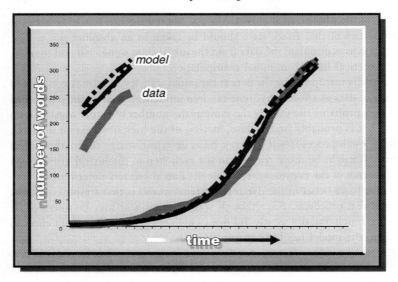

Figure 4.5 The lexical growth data compared with three curves with 5 per cent random effect per data point.

The growth of memory and the manipulation of feedback delay

Everybody who has ever asked the way in a strange town, for instance how to get to the convention centre where the Pan American Society for the Study of Memory holds its biannual meeting, has experienced human beings' limited attention span. While the person asked goes on explaining, the listener usually loses track after two blocks right and one to the left. The amount of new information one can store in short-term memory is limited to the magical number seven, plus or minus two, as Miller once remarked (Miller, 1956). Instead of attention span, investigators use the more common term 'working memory'. There is ample evidence showing that the size of working memory increases during development. One way of testing a child's working memory is to let him or her count dots on a card, and ask the child to remember the number for later retrieval. With only one card, the memory task is trivially simple, but with seven or eight cards, each of which contains a series of dots that have to be counted and remembered, the task becomes virtually impossible even for most adults.

In a paper dealing with the relation between brain growth and cognitive growth, Case has summarized a variety of investigations on children's working memory, using different types of tasks (Case, 1992a). One series of data shows the increase in working memory based on a counting and a spatial task, between the ages of 4 and $9\frac{1}{2}$ years. I have turned them into a cumulative graph, assuming that the lower limit is 1 (that is, the child remembers one number) and that after the age of 10 the growth of working memory in this task is asymptotic.

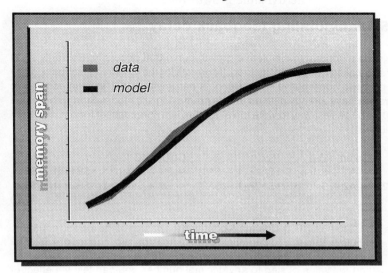

Figure 4.6 Data and theoretical curve for the growth of memory span, for $r = 0.44$ and $f = 6$ months.

The problem with building a growth model for these data is that they are group data, not data on an individual's memory development. I shall assume therefore that the group curve stays close enough to the growth curve of a significant number of individuals, and that it can be considered the curve of a 'typical individual'. I am afraid that this is a rather Queteletian solution, but it is the best we can do at the moment. The actual raw data should be consulted to see whether the individual variation indeed allows for such an assumption.

Figure 4.6 shows the result of modelling the data with a growth rate of 0.44, and a carrying capacity equal to the asymptotic growth level from the data (about 5). The fit between theoretical model and data is remarkably good. It is possible, however, that individual growth curves are much less smooth, but that remains to be tested against the data. A comparable attempt at building a mathematical model has been carried out with data from another test for working memory, memory for consonants (Bleiker, 1991; Case, 1992a). The data again fit the logistic curve very well. It should be noted, though, that the best fit requires that either the feedback delay or the initial level have to be manipulated. Which of both actually corresponds with reality is something that cannot be decided except on the grounds of empirical data.

How can feedback delay be manipulated, given that it is a single iterative step in our spreadsheet model, not a time parameter?

Model 4.5 Manipulating feedback delay

A good and simple algorithm to simulate a growth curve that occurs in arbitrarily small step sizes is the so-called trapezoidal method. It corrects for the remaining feedback delay by averaging over two consecutive steps. Define a parameter name 'step' in addition to the parameters you have already defined for the normal logistic model. Start with a value for 'step' of 0.01. The easiest way to write the algorithm in a spreadsheet format is to work with three columns:

Column A	Column B	Column C
0.01	+ A1 + $step * $r * $A1 * (1 − $A1)	+ B1 + $step * $r * $B1 * (1 − $B1)
(A1 + C1)/2	+ A2 + $step * $r * $A2 * (1 − $A2)	+ B2 + $step * $r * $B2 * (1 − $B2)

$$(4.26)$$

Copy range A2..C2 to A3..C1000. Column A contains the values of the logistic equation. The equations simulate the true differential form of the logistic equation 4.16. The feedback delay is 1/100th of the delay in the normal spreadsheet version (hence the step size 0.01). By setting the value of step to any decimal number, you can test the effect of different feedback delay values. Your test will show that longer feedback delays result in curves that are less steep at the beginning and steeper at the end than curves based on smaller feedback delays. Try step sizes that fluctuate around the value 1.

Signs of chaos and cyclical change?

The growth of the lexicon and of working memory fits remarkably well with a logistic growth process. Given the simplicity of the equation and the very few parameters needed, this is indeed an interesting discovery. Nevertheless, given certain parameter values, the logistic growth model produces curves that are less regular and smooth than the nice sygmoid shapes we have seen in the data. As the growth rate increases, a logistic process enters the domain of cyclical switches and even chaotic change. Is there any evidence for chaotic change in development? In Chapter 4 I have given examples of growth models that clearly showed a chaotic aspect. Empirical examples are the growth of utterance length (Chapter 5, Figure 5.3; Brown, 1973), the growth of the present progressive (Chapter 3, Figure 3.13; Brown 1973) and the rate of word learning (Chapter 3, Figure 3.12; Corrigan, 1983).

In fact, something that looks very much like chaos can also be found in the data on lexical growth from Dromi (1986). The cumulative curve of lexical growth looks quite smooth, but what do we find if we plot the successive growth rates? Figure 4.7 shows that they vary strongly over time. This variation could be the result of random noise or of random external events, but it could as well be the consequence of a chaotic growth pattern of the growth rate itself. The model does of course not tell which of the two possibilities is correct. It just offers a second theoretical possibility – chaotic growth – in addition to the common random noise explanation of irregularity.

The logistic equation not only produces regular evolutions towards a point attractor and chaotic evolutions, it also produces patterns of regular switches between two states

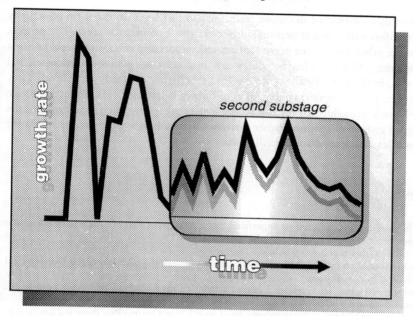

Figure 4.7 Although the growth pattern of Keren's lexicon is very close to a smooth logistic curve, the underlying growth rate *r* varies in a seemingly chaotic fashion. It appears there are two substages in the process, each with different magnitudes of change of *r* over time.

(and between any multiple of two states). Do we find such patterns in mental or behavioural growth?

In fact, many such patterns exist in behaviour, but in general we would not be inclined to put them under the heading of 'development'. For instance, children switch between effort and relaxation, interest and boredom, sensitivity and habituation, activity and rest. Another example comes from the research on the phenomenon of attachment in infancy. It shows, among other things, that children switch between periods of active, individual exploration of the world and periods of seeking comfort and protection with the people to whom they are attached. Mike Apter has described this and similar phenomena in terms of threshold crossings (Apter, 1982). If a girl toddler is secure she may go out and explore something new, such as the neighbours' youngest son. But as she discovers that he is not only quite an interesting boy, but also sometimes very rude, her interest eventually turns into fear. She runs back home to seek the comfort of her familiar place and asks her mother to read from her favourite book. After a while the state of rest and comfort turns into boredom, and she decides to continue her exploration of the world outside. This so-called reversal shift is clearly a carrying capacity phenomenon, in that the child can tolerate a certain upward deviation from the normal level of comfort or security in the form of fear, but that it shifts towards a downward deviation from the comfort level (in the form of actually seeking comfort with familiar persons) if the deviation becomes too great. The process also goes the other way, in the sense that actual comfort and relaxation-seeking turns into boredom. These cycles or shifts are not seen as genuine developmental phenomena, in the sense that they do not lead to a higher or steady-state level. They are, however, part of the normal dynamics of human behaviour. It is interesting to see that the logistic growth equation at least qualitatively explains such switches in terms of a range of growth rate values higher than the ones leading to steady states and lower than those leading into chaotic oscillations.

Notes

1. This is indeed only a popular or superficial interpretation of Piaget's theory, based on the textbook descriptions that emphasize the universality and necessity of the stages. Piaget's own point of view was much more subtle.
2. Everyone should know that there are no ferries to uninhabited islands and the Dutch would have built a bridge anyway.
3. Yes, another Belgian, like Quetelet. I cannot help it that my homeland made such an indelible impression on my work.
4. If you use a spreadsheet under Windows, like Lotus 123 or Quattro Pro, there is a simple way to define all your range names at once. Assuming you have to define four range names, for parameters named 'r', 'd', 'in' and 'K', write those names in four consecutive cells, for instance A1..A4. Enter the corresponding values of the parameters in the range B1..B4 (that is, right to each parameter name). Select the entire A1..A4 block with the mouse. In Lotus, open the menu Range, then Name. An interactive window appears. It has a button marked 'Use Labels' and a small options window, which is by default set to 'To the right'. Just press the 'Use Labels' button, and Lotus knows that the values in cells B1..B4 are named 'r', 'd', 'in' and 'K' respectively. The procedure is very similar in Quattro Pro. Enter the parameter names, then right to those the values. Activate the Block menu, then names, then Labels, press OK. The optional direction is set to 'Right'. If you prefer values left to or below the cells with the names, change the direction option accordingly.
5. The metaphorical term 'cognitive species' is similar to several terms introduced by scholars who have applied evolutionary analogies to the problem of the cultural transmission of knowledge and skills. They have proposed several terms to describe the units of transmission; Dawkins (1976) used the term 'meme' as the cognitive analogon to 'gene'; Boyd and Richerson (1985) speak about 'culture types'; Lumsden and Wilson (1981) use the term 'culturgen'; see van Geert (1985) for an overview.
6. If anyone ever considers translating this concept into French, he or she will practically be obliged to use the word 'croissant'. Finally, developmental psychology deals with something substantial.

5

Transitions and developmental fractals

Transitions and sudden changes

Nur ein Aha-erlebnis, gnädige Frau . . .

Just a sudden insight, Madam. . . . One can imagine Albert Einstein giving this answer when asked how he discovered his theory of relativity ('which one, Madam?' . . .) The German word 'Aha-erlebnis' literally means 'Aha'-experience; after you struggle with a problem for quite some time the solution may dawn suddenly and the usual exclamation then is supposed to be 'Aha!'. Although I doubt whether Einstein got his relativity theory in the form of a sudden insight, it is a common process in creative thought.

There is a famous story about the nineteenth-century German chemist Friedrich August Kekulé. He had been struggling with the problem of the structure of organic molecules until, one night in 1865,[1] he had a dream of a snake, swirling around and biting its own tail. The dream, so the story goes, solved the problem of the six-carbon benzene ring, which in turn made all the problems of organic molecule structure Kekulé had been struggling with for years fall into place. It is interesting to note that the dream sprouted out of fertile soil, since Kekulé had earlier training in architecture, which made him particularly sensitive to spatial structure.

The emergence of sudden insights or discoveries has been of special interest to Gestalt psychologists. They attributed it to processes of pattern reorganization. A good perceptual example is the famous Necker cube, which you see as facing either upward or downward (Figure 5.1). Sometimes it is difficult to change the perception of downward orientation, for instance, but once the organization starts changing, it changes almost instantaneously. Necker cubes are systems with bistable states, and each state functions as an attractor point (Ta'eed, Ta'eed and Wright, 1988). Compare this with another bistable system, such as a rowboat in the water. It is bistable in that it either floats or sinks. Normal perturbations of its balance, such as the movement of the rower, will shift the balance somewhat, but the position of the boat fortunately fluctuates around the balance point. If the perturbation is too strong, for instance if the

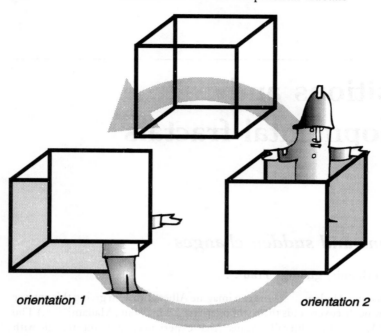

Figure 5.1 The Necker cube (top) is an example of two stable points of organization (perceptual orientation 1 and 2), connected by a sudden-switch-trajectory.

rower stands upright and bends to one side, the boat will topple over and rapidly shift into its other state, sinking. As soon as the equilibrium point is crossed – like the rower bending too much to the right – a positive feedback cycle is set to work and the forces driving the boat towards imbalance will be amplified instead of dampened. Bistable states abound in perception and thinking – at least that is what personal experience suggests. Their characteristic dynamics is that of a long period of stability in one state, then a short intermediate jump to the other state, which is then stable for a long time.

This chapter begins with a discussion of empirical evidence of transitions and sudden jumps in development, which occur at various levels of generalization, measurement or description. The distribution of such transitions over all possible levels of observation leads to a second topic, the fractal nature of developmental processes. Next, I present a mathematical model of sudden jumps or 'strong' transitions and show that these strong transitions bear all the marks of an interesting mathematical object, the cusp catastrophe, which serves as a very general model of sudden state change. Is there any empirical evidence on sudden changes or jumps in development?

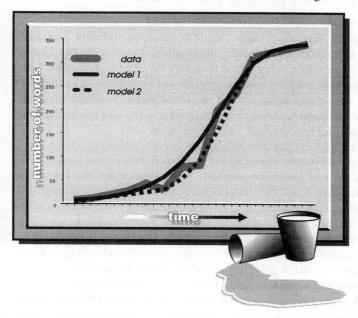

Figure 5.2 Bentler's group data on the growth of conservation as measured by a conservation test, and two logistic model simulations (after Bentler, 1970).

The logistics of conservation growth

Conservation is a good candidate for a sudden-shift type of developmental model. If we look at group data of conservation growth, however, the curves themselves look at first like logistic growth forms (Bee, 1989; Tomlinson–Keasy *et al.*, 1979). The point is that a group curve of conservation development does not say anything about individual development. A child's answer is either wrong or right. But is a child a 'conserver' when giving a correct answer to a conservation question? The conservation answer could be just an accidental hit. It is customary therefore to ask children a series of questions and give them a conservation score relative to the number of questions correct. The Goldschmid and Bentler test of conservation works along this principle.

Bentler (1970) used this test in a cross-sectional study of 560 children between the ages of 4 and 8. Figure 5.2 displays mean scores on the test, compared with two logistic model fittings. It should be noted that I linearly extrapolated the data under the age of 4 years to a minimal score at the age of $2\frac{1}{2}$ years and to a maximal score at the age of 9. The data are again quite in accordance with a logistic growth model. A growth spurt can be clearly observed, but it is not a sudden transition. This conclusion, however, does not do full justice to the available data and is certainly not valid as far as individual growth of conservation is concerned. This follows from Bentler's finding strong evidence for a bimodal score distribution. That is, the scores did not follow a normal distribution, with the majority of the scores evenly distributed around some average. If that would have been the case, development could be expected to follow a gradual increase in the average score. The bimodal distribution, however, shows that a majority of children have either a low score or a high score. The test, therefore, measures the understanding of a principle, namely that of conservation. The children either understand it or not and apply it to all the conservation problems they can identify as such. The group curve shows the gradual shift in the number of children with a high score, resulting in a gradually increasing mean score.

The discovery of the conservation principle appears to take only a little time. This conclusion can be inferred from the bimodality of the scores; the less time it takes for a child to shift from a state of ignorance to a state of understanding, the lower the probability that the investigator will encounter children who are in the transition stage; or, following the same line of argument, the higher the probability that a child will be found in a state of either relatively good or relatively poor understanding. The individual curves, therefore, are much steeper than the group curve. It follows then that the real growth curve of conservation, the curve as it applies to individuals, is more like a strong transition than like a growth spurt of the more elongated type.

Convincing evidence for a sudden jump from a state of non-conservation to conservation comes from the longitudinal study of Han van der Maas (1993). He tested a group of children with a computerized conservation test. The children made the same test repeatedly over many trials. The computer kept track of their scores and in this way a group of individual conservation time series was obtained. The group of transitional children showed a characteristic jump (Figure 5.3). With this particular form of testing we do not see children who regress to the non-conservation state, or who fluctuate between the two states for some time.

States and trajectories of understanding conservation

The question is, however, whether the notion of bistability and the associated sudden jump implies that there are indeed only two states of conservation development, namely conservation and non-conservation.

One of my collaborators, Jan Bijstra, designed a conservation test that could distinguish 'intermediate' conservers from real non-conservers and conservers (the Goldschmid–Bentler does not make this distinction). He investigated a suggestion of Flavell (Flavell, Green and Flavell, 1986) that a significant group of children is not classified as non-conservers if the investigator asks a slightly different question. Instead of asking 'Is there as much lemonade in this container as in the other one, or is there more or less?', the question should be rephrased as follows: 'Is there *really* more lemonade in this glass, or does it only appear to be so?'. The idea is that children who are close to conservation understanding, as measured by the standard testing procedure, already understand that the higher amount of liquid (in the case of a narrower but higher beaker) is a matter of appearance, not of reality. But the standard question confuses them, and if they say 'there is more' they actually mean 'there seems to be more'.

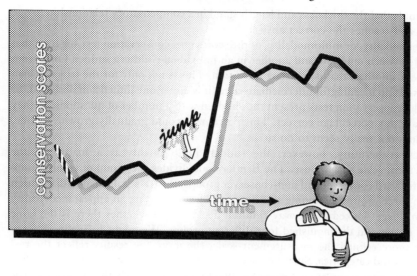

Figure 5.3 Jump in raw conservation scores for 24 transitional subjects (after van der Maas, 1993). The moment of transition functioned as an anchor point for the scores of the individual subjects. As a result, the extremes (beginning and end) are based on data from only a few subjects, and are subject to considerably more noise than the data points around the jump.

Bijstra (1989) confirmed this hypothesis. He also found that over repeated testing sessions, separated by a period of a few weeks, some children tend to shift back from a 'higher' to a 'lower' state. Thus a child who is a clear 'conserver' during the first session is found to be a convinced 'intermediate' during the next session (see also Bijstra, van Geert and Jackson, 1989). This phenomenon occurred with a significant number of children (about 17 per cent). The first tentative conclusion that can be drawn from this observation is that for at least some children, the stable initial state (non-conservation) switches to a non-stable state, which is actually a fluctuation between two or possibly more states, for instance, non-conservation and appearance understanding. Finally, they settle into a stable state, that of conservation understanding.

Piaget (1957; see also Flavell, 1963) actually distinguishes four states, each considered equilibrium states. The Piagetian experimenter shows the child a ball of clay, then rolls it into a long thin sausage or into a flat pancake. He then asks if there is as much clay here as in the ball. In the first knowledge state, the child will concentrate either on the length or on the thickness of the sausage during one testing session and say there is either more or less. In the second state, the child will concentrate on one dimension, thickness for instance, but switch to the other dimension at some point during the testing session. In the third knowledge state, the child will simultaneously look at the thickness and length but will not know how to solve the conflict between the two. These three knowledge states result in a non-conservation answer. They are assumed to succeed one another over a period of a few months. Finally, the child understands that the thickness and length stand in a compensatory relationship to one another and reaches the correct answer.

The bimodality, or multimodality, of the scores on a conservation test suggests that the shift between one state and another in an individual child is a sudden jump from one state to another, that is, a strong transition. This is not only for the trivial reason that there is no meaningful intermediate state (it is either one dimension observed, or two). The conservation tests present the children with a number of questions, so they could have any percentage correct. This percentage could gradually grow over time, but it does not really seem to do so.

On closer scrutiny, however, the sudden jump quality is a matter of the measurement scale that we use. The Bentler scale divides the group of children into straightforward conserver and non-conserver groups. Bijstra's scale made a distinction between three groups, including transitory children, by using an appearance–reality criterion. Piaget looked at the way children decide about whether there is the same amount or not and distinguished four different groups. We might be inclined to say that the more refined the measurement scale, the more the results reflect the real distinctions and categories. Such a conclusion, however, does not reckon with the fact that measurement scales are not chosen in function of how closely they reflect the true distinctions in nature; their choice depends on the specific question asked. It is legitimate to ask whether a child can conserve or not and for that question the Bentler test is the right instrument. If you want to know how children come to their answer, you should employ Piaget's criteria. It is like the famous example of the coast of Britain; its measured length depends critically on the smallest length unit employed. The question which unit that should be depends on what purposes the measurement should serve.

We can imagine that the sudden jump pattern occurs on any level of measurement. If we measure the straightforward conserver–non-conserver distinction, it is likely that the transition from one state to the other takes the form of a sharp transition. If we also take intermediate conservers into account by asking for the appearance–reality distinction, it is likely that we will find a sudden jump from non-conserver to intermediate and from intermediate to conserver.

If the sudden jump indeed occurs between any pair of successive states irrespective of the actual measurement scale – and there is no reason to doubt this fundamental assumption – conservation development is highly reminiscent of a mathematical object that is self-similar over all scales of observation, the fractal.

Fractals and self-similarity in development

Towers and robots

In the previous section, I suggested that conservation transitions occur in a *fractal pattern*: the same transition pattern emerges at all levels of measurement. Let me now turn to a different sort of information about possible self-similarity: microdevelop-

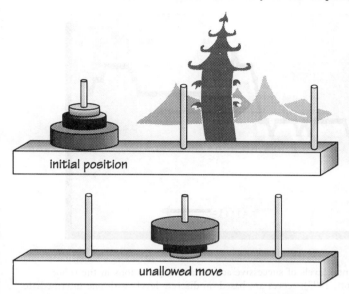

Figure 5.4 The tower of Hanoi in its three-disk version. The combination of disks at the bottom is not allowed by the rules of the game, which do not allow the player to put a larger disk on top of a smaller one.

ment, which involves changes of understanding over the period of a single problem-solving activity. The question is whether the short-term change follows the same basic pattern as the long-term macrodevelopment.

Bidell and Fischer (1993) used 'The tower of Hanoi' – not an adventurous Vietnam movie, but a classic brainteaser game – to study micro–macro similarities. A simple version of the tower problem involves a block with three pegs and three wooden doughnut-shaped disks that can be stacked over the pegs. In the starting position, they form a pyramid on the left peg. The problem is to make a similar pyramid on the right peg by moving one disk at a time. Putting a larger disk on top of a smaller one is not allowed (see Figure 5.4).

If a child is presented with the tower problem for the first time, it is likely to approach it in a way that, on the one hand, depends on its current developmental level, but that, on the other hand, is considerably below the optimal solution level that it will eventually reach. The problem-solving process will therefore show a microdevelopmental path between the entry level, the opening level of problem-solving and the optimal level, which is the level reached after working on the problem with eventual contextual or tutorial support. Children will of course differ in entry and optimal levels and the difference will no doubt depend on the stage of macrodevelopment they are in.

A striking finding is that the children show a sudden shift from inefficient problem-solving characterized by wrong movements, hesitations, etc., to highly efficient acting, resulting in a sequence of correct steps. More precisely, once a child got two steps in succession right, it had all of them right without further hesitation. A state

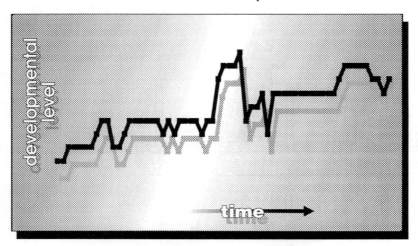

Figure 5.5 Developmental levels of successive actions and explanations in the robot experiment (after Granott, 1993); scores are based on discrete levels with one intermediate score between each two consecutive levels.

of preparation characterized by unsuccessful moves leaps suddenly to a state of correct understanding and mastery of the problem. It is as if the child jumps from a tower; after a long and strenuous march up the stairs to the top it reaches the top and jumps and suddenly the speed of events increases explosively (I admit it is a rather cynical metaphor, but do not worry, the child has a parachute).

A second finding is that the preparation time, the time before the leap, is markedly different for children of different ages. The probable explanation is that the older children start the problem-solving at a higher entry level, with a model or strategy closer to the optimal level. Solving the tower of Hanoi problem requires cognitive functioning at the level of representational systems (in Fischer's terminology). For most children, the entry level is the lower level of representational *mappings*. During the problem-solving act, they construct a representational systems approach in much the same way as they did during the macrodevelopmental process. In this way, micro- and macrodevelopment are qualitatively similar, but differ in the fact that micro-development concerns a shift from an entry to a solution level during an experimental session, whereas macrodevelopment refers to the changes in optimal levels of functioning over the course of years.

A second example of a microdevelopmental process is Nira Granott's robot experiment (Granott, 1993). She presented a small group of adults with a little electronic device on wheels, the robot, and asked them to explain what controls the robot's behaviour. The robots are tuned to react to light, sound, shade and pressure, but their reactions are a rather complicated function of these inputs. I have had the opportunity to play with one of the robots and they are indeed weird little creatures. During the experiment, which is just a free interaction among the participants, all actions and suggestions are videotaped. They are scored in terms of Fischer's thirteen developmental levels. Because the robots are completely unlike anything else the subjects have encountered before, the initial actions and suggestions are at the lowest possible developmental level, sensorimotor actions. The explanations move towards higher developmental levels during the course of the experiment until the groups reach an explanation at an optimal cognitive level (Figure 5.5). The pattern of explanation levels is highly similar to the pattern of macrodevelopment found over the course of twenty-five years. The same stages occur in the same order. Stage shifts occur in the form of sudden jumps, every so often leading to temporary regressions to a lower level of functioning. Granott's experiment shows that we can expect similar patterns at the micro- and macrolevels only if the microlevel poses a sufficiently strong challenge; with familiar objects the subjects would have started at a much higher developmental entry level, possibly their optimal (highest) level. What explains the sudden jumps and strong transitions found in so many developmental phenomena?

Sandpiles, transitions and subcriticality

If they are not polluted by the effluent of sewers or the oil spilled by the many coasters scattered over the horizon, the North Sea beaches offer the contemplative sunbather a beautiful opportunity to carry out experiments with fine, dry white sand. What experiments, the attentive reader will certainly ask and what have they got to do with development? Take a handful of fine white sand and let it slowly glide through a little opening in your fist. The sand will pile up to form a sort of cone. The sand will flow smoothly from the flanks of the cone, but sometimes a little extra sand takes a lot of sand with it in a miniature avalanche. You can of course also take your son's plastic bucket, give him some money to buy himself an ice cream and, after he has disappeared from sight, cut a tiny little hole in the bucket, fill it with dry sand and repeat the experiment under more controlled and scientific circumstances. Meanwhile, think of a good excuse for when the kid comes back.

I admit that the conditions of observation are not really optimal, so it might be better to leave sand and bucket in their original places and read the paper that Per Bak and Kan Chen published in *Scientific American* on the topic of self-organized criticality (Bak and Chen, 1991). In the paper they describe, among others, a comparable sandpile experiment performed by Glenn Held and his colleagues at the IBM Thomas J. Watson Research Center. If sand is dropped grain by grain on a pile, each grain will cause some grains to slide down, but every now and then a single grain may cause a miniature avalanche and it also happens sometimes that part of the pile slides away in a major avalanche (all relative to the size of the pile, of course). The avalanches are qualitatively similar, but quantitatively different. The great majority are very small, involving only a small number of grains. Some are considerably bigger and a few are big enough to affect the form of the pile.

Put differently, the events that change the form of the pile are fractal (avalanches in avalanches in avalanches, etc.) and scale invariant; the small ones are qualitatively similar to the big ones. The causes are quantitatively similar overall, namely the falling of a single grain of sand. Bak and Chen describe the sandpile as a self-organizing system, which evolves towards a state of subcriticality. Subcriticality is the state in which an event (just adding another grain of sand) that would otherwise have only a small effect (some grains sliding down) can cause a major shift to occur (an avalanche).

Two additional facts are well worth noting. The first is that the structure we observe in the sandpile occurs in a large variety of natural events, ranging from earthquakes to traffic jams to simulated biological evolution. It is, in other words, a widely distributed event form and applicable much more widely than to the sands of the North Sea or Long Island Beach. Second, an interesting numerical relationship exists between the frequency of the events (the avalanches) on different scales. If we plot the logarithm of the number of events in each size class (number of very very small ones, number of very small ones, number of small ones, etc.) against the logarithm of the magnitude (magnitude of very very small events, of very small events, etc.), we obtain a tilted line. This means that small changes occur in big numbers and that big changes are few in number. Moreover, the ratio between the numbers is fixed (within statistical boundaries). Let us now turn to the domain of psychological development and see what sandpiles and subcriticality have got to do with developmental states and stages.

In the preceding sections, I have argued that development probably follows a fractal path. That is, the qualitative structure of developments is similar for all possible time-scales. Developmental time-scales may range from very short to very long periods. For instance, at the lower end of the scale we may find single perceptions or thoughts that usually need only a few seconds to come about. Problem-solving events, such as the tower of Hanoi, require a time-scale of minutes. Learning experiments that make use of the so-called microgenetic method (Siegler and Crowley, 1991) last for a few weeks. Major shifts in understanding, such as the skill levels described by Kurt Fischer, require several months to several years, depending on the time in development they occur. At each of these levels the same quantitative patterns occur, be they real transitions, growth spurts or slow linear change. The many little events that occur daily and involve simple problem-solving activities form an interrelated structure. A discovery in one little problem may affect a potential discovery in another little problem, although the relationship between any two arbitrary events is probably quite weak. Such problems may, however, be connected via links that Case calls *central conceptual structures* (Case, 1992b). Domestic problems such as clock reading and dividing a birthday cake are related to these structures, in that each of them weakly positively contributes to that structure. In turn, the structure has a strong positive contribution to each of the separate smaller problem domains, which makes them grow in the form of a marked spurt.

If problem-solving activities, thoughts, perceptions and the applications of skills form an interrelated fractal event structure, there is no reason to doubt that this developmental structure too behaves like interrelated fractal event structures in general. Similar to the sandpile, the daily activities make the structure move to a state of subcriticality. This is a state in which an event that would have caused only a small change under normal circumstances now causes a major shift. The number and magnitude of those major shifts are statistically fixed, but they depend on the actual time-scales at which shifts occur. For instance, getting to understand the tower of Hanoi problem is a major shift compared with the many little shifts during the preparatory stage in the form of much smaller trials and discoveries. The shift from, for instance, having an abstract understanding of an arithmetic operation to an abstract understanding of the relationship between different arithmetic operations, is a major shift in comparison with the smaller ones that occur on a time-scale of weeks or months. Despite major differences in the magnitude of the shifts, however, the magnitude of the causes remains the same throughout the process.

Let me try to use the idea of subcriticality in the cognitive system to arrive at a tentative explanation of why only a limited number of major developmental transitions exist. Most theories, such as those of Piaget, Fischer, Bruner or Case, agree on three to four main shifts, dependent on how they are defined. Fischer, however, usually makes a finer distinction that he calls 'levels' (Fischer, 1980). Thirteen such levels emerge between birth and the age of approximately 25 years.

Fractal development and the quantity of transitions

Why are there only a small number of transitions?

The main transitions, such as the shifts between stages or levels of thinking, seem to occur beyond direct human control or external causation. They emerge by themselves and not because an external agent such as a teacher or a parent pushes the child into a new mode of thought. Small transitions, such as the child's understanding of a particular arithmetic problem, on the other hand, are quite directly manipulable. You can explain to the child how to solve the problem step by step and see to it that it really understands what you mean. Given that parents and teachers control a learning environment in which a certain number of small transitions are supported, how is it possible that the large-scale developmental process boils down to just a few large transitions?

I shall assume that cognitive transitions have a certain magnitude. Just pretend that a certain kind of small transition, such as understanding specific problems, has a magnitude of 1/10 on the scale of Piaget (people studying earthquakes have the Richter scale, so why should developmentalists not have their Piaget scale?). The number of events with magnitude M (which is 1/10 in our case), occurring in self-organizing complex systems of the type discussed here, is given by the equation:

$$N_M = c \cdot 1/M^p \qquad (5.1)$$

that is, the number of events of magnitude M is equal to a constant c times 1 divided by the magnitude raised to a constant power p. Let us, just for the sake of the argument, assume that c equals 1 and that the power parameter equals 1.72 (which is a value found in some related systems; the choice, however, is completely arbitrary; see Bak and Chen, 1991; Schroeder, 1991). If M is 1/10, and p is 1.72, the number of transitions of magnitude 1/10 is about 52 per time unit. Assume that the time unit is a year. That is, whatever the transitions are, they are of the type that takes approximately a week to be accomplished. How many transitions per year would there be, on average, that are 10 times as big? We know that:

$$N_{1/10} = 1/(1/10)^{1.72} \approx 52 \tag{5.2}$$

It follows then that:

$$N_1 = 1/1^{1.72} = 1 \tag{5.3}$$

that is, each year there is on average 1 transition of a magnitude 10 times bigger than the transitions that take place about once a week. By the same token, the number of transitions of magnitude 2 is 1 every 3 years, of magnitude 3 is 1 every 7 years and so forth (Figure 5.6). The number of major transitions (e.g. of magnitude 3) that we can expect over a lifetime is therefore very limited. Between the ages of 0 and 21 years, only 3 transitions of magnitude 3 will occur on average. Put differently, the limitation on the number of major transitions follows directly from the power law that describes their distribution over time. That power law, in its turn, is a direct consequence of the eventual fractal nature of the organization of cognitive change.

What is the point of doing an exercise like the previous one? Recall that the discussion started by asking why there was only a small number of major transitions. Traditionally, the answer to this question has been based on ontological arguments. For instance, there are four major Piagetian stages because they represent the four major steps in the emergence of true scientific thinking. It is the logic of scientific

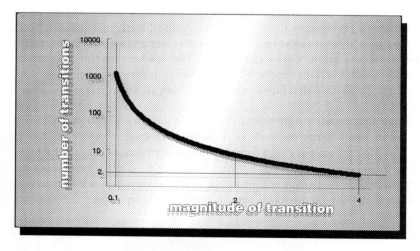

Figure 5.6 If we assume that a transition of magnitude 0.1 occurs once every week, a 22-year-old person will have experienced about 1,200 of such minor transitions. The expected number of transitions decreases drastically with increasing magnitude. That same 22-year-old will have experienced only 2 transitions of magnitude 4 (calculations are based on the assumption that the power parameter is 1.72; note that the y-axis is logarithmic).

thinking that explains why there are four, not five or three, or approximately four. The reasoning behind the current exercise was quite different. It started from the idea that developmental systems have a fractal property. They are transitions in transitions in transitions. If that is true, they should obey the rules of complex fractal systems that change as a consequence of some underlying principle, which, in the case of development, is logistic growth.

A basic rule governing such systems says that the frequency of the changes is a power function of their magnitude. Given the fact that our daily activities and thought processes are like small transitions or growth processes, we should expect a nested structure of bigger and bigger transitions. The number of main transitions – that is, transitions of maximal magnitude – must therefore be very small. More accurately, it is small because of the power law that governs its distribution, but it must be big enough to enable students of development to see a pattern. For some reason or other, the number four seems an optimal combination of both requirements.

Between-transition intervals: evidence of a fractal process?

The empirical evidence I want to discuss here is indirect. It deals with the length of the intervals between major transitions, in other words, with the length of developmental stages. Developmental stages are a tricky issue. Many people believe they are non-existent or highly dependent on the criteria and scales you employ. Stages are surprisingly closely related to the eventual fractal nature of development. I shall take a very pragmatic stand and define a *stage* as any time interval during which a measurable criterion shows a predefined amount of stability. For instance, we might take a measurement scale for social understanding that applies over the whole life span and administer it to children of different ages. If we find growth spurts or sudden changes punctuating longer periods of relative quiet, we may conclude that the scale reveals a stage-wise development. The claim does not extend beyond the measurement procedure, context or task domain. Evidence of similar spurts and plateaux in different domains lends more support to the assumption that the stages are general instead of local and specific properties of behaviour or understanding. Fischer's work on developmental stages, called *levels*, is an example of the procedure I just described. A standardized scaling procedure which is applicable over the whole life span is administered to populations of different ages and with different task domains. Fischer and Rose (1993) present a generalization of findings from different domains that should be applicable to a broad range of developmental phenomena. The stages (levels) and age ranges are given in Table 5.1 below.

I simply took the mean of each transition age, which is indeed a very quick-and-dirty procedure here and transformed them into days. I then graphed the logarithm (to the base 10) of the transition ages. The result is surprisingly close to a simple linear logarithmic distribution (see Figure 5.7). What is so special about this? Linear logarithmic distributions are characteristic of many biological growth phenomena. They are caused by growth processes that are, in some way or another, determined by a component that obeys a power law. An example of such a process is the sandpile

Transitions and developmental fractals

Table 5.1 Fischer's 13 developmental levels with average ages of emergence

Level	Age of emergence
Single reflexes	3–4 weeks
Reflex mappings	7–8 weeks
Reflex systems	10–11 weeks
Single sensorimotor actions	15–17 weeks
Sensorimotor mappings	7–8 months
Sensorimotor systems	11–13 months
Single representations	18–24 months
Representational mappings	3.5–4.5 years
Representational systems	6–7 years
Single abstractions	10–12 years
Abstract mappings	14–16 years
Abstract systems	18–20 years
Principles	23–25 years

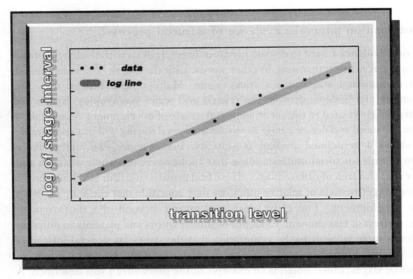

Figure 5.7 A linear logarithmic distribution of inter-transition intervals, based on ages of transition with Fischer's developmental levels.

discussed earlier. It is interesting to observe that a phenomenon determined by both biological and cultural variables, cognitive development, for instance, follows a rule of distribution characteristic of biological growth phenomena in general.

The logarithmic distribution affords for another interesting observation that relates to the problem of 'fractality'. Let me begin with a simple fractal based on the *Lindenmayer system*. Aristid Lindenmayer was a Dutch biologist who conceived of the growth patterns of plants as fractal, repetitive systems based on simple transformation rules. In my fractal example, the transformation rule says that you can grow two branches out of any available branch. The initial state is a single branch. Applying the rule n successive times produces a tree with 2^n branches. Since the tree has to increase in size each time in order to remain strong enough to support the weight of the branches, it takes more and more resources as the tree grows more branches. If the resource supply is a constant (or at least a constant ratio of a variable such as the size of the trunk), the time needed to grow a new generation of branches is proportional to the number of branches it has to grow. The tree is a very characteristic fractal pattern and its growth rule an example of a fractal process. If the time constraint applies, the time between each new generation of branches increases in accordance with the power series:

$$1 \to 2 \to 4 \to 8 \to 16 \to 32 \to 64 \to \ldots \tag{5.4}$$

which is similar to:

$$2^0 \to 2^1 \to 2^2 \to 2^3 \to 2^4 \to 2^5 \to 2^6 \to \ldots \tag{5.5}$$

The logarithmic representation of this time series is a line, namely:

$$0 \to 1 \to 2 \to 3 \to 4 \to 5 \to 6 \to \tag{5.6}$$

Any fractal process where the interval between generations[2] is a function of the magnitude of the fractal pattern (the number of branches, for instance) shows an interval pattern described by a power distribution. That is, its logarithmic representation is a straight line.

The fact that the intervals between major transitions lie on a straight logarithmic line does of course not prove that development is a fractal process. The similarity between the timing of development and that of fractal processes as described here might be a mere coincidence. On the other hand, the logarithmic distribution is yet another clue that increases Miss Marple's suspicion that development and cognitive growth is indeed a fractal process.

What pushes the subcriticality into a major transition?

If you keep adding sand to a sandpile, a moment will come when just a little bit of sand will make a major portion of the pile slide down. An event – adding a little bit of sand – that caused minor changes causes a major avalanche when the sandpile has reached a subcritical state. The physical parameter that determines the criticality is probably the angle of the sand relative to the horizontal surface. What makes the critical shift occur in development, provided development is indeed behaving qualitatively like the sandpile? The answer should be that the event that causes minor shifts will cause a major shift when subcriticality occurs. That is, there is no particular group of developmental mechanisms that is responsible for pushing the system into a major transition. In Piaget's numerous works, lots of examples can be found of how the same information that previously caused children to stick to their old beliefs, suddenly changes those beliefs when a state of disequilibrium has been reached.

Siegler and Crowley (1991) describe a number of microgenetic experiments aimed at letting children discover new strategies. The time of discovery and generalization usually takes a few weeks. Such processes are believed to present a model of developmental processes in a nutshell. The point that Siegler and Crowley make, however, is that the explosive generalization of a new rule or strategy is usually not simultaneous with the discovery of that rule or strategy. What are needed to set in motion the generalization to the whole domain of problems are so-called *impasses* or *challenge problems*. They are the kind of difficult problems that show children that the new strategy they considered as only one of the many possible strategies, is actually the only really good one. Put differently, the discovery of the strategy or rule brings the cognitive system into a subcritical state. Encountering of a challenge problem is the external event that causes the system to pass the critical threshold. Explosive growth of the use of the strategy is the result. The point is, however, that a problem becomes a challenge problem once the subcritical state has been reached, although, of course, not all problems become challenge problems at that stage.

A mathematical model of transitions

The logistic transition

The standard logistic equation is not suited for modelling sudden, steep jumps that follow a period where almost no change took place at all. And the latter is what happens in conservation development or in the tower of Hanoi problem and probably in all processes where sudden developmental state shifts occur.

In our examples of strong transitions, ranging from perceptual shifts in Necker cubes to achieving an understanding of the tower of Hanoi to conservation, we have seen that the initial state is at first very hard to change. It tries to maintain its stability by strongly reducing the probability of events that will cause the state to shift to a different value. Note that this is just a figure of speech: the subject in the tower experiment, for instance, really tries very hard to understand. Nevertheless, he/she remains unsuccessful for the whole preparatory period, in which no real progress is actually made. The same is true with conservation; whatever happens with the form of the clay ball or the liquid column, it confirms whatever belief the child has about the amount being conserved or not. But once the initial state gets pushed out of its attractor basin, the change enters into some sort of positive feedback loop. The further one moves from the stable initial state, the quicker the changes take place, until the process suddenly halts at its new attractor point, which is the alternative perceptual organization, the understanding of the tower strategy or conservation, just to name only two of the possibilities.

What causes such stable states to change? Take for instance conservation. Conservation training is known to have hardly any effect, unless the child is already at a subcritical state (see van der Maas, 1993, for a recent demonstration). How do children ever learn that the amount of liquid does not change in spite of salient form changes? Children are very often confronted with conservation situations. Any transformation of the form of a liquid (milk, lemonade or whatever) or of solid matter (sand, clay, your blanket, etc.) potentially involves a conservation problem: does the amount remain the same, or is it affected by the form? In the majority of cases, the eventually problematic nature of simple domestic acts, such as the child eating mashed carrots and potatoes or smearing them around the dish, goes unnoticed. Consequently, there is no consciousness whatsoever of an eventual problem involving increase or decrease of matter upon changing its form, and, therefore, also no real causative influences that push the belief system into the conservation state.

How does conservation develop, then? Whatever the basis of conservation development, or of many other transitory developments for that matter, it is highly likely that the prompts, conflicts or experiences that push the initial belief or strategy out of balance are randomly distributed. That is, there is no systematic educational effort to teach children conservation around age 5. Some schools, believing in the Piagetian idea, present conservation materials in kindergarten, but children discovered conservation even before Piaget did. More important, the frequency of effective experiences is inversely related to the degree of consolidation of the belief. It is well known in conservation research that 4-year-olds, for instance, can be given quite strong counterexamples, but they simply do not see them as conflicting with their basic belief; they may change their answer in accordance with the suggestion, but fall back on their old answer at the next question. On the other hand, with children who have started to doubt their non-conservation answers, it suffices just to say they are wrong and they will immediately switch to conservation, giving perfectly correct logical justifications (Brainerd, 1973). Conservation training experiments show that the lack of training effects is proportional to the lack of understanding of conservation.

For the next step, I need to introduce the notion of a *learning event*. A learning event is defined as an experience that, for some reason or other, affects the child's understanding or skill level. It could do so for a variety of reasons. For instance, a learning event could be the simple opportunity to experiment with the problem. It could be a problem solution or a reinforcement given after a successful try. It could be a situation that puts the child in a cognitive conflict. It could be a combination of a cognitive conflict arising between two children who solve a common task or problem. In short, a learning event is something whose actual content and effect vary over a wide range of learning, promoting variables and properties. An event that would qualify as a learning event with a child who is close to acquiring an understanding of the conservation principle, probably has no effect at all on a child who has no idea of conservation whatsoever. In fact, the further the child moves from the original non-conservation attitude, the higher the probability that any event involving transformations of quantities will have a learning effect on conservation understanding. All this can be generalized in the principle that the probability of learning (of encountering an effective learning event) is proportionate to the level of understanding or mastery already achieved. A low growth level thus corresponds to a low probability that an effective learning event will take place, that is, with a low chance that anything will be learned. The difference with the logistic growth model is that in the latter, the probability of learning is independent of the growth level. What depends on the growth level is the net effect of growth, since that is the product of growth level and growth rate.

What makes an ordinary event, like drinking your milk or playing with sand and a bucket, qualify as a conservation learning event? We have seen earlier that problem events are determined by a wide variety of control parameters. They cover aspects as diverse as the child's interest and attention to the problem, the salience of the dimensions of the beakers or forms employed, the support and help of a more competent child or adult and so forth. With a specific conservation problem, the child can be highly involved or not, the difference between dimensions can be more or less salient, the adult can give more or less accessible support and explanation. Each of these control variables varies randomly. For a non-conserver all the control variables have to be beneficial for the event to qualify as a learning event (high interest and motivation, attention, high support, salient distinctions, a simple problem and so on). Given the random variability of all these dimensions, the chance that they will all have the required value is fairly low. With children who are closer to an understanding of conservation, it probably suffices that one or a few of the variables are beneficial, but it does not matter too much which ones they are.

A mathematical model of the logistic transition

I shall start with the ordinary logistic equation. Recall that each iteration can be conceived of as a separate learning step. I shall assume that each step now represents an event that potentially qualifies as a learning event. Examples of such events are the child's pouring liquids or sand from one container to the other, playing with clay and so on. The steps in my logistic equation do not represent fixed temporal intervals now, as they did with the feedback delay, but intervals between events; the feedback delay time is now determined by the time between consecutive events that potentially qualify as learning events. From the previous section, I know that there is no growth when the event is not a learning event. How do I model the occurrence of a learning event that is proportionate to the growth level already achieved? I have claimed that the control variables determining a problem event vary randomly. Thus each dimension of the control space corresponds with a random number. For the sake of simplicity, I map all these random variables onto one concatenated variable. The random number that results is needed to determine the probability that an event qualifies as a learning event. Let me assume that the random number varies between 0 and 1. I know that when K is set to 1, the growth level of conservation understanding ranges between 0 and 1. The simplest way to simulate the occurrence of a learning event, therefore, is by using the following rule. For each iterative step in the computation of the growth level of conservation, I pick a random number (between 0 and 1) and compare this with the growth level (also between 0 and 1). When the random number is smaller than the growth level, I decide that this particular iterative step corresponds with a learning event. All these assumptions go into the following simple growth equation:

$$L_{t+f} = L_t \cdot (1 + e_t - e_t \cdot L_t / K)$$
$$\text{for } e_t = 0 \text{ if } L_t < \text{Rand}_t \cdot K, \text{ and } e_t = r \text{ if } L_t \geq \text{Rand}_t \cdot K \tag{5.7}$$

I shall call this the *stochastic transition equation*. It is stochastic because it is based on a random sequence whose effect depends on the preceding steps in the sequence. It is a transition equation because it is able to produce a sharp, jump-like transition, as we shall see in Model 5.1.

It is easy to proceed from this stochastic version to a deterministic form of the logistic transition. From the second part of the equation follows that the growth rate e_t is a linear randomized function of the growth level L_t and some fixed parameter r:

$$e_t = f(L_t, r) \tag{5.8}$$

What is the simplest form in which the function f can be cast? Since the growth level L can vary widely, depending on the value of K, we make e_t a simple multiplicative function of r and of the ratio between L and K, that is:

$$e_t = L_t / K \cdot r \tag{5.9}$$

When I substitute this function in the first part of equation 5.5, I obtain the deterministic form of the transition equation:

$$L_{t+f} = L_t \cdot (1 + r \cdot L_t / K - r \cdot L_t^2 / K^2) \tag{5.10}$$

Model 5.1 Jumps: stochastic and deterministic

In this model, we are going to define an equation that enables you to experiment with either the stochastic or the deterministic version of the transition equation by just changing one parameter.

First, define the following range values and range names (the range names are in boldface, the rest of the text is commentary[3]):

1	**r**	(growth or learning rate)
0.01	**in**	(initial state of grower)
1	**s**	(if $s = 1$, stochastic version works)

Go to cell A10 and type **in**. Cell A11 takes the basic equation:

$$+A10 * (1 + B11 - B11 * A10) \tag{5.11}$$

Note that the growth rate variable is to be found in the B column. Enter the following equation in B11:

$$@if (\$s = 1, C11, D11) \tag{5.12}$$

It says that if the stochasticity parameter is 1, the value of the growth rate is to be found in cell C11. If it is not 1, the value is to be found in D11. This seems a rather cumbersome way of specifying the transition equation, but it will make the steps more transparent.

In cell C11 type:

$$@if (@rand < A10, \$r, 0) \tag{5.13}$$

which states that if a random number is smaller than A10, the cell takes the value of r and if not, it has the value 0.

Cell D11 specifies the value of the growth rate variable for the deterministic model:

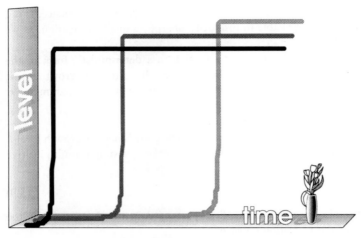

Figure 5.8 Sudden jumps to a higher state level depend critically on the value of the initial state (all other things being equal).

$$+\$r * A10 \tag{5.14}$$

Copy range A11..D11 to A12..D1000 and define a simple line graph for the data range A10..A1000.

Try different values for r between 0.1 and 2.8; with an r of 1, test the effect of the initial state value (try for instance 0.001, 0.01, 0.05 and 0.1).

What kind of growth patterns result from applying the transition equations? Let me take the pattern of change in the tower of Hanoi experiment (Bidell and Fischer, 1993) as an example of a sharp transition. It turns out that the curves based on a sufficiently low initial state (around 0.01) and a high growth rate (around 1) reproduce the tower of Hanoi pattern quite well (Figure 5.8). The initial level remains stable for quite some time, then suddenly switches to a much higher level of functioning. This level is the carrying capacity level, which is by definition the optimal level of functioning. The point in the curve preceding the sudden jump corresponds with the state of subcriticality from the fractal systems described earlier. Second, the length of the initial state, corresponding with the preparatory state, is proportional to the initial state level, corresponding with the entry level in the experiment. If we try a relatively high initial state, like 0.1, the transition takes place immediately, as it did with the oldest children in the experimental group. Third, if the initial state becomes too low, the length of the preparatory state far exceeds any possible problem-solving task, especially with younger children. It follows then that such entry levels will not lead to a discovery of the right stacking principle in the tower task.

With lower growth rates and higher initial states, the resulting curves are quite similar to the ordinary S-shaped curve of the standard logistic equation. With high

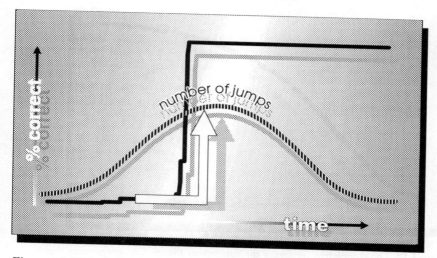

Figure 5.9 With similar parameter values, the stochastic transition model produces a jump at dramatically different moments: small, continuous random effects produce major, non-continuous transition effects.

growth rates qualitative patterns emerge that we have also seen with the standard equation, namely oscillations and chaos.

The stochastic model produces the same sudden jumps as the deterministic version (provided the parameter values are the same; see Figure 5.9). The stochastic element only shows in the moment at which the sudden jump occurs. Whereas the stochastic element appears in each step of the equation, its effect is confined to a specific small time range, the moment at which the jump occurs. In order to investigate the extent to which the moment of the jump is determined by the random element, I ran 1400 simulations of the stochastic model, keeping the parameters constant. The cumulative curve, showing the number of simulated cases which have reached conservation criterion is a typical S-shaped curve which resembles the group data reported earlier (see Figure 5.10). The simulated group data, however, are based on individual growth curves characterized by a sudden leap.

Transitions as catastrophes

The 'catastrophic' nature of transitions

Catastrophe theory is a branch of mathematics that came into vogue in the social sciences after the publication of an influential overview paper in *Scientific American* by Zeeman (1976). It presented a mathematical justification for the existence of sudden changes in, for instance, the behaviour of dogs or people. If a dog is made really nervous, the animal will either attack or flee from the cause of the disturbance. My dog,

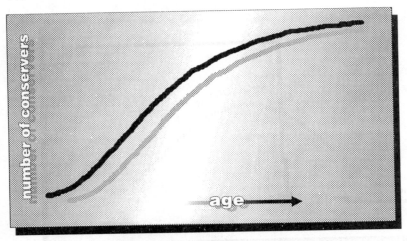

Figure 5.10 The cumulative version of the curve from Figure 5.9, representing the number of 'children' who have reached the criterion: although each individual develops in the form of a sudden jump, the group curve shows a misleadingly smooth, S-shaped growth pattern.

who is very clearly misnamed after a peaceful Belgian cartoon character Guust Flater, who is, I am afraid, not internationally known, has now on several occasions given me the dubious honour of studying Zeeman's catastrophe 'in the wild'.

It is very easy to make Guust anxious, for instance by putting his leash on in the wrong way, exerting too much pressure on his neck. He will try to flee from the threatening feeling, that is, away from the person who holds the leash. This response will, of course, make matters worse. Suddenly his anxiety turns into aggression and he attacks whoever is holding the leash. The attack will loosen the pressure on the leash and reduce the cause of his rage, but this is certainly not enough to calm him down. It really needs a lot of dog psychology, associated with the right sort of physical aggression, to get him back to normal. I have never tried to measure the pressure of the leash around his neck (I am crazy enough to have a dog, but I am not mad), but if I had done that, and plotted the flight or fight reactions against the pressure, I would very probably have found that the amount of pressure at which he attacks is higher than the amount of pressure on his neck at the moment his fear turns into rage.

The sudden shift from fear to rage and attack, or from attack to fear, is an example of a so-called *cusp catastrophe*. The cusp catastrophe is a mathematical form that describes the distribution of equilibrium points. In the case of my ferocious dog, the equilibrium points are different forms of behaviour associated with points on the continuum from fear to rage. His behaviour is either a neutral reaction that is neither flight nor attack, or a choice between flight and attack. Figure 5.11 shows the sheet upon which the equilibrium points are located, relative to a major control variable, namely the fear/rage-inducing variable.

The transition model discussed in this chapter pretends to explain sudden jumps in

Figure 5.11 The plane of behavioural equilibrium points – fight, flight and neutral – and their distribution over a control variable takes the form of a cusp.

a bimodal variable, such as conservation. Does it have the properties specified in the cusp catastrophe model? What are these properties and how do they apply to development?

Catastrophe flags on developmental transitions

Amsterdam is, as is widely known, a city rich in distractions of the most various kinds. Maybe because they wanted to compensate for too tempting outdoor activities, my distinguished Amsterdam colleagues Han van der Maas and Peter Molenaar have turned to the study of catastrophes, a most attractive topic, indeed, but of a less sinful nature than some of the excitements their city has to offer. In a recent paper (van der Maas and Molenaar, 1992), they describe stagewise development in terms of catastrophe theory. The catastrophe model they apply is the cusp discussed in the preceding section. Stagewise development occurs in models like Piaget's, where it is supposed to cover all domains of thought, or in a model like Fischer's, where the stages are strongly domain and context determined. Van der Maas and Molenaar claim that stages succeed one another in the form of real shifts. The shifts are not growth spurts, as Kurt Fischer or I would see them, but real switches as described by the catastrophe model. Just as my dog switched suddenly from flight to fight, the sensorimotor child, for instance, would make a sudden shift to pre-operational thinking, if the Piagetian model were right. The Netherlands is anything but a conservative country, but we do like conservation, and conservation therefore is the example van der Maas and Molenaar employ to show that the shift from non-conservation to conservation understanding is a real catastrophe (in the mathematical sense, of course).

In essence, their argument is as follows. The mathematical study of the cusp catastrophe shows that it has eight distinctive features, that is, properties invariantly associated with the occurrence of a cusp. These properties are called 'catastrophe flags'. If it can be shown that a developmental transition carries these flags too, it is likely to be a catastrophe (since no other change phenomena are known that carry just these flags). Thus, instead of the four horsemen of the Apocalypse, we have the eight flags of the catastrophe to watch for. In his dissertation, Han van der Maas (1993) describes a longitudinal study of conservation development with a computerized test. Since the children had free access to the computers in the classroom, van der Maas was able to collect individual data series with high measurement density.

The first flag is the *bimodal score-distribution*. Children presented with a set of conservation questions tend, in general, to have the majority either right or wrong. We find relatively few children with an intermediate score. Evidence for this comes, among others, from the Bentler data (Bentler, 1970) described earlier. The second flag, related to the first, is *inaccessibility*. A particular score domain, of intermediate scores, is 'inaccessible', that is, it will not appear in the data. The relative lack of real intermediate scores supports this criterion.

The third flag is the occurrence of *sudden jumps*. It is not clear whether the development of conservation shows a real sudden jump, in the sense of a sudden switch. It is likely, however, that the growth pattern is at least one of a marked spurt. Van der Maas found strong evidence for each of these three important flags in his study. Figure 5.3, for instance, shows the sudden jump occurring with the so-called transitory subjects, children who are caught in the middle of the transition process.

The fourth flag is *hysteresis*. It implies that the place where the jump occurs depends critically on the direction of change of the control variable. Van der Maas (1993) found indirect evidence for hysteresis in some of his transitory subjects. He states, however, that conclusive evidence for hysteresis can only be found with an experimental set up, in which an important control variable can be varied continuously (see further, Figure 5.13).

A related, fifth flag is *divergence*. It implies that the magnitude of the jump, that is, the effect of a small change in the vicinity of the transition point, differs over the second control axis (which in Figure 5.11 would be the axis perpendicular to the fear/rage-inducing axis). In the conservation example, this second dimension could well be the amount of support and help during the test. We have seen that real developmental spurts occur only in the case of supportive testing. In unsupported testing the increase is slow and gradual. The evidence from van der Maas' experiment is unfortunately again inconclusive.

The next, sixth, flag is *divergence of linear response*. It implies that perturbations in the vicinity of a catastrophe point will lead to sudden loss of stability and oscillations.

The perturbation that best models this type of event is conservation training, that is, presenting the children with a conservation training programme. It has often been observed that almost all training works very well and very explicitly with children who are already in the transitional state and that it does not work for children who are true believers in non-conservation (Bijstra, 1989).

The seventh flag is *delayed recovery of equilibrium*. It is based on the measurement of the time needed for the system to return to its original equilibrium if it is artificially perturbed. For instance, you can tell the child that another child gave a different answer to the same question. We expect that a counter-suggestion will hardly affect the child if it is far from the transition point to conservation. But, as it approaches that point more closely, the same counter-suggestion will make it think and hesitate longer. This scenario certainly sounds plausible, although there is no direct evidence available. A possibly related effect has been observed in Bidell and Fischer's tower of Hanoi experiment. Just before the jump to complete understanding takes place, many children pause, tap their fingers and the like. It seems that the information they rejected in the previous stage is now causing more and more cognitive trouble.

The eighth and final flag is *anomalous variance*. As the transition point approaches, the structure of the statistical variance changes markedly. That is, the nature of the differences between the children changes as they are ready to make the jump to conservation. Van der Maas and Molenaar (1992) discuss several examples of this anomaly, such as the occurrence of oscillations in the answers, or discrepancies in the reasoning. In van der Maas' experiment no evidence was found for flags six to eight, although there is indirect evidence in his results and the results of others to show that those flags might apply.

In summary, despite lacking evidence for a number of catastrophe flags, there is very good evidence for three essential ones, namely bimodality, inaccessibility and sudden jump and reasonable evidence for hysteresis. I would say that this evidence is strong enough for us to place a higher bet on the catastrophe than on the non-catastrophe case. Some catastrophe flags have been shown in empirical research, others sound quite convincing, yet others are plausible extensions of findings in other domains. The question now is whether the flags apply also to the transition model presented in this chapter.

Is the logistic transition model a catastrophe?

If you do not like mathematical models, I am sure your answer will be yes, of course it is (but I am also sure your reasons for saying so will be based on a different concept of catastrophe). Let us turn to the official meaning of the catastrophe concept, however, and investigate whether the flags apply to the transition model presented in the form of equations 5.7 and 5.10. For a specified parameter range those equations produce typical transition curves. Let me pretend that those curves are simulated data from a longitudinal conservation study. Do the catastrophe flags apply to them?

Assume that we take an age distribution for the children that lies around the transition age, for instance between 4 and 6 years; that is, the time window of the sample is 2 years. Given the steep form of the transition, we may estimate the actual transition to take place within a much smaller period. For instance, let us assume it takes about 10 per cent of the age range over which we sample (that is, on average 0.2 years or roughly $2\frac{1}{2}$ months). The probability that we are going to find a child who is right in the middle of a transition is 10 per cent.

Consequently, the probability that we shall find a child in the state of either non-conservation or conservation will be 45 per cent. Put differently, we will find a highly bimodal distribution. The intermediate scores on the test (some items correct, some wrong) will occur very infrequently in the sample. Children who are right in the middle of the transition may respond inconsistently over the items, but they may as well be consistent in either a conservation or a non-conservation strategy. That is, a large part of the score variation (the intermediate scores) is inaccessible. Third, the developments take place in the form of a sudden jump. We have seen, however, that if many individual scores are added the underlying spurt turns into a much more gradual S-shaped growth curve. The averaged group data will definitely obscure the transitory character of the change, but we know from each individual simulation that the transition is a very sharp growth spurt. In summary, three important catastrophe flags are found in the transition model.

What about hysteresis, the fourth flag? Figure 5.11 shows how hysteresis occurs over the 'fold' of the equilibrium sheet. If we move to the back of the folded sheet, the hysteresis effect becomes smaller and smaller and finally disappears. In the example with the dog, the left-to-right variable was the fear/rage-inducing factor. The front-to-back variable was assumed to be the dog's level of excitement. In the transition model, the variables are of course very different. From left to right runs the time variable. From back to front runs the growth rate variable, with the lowest growth rate in the back. The problem is that, whereas the left–right axis could be varied in either direction in the case of the dog's attack catastrophe, this is not possible in the case of time (trivially, you cannot run time backwards). That is, there is no empirical interpretation of eventual hysteresis phenomena in case the control variable is time, which it is in developmental transitions. I discussed this matter with Han 'Catastrophe' van der Maas, and he showed me a mathematical technique for demonstrating eventual hysteresis effects in dynamic models. In essence, it amounts to letting an external factor affect the critical part of the dynamic equation, for instance, by adding an increasing value to each outcome of a sequence of iterative steps. You then let the sequence run backwards while adding an external factor that decreases in the same way as the first one increases. It is possible to compute the range of external variable values for which hysteresis can be found.

The result of this can be seen in Figure 5.12 where one line represents the forward and the other the backward loop of the external variable. The model simulates what would happen in a microdevelopmental investigation of conservation. For instance, when a critical control parameter, the difference between length and height of the containers involved, is varied from highly different to about the same, the child would persist in non-conservation until it reached a pair of beakers that were virtually identical. But if the difference between the dimensions is varied from almost the same

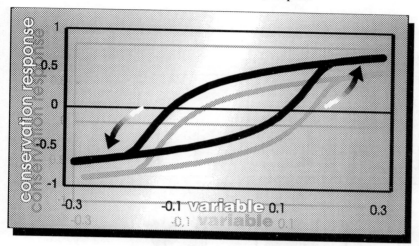

Figure 5.12 Adding an increasing or decreasing external effect to the transition model results in hysteresis: the growth levels either drop back to or escape from a minimal level at different places, which depend on the direction in which the control variable has been changed (left-to-right versus right-to-left in the diagram).

to very different, the child would first conserve, then switch to non-conservation with a pair of beakers that are very different in shape. In summary, although hysteresis does not apply to the transition model when time is taken into account, it does apply when you simulate the effect of an external control factor. That is, the fourth catastrophe flag applies to the model (Figure 5.13).

The next catastrophe flag, divergence, marks the difference in effects of small perturbations, depending on where in the catastrophe model the perturbations are applied. Recall that I suggested employing the growth rate variable as the back-to-front dimension in the transition catastrophe. If the growth rate is small, a single step forward along the transition curve (which is then actually very similar to a smooth growth curve) exerts no significant effect. As the growth rate increases, however, the same small step, if it occurs near the transition point, will magnify into a sudden leap to the higher equilibrium state.

It is difficult, however, to show whether or not the additional catastrophe flags, divergence of linear response, delayed recovery of equilibrium and anomalous variance apply to the logistic transition model. This model offers no description of the underlying cognitive processes and these might well be needed to explain the effects of external perturbations such as counter-suggestions on the child's thought process.

In summary, the transition model seems to fit a significant majority of catastrophe indicators, the so-called flags. We may conclude, therefore, that it can be subsumed under the broad class of models that display a cusp catastrophe and therefore describe switches between bistable states.

Chapters 4 and 5 have been devoted to two different forms of increase, namely the

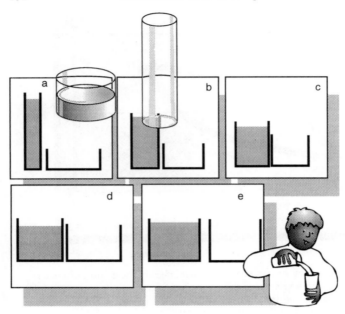

Figure 5.13 Hysteresis in the conservation jump can be demonstrated by presenting children with an ordered series of conservation questions with different pairs of containers; containers are ordered from very salient difference to almost no difference. It is assumed that the jump from or to the conservation answer will depend on whether one starts either with the almost similar or with the very different pair.

logistic growth and the logistic transition form. Later, they will serve as building blocks of more complicated models. They will describe developmental ecologies, where the variables entertain relationships of mutual support or competition. Before proceeding to the issue of dynamic developmental ecologies, I shall describe a third building block, namely the oscillation.

Notes

1. That must have been shortly before or after he left the University of Ghent (in Belgium, yes, where we met Quetelet, among others) where he had taught from 1858 on. I am afraid the Belgian Connection keeps haunting me.
2. A *generation* is the result of applying the transformation rule once, for instance, 'every branch produces two new branches'.
3. If you define Range Names with the automatic procedure described earlier (see note 4, Chapter 4), put your commentary in a different cell (for instance, the cell to the right of the one where you put the corresponding range name).

6

Oscillations

Oscillations in development

'What goes up, must come down . . .'

My wife and I share a little foible with a couple of our dearest friends: we love to spend hours singing old 1960s songs. I admit it is a little pathetic, some old guys and girls immersed in their collective adolescent nostalgia, but who cares – our neighbours live at a safe distance.[1] One of our favourites is a song by Blood, Sweat and Tears that starts with 'What goes up, must come down . . .' and it immediately goes on to offer an almost Buddhist explanation in the second line, 'spinning wheel got to go 'round'.

If you are a developmental psychologist, you are probably particularly interested in 'what goes up'. If you are in the life-span business, 'must come down' should also appeal to you. But if you are in dynamic systems, the spinning wheel should tell you that things go up and down all the time and progress in spinning the wool is a result of that incessant oscillation. Technically, a spinning wheel is a device in which a rotation results from an up- and downward oscillation that is equal to the sine of the rotation point. Sine functions are frequently used in dynamic models to introduce a regular oscillator to some changing function. If you write a sine function in your spreadsheet and graph a time–delay phase space (which was explained earlier), you will notice that it forms a cycle.

I admit it is a bit tricky to take a campfire song as a source of deep wisdom, but there is still an attractive aspect to the idea that things progress, if they progress at all, by going up and down. In nature, it seems, the shortest line between two points is the wiggle. In this chapter, I shall first present some evidence of oscillations in development and of the cyclical nature of resource allocation. The rest of the chapter discusses a few speculative models of resource oscillations and their effect on developmental and growth processes.

Oscillations in development

The research data abound with evidence for a wiggling developmental path, but for some reason or other, we have tended to overlook that fact. Development is usually seen as a great march towards a higher way of being. Whatever irregularities occur along the way are not caused by the marching of the troops but by unintended external disruptions. Nevertheless, the oscillatory and fluctuating movement could as well tell a basic fact about the way change in nature is organized. It is possible that processes just need to go up and down in order to maintain their dynamics over time. Let me first discuss some empirical evidence for oscillations in various developmental domains.

In Chapter 4 (on the logistic growth equation), I discussed Dromi's study of the lexical development of her daughter (Dromi, 1986). The cumulative data, referring to the increasing number of words the child used and understood, showed a nice logistic S-shape. But, if we graph the growth rate per observation period, the image changes dramatically. What we see is an irregular fluctuation over time. The first substage of learning words is characterized by rather large swings, whereas the second substage shows much smaller oscillations (Figure 4.7). In a comparable study, Corrigan (1983) found similar oscillations in the rate of word learning. After an initial period, in which the first elaboration of the lexicon takes place, the increase changes into an irregular fluctuation (see Figure 2.11). The net result, the additive growth curve, however, closely resembles a smooth S-shaped curve. The additive nature of word learning conceals the fact that the increase process itself oscillates quite markedly.

Oscillations also occur in other domains of language development. Take for instance the growth in correct use of a syntactic rule over time. Data from studies on interrogative questions (Labov and Labov, 1978) and on inflections, such as the present progressive (Brown, 1973), show a similar qualitative pattern. The average number of structures used correctly varies widely over time, until it settles down at an equilibrium level that is 100 per cent correct (Figure 2.10).

Kurt Fischer's studies of the growth of understanding in various cognitive domains, such as arithmetic understanding or reflective judgement, show strong oscillations. For instance, in a study on reflective judgement, children were given an ill-structured problem and were asked to reason about their thinking process. Two different test scores were compared, one score on understanding *abstract mappings*, another on *abstract systems*. In abstract mappings, children justify their thinking by referring to the context in which the problem occurs. Abstract systems require a coordination of mappings and require the child to compare and contrast different contexts, or different sides of an issue. The increase in the scores oscillates over the zero line; that is, there is real regression (Kitchener *et al.*, 1993; see Figure 6.1). The pattern is highly similar to that of arithmetic understanding, more precisely the child's understanding of how operations such as addition and subtraction relate (Fischer, Kenny and Pipp, 1990; see further, Figure 6.2).

The data are based on cross-sectional research, not on individual case studies, as in the examples from lexical and syntactic development. Nevertheless, the group data must be based on individual data that show at least the same sort of variation over time,

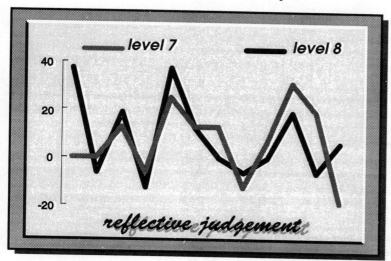

Figure 6.1 Oscillations in the yearly increase in scores on reflective judgement (after Kitchener *et al.*, 1993).

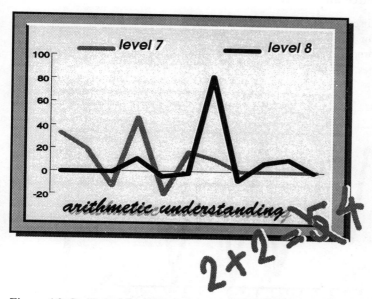

Figure 6.2 Oscillations in difference scores of arithmetic understanding (after Fischer *et al.*, 1983).

although individuals may vary as to the amplitude of those oscillations (see Figures 6.1 and 6.2).

Oscillatory increments are also found in brain growth. Matousek and Petersen (1973) measured changes in the relative power of the alpha frequency band for the occipital–parietal region and found a series of characteristic oscillations between the ages of 1 and 20 years (see Figure 6.3). As Fischer and Rose (1993) have noticed, these changes show a striking correspondence with periods of rapid change in metabolic and ERP measures. In a recent series of studies, Bob Thatcher has shown that the process of cortical organization, far from taking place in a linear and continuous manner, follows a complicated cyclical path, with several reorganizations that repeat the structure of the preceding cycles (Thatcher, 1992).

In summary, data from various domains show that the process of growth is not a simple increase, but it takes place in the form of incremental steps that are very clearly oscillatory. Before trying to explain where these oscillations come from, I shall take a look at a domain where you would intuitively expect marked oscillations, the energy and attention resource functions.

Cycles of resource allocation

In Chapter 2, I discussed several forms of long-term cyclical change found in models such as Piaget's or Fischer's. Next to these long-term cycles, there is a vast range of shorter cyclical processes, related to the way in which resource functions are allocated to human activities. The most general and encompassing timing of resource allocation

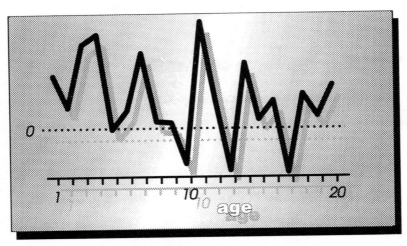

Figure 6.3 Changes in the relative power of the alpha frequency band for the occipital-parietal region (after Matousek and Petersen, 1973).

is the pattern of waking and sleep, governed by the circadian rhythm of our biological clock. The study of these biorhythms is a science in itself, and I shall not go into the complexities of this field (see for instance, Winfree, 1987, for an introduction relating the experimental study of biorhythms to processes of self-organization in coupled oscillators).

Let us take a closer look at attention, which, as everyone would intuitively agree, represents a main resource for learning and developing. Three aspects can be distinguished (Olson and Sherman, 1983). The first is called *arousal* and it refers to the overall level of activation, ranging from being asleep to being very active. It is related to the amount of 'energy' a person invests in a specific task. The second sense of attention is *selection*. Our brains are not capable of taking into account everything that occurs at a given time, or that could possibly be relevant to a particular problem. People select specific aspects or domains that they can keep track of, and these are highly limited chunks of the information available or potentially relevant. The third aspect involves the notion of *effort*. Effort is closely related to arousal, but it contains a more straightforward reference to the amount of mental energy – whatever the nature of that may be – allocated to a specific task.

By their very nature, the three aspects of attention are oscillatory functions. Our arousal state goes up and down with alertness and fatigue and is determined by the interaction between physical events, effort spent on tasks and a biological clock that takes care of the general pattern. If we focus on the selection of a particular learning task or content, the oscillation occurs in the form of cycles of sensitization and habituation. Since we are limited in the intake of information and the range of the contents we focus on at a time, each specific learning content shows a pattern of alternations between selection and deselection (when some other content is selected). For instance, a child's learning of arithmetic is anything but a continuous activity function (and in some children it is very discontinuous, because they do not like maths at all). It is an alternation of short periods of selective attention and effort and comparatively long periods in which a child allocates its interest and effort to other subjects. It follows then that since the growth rate of arithmetic learning probably depends on resources that oscillate, parallel oscillations of the resulting growth process may be expected. Finally, effort too is based on limited energy resources. Spending time, attention and effort in carrying out a task leads to fatigue or even exhaustion and then at least some time is required to recover and reload.

There is, as far as I know, hardly any evidence on the natural fluctuations of attention and interest in individual subjects. The most revealing data I could find come from a study that is almost one hundred years old. In 1898, John Perham Hylan, instructor in psychology in the University of Illinois, published a little monograph supplement to the *Psychological Review* (Hylan, 1898). He presented several experiments on the natural fluctuation of attention, the fluctuations not determined by external events and disturbances. The copy I read bears the bookmark of Gerard Heymans, first professor of psychology in The Netherlands, who founded his Groningen laboratory only a few years after Wundt. Hylan employed experimental data as well as diary data and subjective ratings from his subjects. Hylan asked his subjects to add series of columns of numbers and observed the time it took them to add each column and how many errors they made. In another experiment, he showed his subjects – there were never more than a few – a series of pictures, once a day and over periods ranging between one and two months. Hylan noted how much time his subjects spent looking at those pictures. But he also asked a few subjects to select a topic of personal interest and to write down every day to what extent they felt interested in that subject, or liked or disliked it. The topics ranged from work, eating and physical exercise to family members and the progress of a love affair. Just for fun, I show a diagram of one subject's rating of how much (s)he liked two family members, x and y, beginning with 29 December and ending 18 January, almost one hundred years ago (Figure 6.4). It is interesting to note that all the curves are very similar, irrespective of the domain to which they apply (love, arithmetic, etc.) and the time-scale at which they figure. The pattern is always an irregular oscillation.

It is of course very easy to discard these and comparable data, because they are subjective, or just accidental and coincidental variations, best explained by invoking the notion of randomness. But the subjective nature of – at least some – of these data is an essential feature and the explanation by reference to randomness is no explanation at all, since 'random' simply means 'I do not know'. It goes without saying that some of the variation is clearly coincidental. Hylan reports some accidental disturbances during the experiments, for instance, that, in his words, exaggerated the fluctuations. The basic pattern, however, is a genuine, irregular oscillation of the attention, effort and energy phenomenon itself.

The patterns of resource allocation and the nature of the oscillations are subject to a

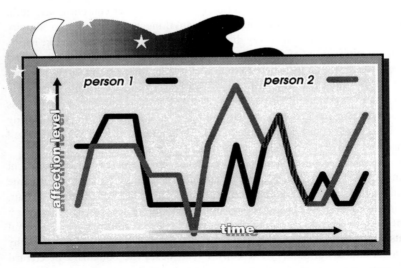

Figure 6.4 Changes in a person's affection for two family members (after Hylan, 1898); the 'affection level' is the person's intuitive estimation of his current affection towards the family member in question.

long developmental process. Take for instance the pattern of arousal. Newborns show a cyclical pattern of alertness states: regular sleep, irregular sleep, drowsiness, alert inactivity, waking activity and crying (Olson and Sherman, 1983). On average, the state of alertness in newborn infants does not last longer than about ten minutes. The younger the infants, the more erratic the cycles of states and the shorter the duration of alertness. The aspect of selection undergoes developmental changes too, as does effort allocation. Children have to learn to organize their attentional function (Brown *et al.*, 1983). A particularly important aspect is the fine-tuning of attention allocation, for instance how to adapt the level of effort to the degree of difficulty of the task. Another aspect concerns the allocation of effort and attention to the various learning tasks that children have to accomplish and to find a good balance between the tasks, dependent on the degree of difficulty of the task and the child's own level of mastery. Attention allocation is important because it involves the distribution of a main resource, effort and attention, that directly affects the quality and speed of learning. In this chapter, I shall present several rather speculative models that produce oscillations in a dynamic way. The first is based on the metaphor of a resource well.

The well model

There's a hole in my bucket . . .

When my father was a schoolboy, one of the horrors of his day was a maths problem that involved exactly the kind of bucket described in the old song. It featured a water tap from which flowed a certain amount of water per time unit in an attempt to fill the bucket with the hole in it. The hole in the bucket had a certain diameter and, given all this formidable information, my father and his peers had to calculate how long it would take for the bucket to fill (or something like that; he must have been so horrified by this problem that he never told me the exact details). A resource such as attention and effort is like the leaky bucket. Assume the water is the resource, and the water that flows out through the hole is the amount of resources needed. The tap filling the bucket with fresh water can be compared to some sort of recovery function. The question is how the opposing tendencies – depletion and recovery – behave over time.

A similar comparison invokes the metaphor of a well. The water is again the resource function, comparable to effort or energy that a person invests in some task. Just assume that Victor, a farmer in the San Joaquin Valley, needs a certain supply of water, say S, to do a particular job, such as irrigating his vineyard. The well on his farm is fed by an underground stream with a volume R per time unit. If the vines need a lot of water, Victor will soon reach a point where the well is empty, which obliges him to wait for a period equal to S/R. A single irrigation round of the land will again empty the well and our farmer will have to wait until there is again enough water to do his work, and so on, *ad infinitum*, since there is no end to the farmer's labour. Compare the water with effort or energy, or whatever is needed to perform some task and assume that the task requires a minimum amount of effort or energy to be performed well. If effort or energy recovers more slowly than it is retrieved, a resource oscillation will occur similar to the oscillation of the water from the well.

Let us assume, however, that the demand for a psychological resource, such as effort and attention, is a function of the amount of resources available. That is, if you are alert and energetic, there is most probably a higher demand than when you are tired or drowsy. This follows intuitively from the fact that people initiate activities that require an energy demand that suits their current state. Assume then that the initial amount of resources available is R_t and that the demand is equal to a ratio m of the available resource:

$$R_{t+1} = R_t - mR_t \qquad (6.1)$$

and so on. For the sake of symmetry, let me assume that the rate of recovery r is also a function of the available supply, that is:

$$R_{t+1} = R_t + rR_t \qquad (6.2)$$

What would happen if the recovery is not immediate, that is, if some recovery time is needed for the supply to be refilled? If the recovery time is equal to a delay of d, the equation then becomes:

$$R_{t+1} = R_t - mR_t + rR_{t-d} \qquad (6.3)$$

Model 6.1 A resource well

Equation 6.3 is easy to model. Go to cell A100, for instance, to make sure you have enough empty cells preceding the initial state point. You will need them to define the length of the delay. Go to cell D100, write down the range name 'm' and enter the value of m in cell C100. With Range Name Create (or any other equivalent instruction dependent on the spreadsheet you use), define range name 'm' as referring to cell C100. Set A100 to 1 and specify the following equation in cell A101:

$$+ \text{A100} - \$m*\text{A100} + \$m*\text{A75} \qquad (6.4)$$

Copy it to the range A102..A300. The recovery time is 25 time units, since each cell represents a time unit. Note that in this model parameters m and r from equation 6.3 are represented by one value (m). You can of course try models with different values, if you define a range name r.

For m, try values ranging from 0.1 to 1. Figure 6.5 shows one of the curves, based on a value of 0.3 for m. Try different delay times, for instance A90 or A60. Change the value in cell A101 and copy it to the A102..A300 block each time you make a change in the recovery time.

Instead of applying the difference form you could also try a differential form of the equation by employing the trapezoidal method described earlier. You might also want to try another version of the difference equation. In its present form, the range of cells preceding the initial state (A100) is empty. Go to cell A1, type in some small number (0.01 for instance) and write a sequence of logistic growth equations that fills the range A2..A99. Take a growth rate that allows for a gradual increase over the whole range.

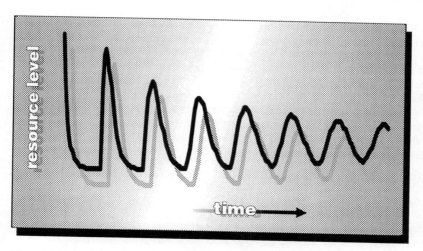

Figure 6.5 Oscillations resulting from a resource based on the well model.

In summary, the well model of resource depletion and recovery produces an oscillating pattern. That is, the resource level – take for instance a child's invested effort and interest in a particular task – goes up and down over time. A peculiar aspect of this model is that, as the depletion and recovery go on undisturbed, the process finally moves towards an equilibrium point where recovery and use are in exact balance. What does resource oscillation mean for learning or development?

Oscillating resources and cognitive growth

All other things being equal, the learning or growth effect of a task depends on the amount of attention, effort or interest invested. With a child who is more alert and interested, paying attention to what it sees and hears and willing to invest a lot of effort in learning tasks, we should certainly expect better school results and more rapid learning than with a less alert, less interested and less industrious child. It is quite natural, therefore, to relate the growth rate parameter in a cognitive growth function – such as the one describing the growth of the lexicon – to the level of attention, effort and interest spent during the actual learning process.

For the sake of simplicity, just assume that the growth rate r is linearly proportional to the resources invested in the growth or learning process. That is, the more resources invested, the bigger the increase of whatever increases as a result of a particular learning activity. Take lexical growth as the standard example. What is the form of the growth curve that results from applying a growth rate that oscillates?

Model 6.2 Growth under oscillating resources

Our starting point is the difference form of the oscillating resource function demonstrated in Model 6.1. It covers 200 consecutive steps (spreadsheet cells). For simplicity, let us assume that the time range of these 200 steps is also the time range of the growth or learning process that depends on the oscillating resource.

The resource – which could be attention, effort, interest or a combination of them – oscillates between a minimum and maximum value. The absolute values have no intrinsic meaning in terms of growth rate values and should be brought back to a normal form. The normal form is one in which the minimum is set to 0 and the maximum to 1. A simple way of normalizing the oscillatory value goes as follows. Let A100 be the first cell. In the adjacent cell B100 enter the following equation:

$$+ (A100 - @min(A\$100..A\$300))/(@max(A\$100..A\$300) - @min(A\$100..A\$300)) \quad (6.5)$$

Copy it to B101..B300. This is the range in which you will find your normalized oscillation values which vary between 0 and 1. The functions @max and @min are built-in spreadsheet functions; they will give you either the maximal or the minimal value in the range to which they apply (e.g. range A100..A300 in @max(A100..A300)).[2]

The oscillating function will act as the variable growth rate parameter for a grower. It does not matter too much what grower this is. Just assume it is lexical growth. In cell C100, enter the starting value, for instance 0.01 (assuming that the carrying capacity level is 1). In cell D101, enter the logistic equation. It should refer to the varying growth rate in the range B100..B300:

$$D100*(1 + B101 - B101*D100) \quad (6.6)$$

Copy this to the range D102..D300. In this equation, the growth rate is the value of the adjacent B cell, that is, B101 for cell D101, B102 for D102 and so on.

The growth rate varies between 0 and 1, because it is the normalized oscillation. You probably want to experiment with different values, such as a growth rate that varies between 0 and 0.2, or − 0.5 and 2. In order to achieve this, change the equation in the range B101 as follows:

$$+ ((A100 - @min(A\$100..A\$300))/(@max(A\$100..A\$300) - @min$$
$$(A\$100..A\$300)) + \$AR)*\$DR \quad (6.7)$$

(do not forget to copy this changed equation to B101..B300). The equation makes no sense until you have told the spreadsheet what *DR* and *AR* mean. Go to the range where you have put your other parameters and define the range names *DR* and *AR*. If *DR* is 1 and *AR* is − 0.5, the normalized values of your oscillating resource will vary between − 0.5 and + 0.5 (if *DR* = 0.5 and *AR* = 0.2 they will vary between 0.1 and 0.6 and so forth; see Figure 6.6).

Why would we want to let the growth rate value vary between a negative and a positive number? The idea is that if a child invests too little effort and attention in a learning task, the effect may be the reverse of learning: performance may drop instead of increase.

Try different values of both *AR* and *DR*, but begin with an *AR* value of 0 and a *DR* of 0.1. If *AR* is negative (e.g. − 0.2), the growth curve will show dips. Try different values, for instance a high *DR* value (which, however, should never be bigger than 3). Try also the effect of a high *DR* (such as 2.5) and a negative *AR* (such as − 0.2).

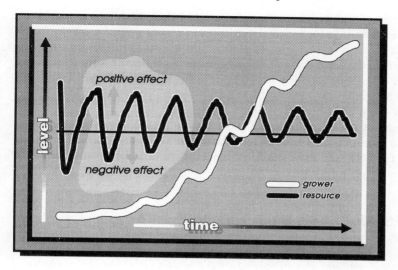

Figure 6.6 Growth based on an oscillating resource curve, for AR = − 0.15 and DR = 0.12; the resource curve is based on the well model.

Is there any evidence for the existence of growth curves that show the irregular pattern demonstrated in Model 6.2? Well, we have seen several examples already. Take for instance Keren's lexical growth curve. Overall, it fitted the logistic form very well, but it showed small irregularities over time. This became particularly clear when we computed the underlying growth rates. The pattern of growth rates did indeed resemble an oscillatory pattern; the biggest oscillations occurred at the beginning. Very similar data can be found in Corrigan's study of the growth of the lexicon and the growth of the mean length of utterance (Corrigan, 1983). A nice qualitative fit of these data can be achieved by modelling them with an oscillating resource (van Geert, unpublished paper). In the next section, I shall explain that different intuitively plausible models of resource depletion and recovery all lead to a similar pattern, namely oscillation over time.

From credit cards to predators

The credit card effect

A basic idea of the logistic growth model is that a delay exists between the first occurrence of a causal factor or mechanism, and its actual expression in the psychological variable it determines. This *feedback delay* can be explained in a number of ways. For instance, it could be the effect of an intervening learning period, or of a certain resistance of a conceptual network to change. It could also be the consequence of an intervening planning and preparation stage. Before actually carrying out an activity in response to environmental conditions, we must plan the action, recruit means for its execution or prepare ourselves in any way required by the goal. It is conceivable, therefore, that there is a class of resource-consuming learning activities that involves this significant delay between the onset of the planning and the actual execution. The principle is very similar to buying something with a credit card: buy now and pay later. The activities to which this principle applies are probably of the kind that requires a lot of information gathering, preparation, the use of different cognitive and material means to attack the problems at hand and so forth. Let me first take you to Toad Hall and show you how a model of resource depletion based on the credit card principle might work.

Model 6.3 Mr Toad's bank account

A week or so ago as I strolled through a Palo Alto flea market, a little brown book caught my eye. It was Kenneth Grahame's *The Wind in the Willows*, a book I had always wanted to read just because its title evokes a tranquil feeling of sitting on the marshy borders of a creek in the shade of old trees. While reading the book, I was especially taken with one of the characters, the wealthy but also rather pathetic Mr Toad of Toad Hall. The following story could very well have happened to Mr Toad. It involves his bank account and his more than unfortunate discovery of the credit card.

Mr Toad is indeed a very rich toad and his capital, well invested and taken care of, grows in accordance with classic neo-liberal economic laws, exponentially. When old Mr Toad died he left his son a starting capital of 0.01 Megadollars. Since the bank manager has a spreadsheet file of Mr Toad's capital, he enters this starting amount in cell A100. Good investments in the stock market make this capital grow at the memorable rate of 0.2 a day! The happy bank manager writes down:

$$+ A100 * (1 + \$r) \tag{6.8}$$

in cell A101 and copies this to the range A102..A1000, after having defined a range r that is given the value 0.2. And then, a few days later, the unimaginable happens. Young Mr Toad discovers the credit card. 'How could I ever have lived without it', he exclaims, 'All those wasted years that lie behind me! From now on I shall devote my entire life to the use of the credit card.' The bank manager is a bit concerned and bids Mr Toad be very cautious. 'How, sir,' he asks, 'are you going to pay your debts back?' 'Well my good man,' says Toad, 'I shall spend my entire capital on my credit card every day, and I shall pay you back any debt I incur after twenty days, but what I shall pay you back will of course always be a function of what I possess at that moment.' The bank manager grumblingly submits to the wishes of his best customer and changes the equation in cell A101 as follows:

$$+ A100 + \$r * A100 - B101 \tag{6.9}$$

which he then copies to the range A102..A1000. In cell B101 he enters the following equation:

$$+ \$d * A80 * A100 \tag{6.10}$$

which he copies to B102..B1000. He defines a range named *d* which is given the value 1, after ample and painful negotiations with Mr Toad, who has a much larger figure in mind. Equation 6.10 is the amount that Toad has agreed to spend on paying back his debts on the credit card made twenty days earlier. To his surprise, the bank manager sees that Toad's bank account oscillates (see Figure 6.7). Spikes of high income are separated by periods where Toad is as poor as the local churchmouse.

How do Toad's financial problems apply to a model of psychological resources? Equation 6.8 implies that a person's resources grow, because there is an external input. For instance, people acquire better and faster ways of information processing, attention span, effort allocation and so forth. They rest and relax to substitute any resources they may have consumed earlier. The second part of the model says that next to the repletion there is also a depletion of resources. Resources are consumed, because the person is investing effort and attention. The third part of the model, equation 6.10, says that the repletion of resources is a function of an earlier decision, action plan, etc., on the one hand and of the present state of available resources on the other. The model applies to all forms of resource investment that are based on action plans or decisions that require a considerable preparatory stage, causing a significant delay between decision and actual performance.

Let us see what kind of growth curve would result from a growth or learning process that used this oscillating resource. Go back to the spreadsheet, enter an initial level in cell C100 and write the following equation in cell B101 (to be copied to the range C102..C500):

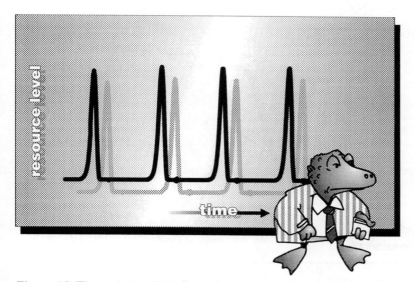

Figure 6.7 The evolution of Mr Toad's bank account based on his agreement with the bank manager; the magnitude and distribution of the spikes depend on the parameter values chosen.

$$+ \text{C}100 * (1 + (\text{A}101 + \$\text{AR}) * \$\text{DR} * (1 - \text{C}100)) \qquad (6.11)$$

and define range names *AR* and *DR* which take, as default values, 0 and 0.05, respectively. The resulting growth curve will be like the one in Figure 6.8. It has the form of a simple stepwise function consisting of plateaux alternated by rapid growth spurts. The stepform is a consequence of the resource release in the form of sharp spikes, typical of this model.

Earning money, paying debts . . .

The credit card concept provides a simple model of growth processes that depend on exhaustible but recoverable resources. For instance, I use energy to support my activities during daytime, but I have to pay back in the form of inactivity and rest during the night. I consume interest and attention resources as long as I am interested in a specific subject or activity, but I pay back in the form of habituation and temporary loss of interest in that particular subject. In the previous section, I modelled the trajectory of an exhaustible resource such as energy and attention. I found an oscillating function, which I connected to the growth rate parameter of a grower, resulting in a stepwise process. The following model is an extension of the credit card concept.

It is obvious to assume that the progress we make is proportionate to the amount of effort and attention spent in that process (although any developmental progress depends on more factors than attention or effort). In the preceding sections, I assumed

Figure 6.8 An imaginery growth curve of a complex skill (playing volleyball, for instance). The curve is based on the bank model (Figure 6.7) and forms a pattern of sudden increases followed by temporary stability.

that we must pay back the exhaustible resources consumed, in the form of rest, or a temporary decrease in learning or progress. I also assumed that there is a certain delay between the actual consumption of the resource and its replenishment, for instance in the form of a rest period.

Let us take a simple logistic equation. We know that the increase in the growth level L_t is determined by the function $(r - r \cdot L_t)$. I have assumed, however, that you pay back for resources consumed earlier, which implies that some of the resources that would go into the learning or growth process have to be invested in replenishing the energy or attention resource used to feed the preceding growth stages. Since that amount is a function of the amount of previous growth, that is, increase in level, we end up with a logistic growth equation that has the following form:

$$L_{t+1} = L_t \cdot (1 + r - r \cdot L_t - d \cdot \Delta L_{t-n}) \tag{6.12}$$

The function ΔL_{t-n} is the increase in the growth level L at time $t - n$, that is, n time units ago. The delay time n is the average delay in repletion of resources characteristic of the current system. The parameter d determines to what extent the growth process suffers from the growth in the past. What is the form of the ΔL_{t-n} function? It could simply be the increase in L, n time units ago, or an average increase, or any weighted function of the increase. Instead of reckoning with the absolute increase, we can also work with the relative increase. The idea is, then, that the resources needed to make a certain amount of progress depend on the level already attained; learning 5 words requires more effort when you know only 50 words than when the lexicon is, for instance, 2000 words. I am not sure whether the relative increase assumption holds for word learning, but it seems reasonable to assume that it is true in at least some forms of learning or development.

Model 6.4 The fluctuation of attention

This model lets you experiment with four different versions of the fluctuation equation: the cubic and the quadratic version of the logistic equation and the relative *versus* absolute increase model. You will need the following list of parameters: *ini, r, d, r_ini, div, cub* and *rel_A*. The maximal delay your model affords is 100 cells. This means that the first 100 cells are a sort of take-off for the actual model. In A1, enter:

+ ini/div (6.13)

The parameter *div* is a divisor determining which fraction of the initial level the take-off phase starts with. Since the actual starting point of the model is set at cell A100, we let the initial state level grow towards its starting level. In order to do that, enter:

+ A1 * (1 + $r_ini − $r_ini * A1/$ini) (6.14)

in cell A2, and copy this to A3..A99.

In cell A100 write " + ini".

You will use the B column to keep track of the increase or decrease in A, defined either absolutely or relatively. In cell B2, write:

$$+ (A2 - A1)/@if (\$rel = 1, A1, 1) \tag{6.15}$$

and copy this to B3..B3000.

The actual model equation should be entered in cell A101:

$$+ A100 * (1 + \$r * (1 - A100) * @if (\$cub = 1, A100, 1) - \$d * C101) \tag{6.16}$$

Cell C101 is where you specify the ΔL function. One possibility is:

$$+ (B50 * 1 + B51 * 2 + B52 * 3 + B54 * 2 + B55 * 1) \tag{6.17}$$

You can change the delays and weights as you wish. Copy C101 to C102..C3000. Each time you change the ΔL function, C101 should be recopied to:

C102..C3000.

For a start, try $ini = 0.01$; $r = 0.05$; $d = 0.12$; $cub = 0$; $rel = 1$.

More complicated weighted functions are possible, for instance with five different values and weights ranging from 1 to 3. The delays and parameter values can be very different, but the result is almost always fascinating. With low parameter values, especially low values for the damping parameter d, the resulting growth curves are regular S-shaped curves. For somewhat higher values, the curves grow in an oscillatory way, which strongly resembles the growth curves of morpho–syntactic structures discussed earlier. For still higher values, the curves settle into chaotic oscillations. They differ from the chaotic oscillations of the unaltered logistic equation. With the latter, the levels jump from one state to another. With the current altered form, the chaotic oscillations are smooth. They make beautiful phase space representations (Figure 6.9). The model is very rich (but hopefully not too rich) and produces a large variety of different growth patterns, most of which have the kind of irregularity typical of many empirical growth phenomena.

One characteristic pattern consists of an irregular oscillation which occurs after the process has reached its carrying capacity level. It often starts with small oscillations that magnify and then vary between upper and lower boundaries. It is interesting to note that these oscillations are very similar to the oscillations in attention that Hylan found in 1898 (Hylan, 1898). This is probably more than just an accidental similarity. Hylan's model and mine follow the same assumptions: attention and other exhaustible resources need recuperation and there is often a significant delay between the use and the actual recuperation of the resource.

Le secret de l'urinoir . . .

When I was a kid, I used to accompany my parents on their Sunday night visits to the pub. This was just the Flemish way, and nobody saw any harm in letting the children taste the divine fruit of the brewery, the Trappist beer, made and sold by Trappist monks and a proof of the fact that God blesses those who love Him. Anyway, the beer had a pronounced effect on my inexperienced bladder, and it was in the men's toilet that I was confronted with an interesting technical problem. As anyone knows, the

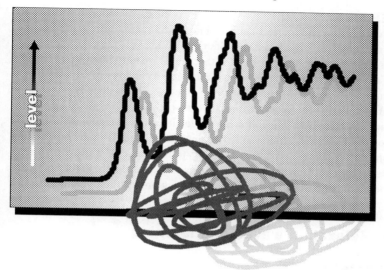

Figure 6.9 A logistic model is altered in accordance with the resource recovery concept: the resulting growth curve shows chaotic oscillations that die out towards the end. The coil in the foreground is the phase representation of the oscillating growth curve.

male anatomy requires two different kinds of plumbing equipment and it was that aimed at the fulfilment of the smaller needs that caught my attention. Nowadays, these things are equipped with a flush button or even an electronic beam, but the older ones either had no flush at all, or flushed at regular intervals not caused by any human intervention. I remember that I spent quite some time trying to reconstruct the secret behind that regular automatic flushing. One of my designs involved a complicated system of clocks and levers. It was only much later that I learned that the secret behind the flushing is very simple and that it is technically subsumed under the class of so-called relaxation waves, an unintended but appropriate name given the context where I first discovered one.

Relaxation waves apply to resources, such as the water container, that recover at a constant rate (the tap filling the container). The resource is released when a threshold level is crossed, which, in the case of the container, is when the overflow pipe gets filled with water. Since the pipe has a form of a siphon, the water will start flowing and will continue to flow until the level in the container reaches the opening of the pipe. Then the container will fill up again and so on.

It is highly probable that at least some forms of attentional resource functions behave in accordance with the principle of a relaxation wave. Take for instance a person's interest in a specific subject. Prolonged activity and involvement in that subject will finally lead to saturation. As the saturation level reaches a certain threshold, the person will quit that activity and proceed to something else. Then motivation and interest in the subject will build up again, until they reach the threshold needed to initiate the activity again. This is just a speculative model, but it fits our intuition of how attention and interest behave. The model is also quite reminiscent of the reversal shifts described by Apter and Smith (1982).

An interesting aspect of the model is that the thresholds are most likely stochastically determined. That is, the actual point of ceasing an activity following saturation is at least codetermined by environmental or activity-specific events that are to a large extent random. Similarly, the renewed initiative to pick up the activity again also depends on coincidental events. The following model describes a version of the logistic growth equation to which a relaxation wave effect has been added. It shows how adding a small random perturbation may affect the long-term course of a growth process mainly because the random factor has a major impact on events that lie at the boundary of the attractor points and is unable to affect other regions of the dynamics.

Model 6.5 Relaxation waves and learning

The model of the relaxation wave may seem a bit awkward at first, but it is only a disguised version of the logistic growth equation. It consists of two coupled equations. One describes the growth of the resource function that is supposed to go up and down; the other specifies the change in the growth rate of that growth function. Let us begin with the latter equation.

The growth rate must be positive when the dependent grower – the resource – goes up, and negative when it goes down. In this way, the resource will keep growing as long as it grows and it will continue to decrease as long as it decreases. Let A2 be the starting cell of the growth rate, with value 0.5, and B2 the starting cell for the resource, with value 0.01.

The growth rate changes in accordance with the following equation:

@abs(@abs(A2) * (1 + $r_r − $r_r * @abs(A2))) * (B2 − B1)/@abs(B2 − B1)   (6.18)

which has to be entered in range A3..A1000.

Range B3..B1000 takes the equations for the growth of the resource. In B3 enter

+B2 * (1 + A2 * $d_r − A2 * $d_r * B2) + (@rand − @rand) * $d_rand   (6.19)

First, all the range names necessary to make the model run must be named and specified. The range name d_r contains a parameter damping the effect of the growth rate values in A on the resource in B. The parameter d_rand modifies the extent to which the random component affects the resource growth. The r_r parameter specifies the rate of change in the growth rate. Suitable values for each of them are: $r_r = 0.01$, $d_r = 1/4$ and $d_rand = 1/200$. The graph of range B2..B1000, where the resource levels are found, should look like the oscillations in Figure 6.10. Hit the recalculation button a few times (F9 in Lotus 1-2-3 for Windows) to see how the small random factor changes the macroscopic outlook of the resource spikes (or humps). The smaller you make d_r (e.g. 0.1), the more clearly the random effect may be observed.

Assume that the resource is a major component of a growth rate in an ordinary logistic growth equation. To model such a dependent grower, use the equation:

+C2 * (1 + B2 * $d_g − B2 * $d_g * C2)   (6.20)

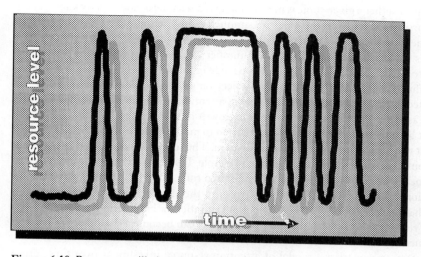

Figure 6.10 Resource oscillations based on the principle of the relaxation wave: the length and distribution of the waves depend on small random factors acting throughout the whole process.

that starts with an initial value of 0.01 in cell C1. Define the growth rate damping parameter d_g and give it the value 0.01, or at least a value small enough to smear the growth out over the 1000 consecutive cells.

This model shows very clearly how a small random factor which ranges between plus or minus 0.5 per cent of the maximal level of the resource is active only in the vicinity of the attractor points, that is, at the levels 1 and 0. The random factor is equally active over the whole range of resource levels, but its effect is sensed in limited regions only. They are the regions where the changes are of the same magnitude as the random influences. The random factor actually either prolongs or shortens the length of the equilibrium stages, the regions where the resource value is close either to 1 or to 0.

Interest contagion

Most of the subjects that people can pay attention to and into which they are likely to invest effort – like a psychology course, another person's habits and character or a playground – are complicated structures. They contain a large variety of potential aspects, components and details. We never pay attention to all these aspects at the same time. That would simply far exceed the space of our human working memory. It follows then, that a model of attention resources, instead of describing a person's attention investment in the broad subject as a whole, should try to capture changes and fluctuations in attention and effort spent in dealing with separate aspects of that subject domain. There is no natural division of a subject range, say a psychology course, into a set of neatly distinguished elements. Nevertheless, any student will be able to recognize whether a given topic is new or not, given what he or she already knows about the course. Let me, for the sake of simplicity, just assume that the number of components or aspects that can be discerned in a broad subject is determined by a person's subjective decision. I take that number as a person-specific reference point.

There are three assumptions that can be made in this model. The first is that interest in or effort spent on some aspect of a subject range is *contagious*. That is, as we get interested in a particular aspect of a problem, attention will be directed to other slightly related aspects. Put differently, there is a growth of involvement in some domain of interest because each element we pay attention to makes it more probable that another element will become part of the interest domain. The second assumption is nothing but a version of the habituation or saturation principle. It says that a person is interested in some specific aspect or subject for only a limited time. After that time, habituation or saturation will turn attention to another part of the subject domain. Third, once an aspect has been rejected as a consequence of saturation or habituation, it will require a certain recovery time before that particular aspect can become a candidate for interest investment again.

It is easy to construct a model of attention resource investment over time, given these three assumptions. Let the total subjectively distinguished number of aspects or elements in a subject range be normalized to 1 and any number of aspects actually paid attention to, to a fraction of 1. Call this fraction A. Assume that the average 'contagiousness' of attention investment is described by the parameter c. If A_t is the initial number of aspects attended to, the increase in number of aspects interested in is given by:

$$A_{t+1} = A_t(1 + c \cdot S_t) \tag{6.22}$$

The variable S_t is the number of aspects that are susceptible to becoming a new focus of attention. What is its magnitude?

Recall that a topic remains interesting only for a limited amount of time, say a time period p. After that topic has been left, it will require another period of time before the habituation or saturation that occurred as a consequence of the earlier involvement has been dissipated. Let us call this recovery time q.

If t is the time of the initial state occurrence, at time $t + 1$ the number of susceptible aspects is:

$$S_{t+1} = 1 - A_t \tag{6.23}$$

and at any later time it is:

$$S_{t+2} = S_{t+1} - (A_{t+1} + A_t + A_{t-1} + \ldots + A_{t-p+1}) + A_{t+1-q} \tag{6.24}$$

The sum of As within brackets is the sum of aspects attended to for the total time period of p. The variable A_{t+1-q} is a set of aspects we were interested in and that has now recovered from the saturation that was a consequence of that earlier involvement (for a recovery time of q). This set of coupled equations will by itself run into an oscillatory movement, as can be seen in the following model.

Model 6.6 Contagious attention

You need three columns of data to model this concept of contagious attention. Start with cell A99 and enter the following titles and equations:

	column A	column B	column C
row 99	new topics	potential topics	total topics
row 100	@RAND/$E	$N − A100	@SUM(A100..A93)
row 101	+ C100*$A* B100	+ B100 − A100 + A10	@SUM(A101..A94)

$$(6.25)$$

In order to make the model run, you need to define a set of parameters and values (between brackets): A(0.3), N(1), D(1), E(100), R(20), Random(0). Copy the cell values in A101..D101 to range A102..D1000.

If each cell represents a tick of the clock (and such a tick could correspond with a day, a week, a month, etc.), the time a particular topic stays in the pool of topics in which we are interested is eight ticks. It requires a long recovery time, however, before a topic that once belonged to that pool re-enters the pool of potentially interesting topics again, namely ninety ticks. These values can be found in the form of cell references in cells B101 and C100, respectively. The model with the parameter values described here produces an oscillation of sharp spikes of interest in an increasing number of topics all belonging to a broad subject domain (see Figure 6.11). Experiment with different parameter values, for instance $A = 0.15$ or $D = 10$, and with different delay values. For instance, in cell B11 specify the value A50 instead of A10, but do not forget to copy this equation to the entire B range). Define the graph for range C100..C1000.

You can enter a fourth column, called 'Total constrained', which allows you to enter the effect of working memory limitation on the number of topics entertained simultaneously,[3] or the effect of a random perturbation (if $D = 2$, the maximal number of topics entertained simultaneously is 50 per cent of the total number represented by the parameter N). If you use the D-column, replace 'C' by 'D' in the A-column.

The equation for range D100..D1000 is a bit awkward, unfortunately:

$$@ROUND(@IF(C100 > \$N/\$D, \$N/\$D, @IF(C100 < 0, 0, C100)) + \$RANDOM*(@RAND − @RAND)/\$E, \$R)$$

$$(6.26)$$

You can also make the number of possibly distinguished topics smaller by rounding-off. For instance, if you round-off to one digit behind the decimal point, the total number of possible separate topics that a person could attend to in a specific attention domain is ten. Range D100..D1000 can be plotted separately to show the effect of the constraints you imposed on your model.

Just as with the previous models, you should make a grower dependent on the oscillating resource by making its growth rate a function of the resource. The result is

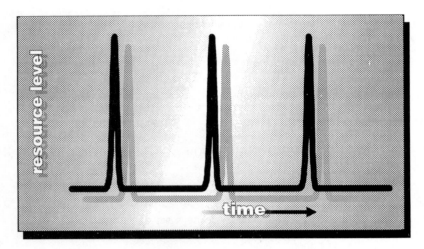

Figure 6.11 Resource oscillations based on the model of 'contagious' attention, saturation and recovery; the magnitude and distribution of the spikes depend on the parameter values chosen.

very similar to the growth curve based on the credit card model. It shows characteristic stepwise changes, very similar to those from Figure 6.7, based on the credit card metaphor. The spike form of the resource release produces the characteristic stepwise growth. Many forms of learning, for instance learning in school, follow this temporal organization: relatively short periods of learning and increase in mastery followed by long periods of rest or stability. The resources not utilized during the periods of rest can be used for other processes of learning that follow the same temporal pattern. This particular form of resource allocation might explain why our natural form of learning consists of a succession of many small learning episodes, devoted to different topics, that succeed one another rather abruptly.

The predator–prey relationship between attention and effort

In the morning, when I enter the redwood cabin that serves as my office at the Center for Advanced Study – which one of my fellow Fellows called the Center for Ridiculously Advanced Study after having seen what other people were doing – I am in general eager to start writing. An unfinished chapter is waiting for completion and while I am biking to the Center a lot of possibilities and ideas come to my mind. As I start working, I soon become completely immersed in the problems of cognitive growers and non-linear relationships and other fancy things. But as the day runs to its end, I begin to feel some saturation; the Lotka–Volterra models that in the morning completely filled my mental horizon are now gradually losing their glittering attraction and I start longing for a glass of wine and some bread with Italian salami.

The present scenario – with or without Lotka, Volterra and salami – should sound familiar to many readers. I have mentioned it because it contains a potential model of resource oscillations. In the sort of activities described above, motivation and willingness to spend effort on a task build up. It is because you have the motivation to carry out a particular activity that effort and energy resources are allocated and actually invested in doing the task. But, as you go on, the investment of energy and effort lead to fatigue or saturation, which in turn decreases the further allocation of resources to the task. That is, the investment of effort and energy in a task decreases as a function of time spent on that task. Let E be the effort or energy invested in a task. It decreases over time but increases as a function of attention, motivation and interest. Let me express this in the form of the following equation:

$$E_{t+1} = E(1 - f + m \cdot A_t) \tag{6.27}$$

for E the energy or effort level, f the parameter that specifies the rate of fatigue, A the level of attention or interest in the task, and m the positive effect of attention on the allocation of energy resources.

What about the change in A, that is, the attention, motivation or interest level? Let me assume that it grows towards an asymptote. That is, it increases over time and levels off as it reaches a maximum (which is probably person- and context-dependent). The investment of energy or effort eventually has a negative effect on attention or motivation, for instance, because it leads to fatigue or saturation. Let me write these assumptions in the form of the following equation:

$$A_{t+1} = A_t(1 + r - r \cdot A_t/K - d \cdot E_t) \tag{6.28}$$

which means that attention grows in accordance with the principle of logistic growth (hence the growth parameter r and the carrying capacity K for the asymptote) and that it decreases meanwhile as a consequence of the amount of effort and energy invested in a task, mediated by a parameter d.

This model is similar to the predator–prey model that describes the dynamics of a population of prey (say rabbits or ranunculus) and predators (say foxes or rabbits, respectively). It has been developed and studied by an Italian and an American mathematician whose names are Volterra and Lotka (they could have featured as a comic duo with names like that, but instead they chose to enrich the world with what is probably the oldest example of a coupled dynamic equation). If you want to see what this model does, go back to Chapter 2 and the section on singing in Yeltsingrad. The model describing the evolution of performance in the happy singers is exactly like the present one describing the relation between attention and effort. As can be seen in the figures, both variables are locked into oscillations that are slightly out of phase.

Try the equations in spreadsheet form with the following set of parameters. Take 0.9 as initial value for A and 0.1 as first value of E. Define range names r, d, f and m, and give them the values $r = 0.03$, $d = 0.04$, $f = 0.03$ and $m = 0.1$. Try different values for each parameter, but change them in small increments.

What about an eventual learning process that depends on the oscillating attention and effort? Its growth rate probably amounts to some combination of both variables, of attention and effort. Assume both make a similar contribution to the growth of, for instance, the child's lexicon. The equation for the growth of a skill or knowledge domain dependent on attention and effort would then be:

$$L_{t+1} = L_t \cdot (1 + d \cdot (A_t + E_t) - d \cdot (A_t + E_t) \cdot L_t) \tag{6.29}$$

for d a damping parameter that mediates the effect of attention and effort on growth.

Figure 6.12 shows the result of a simulation based on an initial value of 0.001 for L and 0.012 for d. The number of cells is equal to that used for computing the resource oscillation, namely 1000. Next to the theoretical curve is the empirical curve based on Keren's lexical growth (Dromi, 1986). I have not attempted to find a better fitting theoretical curve, since I just wanted to show the qualitative similarity between the curves.

Summary: Towards connected growers

The models presented in this chapter are quite speculative, to say the least. My aim was to show that various intuitively plausible models of resource retrieval and repletion all lead to the same pattern, an oscillation over time. Each of the models contained a parameter – or a few parameters – that accounted for qualitatively different patterns.

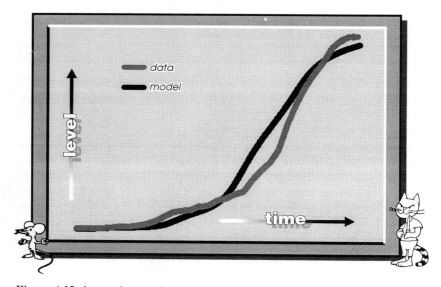

Figure 6.12 A growth curve based on the predator–prey resource model compared with Keren's lexical growth curve. No effort has been made to estimate parameter values that would have led to a better fit between simulation and empirical data; the simulated curve shows that patterns qualitatively similar to the empirical curve result directly from applying the predator–prey model.

In general, if the value of such a parameter is low, the oscillation is likely to consist at the beginning of a (few) large wave(s) that soon dampen out. If it is big enough, the oscillations take the form of waves, ranging from regular wave patterns to sharp spikes separated by relatively long periods where the resource level is near zero.

The resource models are not developmental in the pure sense of the word. They do not model the development of alertness between babyhood and childhood, for instance, or the allocation of attention and effort resources for classroom tasks. They are just speculative models that describe the oscillation of those resources over time in the form of rest/activity or attention/boredom cycles. Their main purpose is to provide a model for changes in the growth rate function of growers that depend on attention and effort resources. In this chapter, the coupling between the change in resources and the growth of a dependent variable was asymmetric. The resource changed by its own internal logic, not because of the change it promoted in the dependent grower. In reality, however, we should expect the resource to change as a consequence of the effort and attention spent in the learning or growth process. The relationship, therefore, is one of reciprocity. Both growers (resource and dependent grower) affect each other continuously, although the way they do so differs. The notion of connected growers and mutual determination will be the main theme in the chapters to come.

Notes

1. Well, that did not seem to be the case in Menlo Park, California, where an evening of (in our perception very quiet singing) was ended by a policeman whose heart no doubt was with *Let it Be*, but whose mind was on his profession.
2. It is actually much more convenient to define two range names, min and max. The value of the min parameter is the equation

   @min (A100..A300) $\qquad$ (6.30)

   and the value of max is

   @max (A100..A300)

   You can then replace the @min (A100..A300) and @max (A100..A300) expressions in your equations by $min and $max respectively.
3. By simultaneously I do not literally mean all at the same moment, but something like 'in the same time period', which could involve days or weeks during which a set of topics alternates.

7

Connected growers

Development and uncertainty

Butterflies of Jasper Ridge and butterflies of Lorenz

Not very far from the Center where I hope to finish this book[1] lies a beautiful biological preserve called Jasper Ridge. It is owned by the nearby Stanford University and the other day I was invited there on a nature walk. The guide explained a lot of things about plants and gophers and seeds and also mentioned that this very preserve was the place where Paul Ehrlich did a great deal of his fundamental study of population dynamics and evolution. I had just begun to read Ehrlich's book *The Machinery of Nature*, which describes, among others, his ecological studies on a population of Bay checkerspots, a species of butterfly that lives on the Ridge (Ehrlich, 1986). Ecology is a good example of a discipline that has successfully applied the principle that (almost) everything depends on (almost) everything else and the studies of the butterfly populations demonstrate how the same basic principle of ecological codetermination may work out in a multitude of ways. Even in a small region like Jasper Ridge, the checkerspot population seems divided into several smaller subpopulations, each of which follows its own growth dynamics over time. The populations evolve in answer to an intricate web of local interactions between the animals and their food sources and hiding plants within different microclimates and on different soils.

It is highly likely that in their abstract form the mechanisms that govern the subject of developmental psychology are very close to those of ecology. Both are concerned with intricate webs and networks of mutual interaction and with changes over considerable time periods. If we must deal with such structures, we are going to need the right sort of equipment and method to discover the rules that lead their dynamics. An interesting property of interwoven structures is that their behaviour shows unexpected combinations of high regularity and unpredictability.

Thanks to Gleick's fascinating book *Chaos* (Gleick, 1987), many people have now heard of the incredibly mighty butterfly of Lorenz. If Lorenz's butterfly flaps its wings in Singapore, a tornado may occur in Texas. This sounds dramatic, but it is only an evocative literary illustration of a basic principle in non-linear dynamics. It says that some dynamics are extremely sensitive to initial conditions and amplify them to a scale where they completely determine the macroscopic events. The butterfly in Singapore represents a very, very small event in a region where tropical storms are born, and if it had not moved, the Texan tornado might not have happened. This discovery puts a terrible moral burden on butterflies, but they do not seem to worry too much, fortunately.

Lorenz, a meteorologist who started to work with computers in the 1950s, described his discovery of the butterfly effect as follows. He had worked on a series of equations that described atmospheric movements and simulated them numerically on what was still considered an electronic miracle machine in those days. Once he wanted to examine the results of such a computation in more detail and typed in the starting numbers of a previously computed simulation, rounding the numbers off to a few decimal points. In the beginning of the simulation, the resulting curves were of course practically like those from the first run, since they were based on starting numbers that were almost the same as the original ones. But soon the curves began to diverge and the whole system ran into a completely different path. The effect of rounding-off, which was (with some exaggeration) like a butterfly flapping its wings, had magnified to the scale of the simulated events, the atmospheric currents and winds.

Lorenz's equations were coupled equations and if they described development we would have called them connected growers. Was it because of the connection and mutuality of effects between them that they ran into unpredictable results, given only a small error at the starting level? If so, are we not going to run into comparable and even worse problems in developmental psychology, abandoning all hopes for a science that is capable of making predictions on the basis of good developmental theory? To answer this question I shall discuss several examples of coupled growers. They all start from a similar assumption about how the carrying capacity, defined as the level and form of a tutor's or adult's help and support, would evolve as a consequence of changes in the tutee's learning level.

This chapter presents a basic model of connected, non-linear growers and discusses characteristic patterns in the simplest possible connected model, namely one with two, reciprocally connected growers. First, however, I shall go somewhat deeper into the question already raised in this section: Given that very simple models are already so complex, will connected growth models not be even more complex? Will their outcomes be predictable at all?

Predictability in non-linear models

Maintaining a good level of environmental resources is not free. Take for instance a school. A high teacher-to-pupil ratio, a good library full of recent books and glossy educational magazines, lots of computers and materials to experiment with are indeed costly. Now assume that the pupils' average learning results remain low and that they do not seem to take much advantage of the information present in the library and the attractive videotapes about foreign cultures. The rational reaction to this situation would be to cut down on the expensive resources, since in spite of all the investments they appear to have produced no results.

How are we going to decide on the resource reduction, what information will be used and how will the process be paced? A simple model for the adaptation process is one in which K (the carrying capacity, which is linearly related to the resources) decreases as a function of the distance between K and the learning or growth level achieved. The relationship between growth and learning, say of a number of scholastic skills (represented by L) and the available amount of external resources, such as books and AV media (represented by K) would be as follows:

$$L_{t+1} = L_t \cdot (1 + r - r \cdot L_t/K_t)$$
$$K_{t+1} = K_t \cdot (1 - d \cdot (K_t - L_t)/K_t) \tag{7.1}$$

I assume most readers are now sufficiently familiar with the spreadsheet format to model this set of equations on their own. It is worthwhile trying two identical sets of coupled equations, and examining the difference between different d and r values. Good starting values for the variables are: $d_1 = 0.01$, $d_2 = 0.01$, $L_1 = 0.01$, $L_2 = 0.01$, $r_1 = 0.1$ and $r_2 = 0.2$ (the subscripts 1 and 2 refer to the first and second set of growers, respectively; if you wish, you can compare three or four at the same time). What you will see is a growth pattern like Figure 7.1. By experimenting with different values for r and d you can easily grasp the general principles underlying this dynamics. Small differences in initial state or parameter values will result in only small differences in the growth patterns. The model, therefore, is pretty close to a simple linear model and once you have a reasonable guess of the magnitude of the values involved, it is relatively easy to predict the outcome.

What happens, however, if the growth rate pushes the growth pattern into the chaotic domain? This is the situation where the growth level alternates between overconsuming and underconsuming the available resources. The continuous pattern of loss followed by rebuilding the level, loss again and so on, is very expensive in resources invested. The answer to this question is somewhat counterintuitive. Whereas the adaptation parameter consisted of a small negative adaptation ratio in the first case, it should now be a big positive number. That is, we should simply increase the resources, dependent on where the growth level is. This leads to an unexpected situation where the system soon settles into an equilibrium point. This pattern is quite counterintuitive, since a strong upward adaptation to a growth process that changes very rapidly and tends to overshoot its carrying capacity anyway would be expected to lead to an exponential explosion.

Try the following parameters: $d_1 = -1.06$, $d_2 = 1.4$, $L_1 = 0.3$, $L_2 = 0.3$, $r_1 = 3$ and $r_2 = 2.4$ (note that the negative value of d makes its effect positive in equation 7.1, since d is preceded by a minus sign). Experiment with some different parameter values and also try different initial states. If they are small (say 0.01), the equilibrium state occurs at a much higher level than with relatively high initial states, such as 0.3; see Figure 7.2. Overall, however, this model still behaves linearly, in that small differences in a parameter value (between one set of equations and another) result in small differences between the actual outcomes. The model behaves, however, rather

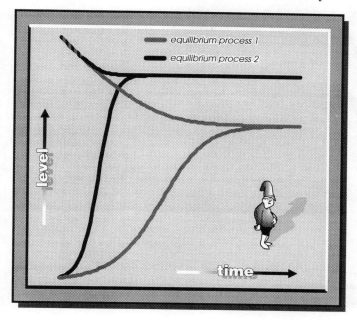

Figure 7.1 Different growth rates correspond with different equilibrium points when carrying capacity adapts itself to the speed with which the growth level approaches the carrying capacity level.

counterintuitively and requires actual numerical experimentation to find out what it does, given different values. It therefore exceeds the limits of purely verbal extrapolation, but it still allows us to make successful predictions even if the starting conditions are known only approximately.

In the previous models, the carrying capacity adapts to the growth level with a rate, $K - L$, which is big at the beginning and decreases as the growth level approaches the equilibrium level (when $K - L$ becomes an increasingly small number). We would like to know what happens if the adaptation occurs the other way around. That is, adaptation is small in the beginning, because the environment providing the resources might want to wait and see how the learning or developing proceeds before adjusting its resources. As it becomes clearer where the learner will aim in the end, adaptation of the resources provided is supposed to occur faster, inversely dependent on the distance between growth level and carrying capacity. This model can be described in the form of the following set of equations, which are only slightly different from those in equation 7.1:

$$L_{t+1} = L_t \cdot (1 + r - r \cdot L_t / K_t)$$
$$K_{t+1} = K_t \cdot (1 - d \cdot K_t / (K_t - L_t))$$

(7.2)

Whereas the first model behaved very nicely, allowing for prediction and rational

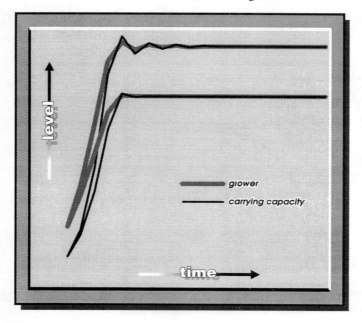

Figure 7.2 With chaotic growth rate values, the growers settle into an equilibrium state if the K-compensation is positive instead of negative.

understanding of what happens on an overall scale, this model behaves strangely. In order to experiment with the model, start with an initial K of 1 and an initial L of, for instance, 0.99 and an r of 0.3. The d parameter should be a very small number, for instance 10^{-15}. It is worth comparing two $L - K$ couples that differ from each other only in the d parameter. That difference should again be very small if you want to see something comparable to the butterfly effect. For instance, if d_A is 10^{-15}, make d_B $(1 + 10^{-14}) \cdot 10^{-15}$. Instead of a parameter difference, you can make the initial state of one L variable slightly different from the other, for instance, with a difference of 10^{-15} (see Figure 7.3). The model produces patterns of meandering changes.

The meandering change model defeats any claim to prediction for at least two reasons. The first is that it shows sudden jumps up and down at unexpected places. That is, there are no observable signs announcing the jumps; they just occur and an adjacent growth curve with very similar values does not show them. Second, growth patterns based on ridiculously small parameter or initial state differences run together for some time, but suddenly become magnified, often to an extent that exceeds the average fluctuation of the curves. This happens suddenly and is again not announced by observable indications. There is a third sense in which such models behave differently from the ones we are used to. If you add a very small error term to each (or some) of the steps in the computation, you will see the same divergence from the comparative path as with the small parameter or initial state difference.

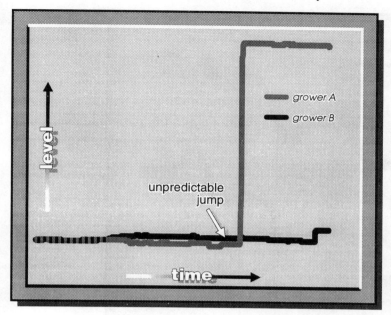

Figure 7.3 In a non-linear system, very small initial state differences become magnified at an unpredictable moment; the two growers that differ only in a very small initial state difference grow together for some time, then one of them suddenly jumps to an entirely different path.

In what sense, however, does this defeat prediction? Is not the model completely deterministic and therefore completely predictable? Does not each computer run give you the same numbers, provided you started with the same initial state conditions as with the previous run? The answer to these questions is affirmative, but that does not affect the major problem. Prediction is about real states of affairs in the world and is based on observations made about these empirical states. Observation is accurate only to a limited extent and however accurate it is, there is always a range of error. If a mechanism is non-linearly affected by influences whose magnitude lies well under that error limit, its behaviour is unpredictable.

There is no real problem if the mechanism is affected in a linear way. In that case the prediction error always lies within a band of equal width around the predictable pattern (see Figure 7.4) and is in general proportional to the measurement error. This is the standard situation, which we traditionally expect to occur. Thus, once we have a good model, the predicted outcomes are as good (or as bad) as the measurements we have made of the conditions on which we have based those predictions. But we have just seen a simple model of connected growth where the error is not linearly distributed. The differences between the two patterns, based on only tiny initial state or parameter differences, are sometimes very small and sometimes very big and no

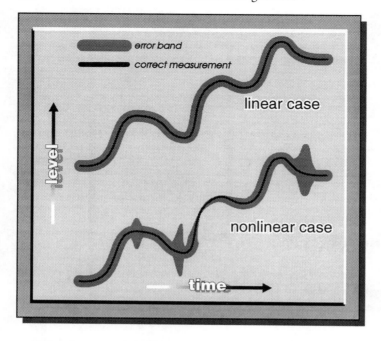

Figure 7.4 In a linear model, errors are distributed evenly around an average process line; in a non-linear model, major bouts of error or noise may occur in unexpected places.

observation-based principle exists that will tell you where and when those differences will occur. In summary, despite its simplicity, the non-linear meandering change model we just tested is by definition not predictable in the empirical sense of the word.

Should we conclude, therefore, that all models consisting of connected growers (specified by coupled equations) are unpredictable? Of course not. Earlier in this chapter, I described another model of resource adaptation, which was superficially similar to the meandering change model but which provided perfectly predictable patterns although it is non-linear. Should we conclude then that unpredictability is a property of a subset of non-linear connected growers? Would the unpredictability increase with increasing numbers of interacting variables involved? We have seen that this is not the case (Model 4.3). The chaotic regime of the simple logistic growth curve is extremely sensitive to very small initial state differences. Logistic, chaotic growth patterns that are similar except for a tiny initial state difference will remain similar for a considerable amount of time, and then, suddenly, divergence sets in. If we compute the difference between the corresponding states of the two series, that difference is almost zero in the first part and suddenly magnifies to a level where the difference becomes about as big as the varying growth levels themselves (Figure 7.5).

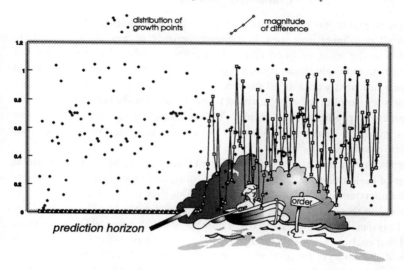

Figure 7.5 The dots scattered over the diagram represent growth levels of two different growers; the levels vary chaotically over time. The points refer to two different growers that start with a minute difference in initial state level. The difference between the two growers is very small at the beginning, but explodes suddenly and becomes as big as the chaotic variation itself. The dots represent the variation of the growth pattern, the blocks connected by a line show the difference between that pattern and one with a slightly different initial state level. The point where differences are magnified explosively is the 'prediction horizon'.

The prediction horizon and the function of uncertainty

What the previous models illustrate is the existence of a so-called *prediction horizon*. The prediction horizon is the period of time over which our predictions are a linear function of the measurement errors made. That is, for a given time period, small measurement errors will lead to only small prediction errors. Beyond that time period, however, the error magnifies exponentially and will rapidly become as big as the signal itself. Beyond that point, predictions on the basis of a good model and highly reliable (though very slightly erroneous) measurement will be as good or as bad as prediction based on Tarot cards or dice.

The existence of a prediction horizon is a theoretically inferred fact. We have seen that it exists in a variety of non-linear models. A practical illustration of it is the mathematical models on which the daily weather forecast is based. They too have a prediction horizon, which is about five days. Is there any evidence for prediction horizons in developmental psychology? It is true that we do not know how to predict people's life courses very well, but is this because our models are poor, or because the information on which the predictions are based is flawed? Or is it because development is a domain haunted by the kind of non-linear models that have very short prediction horizons?

Let me try to tackle this question by repeating the conclusion from the previous section: not all non-linear processes of connected growth or growth in general are unpredictable in the sense outlined above. It is quite probable that many forms of connected growth in development are of a type that enables good prediction, provided that we have a sufficiently reliable estimation of the parameters. It is also possible that the prediction horizon lies far enough ahead to enable us to make sufficiently reliable and still practical predictions of children's developmental careers. Given these possibilities, however, what would we expect to be the case, in view of what we know about human development?

People are both very similar to and very different from one another. They are similar in a number of basic things, such as their bodily form, basic social habits and behaviours, basic understanding of the world and so on. But they differ a lot in the specific ways that build on those basic things, in the skills they master, the knowledge they have and so on. This means on the one hand that a number of developmental processes must be of a kind that enables reasonably faithful reproduction of an existing form. Although the growth of the embryo, for instance, is an extremely complicated pattern of mutually interacting components, involving environmental as well as genetic information, the process as a whole is robust. In most cases, it will lead to a very predictable outcome in the structure and functioning of the physical body that results from it. The same principle holds for the acquisition of basic skills, such as social behaviour, language and a basic cognitive understanding of the world. They are robust processes in the sense that they are successful generation after generation, even if they are accompanied by individual variation and long-term historical and phylogenetic change.

On the other hand, think of the many domains and characteristics over which people may differ. They differ in personality, expertise, their attitudes towards life, temperament, profession, interests, social position and so on. Different traditional explanations exist for these individual variations. We could claim they are based on different aptitudes or innate predispositions. I do not doubt many of them are. It has also been claimed that individual differences arise from coincidental environmental differences. If you are the son of a baker, you are likely to have a child whose father was a baker too. Or, finally, individual differences could be just random variations, random ripples in the great pond of society. These explanations are still question-begging in the sense that they simply assume the existence of variation; genetic variation in the case of different genetic endowments, or environmental variation in case the individual is considered a product of the environment. But where does this variation come from? If every dimension of difference – say a personality dimension, or a cognitive, affective or social dimension, etc. – evolves according to a robust dynamic mechanism, variation will be non-existent, since these dynamics tend to drift inexorably towards one favoured equilibrium state.

If the mechanism of development were a mixture of robust models, leading to similar end states in spite of highly varying conditions and 'chaotic' models, which are extremely sensitive to initial state or environmental conditions, we would have the best of both worlds. The robust mechanisms would keep everything within manageable bounds, whereas the chaotic mechanisms would produce extensive variation out of what, for all practical purposes, are almost identical starting conditions. In the jargon of dynamic systems, chaotic dynamics is a great means for exploring possibilities in a vast domain of potential differences.

Variation seems a necessary condition for life. If you get stuck in a highly particular ecological niche and you have no sources for experimenting with different forms of life maintenance, you might be quite well off as long as the circumstances remain similar. Once the world begins to change, however, you are in serious trouble. The same is true for the discovery of new ideas and principles. Old ones work fine until you encounter an unsolvable problem. Then you need a mechanism of variation that produces a range of possibilities for you, which you can then explore and select dependent on whether they are successful or not. In summary, adaptation to the vagaries of life requires mechanisms that produce novelty. The cheapest are the chaotic ones, that is, mechanisms that produce very different patterns given only very small – sometimes infinitesimally small – variations in the starting or environmental conditions.

Some basic mathematics of connected growth and development

Steps of the mind's staircase

On the cover of Robbie Case's *The Mind's Staircase* (1992b) is a picture of the Case children. They look at you from behind the corner of what must be the staircase of the Case house (lots of cases here, indeed). The picture lets you look at the children from above: you are on the upper floor; they still have a lot of steps to go. What Case and his collaborators mean by the mind's staircase is a structure of levels of increasing cognitive complexity. The knowledge at each of the levels is domain- and con-text-specific, but each of the items of knowledge or skill is supported by what is called a *central conceptual structure*. This structure is 'a network of semantic nodes and relations that plays a central role in mediating children's performance across a broad range of tasks (though not all), and that also plays a central role in their development' (Case, 1992b, p. 352).

If we were to try to apply a dynamic growth model to this notion of development, a feat Robbie has actually accomplished during our cooperation at the Center for Advanced Study, we could not take only this central conceptual structure into account. Growth and change apply to the relatively separate domain- and concept-specific knowledge and skill structures, as well as to the central structure that supports and finally underlies them. In Robbie's own model, each domain-specific structure has a moderate supportive and stimulating effect on the growth of the central conceptual structure, whereas the central conceptual structure in its turn has a much greater supportive influence on each of the separate domains.

I shall not concentrate on the Case theory of development here, but use it as an example of a network of connected growers and show a number of possible ways in which the connections could be worked out. Before doing so, let me describe some domain-specific forms of knowledge that can be considered as separate growers, although they all contribute to and benefit from an underlying central conceptual network. The examples come from what Robbie Case calls the *dimensional stage* of thinking, which occurs in most children between the ages of 5 and 12 years, and which is roughly similar to Piaget's stage of concrete operations.

In order to test a child's mastery of dimensional thinking, Case and his co-workers use a set of different tasks. They could have used more, no doubt, but these seem to constitute a representative sample. Six have been used in a study about parallels in development. One is the birthday party task. A child is presented with a story about two children celebrating their birthday. The child has to decide how happy each of them is, using information about which presents each of the party birds wanted in the first place and what they actually got. The reward distribution task features two children who volunteer to stay after school to make postcards for children in the hospital. The volunteers differ as to the number of days they came in to help and the number of postcards they made. The child is then asked to decide what reward the teacher should give to each of them. The balance beam task involves a judgement about which side a balance beam will tilt to, given different weights attached at different distances from the centre of the balance beam. The fourth task concentrates on children's ability to tell the time and on their knowledge of different durations. Clock reading is an important aspect of this skill. Similar to time telling, the fifth task, money counting, is of considerable cultural and practical importance to the children. It involves knowledge of the structure of numbers based on coins and banknotes of different values. The sixth task, number knowledge, asks for different forms of numeric understanding, the decimal number system, ordering of numbers and so on. It is a task that depends on extended school training. The six tasks represent the child's understanding in the general numeric domain, which is of course only one of the several domains that develop in children.

Each of the tasks has its own developmental or growth path, even if the reported correlations between scores are relatively high (Case, 1992b). Moreover, considerable individual differences exist between children's understanding of the various task domains. Each of the tasks has its own specific resources in the form of specific information, training at school, the individual child's interest in and affinity for the task at issue, cultural support and valuation of the task and so forth. In addition, each of the tasks is related to its central conceptual structure in that it contributes a little to the growth of that structure, but in turn profits a lot from it.

Finally, we can ask about the relationships between different central conceptual structures. For instance, some children are clearly more 'talented' – whatever that concept finally amounts to – in the numeric domain, whereas others show closer affinities to the social and practical domain.

In summary, there are a lot of different things out there that we may consider independent growers in the sense that they follow their own paths of change and have their own access to specific resources. But the independence goes hand in hand with an intricate network of reciprocal dependence. Some growers will benefit from others and will compete for time and effort resources with still other growers. Some growers, such as the central conceptual structures, lie deep under the surface of actual behaviour and problem solving and address their resources in very indirect ways, whereas others take the form of observable activities that profit directly from the information and training given. How shall we build a model out of these many building blocks?

The form and magnitude of the relationships between connected growers

In Chapter 2, I explained that the dynamic systems approach I employ in this book is actually a very simple sort of theory. It deals only with increments and decrements in what are called 'growers', that is, aspects of development that follow their own paths of development and that have their own specific access to their resources. It follows then that a relation between two growers is at bottom either a *supportive* or a *competitive* *relationship*. If the relation is supportive, grower A contributes to the growth of grower B. If it is competitive, grower B suffers from the growth of A. The relationships also differ in magnitude. The support or competition can be strong or weak. If it is zero, the relation between the two growers is *neutral*.

The relation can also be *conditional*, in which case it is a combination of competition and support. If A is a condition to the growth of B, A will prevent B from growing, as long as A is below some threshold level. As soon as that level has been crossed, A will support the growth of B. The conditional relationship covers what is traditionally called a *prerequisite* or *precursor relationship* in development. It refers to a skill or knowledge whose presence is conditional to (but not necessarily sufficient for) the emergence of a dependent grower. In the standard account of prerequisites or precursors, the relation is defined in a qualitative way; the child must have this or that form of understanding before a more complex overarching form of understanding may emerge. In the dynamic systems model that deals with 'mores' and 'lesses' only, the prerequisite relation is specified in the form of a quantitative threshold level, above which the growth rate of a dependent grower turns from a zero into a positive value.

Finally, the actual positive or negative effect of a grower A on another grower B is the result of (at least) three components: first, the magnitude of the relationship, and second and third, the growth levels of A and of B at the time the effect is exerted. This follows from the size-related concept of growth, which says that increase or decrease is a function of the size already achieved and not of some absolute addition or subtraction. It applies to development in that development is a process where each next step is a function of the preceding one, or a previous step, dependent on the time delay of the effect. The state-related nature of the connections between two growers is a sort of default option of the model. Different options, such as mere addition and subtraction, or optimality relationships are possible and may be defined in the model you construct out of the given building blocks.

The matrix of connected growth

Let me, for the sake of simplicity, confine the discussion to the six numeric tasks and their underlying central conceptual structure. Because these tasks and structures are

Table 7.1 A table containing four theoretical assumptions about relations between growers in the form of cell values

Rate	P	B	D	M	N	T	C
P							
B							
D							
M							
N	− 0.01 (1)			+ 0.1 (2)			+ 0.1 (3)
T							
CN	+ 0.2 (5)				+ 0.5 (4)		

only examples of a more general principle, I shall call them by single capitals, namely B for balance beam, P for birthday party, D for distributive justice, M for money knowledge, T for time telling and N for number knowledge. The central conceptual structure for numeric knowledge is called C.

Provided we know for each pair of tasks or structures how they quantitatively relate to one another, we can set up a matrix of relationships that will specify a whole model of connected growth. The matrix consists of a set of columns bearing the names of the growers, and a set of rows equally named after the growers in the model. Each cell, therefore, is at the crossing of two growers and contains information about how the grower named in the row affects the grower named in the column (see Table 7.1). Put differently, a cell specifies a theoretical assumption about how one grower relates to the change of another.

Table 7.1 contains four numerically specified assumptions about the relations between a number of growers in the Case model. The cell contents are read as follows. Take for instance the cell numbered (1). It contains the value − 0.01 and is at the crossing of the P column and the N row. It means that numerical understanding negatively affects the understanding of the birthday party problem, although the magnitude of the effect is small (0.01). A possible theoretical justification behind this figure is that the birthday party problem involves social and personal understanding, and reasoning with pure numbers, as is taught during the arithmetic class, is supposed to interfere with it slightly. Of course this is just an assumption, which is not supported by any available data, but I am only demonstrating a process of dynamic model building. Similarly, numerical understanding is supposed to have a positive, that is supportive, effect on the understanding of money problems (cell 2), and a similar effect on the central conceptual structure of numeric understanding (3). In turn, the central conceptual structure of numeric understanding has a large positive effect on the understanding of the number system (cell 4). Finally, the central conceptual structure is supposed to have a strong supportive effect on the understanding of the birthday problem (cell 5), although the magnitude of the effect is considerably smaller than with numeric understanding (cell 4).

The whole matrix should be filled in with numbers specifying the relationship between any two variables involved. In the first step of matrix building, the numbers are only rough estimations. They have no function other than roughly to compare the magnitude of the relationships. For instance, we could decide to take the number 1 as the smallest possible relationship figure (except for zero, which represents the case of neutral, that is non-existent, interaction). All the other figures in the matrix – 2, 5, 10, etc. – represent estimated multiples of that smallest number. The real numbers depend on the actual equations we will write and should be determined once the equations are available and put in the form of a dynamic model.

Two aspects of the matrix need some further consideration. The first is the second, unnamed column, which contains the values of the r (growth rate) parameter of the variables specified on the left. The other is the diagonal, that is, the series of cells where a variable determines itself. The diagonal cell contains the value of the logistic a parameter, which indirectly specifies the carrying capacity value for the corresponding variable (since $K = r/a$).

The standard mathematical format of connected growers

Any positive or negative effect on a grower (for instance P, for birthday party problem understanding, for instance) is treated as a separate variable in the logistic or transition equation for that grower. Let us have a look at grower P in Table 7.2. This table is an extension from Table 7.1 and covers all the influences on P from any of the additional growers in the model.

From Table 7.2, we can reconstruct its growth equation as follows:

$$P_{t+1} = P_t \cdot (1 + 0.2 - 0.2 \cdot P_t + 0.1D_t - 0.02 \cdot M_t - 0.01 \cdot N_t + 0.2C_t) \quad (7.3)$$

which, by way of definition, is the same as:

$$P_{t+1} = P_t \cdot (1 + 0.2 - 0.2 \cdot P_t + \Sigma(G_t)) \quad (7.4)$$

provided that $\Sigma(G_t)$ means the sum of the effect of all additional growers at time t on grower P at time $t + 1$.

This equation has a natural meaning in terms of the growth rate and carrying capacity of the affected grower P. In order to explain this, let me go back to an abstract, canonical form of the logistic growth equation, which is:

$$L_{t+1} = L_t \cdot (1 + r - aL_t) \quad (7.5)$$

Table 7.2 The effect of all additional growers on the grower 'birthday party' P. The growth rate of P is 0.2 and its default carrying capacity $0.2/0.2 = 1$

	Rate	P	B	D	M	N	T	C
P	0.2	0.2						
B		0						
D		0.1						
M		− 0.02						
N		− 0.01						
T		0						
C		+ 0.2						

The growth rate r can be the sum of any set of contributing variables, for instance:

$$r_{t+1} = r1_t + r2_t + r3_t + \ldots \tag{7.6}$$

In equation 7.4, the effective growth rate, therefore, is the sum:

$$r + \Sigma(G_t) \tag{7.7}$$

This means that the effect of connecting growers to the growth of, say, P results in an increase in the growth rate of P with the factor $\Sigma(G_t)$, which is the sum of all the influences of the additional growers on grower P at time t. The additional growers also affect the carrying capacity of P. Recall that given equation 7.5 the level of the carrying capacity is: $K = r/a$ $\hspace{3cm}$ (7.8)

Since the effective growth rate of, say, P is given in equation 7.7, it follows that:

$$(r + \Sigma(G_t))/a = K + \Sigma(G_t)/a \tag{7.9}$$

This means that the effect of all the additional, connected growers on P is not only that P's growth rate is increasing, but also that the carrying capacity or maximum equilibrium level of P increases.[2] This result is in perfect accord with the definition of the carrying capacity, namely the maximum equilibrium level achievable under the currently available resources. Any supportive grower in the connected network acts as a resource-enhancing variable and thus increases the maximal level the dependent grower can achieve.

There could be theoretical reasons for confining the effect of the connected growers to the carrying capacity of the dependent grower, thus leaving the latter's growth rate at a constant level. To do so, a coupled equation should be used, which is as follows:

$$\begin{aligned} L_{t+1} &= L_t \cdot (1 + r - rL_t/K_t) \\ K_t &= K + \Sigma(G_{t-1}) \end{aligned} \tag{7.10}$$

We could also make the growth rate dependent on the connected growers and leave the carrying capacity as it is. It goes without saying that whatever equation we choose, it should be based on a theory of development of, for instance, cognitive growth and not on mere mathematical preferences. If there is reason to assume that the effect of some connected growers consists of increasing (or decreasing) the rate of growth in a dependent grower, then we should write an equation in which this model is specified.

Non-linear effects, prerequisite relationships and combined positive and negative influences

In Tables 7.1 and 7.2 each cell specifies a simple linear relationship between a dependent grower (for instance, the birthday party problem) and a connected grower (for instance the central conceptual structure for numeric understanding).[3] The linear relationship takes the form of a parameter that moderates the effect of the connected grower on the dependent one. Some growers, however, have an effect that depends on an optimal value. Assume that self-esteem would be a separate grower in the Case model. Self-esteem is partly dependent on personal success or failure experiences, partly on personality and environmental (family) aspects. Let us pretend it is a separate and measurable part of the child's perception of self. There is no doubt that positive and realistic self-esteem has a positive effect on learning and achievement (see for instance Harter, 1978, 1983; Kunnen, 1992). Increasing self-esteem should therefore have an increasing effect on learning. But what if self-esteem keeps increasing and goes far beyond a realistic and acceptable level? We would expect its positive effect to decrease markedly and finally to become negative. Unrealistically low self-esteem would also have a negative effect on achievement and learning and turn into a positive effect only beyond some minimal threshold.

Provided you define the required parameters, the following equation specifies the self-esteem effect function as depicted in Figure 7.6:

$$\text{effect (esteem)} = exp \left[\frac{-(\text{esteem} - \text{optimum})^2}{sqrt(-1 \cdot \text{width} \cdot ln \ (\text{threshold}))} \right] - \text{threshold} \quad (7.11)$$

Note that *exp* means 'exponent of', *sqrt* stands for 'square root' and *ln* for 'natural logarithm'.

What if the theory describes a prerequisite relationship? For instance, it could claim that a minimum level or threshold (*T*) of representational understanding *R* is

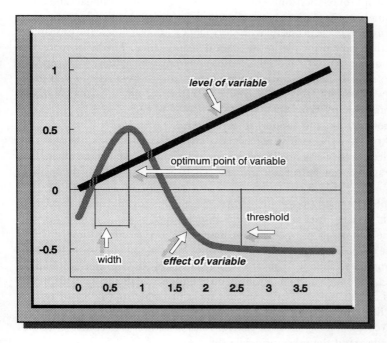

Figure 7.6 A variable such as self-esteem is assumed to have an optimal positive effect corresponding with a certain optimal value, but a negative effect when that value is exceeded.

necessary before abstract thought A can emerge. The cell that specifies the effect of representational (R) on abstract (A) understanding should specify first to what extent A benefits from R (or even suffers from R, if the two compete) and second, should also contain a prerequisite equation. In its simplest form, the prerequisite equation is a function that keeps the growth rate of abstract thought A zero as long as the threshold T of representational thought R has not been passed:

$$\text{if } R < T, r_A = 0, \text{ if not } r_A = \text{any positive number} \qquad (7.12)$$

for r_A the growth rate of the grower abstract understanding A. It is also possible to write a more complicated function for the prerequisite relation, but the simple yes or no form in equation 7.12 functions very well.

Finally, it is possible that the relationship from one grower to another is both supportive and competitive at the same time. Just assume a child is learning simultaneously about time telling and money. Both learning activities require evanescent resources such as time spent on task, effort, attention and interest. Whatever time spent on learning one skill cannot be spent on learning the other. Preferences for one or the other learning task will negatively interfere with effort spent in doing the other. On the other hand, however, it is easy to defend the claim that they also support each other. They both require the understanding of a comparable hierarchical principle of relationships between hours and minutes, or dollars and cents. Adding up dissimilar units of time or money works in accordance with the same general strategies. Discoveries made in one domain – say money – may increase the probability of discovering that same principle in the other domain – time. The tasks contribute independently to the central conceptual structure from which they, in turn, both profit. In that sense, a simultaneous supportive and competitive relationship exists between the two growers (this is of course just theory, not a statement about empirically established relationships). What if I wanted to enclose this hypothesis of simultaneous competition and support in my matrix?

One possibility is that the positive and negative effects simply add up. The net result is either a smaller negative or a smaller positive interaction from one to the other. This interaction parameter can be specified in the cell that corresponds to the growers involved.

A second more interesting possibility is that the competition and support relate to different aspects of the grower at issue. In the simplest case, the competition between money and time telling is a competition for limited resources such as time, effort or attention. Time spent learning about money cannot be used to improve skills in time telling. For simplicity, assume a linear relationship between the 'consumption' of resources such as time and effort on the one hand and the actual increase in a grower on the other hand. The supportive effect relates most plausibly to a different type of resource. It is likely that the understanding of one principle (of time, for instance) contributes to representations of more general rules or central conceptual structures that help us understand the other principle (of money).

We may now summarize this discussion in a model that relates the competitive parameter to the *increase* (or decrease) in the variable, and the supportive parameter to the absolute *level* of that variable. For instance, let money (M) be the dependent variable, and time (T) the variable on which it depends:

$$M_{t+1} = f_{comp}(T_t - T_{t-1})$$
$$M_{t+1} = f_{sup}(T_t)$$

(7.13)

We shall see later that this principle is useful in modelling the growth of hierarchically related growers, as in Kurt Fischer's model.

The unexpected complexity of simple reciprocal dynamics

Time and money

In the preceding section I used Robbie Case's tasks for numerical understanding during the dimensional stage of development as an example of a set of connected growers. Let me now concentrate on two tasks, money counting and time telling.

We have seen that both money counting and time telling rely on the same underlying conceptual structure, that of hierarchy and embedding. Seconds go into minutes, minutes into hours. Cents go into dollars, one dollar bills into five dollar bills and so on. They both require the use of general numeric knowledge and strategies. Units add up to higher order units. Thus whatever general principle you discover in one task would certainly benefit growth and learning in the other. Familiarity with one task may accelerate getting acquainted with the other, if the latter is presented later as a new task. Once a child gets interested in one kind of problem – such as money counting – the interest taken in this type of task might easily transfer to other domains, such as time telling. Put differently, the relationship between the time and the money tasks is one of reciprocal positive influence, that is, reciprocal support. In the matrix model, their relationship would take the following form as shown in Table 7.3.

Table 7.3 specifies the magnitude of the reciprocal effects. It says that time benefits twice as much from knowing about money counting as money counting benefits from time telling. This is just an example and I have no theoretical justification for it. In Robbie Case's model reciprocal support exists via a third, underlying structure acting as an intermediate, the central conceptual structure.

Positive interaction between two growers is highly likely to occur with bright and

Table 7.3 A reciprocal positive (supportive) relationship between time telling and money counting, with different magnitudes for the estimated effects

r	Time	Money
Time		+ 0.1
Money	+ 0.2	

interested children working in high quality educational situations. They are able to discover and understand general principles and strategies underlying both task domains. Mentally retarded children, on the other hand, have great difficulties understanding general abstract principles. They have similar difficulties reflecting on their own thinking processes and how and why they came to a specific result. The probability that their learning how to count money will positively affect their time telling skills and vice versa is very low indeed. It is more likely that the opposite will hold. Time telling and money counting are similar in their underlying principle, but different in how the principle is applied. Time is based on a divisor of 60; money has a decimal divisor. The units have different names and relate to one another in different ways. We may expect, therefore, that the relation between the two tasks is reciprocally negative. That is, learning about money might negatively affect time telling and vice versa simply because any progress made in one task has a chance of creating confusion in the understanding of the other.

The previous forms of reciprocity were symmetric as far as the nature of the effect is concerned; the relations were either both positive (supportive) or both negative (competitive). An asymmetric reciprocity, on the other hand, involves a positive (supportive) relationship from, for instance, money counting to time telling and a negative or competitive effect of time telling on money counting.

Is this asymmetric relationship conceivable with the tasks I used as examples before, money counting and time telling? One possibility is that the positively affecting task, money counting, has been learned first and some generalizations have been made and understood about how counting with units works, applied to magnitudes such as dollars, quarters and dimes. This knowledge may then help a child to understand a new task, time telling. But, time invokes a different sort of unit with a divisor of 60, which might confuse the child and negatively interfere with the skill in money counting. I admit that this scenario is not very likely to occur, but I present it as an example of how we could hypothesize a relationship between growers that relate in this asymmetric way.

In view of the networks that constitute the ecologies of real developing children and their environments, the reciprocal relationships look ridiculously simple and straightforward. Nevertheless, I have discussed several models where the complexity of behaviour was unrelated to the simplicity of the underlying equations. The next section will explore the basic dynamics of reciprocally connected growers.

Reciprocal support

The matrix for the reciprocal support can be generalized as shown in Table 7.4.

The parameter $S: A \leftarrow B$ should be read as 'the extent to which grower A is supported by grower B' (and $S: B \leftarrow A$ means 'the extent to which grower B is supported by grower A'). In the simplest form, which is also what we are going to explore, this parameter is a positive number, for instance 0.1.

In accordance with the general equation for connected growth explained in this chapter, the *standard logistic equation* for reciprocal support takes the following form:

Table 7.4 The generalized matrix of reciprocal support

	r	A	B
A	r_A	1	S: B ← A
B	r_B	S: A ← B	1

$$A_{t+1} = A_t \cdot (1 + r\_A - r\_A \cdot A_t + S: A \leftarrow B \cdot B_t)$$
$$B_{t+1} = B_t \cdot (1 + r\_B - r\_B \cdot B_t + S: B \leftarrow A \cdot A_t) \qquad (7.14)$$

We know that in the *logistic transition model*, the effective growth rate is dependent on the level of the grower (divided by the carrying capacity, which is set to 1). The simplest thing to do is just to substitute $r\_A \cdot A_t$ and $r\_B \cdot B_t$ for r_A or r_B, respectively:

$$A_{t+1} = A_t \cdot (1 + r\_A \cdot A_t - r\_A \cdot A_t^2 + S: A \leftarrow B \cdot B_t)$$
$$B_{t+1} = B_t \cdot (1 + r\_B \cdot B_t - r\_B \cdot B_t^2 + S: B \leftarrow A \cdot A_t) \qquad (7.15)$$

But a second possibility exists. Formally, the effect of a positive supporter is to increase the growth rate of the dependent grower. By doing so, it also increases the carrying capacity. Since in the transition model the growth rate is assumed to be a function of the level already achieved, any factor increasing the growth rate must, by definition, also be a function of that growth level. The equation expressing this state of affairs takes the following form:

$$A_{t+1} = A_t + A_t^2 \cdot (r\_A - r\_A \cdot A_t + S: A \leftarrow B \cdot B_t)$$
$$B_{t+1} = B_t + B_t^2 \cdot (r\_B - r\_B \cdot B_t + S: B \leftarrow A \cdot A_t) \qquad (7.16)$$

Let me call this the *strict transition version of reciprocal support* and the model in equation 7.15 the *intermediate transition version*, since the support term added to the equation behaves as a logistic growth rate.

The numerical study of the behaviour of the support model does not differ from the other reciprocal models. In the following tutorial, I shall describe a spreadsheet format that can be used to test each of the models, without having to change the equations.

Model 7.1 A universal model for reciprocal interactions

Start your spreadsheet by defining a number of parameter values, in the form of range names. The range names you will need are shown in Table 7.5.

If the value of $P: A \leftarrow B$, for instance, is a negative number, A suffers from B, or, put differently, B has a negative or competitive effect on A. If it is a positive number, the effect is supportive. By giving the variable *trans* the value of 1, you define the model as a strict transitional one. If *int* is 1, the model is intermediate transitional, but only if the value of *trans* is also 1 (if *trans* = 0, the value of *int* is always read as 0, even if it says 1 in the value column).

Table 7.5 The parameters needed with the universal equation for reciprocal interaction

Value	Range name	Description
0.01	in_A	Initial level of grower A
0.01	in_B	Initial level of grower B
0.2	r_A	Growth rate of A
0.3	r_B	Growth rate of B
0.2	P: A ← B	Extent to which A benefits or suffers from B
0.15	P: B ← A	Extent to which B benefits or suffers from A
0	trans	If value = 1, the model is transitional
0	int	If value = 1, the model is intermediate transitional

It is possible that the value of the equation will drop below zero and become negative. This situation has no analog in reality; children never know a negative number of words, or have a negative skill. We should consider the initial state value of each of the growers as its minimal value. I have introduced this concept of minimal value earlier and called it the minimal structural growth level. You can apply a trick to keep the growth levels equal to or above the minimal structural level. The trick is to spread the grower out over two columns. In column A enter the basic equation for the first grower; in column B enter the condition that the growth level should never be smaller than the structural minimum, which happens to be the initial state level. In cell A1, enter in_A, and in cell A2:

$$B1 + B1 * @if (\$trans = 1, B1, 1) * (\$r\_A - \$r\_A * B1$$
$$+ \$P: A \leftarrow B * D1/@if (\$trans = 1 \# and \# \$int = 1, B1, 1)) \tag{7.17}$$

Note that the formula does not refer to the previous cell in the A column, but to that in the B column. This is so because the B column contains the constrained value of the equation. In cell B1 enter the following formula:

$$@if (A1 < \$in\_A, \$in\_A, A1) \tag{7.18}$$

This 'if' statement defines a value that is *in_A* if the value of *A1* is smaller than zero; if it is not, the value is just *A1*.

This equation makes the result of the growth equation in the corresponding cell *A1* equal to the initial level value if its value is lower than *in_A*. The first if statement in equation 7.17 turns it into the transition version, given that the value of trans is 1. The second if statement makes it an intermediary transition model if both *trans* and *int* are 1. In cell *C1* type *in_B*, in cell *D1*:

$$@if (C1 < \$in\_B, \$in\_B, C1) \tag{7.19}$$

and copy this to cell D2. In cell C2, enter:

$$D1 + D1 * @if (\$trans = 1, D1, 1) * (\$r\_B - \$r\_B * D1$$
$$+ \$P: B \leftarrow A * B1/@if (\$trans = 1 \# and \# \$int = 1, D1, 1)) \tag{7.20}$$

Copy cell range A2..D2 to A3..D1000.

Before starting the process of model testing, you should define a few different graph types. Define a graph with the name 'timeseries', and one with the name 'phaseplot'. Timeseries is a normal line graph that depicts the values B1..B1000 and D1..D1000. Phaseplot is a state space diagram. Define it as an xy graph. The value for the x-axis is

B300..B1000; for the y-axis it is D300..D1000. I suggest you start with cell 300 to cut off most of the introductory cell values. The phase plot is interesting only if you hit the chaotic domain with your values. The route to chaos should in general not be longer than the first 300 cell values.

You test the model by first specifying all your parameter values in the value list (do not forget to define the range names for the correct cells, namely those that contain the values, not the parameter names). Then change the value of one parameter in small steps. It is possible to automate this process by writing a macro; if you are not familiar with this, consult the spreadsheet manual.

What will be the equilibrium level of A and B, if any (that is, given they do not run into oscillation or chaos or something else)? It is the point where the difference part of the equations becomes zero. It can be shown that for the standard logistic form, the equilibria for the growers A and B are:

$$K_A = (r\_A \cdot r\_B + P:A \leftarrow B \cdot r\_B)/(r\_A \cdot r\_B - P:A \leftarrow B \cdot P:B \leftarrow A)$$
$$K_B = (r\_A \cdot r\_B + P:B \leftarrow A \cdot r\_A)/(r\_A \cdot r\_B - P:B \leftarrow A \cdot P:A \leftarrow B) \qquad (7.21)$$

Now that the preparatory work has been done, we can start testing the behaviour of the reciprocal support model. I suggest you begin with values from Table 7.5. Since *trans* = 0, the model behaves as a straightforward logistic growth model, with symmetric support. What you will see with these parameter values is probably what you have expected. Both growers stabilize at an equilibrium point that lies higher than the level they would have achieved without the reciprocal support. To see how the level depends on the value of, for instance, the support parameter, change both $P:A \leftarrow B$ and $P:B \leftarrow A$ to 0.05. You might find it counterintuitive to see that the grower with the highest growth rate profits the *least* from the support (try 0.3 for r_A and 0.2 for r_B) (see Figure 7.7, which represents the first 100 steps of the computation).

Increase the value of the $P:B \leftarrow A$ parameter by increments of 0.01. Check the resulting curves for each increment. You will see that the curves start to show the two–state flip-flop we also saw in the standard logistic growth equation. Then suddenly chaos sets in. A nice form of chaos can be seen for $P:B \leftarrow A = 0.2$. The phaseplot (more precisely, the state space plot you have defined) shows two separate oval forms. With still higher values, the oscillations become bigger and bigger, until the whole process ends in an exponential explosion. For the series of parameter values 0.01, 0.01, 0.05, 0.03, 0.0235, 0.06, 0 and 0 (in order of appearance in the value list), a very different form of chaos can be seen, consisting of irregular oscillatory jumps (see Figure 7.8).

If you get chaotic or even explosive processes with the standard logistic form of the equation, try the same parameter values with different models. For instance, with *trans* = 1 and *int* = 0 you simulate a transition model, and with *trans* = 1 and *int* = 1 you have the intermediate transition model. Overall, the intermediate transition model is the most robust of the three models, in that it tolerates much higher parameter variation (especially of the support parameters) before it runs into chaos or explodes. The intermediate model is particularly interesting if you start from different initial state values, for instance $int\_A = 0.01$ and $int\_B = 0.001$. With sufficiently low

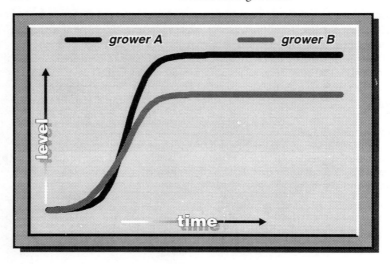

Figure 7.7 Reciprocal support normally results in a higher equilibrium level for both growers.

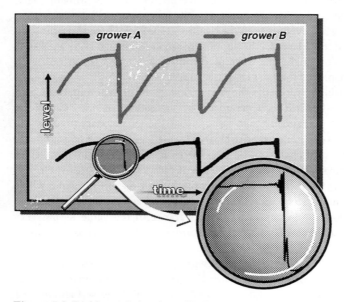

Figure 7.8 Besides real chaotic oscillation, reciprocal support sometimes falls into a quasi-chaotic oscillation resembling a relaxation wave (this figure); in other cases its growth pattern resembles a chaotic oscillation.

support parameter values, a stepwise growth process results. A good empirical example of this model is Kurt Fischer's levels and tiers model of development. I will leave this example for Chapter 8.

Reciprocal competition

The logical counterpart of reciprocal support is of course reciprocal competition; both growers have a negative effect on one another, which technically means that they have a reciprocal competition relation.

I suggest you start with growth rate values greater than 0.2, and with the following set of parameters: $in\_A = 0.03$, $in\_B = 0.03$, $r\_A = 0.2$, $r\_B = 0.15$, $P: A \leftarrow B = -0.1$, $P: B \leftarrow A = -0.1$, $trans = 0$, $int = 0$.

Before studying the behaviour of these growers, you must disable the function that kept the growth rate equal to or above the initial state level. With this function still working, the qualitative patterns will be different. Go to the columns B and D of your spreadsheet, and alter the function as follows:

$$@if(A1 < 0 \# and \# \$min = 1, \$in\_A, A1) \tag{7.22}$$

This equation makes sense only if you first define a parameter with the range name *min*. If $A1$ is smaller than 0 and the value of *min* is 1, equation 7.22 returns the value in_A and the value $A1$ in any other case. Enter a comparable equation in the D column; copy it to the entire columns B and D. Thus, by setting *min* to zero you can disable the function that kept the growth level at a minimum that was equal to its initial state level.

The pattern you will get is characteristic of reciprocal competition with relatively high growth rates (greater than 0.1; Figure 7.9). You will see that both growers stabilize at a level well below the carrying capacity they would have reached if it were not for the negative effect of the other grower. In this particular case, one grower (A) regresses a bit, in response to the growth of B. This pattern, by the way, is similar to the one produced by weak mutual support, that is, when mutual support does not increase the carrying capacity. Try the transition version of this model by entering the value 1 for the *trans* parameter. This model produces a more dramatic shape, with the beginning of a stepwise flattening in grower B. As a next step, give all parameters similar values for the two growers, namely 0.03, 0.03, 0.15, 0.15, -0.1, -0.1, 0, 0 (in the order of Table 7.5). Then start decreasing the value of $P: B \leftarrow A$, that is, the parameter specifying to what extent B suffers from A. Go with increments of -0.01. If the competition value reaches -0.15, the B grower drops down to about zero level. For all practical purposes, it disappears as a behavioural alternative in the repertoire.

It is interesting to try compensatory values. For instance, try to increase the initial state level whose competition factor is bigger than the other. Can initial state level compensate for higher competition?

For smaller growth rates, for instance $r\_A = r\_B = 0.05$, the situation changes qualitatively. For the higher growth rates, the system of two growers could have any attractor point; that is, each grower could stabilize at any level between 1 and 0. For the smaller growth rates, this is no longer the case. The system has only two attractor

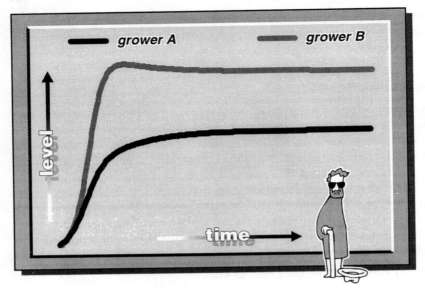

Figure 7.9 A typical pattern of mutual competition, based on growth rates bigger than 0.1.

states, either ($A = K$; $B = 0$) or ($A = 0$; $B = K$). For some values, the growers stay together for some time at what seems to be an equilibrium level, but they will eventually separate and one will grow towards zero; that is, it will disappear as a behavioural alternative. Try, for a start, the values 0.03, 0.03, 0.05, 0.05, − 0.1, − 0.10001, 0, 0 (in the order of Table 7.5). The tiny disadvantage of the B grower will finally lead to its disappearance.

The small growth rate values (e.g. 0.05) allow for a number of interesting compensatory relations. That is, a higher competition can be compensated for by a higher initial level or higher growth level. Try for instance 0.03, 0.05, 0.05, 0.05, − 0.1, − 0.135, 0, 0 (see Figure 7.10). The existence of such compensatory relations in addition to the binary attractor of the system explains why it is full of threshold levels. That is, under some level of, say, competition, the result of the dynamics is invariably that A disappears. But beyond that level, A wins and B disappears. In the vicinity of those thresholds, small differences in other variables may change the outcome dramatically, in that a little higher initial state (for instance) may compensate for a little higher competition factor. The situation becomes even more complicated if you add an extra variable, carrying capacity. In the present model, K is by default 1, but it could easily be added as a variable.

Just assume that this model would apply to a developmental domain where compensatory actions are taken to counterbalance the negative effect of children's environments. For instance, children growing up in very poor economic and social circumstances have a future that is like a bistable state: it is either finishing school and

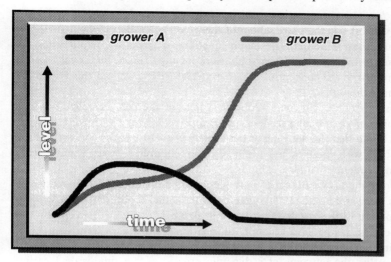

Figure 7.10 In a low-growth-rate situation, reciprocal competition allows for a variety of compensatory effects: the initial dominance of the first grower is compensated by a slightly higher carrying capacity level in the second grower, leading to the final 'victory' of the latter.

taking a reasonable job, or not finishing school and ending up in asocial or even criminal activities; I exaggerate, but there are too many youngsters for whom these are the alternative choices in life.

If the system determining the outcome of the process is in general similar to the bistable reciprocal competition system – and it could be, given the mutually exclusive nature of the alternative futures and the number of factors influencing the choice – it will be notoriously difficult to handle that system and navigate it in the direction society wants. In view of the complexity of the situation, it will be very difficult to predict whether one or another compensatory educational measure will work. It will work under some circumstances, and not under others and it will be very difficult to generalize. This does not mean that, if this model is right, compensatory education and action are no longer possible. It is rather the other way around: the model predicts that compensatory effects will occur in a variety of ways. But it also shows that the effects and nature of the compensatory action are very context-dependent and only work if it passes a threshold value.

An empirical example of reciprocal competition: the meaning of 'big'

If you are shown two different objects at a time, and you are asked to pick the *big* one, you would probably take a number of aspects into account. What sort of object is it, is an object of that size and dimensions usually called big, or would you use another word, such as *tall* or *long*? If it is a geometric object, such as a rectangle, which dimension – horizontal or vertical – is the more salient of the two? Earlier developmental studies suggested a curvilinear trend in the development of big. Whereas 3-year-olds interpret big as referring to overall size, 5-year-olds were inclined to see big as tall. Later, children will return to the concept of big as an overall size word and this is also the typical pattern with adults.

Sena and Smith (1990) not only replicated some of the older studies, but also presented their subjects, ranging from age 3 to adulthood, with a variety of different objects. They found that the meaning of big depended greatly on the context and the objects used, both with children and adults. Overall, children between 3 and 7 years showed a strong tendency to interpret big as tall. Adults sometimes interpret big as tall, as long, or as referring to overall size. Finally, significant individual differences exist for some contexts. Sena and Smith (1990) suggest that the actual application of the word to a particular object is the result of a dynamic process, involving perceptual and cognitive processes, taking into account information from a variety of contextual sources. Calling something big is not just the immediate expression of a present concept, but rather the outcome of a dynamic process over a time-scale I earlier referred to as microdevelopmental. The macrodevelopmental changes, for instance from the 5-year-old's preference for tall to the adult's use of a variety of contextual cues, boils down to a process of changing the parameters and eventually the rules of the microdevelopmental dynamics. This macrodevelopmental process is likely to follow a type of contextual dynamics similar – but on a different time-scale – to the microdevelopmental process.

The outcome of the microdevelopmental process – which is an actual decision about which object is big – can be described as an attractor state in a state space consisting of the major decision dimensions for big, namely the length (or width) and height dimensions. At the beginning of the decision process, you have not decided yet for either length, height or a dimensional combination of both. The decision amounts to pinpointing a particular dimension or combination of dimensional values as your decisive criterion for big in the given context. I shall explain how this process can be modelled by using the idea of a reciprocal competition dynamics.

The dynamics that we need is one that results in the specification of two values: one value for the importance attributed to the height dimension, one for the importance of length. If the outcome of the process is ($H = 1$, $L = 0$), only height would be considered the distinctive feature for big in the particular problem situation at hand. If ($H = 0.5$, $L = 0.5$), height and length are considered equally important (in evaluating a surface). The deviation of the values from 1 would say something about how important other dimensions, aspects, or considerations are with regard to determining whether something is big. The higher those values, the more exclusive the attribution of big to the dimensions for which these values hold.

To see how the dynamics work, take the parameter values that produced the pattern as in Figure 7.10 (0.03, 0.05, 0.05, 0.05, -0.1, -0.135, 0, 0). Assume that the A grower stands for the height dimension, and the B grower for length. A state space plot with A as y-axis and B as x-axis is shown in Figure 7.11. It represents a

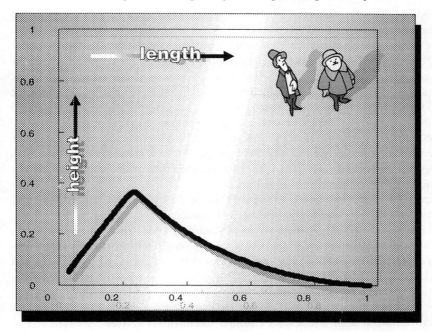

Figure 7.11 Phase plot of a decision process: after a period where both height and length were taken into account when the child had to make a decision about how *big* an object is, the child finally focuses on one particular dimension to make a decision (the choice of the dimension depends on the context in which the *big* question is asked; in this particular case the preferred dimension is the length of the object).

microdevelopmental process, namely the growth of the decision about which dimension – height, length or both – should determine the choice for big in a particular problem situation. In this simulated decision process, both height and length (surface) are taken into consideration for some time, but then the length dimension gains more and more support. The final outcome is that length accounts for 100 per cent of the decision about which of two presented objects is the big one. Change the value of the growth rates of A and B to 0.2 and you will observe a very different situation. The outcome of the decision process would be that ($L = 0.75$; $H = 0.50$). That is, big is clearly attributed mainly to the surface (a combination of height and length), but in this particular case length is considered more important than height in the decision about which object is the big one. You can go on changing the parameters and studying the phase plots of the trajectories.

How do the parameters and variables in the reciprocal competition relate to the perceptual, conceptual and developmental processes that Sena and Smith (1990) described? I see the reciprocal competition model as a general, abstract model for a microdevelopmental process whose detailed format could be modelled after a neural network or a symbolic information processing program, to mention only two possibilities. The parameters and variables should therefore be given a meaning that makes sense in terms of the short time period the equations are supposed to model here. A low growth rate leads to a situation in which only one of the dimensions, height or length, is chosen. This is, moreover, the response pattern most characteristic of the youngest age group. The most plausible assumption then is that growth rate in the equation stands for a general variable that changes during development. That variable could be information-processing speed. It could also be working memory, associated with the ability to take into account more than one dimension in finding the solution for a problem. The magnitude of that processing variable, corresponding with growth rate in the equations, is supposed to increase with age. We have seen that a higher growth rate results in an equilibrium state where both variables, height and length, survive and contribute to the impression of big. This is exactly what has been found with older subjects, although they sometimes use only one of the dimensions. In order for this result to obtain, the competition parameter of one dimension should be pretty high, given that the growth rate is high. As for the other variables, they probably relate to contextual and object-specific properties of the objects given in the decide-which-one-is-big experiment. We may assume that the perceptual salience of either the horizontal or the vertical dimension of the objects corresponds with the initial state of the dimensions in the reciprocal competition model. The higher that initial state, the higher the probability that it will become the dominant dimension when the process has settled into an equilibrium state. Cultural and linguistic conventions as to what is called 'big' may correspond with different carrying capacity levels for each of the dimensions in the equation. A higher carrying capacity corresponds with a stronger attracting force and could counterbalance the negative effect of initial state, that is, of perceptual salience.

Asymmetric reciprocity: competition and support

The preceding reciprocal models were symmetric in the sense that both were either positive or negative. The present model is asymmetric and involves a negative effect of one to another that positively affects the first.

The following list of values provides a good starting point for experimenting with the asymmetric reciprocity model: $in\_A = 0.01$, $in\_B = 0.01$, $r\_A = 0.1$, $r\_B = 0.1$, $P: A \leftarrow B = -0.01$, $P: B \leftarrow A = 0.1$, $trans = 0$, $int = 0$ $K\_A = 1$; $K\_B = 0.4$.

Try the outcome for these parameter values by changing $P: A \leftarrow B$ from -0.01 to -0.25 in steps of -0.025. You will notice that the qualitative behaviour of the model is very similar to that of reciprocal competition with sufficiently high growth rates (say $r > 0.1$), in that the variables stabilize at some level. If you increase the value of the competition factor of A (that is, the extent to which A 'suffers' from the growth of B), you will reach a point where A, after a period of introductory growth, slides back to its minimal level (which by default is the initial state level) (see Figure 7.12).

There are two differences with the reciprocal competition model. The first is that this model does not change its attractor behaviour with decreasing growth rates. Recall that the reciprocal model could give you any combination of values for the variables

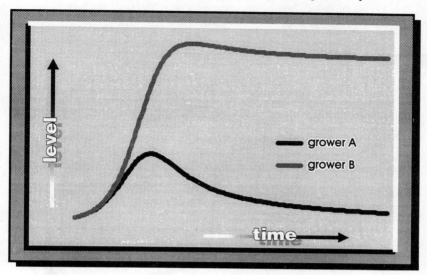

Figure 7.12 Grower B replaces grower A, which virtually disappears. The pre-transitory dip is followed by a post-transitory bump. The competence level is the highest performance level of either A or B.

involved if the growth rate was high enough. Below a certain growth rate limit, though, the endpoint of the process was that one variable survived on a maximal value and the other disappeared, even when both growers had stayed on the same level for a while. In the asymmetric model there is no such discontinuity. Second, the reciprocal competition model often produces a 'hump' in the grower that retains the higher value of the two (see Figure 7.9). In the asymmetric model, both growers show the hump, which sometimes amounts to a significant rise, preceding the levelling-off towards the equilibrium points.

The next section explores the asymmetric model further for the transition model. Recall that in the strict transition model, growth rate and the parameter value specifying how much an adjacent grower affects the grower in question is a function of the growth level already achieved. In the weak transition model, growth rate is a function of the growth level, but the parameter specifying the effect of another grower is a constant.

An empirical illustration: take-over phenomena

Try the following list of parameter values $in\_A = 0.1$; $in\_B = 0.01$; $r\_A = 0.1$; $r\_B = 0.1$; $P{:}A{\leftarrow}B = -0.1$ $P{:}B{\leftarrow}A = 0.1$; $trans = 1$, $int = 0$. Notice that the initial

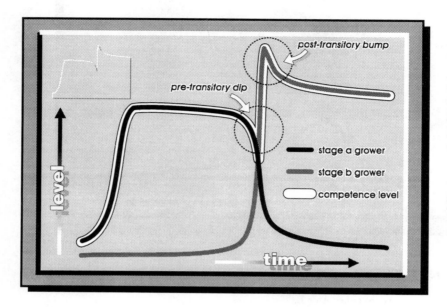

Figure 7.13 With the right parameter setting, an asymmetric model results in the survival of a grower B, at the cost of the disappearance of a grower A (the end result is similar to that of a reciprocal competition dynamics with low growth rates; Figure 7.10)

states of the growers are quite different: the first grower starts much higher than the one it supports (0.1 *versus* 0.01). On the other hand, the first one suffers from the increase in the supported grower. By replacing the last number, 0, by 1 your equation will turn into the other transition form, namely the intermediate one. Figure 7.13 shows the trajectory of the growers. It is highly reminiscent of what happens in what I call *take-over phenomena*. By take-over, I mean that a new skill, strategy or problem-solving procedure is taking over the range of problems that were dealt with by an earlier and in general weaker and more primitive skill, strategy or procedure. As a result of the take-over, the previous developmentally more primitive form is supposed to disappear.

Language is an example of a domain where lots of such phenomena occur. Beginning speakers make mistakes that are not just random errors. They reflect genuine rules of language production and understanding that are indicative of the level of linguistic skill the child has reached at that moment. Those more primitive rules are replaced by others that in general more closely reflect mature language use. Once a more developed rule has been mastered, the old predecessor rule is rarely used any longer and usually it is abandoned completely.

Similar processes are assumed to occur in domains where development can be described in structural cognitive terms. Take for instance the stages of moral development discerned by Kohlberg (1969). If a child is presented with a story containing a moral dilemma, such as whether you are allowed to steal food if your poor old mother is starving and she has no money to buy any, children may base their judgement on moral conventions and rules. This is basically what they do during the stage that corresponds with Piaget's concrete-operational stage. They may also judge on the basis of universal ethical principles and decide that life is a more important good than someone else's money. This is what we could expect during the formal operational stage. The higher form of moral judgement simply replaces the preceding form in the moral dilemma situations. Thus, as far as thinking about those dilemmas is concerned, a take-over process has occurred, substituting the higher form for the lower.[4]

It has often been observed that take-over phenomena are accompanied by temporary regression in performance. Sydney Strauss has done a lot of research on transient performance regression and has coined the term *U-shaped growth* to describe it. Strauss (1982) and Bever (1982) both edited books containing a variety of papers on regression in different domains. An explanation that keeps coming back in almost any paper that deals with it is that the performance regression is the consequence of internal reorganization processes. As the child starts to build up a new mode of representation or thinking, for instance, thinking in terms of ratios instead of qualitative identities, he or she must reorganize and redefine the rules and strategies used to solve problems in the domain at issue. This reorganization causes a temporary fallback in performance, followed by a higher performance level, due to the new and usually better cognitive structure. It is like a three-star restaurant serving junk food while its kitchen is under renovation and getting a fourth star as soon as the chef has got used to the new equipment. Anyway, the general pattern of such take-overs is the appearance of a performance pattern that disappears as a new performance pattern takes over. This take-over is usually accompanied by a temporary regression. This qualitative pattern is exactly what the intermediate transition form of the asymmetric reciprocity model produces, as can be judged from Figure 7.13. But is this resemblance supported by a good theoretical basis?

In a take-over, a more mature or more highly developed form substitutes for a more primitive, earlier one. The earlier form can be assumed to support the later one. For instance, in one of Strauss' experiments, children have to judge how hot the water in a jar will be, basing their answer on the number of candles heating it (Strauss and Stavy, 1982). They should understand, for instance, that it does not make any difference when you add another cup of water if you also add an extra candle. Four- to five-year-old children typically reason on the basis of qualitative identities. They will say, 'You only added some water and you put an extra candle under it'. In a significant number of cases, this simple strategy will result in a significant number of correct answers. More important, however, is whether it will also help the child discover and understand better the more advanced, quantitative ratio strategy (x cups divided by x candles is the same as one cup over one candle, etc.). This will be so if, for instance, the older reasoning strategy leads to an agreement with the newer strategy when the latter is still under construction. Bryant (1982) has argued that agreements between existing and new strategies are of considerable importance in establishing and developing that new strategy. But will the later strategy also support the older one? Probably not. The quantitative strategy, once established, will lead to a different answer from the qualitative one in a variety of more complex problems. It will conflict with the older one, in other words and so contribute to its decay.

In summary, take-over phenomena, at least of the type often described as the U-shaped form, comply with the asymmetric reciprocity format. Are they also based on the transition form of growth? There is a good chance they are. The transition form requires that the chances of making developmental progress in some field are positively related to the level of understanding already built up. The less you know about ratios and compensations between dimensions, the less likely it is that an arbitrary encounter with such a problem, in real life or in a tutorial situation, will teach you anything about those principles. If it can be shown that this is indeed the case with the examples of domains in which U-shaped growth has been found, the asymmetric reciprocity model would be a good candidate for explaining the phenomena.

Finally, notice that the pattern described as a take-over, showing an intermediary performance dip, is also produced by the reciprocal competition model. Under specific parameter values, the earliest grower increases, then starts to fall back as the later grower takes off. It appears, then, that very different models produce the same predictions and outcomes. They cannot both be correct, since they start with different assumptions about what is going on. The way out of this conflict is to start with a theoretical assumption, for instance, one that tries to establish the nature of the relationship between two growers. Is it a reciprocal competition, or is it asymmetric? Once the nature of the relationship has been determined, one should try to find out whether a model based on that type of relationship can indeed produce the empirical trajectory found in research. The other way around, starting from a model that produces an empirically found pattern, then deciding that this must be the model that explains the pattern, will often lead to mistakes and overexplanatory models. The theoretical model of the mechanism should be the starting point for the building of a dynamics model.

Simultaneous competition and support

In all the previous models competition and support were a function of the level of the grower. For instance, the extent to which the time-telling skill suffered from money counting (or the extent to which it benefited, depending on the model at issue) was a function of the level of skill in the money task. Earlier we have seen that it is not necessarily the level *per se* that determines the growth pattern of another grower. It could also be the change, that is the increase or decrease per time unit, that affects a dependent grower. Let us assume that a moderately bright and interested child is learning about money counting and time telling. It is likely that the two tasks will not develop completely simultaneously. That is, there is a good chance that one will be ahead of the other. We can still assume that the two task domains will benefit from one another. Maybe the beneficial effect runs via an intermediate grower, such as the central conceptual structure of numerosity, that Robbie Case sees as the responsible factor here. But there is also a reciprocal competition. Let us assume that the time children spend on learning skills such as money counting and time telling is quite limited. If there were few other skills and activities the child had to learn, there would be ample time to spend on both the money and the time tasks. In practice, however, there will be considerable competition for evanescent resources such as time or attention. Time, effort and attention are resources needed for the learning of skills. We may therefore assume that the amount of resources consumed is a function of the increase in the growth level, not of the growth level *per se*. That is, all other things being equal, rapid learning and acquisition of more information will require more resources than slower or smaller increases.

There is another sense in which a competition can exist between, say, money counting and time telling. We have seen that the underlying principles are similar, but also different enough eventually to cause confusion. Thus the switch from money to time could have a negative effect on the learning of the latter, because that requires a reorganization of knowledge. For instance, the word *quarter* refers to a collection of 25 units of money, but 15 units of time. The amount of confusion, however, is most likely not dependent on the absolute level of either the money or time knowledge, but on the actual increase in that knowledge. The increase involves the establishment of new principles, facts and rules. Once they are firmly established, for instance, in the case of money, they will not negatively interfere with an additional grower, such as time, any more. Thus it is the learning itself (that is, the change) that is responsible for the eventual negative interference.

If I summarize this model, I end up with a model already presented under equation 7.13, one where there is simultaneous competition and support. The competition is a function of the increase or, in general, the change in the grower. The support on the other hand, can be considered a function of the level of that grower. Equation 7.13 presented this model in only the most general form. Here is a more specific one, for M the money and T the time task:

$$M_{t+1} = M_t(1 + r_M - r_M/K_M + s_{M \leftarrow T}T_t - c_{M \leftarrow T}(T_t - T_{t-1})/T_t)$$
$$T_{t+1} = T_t(1 + r_T - r_T/K_T + s_{T \leftarrow M}M_t - c_{T \leftarrow M}(M_t - M_{t-1})/M_t) \tag{7.23}$$

The interpretation of the parameters is straightforward: r_M is the growth rate of M, K_M its carrying capacity, $s_{M \leftarrow T}$ the parameter for the support that M gets from T and $c_{M \leftarrow T}$ the parameter for the competition that M experiences from T (see Figures 8.4–8.6 in Chapter 8 for examples). Note that the competition is a function not of the absolute increase or decrease in T, but of the relative increase, that is of $\Delta M/M$. One could as well argue that the competition is a function of the absolute increase, then skip the M_t divisor. I shall describe the simultaneous support and competition model at length in Chapter 8, where it will be used as a major component in a model of long-term development.

How to build your own house

Chapters 4 to 7 have been devoted to explaining basic building blocks for dynamic systems models of development and growth. We have seen that despite their simple appearance, the building-block equations could create stunning and unexpected patterns. The ecological principle requires that such building blocks be connected in models which do justice to the manifold interactions and reciprocities that shape and explain the course of development. In this chapter, I have reviewed the general principles of how growers should be connected into networks. I discussed very simple networks consisting of two growers. It seemed as if even simple networks could explain local developmental phenomena, such as a single stepwise increase, or a performance regression preceding a jump towards a higher level.

So far, however, I have not explained how to build a model for a more complex developmental process, for instance, of cognitive development between birth and adulthood. How should we proceed, given empirical data on the developmental trajectories and at least some theoretical assumptions about the underlying mechanisms? Can we build our own houses, or should this be left to the contractor, that is, the expert model builder whose thoughts and actions are virtually inaccessible to all those who are immersed in the data and the problems of empirical research? It is my firm belief that building models is not really difficult, certainly not more difficult than doing your own statistics, given the wealth of relatively friendly computer programs now available. In the tutorials presented so far, I have guided the reader step by step and tried to explain how you can build your own small models. As far as building the big models is concerned, I do not believe there is a general strategy, at least not one that can be explained concisely enough to fit the scope of this book. Instead, I have opted for a case story, namely the building of a model of Kurt Fischer's tiers and levels of development in the form of a hierarchic network of growers. This is what Chapter 8 will discuss.

Notes

1. Well, this puts me into a sort of logical entanglement, since by the time this line will be read, the book will have been finished and then the line should have been in the past tense, which however is wrong at the time of writing. I used to be fascinated by these sorts of unsolvable puzzles.
2. Or decreases, if the value of $\Sigma(G_t)$ is negative, which is the case when the negative effects are bigger than the positive ones.
3. Recall that in this model every grower is at the same time a *dependent grower* (dependent on the values of all the other ones) as an independent grower (contributing to determining the value of the growers to which it is connected); the model is thus fundamentally different from a classic dependent/independent variable model.
4. Note, however, that the take-over probably applies to this particular domain only, namely explicitly stated, highly cognitively laden moral dilemmas. The person who thinks on the basis of universal principles here may be very authoritative and punishment-oriented as soon as the problem concerns a criminal act of which he or she is the victim: 'a conservative is a liberal who has been mugged'.

8

Building a model: a case history

The first steps

A day at the farm

In the summer of 1989, Kurt Fischer was teaching a course somewhere in South Germany. He suggested he might stop at my house to discuss an article of mine on dynamic growth models in cognitive and language development (see van Geert, 1991). When I told my neighbours – hardworking, traditional Dutch farmers, very nice people – they almost fainted. South Germany was the end of the world for them, and just the idea that somebody from the United States could say that he was in the neighbourhood anyway and was going to make a detour via The Netherlands made them shiver with awe. They were truly impressed by this demonstration of international scientific cooperation, although they were in general more impressed by the fact that I grew good vegetables. Kurt arrived and we spent a day at my house. Nothing had changed since it was a working farm, so we first made the obligatory walk in the vegetable garden, visited the horse stables and admired the lanes and trees of the old and rural part of The Netherlands where I live. Kurt spent the night in the sheep shed, which, I hasten to say, had long since been adapted to cater to the needs of our species and no longer serves those of the genus *Ovis*.

The next day we had a most interesting discussion. Each of us explained the other more than a single person could swallow in a week. By the time Kurt left, we both felt that we had much more to learn and understand from each other's work, although we were convinced there was enough commonality to make eventual cooperation worthwhile. At that time I was head of the large Psychology department of Groningen University (it is amazing how many psychologists there are in The Netherlands; I still wonder what they are all doing to make a decent living) and for the next two years I was busy organizing and managing things that probably would have organized and managed themselves if I had not been around. About two years later I heard the wonderful news that Kurt had planned a group on Modeling and Measuring Development at the Center for Advanced Study in the Behavioral Sciences at

Stanford, and that my name was on the list. After I had fulfilled my duties, my university sent me on a long and well-deserved vacation to California.

Our working group at the Center consisted finally of Kurt, Robbie Case who was professor of education at Stanford University at that time and me. Every Wednesday afternoon, Robbie would climb up to the Mount Olympus of the Center and after they got me off the volleyball court – not without considerable pressure, usually – we would discuss modelling development, scribbling on the blackboard and filling it with the humps, the jumps and the bumps we thought characteristic of development.

In the course of that year, we managed to build a dynamic growth model of Kurt's theory of skill development (when I say *we*, I should add that Kurt did the hard and tedious work). In addition, Robbie worked on a model of his central conceptual structure and the task domains associated with it. The growth of these models during the year, especially of the complicated Fischer model, provides a good case history of model building and I hope that telling how the model came about may throw more light on the process of dynamic model building than formal instruction would do. I shall first discuss some basic aspects: what Fischer's theory says, how we decided on basic building blocks of the model and what kind of empirical data were available. I shall then describe the steps we took towards the construction of the dynamic growth model, which, at the time this book was finished, was still in the process of further elaboration.

Fischer's model of skill development: some basic principles

The Fischer model of skill development is a combination of flavours from very different origins. First, it is obviously a structural theory with a firm deductive basis. This puts it clearly in the tradition of Piaget. When Kurt's theory is given a label in the literature, it is almost invariably called neo–Piagetian. Second, it is concerned with growth and learning, that is, with the quantitative-temporal aspects of development. Transitions from one 'stage' to another are seen as growth spurts. Thus the qualitative changes are clearly correlated with quantitative leaps. Third, it sees a person's developmental level as a context-dependent property. A person can be at different developmental levels at the same time, because the levels make sense only in the context of actual thinking or acting. The second and third aspects place the theory more in the perspective of learning theory and behaviourism, which were the theories Fischer worked with at the beginning of his scientific career. Fourth, it places a strong emphasis on the dynamic aspects of development. This is clear from the contextual aspect of, for instance, cognition, defining cognitive level as an interplay between the person's capacities and the context in which those capacities become manifest. But it is also present in the concept of skills, which are structures of elements interacting in accordance with the principles governing dynamic systems. Finally, the theory tries to relate major changes in behaviour and the underlying control systems to changes in brain capacity and brain growth. The relation is believed to be reciprocal, not from brain to behaviour alone.

The key to the structural part of the theory is the notion of coordination into a higher order structure. Take a representation. At the lowest level, we use it in the form of a *single representation*, for instance, a child's representation of his or her dad. Given several representations, you can try to coordinate them in the form of a relationship. For instance, you can pretend that one doll is Dad and the other doll is Mom and you let them act out some event. A relation between two representations (or any other unit, for that matter) is called a mapping and this is also the name of the second level of development. Once you understand these mappings, you can coordinate two mappings in a representational system. For instance, you understand that your dad, who owns a pet shop, is also a salesman and a shop owner and he sells a goldfish to the mother of your best friend Nancy, so you know that Nancy's mother is a customer. Finally, you can coordinate mappings, that is, relate them to one another in a structure called an abstraction. Abstractions are qualitatively different from representations, but are built out of them. They are, so to speak, fourth-order representations, since the single representation was a first order, the mapping a second order and the system a third order representation. For instance, you have obtained an abstract and generalized notion of a father role, or the role of a shop owner. The whole process will now repeat with abstractions instead of representations as building blocks.

Representations and abstractions are called tiers, that is, they are basic types of behaviour control systems that are qualitatively different from one another. The basic control system at birth is the reflex. Reflexes get coordinated in the way I described for representations. The fourth-order coordination transforms the reflex into a control system of a different nature, the sensorimotor system. Four coordinations further the sensorimotor has turned into the representational system, which in turn shifts towards the abstract tier. The whole structure of tiers and levels[1] – which are the steps of coordination – looks very deductive and almost algebraic (Figure 8.1).

Over the years, Fischer and his collaborators have gathered ample evidence for the assumption that the qualitative changes (the leaps from one level to another) take place in the form of growth spurts. These spurts take place in a relatively narrow age range. The spurt is of course indicated by a quantitative measurement, which usually amounts to a score on a test aiming at a particular level, for instance the level of mappings of representations. An ordinary test, however, will not show the spurt at all, but will demonstrate a pattern of monotonic and gradual growth. Only a test that captures the child's highest performance level will be able to reveal the increase in rate that characterizes a growth spurt. This type of test requires that the child is supported, given information and presented with the right type of prompt. In Chapter 1, I explained that both growth levels, one measured with an ordinary test and the other under practice and support, are both real properties of the child's skill level.

There is something peculiar with the growth spurt, however. Figure 8.2 shows the growth curves for arithmetic understanding (under supportive testing conditions). They resemble an S-shape only very roughly (note that the first part of the S is missing for the level 7 data). The curves seem to consist of an S-shape built from smaller S-shapes that are added on top of one another. In fact, each of the curves is the result of repetitive growth spurts. Each time a new level emerges, the preceding level receives extra input from the successor. It sets into a new spurt and stabilizes at a higher level,

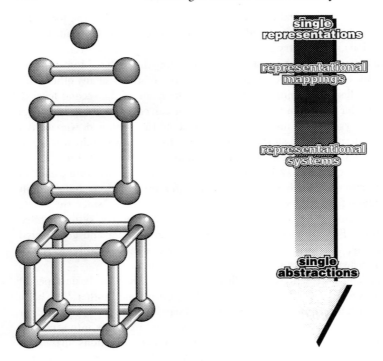

Figure 8.1 A spatial representation of the structure of the four levels in each tier: a level is built out of 'atoms', which form 0-, 1-, 2- and 3-dimensional structures.

until a second new level emerges, which makes it increase again and so on. This growth pattern is indicative of the connected and coordinated nature of the levels. Finally, the growth curves are showing not only spurts and plateaux, but also real regressions, performance dips. This is quite clear from the level 7 data, for instance, but it can also be found in data on reflective judgement (Figure 8.3).

In summary, Fischer's theory of dynamic skill development combines a qualitative structural view, offering clear-cut definitions of the components and elements to be discerned, with a quantitative growth pattern that is varied and complicated in an interesting way.

Foundations for model building

The structural nature of the model and the definition of 'growers'

The starting point of a dynamic growth model should be a set of theoretically and empirically justified assumptions about the mechanisms underlying the development

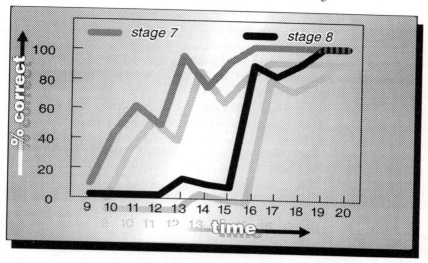

Figure 8.2 The growth curves of arithmetic understanding at levels 7 and 8: an alternating pattern of increases and decreases constitutes a global step-wise process.

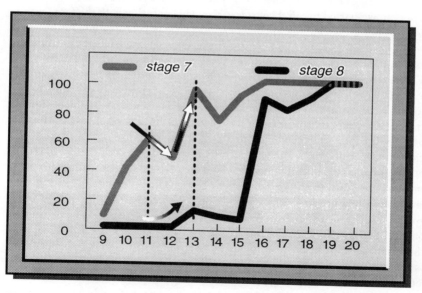

Figure 8.3 The relationship between growth in two succeeding levels follows a pattern of positively and negatively correlated switches in growth direction (increases and decreases).

empirically studied. In practice however (and this also happened in the project that Kurt Fischer and I undertook), some theoretical problems remain unanswered or at best partially answered by the time the computer generates the first curves. This is an acceptable procedure as long as the model building and the theoretical reflection maintain a sort of dialectical tension and one continues to inspire the other.

A basic weakness of the growth model is that it cannot explain the dynamics behind the qualitative emergence of new levels. Why does a coordination of reflex systems lead to a structure that we recognize as a sensorimotor action? There is no way for the dynamic growth model we have explored in this book to answer those questions. In fact, we have to take the qualitative distinctions for granted. The only thing we may hope to model is the time of their onset and the form of their growth curve.

A great advantage of a structural theory is that it enables the model builder to determine easily what the growers of the model will be. Recall that a grower is any component in the model to which a growth equation applies. Fischer's theory makes a distinction between potential growers at different levels of generality. The most general distinction is that between tiers: reflexes, actions, representations and abstractions. In principle, it is possible to specify a dynamic growth model for these four basic control systems. They form the highest level of aggregation in the model (and to avoid confusion with yet another meaning of level, let me call them *aggregations*, instead of levels of aggregation or levels of generality). The next aggregation is what Fischer calls *levels* (later on, we started to call them *stages*, to avoid confusion with the term *quantitative level*). They are a combination of a tier and a level of coordination, for instance, the level of abstract mappings. There are thirteen such levels and they define the growers in a model that is one aggregation level below an eventual growth model of tiers. The next aggregation is that of general task domains, such as arithmetic knowledge or reflective judgement. It is further subdivided in different tasks or tests. Below – or I should say next to – the aggregation of the task level is the aggregation of support context. In a sense, support context is a dimension that cuts through the other aggregations because it applies independently to all other aggregations.

Fischer and I decided to take the empirically measured variables as the growers in the model we wanted to build. These variables were performance measures of tasks in different domains (arithmetic, reflective judgement), administered under either 'spontaneous' or 'practice and support' conditions. We never asked ourselves whether the growers we discerned were 'real' in the sense that they were the real independent components of cognition. The reason is that there are no such things as independent units that can be separated from one another by an absolute distinction. In biology, you can distinguish units in the form of species and use the criterion of reproductive isolation, but not in the domain of psychology. What we define as a unit is determined by the choice of an aggregation level and by the distinctions that can be justified there. The identification of a grower is a matter of justifiable theoretical definition, empirical data and common sense. I believe that we can choose for many different levels of aggregation or description and build a model either at the level of tiers or at the level of highly specific tasks and still uncover the same basic dynamics and the same basic principles of change.

Empirical data and theoretical time series

A dynamic growth model generates a time series for an eventual individual subject, not a group. The parameter values it uses are properties of a single person. The data that Kurt Fischer and I used, however, are based on cross-sectional research designs. We had no individual data that span the total age range of 25 years. There is very little hope that such data will ever become available. Moreover, it is plausible that a longitudinal study of the kind of developments we were interested in is impossible in principle. It is likely that the procedure used in the longitudinal data collection itself, testing under help and support conditions, considerably affects the course of the growth pattern it is supposed to measure. This is no major disadvantage from the point of view of a dynamic theory, since such a theory would incorporate the testing itself as one of the beneficial factors. It is devastating, however, as far as generalization of the data over the untested population is concerned. I have said earlier in this book that generalization over a population is not the first concern for developmental psychology. What we should seek is generalization over time, that is, over how mechanisms operate, not necessarily what in a majority of cases they produce. I am afraid I have not been able to convince my working partner of this view, but I have not tried particularly hard either.

How can cross-sectional group data be used in building a model that seeks to reconstruct the mechanism of change as it applies to individual cases? First, the group data provide a reasonable idea of developmental successions: What comes first, what follows what? Second, they can be treated as constraints on possible individual patterns. For instance, if the data show a dip followed by a leap, it is highly likely that a dip will occur in individual data, although its magnitude may show considerable differences. Finally, the variance for each measurement point indicates how much individual variation we can expect at different ages.

I must admit that, in the course of our discussions, Kurt and I never really bothered about the fact we were using group instead of longitudinal data. In the Queteletian spirit, we simply took the group curve as a typical individual curve that we would try to model. Once a reasonable model had been worked out, we could start varying the parameters and study their effect on the form of the curve. The theoretically produced variation could then ideally be checked against the data, for instance in a comparison between the theoretical variation and the corresponding empirical variance.

What do the available group data mean in terms of a person's potential growth level? The data were of two different kinds. The first type consisted of percentages of tasks passed in an age group. For instance, subjects were presented with two different reflective judgement tasks. Their answers were scored on the 'single abstractions' pass level. That is, if the subjects used single abstractions in their explanations they received a score '1' on the criterion *single abstractions*. The maximum score of a subject was 2, because there were two problems. The sum of scores over the group – say 12, out of a maximum of 2 for each of 10 subjects – would then amount to a percentage score of 60 per cent (12/20). We assumed that the group score could be taken as an indication of the knowledge or skill level of our imaginary subject. Our imaginary subject, we reasoned, would have a probability of 60 per cent to answer a reflective judgement problem at the single abstractions level. Whatever the knowledge or competence of our subject might be like, it would be represented by this probability. In Chapter 3, I introduced the notion of a pass level dimension. It was considered an abstract measure, concatenating all possible control variables affecting a person's answer to a reflective judgement problem. The score of 60 per cent means that from the collection of all possible problems in all possible combinations of control variables, the subject would answer 60 per cent correctly. Of course, we do not really know at the moment whether this inference from group data to potential individual characteristics is justified. At present, however, it is about the only thing we can do, since there are no individual time series data available. The second sort of growth curve that we used was based on a mean score. Raters gave stage or level scores to the responses of the subjects. For instance, in the reflective judgement study they estimated the skill level demonstrated in each of the questions asked by the experimenter. The levels were added over questions, problems and subjects and resulted in a sort of Guttman-scale score for each age group in the study. This score represents the highest level that can reliably be attributed to the subject. The attribution of levels is completely defined by the available scales and tests. For instance, if a score of 75 per cent correct on a level 7 task is defined as a a a reliable indication of the subject's correct understanding of level 7 rules and principles, then level 7 is what the subject is.

What we did more or less implicitly here, using a group score as an approximation of potential individual scores, is common practice in developmental psychology, or psychology in general for that matter. The problem is, however, that we have no justification for the belief that a sequence of average scores over age ranges resembles a succession of scores in a potential single subject. Subjects could very well show very different magnitudes of oscillations over time. We have seen that sudden transitions in individuals add up to a smooth S-shaped growth curve. Averaged chaotic oscillations would very closely resemble a stable state. But, since the group curves are all we have, there is no other choice than to use them, even if there is a chance they might be quite misleading. As my grandfather, who even you will recall managed to build wooden shoes out of concrete, would have said, 'If there's no concrete to build with, use wood and if there's no wood, find yourself some tobacco to chew on'.

The characteristic data pattern and the dynamic building block

Combined support and competition

One of the first steps in setting up a dynamics model of development is to form an idea of what is characteristic in the data. Which characteristic pattern should be the focus, or rather the starting point, of the model building? Since my Belgian culinary background still colours my imagination, I sometimes feel that the decision about what is characteristic in the data amounts to deciding whether a glass of beer is half full or half empty. Which of these two descriptions is true of the actual glass of beer depends on what has happened before you observe it. If the glass has been with the drinking customer, then it is already half empty. If it is still in the hands of the bartender, you had better say it is still only half full. Especially if we look at developmental data, we should take the time course into account and try to understand what happens at a given moment in the context of what preceded it and of what follows.

Nevertheless, the theoretical expectation often determines what is viewed as characteristic in the data. It is customary, for instance, to see a developmental curve as the distorted representation of a linear and monotonic trend towards a steady-state level. The fluctuations along the way are consequently attributed to error variance. Alternatively, the data can be seen as a set of sudden jumps to a new qualitative overall level and invoke the notion of *décalage* to explain away, in a sense, evidence for smoother and more gradual change. One of the great advantages of a dynamic model is that the theoretical study of dynamic interaction patterns, for instance of connected logistic or transitory growers, reveals a rich collection of different growth and change patterns. When attempting to come up with a model for an empirical curve, we not only have all these different patterns in mind, but also know the dynamics and parameter values that characteristically produce them. It is the combination of the empirical fluctuations on the one hand and on the other the model we expect to operate in the data domain in question, that guides our intuition in determining what the characteristic pattern in the data will be.

At the beginning of our cooperation at the Center, Kurt and I started from different backgrounds that, we knew, had to be reconciled for us to build successful models. Kurt was familiar with structural theory and the data, knew how they had been acquired and put together and knew how they related to one another in the many domains he and his collaborators have been studying over the years. I was acquainted with the particular brand of model building I had developed, with its possibilities but also with its lacunae and problems. We both believed in the importance of explaining growth curves and in the ecological framework of resource-dependent growers that either competed with or supported one another to different extents.

We believed that the basic pattern in the data was a combination of support and competition between different levels (or 'stages'). If you take a closer look at the first half of the growth curves in Figure 8.3, you will notice that the curve for level 7 goes up first, then down, then up again. Its decrease precedes the first increase of its successor, the level 8 grower. Then, as level 8 increases more and more, level 7, the predecessor goes up again. Although the idea grew along with the later model-building efforts, we soon agreed on the following basic pattern. Although the predecessor (level 7) is clearly conditional for the emergence of the successor (level 8), the predecessor also profits from the growth in the successor. For instance, understanding the relationship between addition and subtraction will, in general, improve your understanding of addition and subtraction separately, and therefore have a positive effect on the level 7 test score, which measured these separate understandings. But then there was something else we had to cope with, the persistent and consistent dip in the predecessor curve announcing a leap in the successor.

If you have two growth curves of growers that you know are in some way connected or related to one another and both curves go up, then there is reason to expect a supportive relationship from one to another. If one goes up while the other goes down, there must be a competitive relationship, for instance, when both feed on the same basic resource such as time and the time spent in mastering one skill is, by definition, subtracted from the time you could have spent in mastering the other. The problem was that the empirical curves showed both increase and decrease, that is, both competition and support. If competition and support are added, they behave like the result of two opposing forces, or like the sum of a negative and a positive number, the result of which is, trivially, either negative (competition), positive (support) or zero (neutral).

Previously, I had worked on models in which the competitive or supportive effect was not related to the actual growth level of the supporter or competitor, but to its increase or decrease per time unit (see van Geert, 1991). For instance, a parent may adjust his or her amount of help to a child, not to the actual competence level that the child has achieved, but rather in relation to how much the child has learned or improved over a past period of time. I figured that this model could solve our problem. We assumed that the previous level, say understanding of addition or subtraction separately, profited from the degree of understanding at the next level, that is, of how addition and subtraction relate. But the discovery of how addition and subtraction relate to one another requires time and attention and probably also a reorganization of the knowledge about addition and subtraction separately. Time, attention and reorganization of knowledge are related not to the actual level of knowledge acquired, but to the *increase* in the knowledge, that is, to the effort and time invested in the actual learning or mastering. We started with the simple assumption that the negative effect of level 8 knowledge on the preceding level 7 knowledge was proportional to the amount of increase in level 8 knowledge. The positive effect of level 8 on level 7, on the other hand, should be proportional to the actual growth level of level 8. Remember that I discussed this model in Chapter 7, but at the time we were struggling with this problem that chapter had still to be written.

The logistic growth equation for a grower L_n at a developmental level n, is defined as a function of three parameters: its own preceding growth level, a positive parameter operating on the growth level of a succeeding grower L_{n+1} and a negative parameter operating on the increase or decrease of the succeeding grower. If the grower is level 7, for instance, it would depend on level 8, level 8 would depend on level 9 and so forth. This sort of chainwise connection between growers became our standard model for hierarchically connected growers, that is, of connections between growers at different levels of complexity or cognitive hierarchy. We employed the following growth equation for a connected grower:

$$L_{n(t+1)} = L_{n(t)}(1 + r_n - r_n L_{n(t)}/K_n + sup\, L_{n+1(t)} - comp(L_{n+1(t)} - L_{n+1(t-1)}))\ (8.1)$$

Recall that there is a second form of growth, which specifies a much sharper transition pattern. We started the model building with this equation which we called the 'ordinary' version. Some time later, when I had worked out the transition version of the growth equation, I explained its logic to Kurt and showed the different growth patterns it generated. At the onset, he was not convinced of the value of the transition version, because he suspected that the ordinary logistic equation already did what I wanted this new model to do, namely make the growth rate dependent on the growth level already achieved. My main justification for this new transition model was that I assumed there existed a class of growers whose actual growth depended on what I called 'learning encounters', that is, actual encounters with a context that enables the child to learn. I claimed that the probability of running into such a learning encounter was a function of the growth level already achieved. Imagine a child of three who understands only very little about conservation. The child will encounter a lot of conservation events – playing with water or sand and containers, for instance – but most of these events will go unnoticed and will not be detected as potentially problematic. Only very few conservation events are simple and salient enough for the 3-year-old to be detected as potentially problematic and learned from. Thus, even if this child is a fast learner, able to make quick and correct inferences from the information given, he/she would have little chance to practise these learning capacities as long as his/her knowledge about, for instance, conservation, is still very immature. In the transition model, the growth rate function is defined by a parameter and a variable. The parameter is the intrinsic speed of learning and corresponds with the familiar growth rate r; the variable is the probability of encountering a learning experience, which is a function of the growth level attained (relative to the carrying capacity). The equation for the transition version is the following:

$$L_{n(t+1)} = L_{n(t)}(1 + r_n L_{n(t)}/K_n - r_n L_{n(t)}{}^2/K_n{}^2 + sup\, L_{n+1(t)}$$
$$- comp(L_{n+1(t)} - L_{n+1(t-)}))$$
$$(8.2)$$

Fischer and I agreed that the transition version was at least a plausible alternative to the conventional logistic model. We decided to build two parallel versions of our developmental model, one based on the standard logistic, the other on the transition version. We called the transition model the *cubic version* because it contains a cubic term, $L_{n(t)}{}^3$, resulting from multiplying the $L_{n(t)}$ just preceding the brackets with the $L_{n(t)}{}^2$ inside the brackets.

Precursor connections between growers

With equations 8.1 and 8.2, the growers are connected in a way that appears to be opposite to what you would expect intuitively. The equations make the predecessor dependent on the successor for further increase and temporary decrease. Put differently, an earlier level profits from a later one. We thought we had good reasons for this, from both the available data and probable mechanisms. For instance, when you understand the relationship between addition and subtraction (a later level), you are likely to achieve a better understanding of addition and subtraction separately. For instance, you are capable of checking the result of a subtraction by making an inverse addition, and by doing so you may correct or avoid errors.

In a hierarchical model such as Fischer's, however, the most obvious connection between any two growers would be between a predecessor and its successor. For instance, understanding about addition and subtraction separately is a precondition for acquiring an understanding of how they both relate in a more abstract sense. In fact, the whole structure of levels is based on the idea that the predecessor is a necessary building block of the successor. Each successor integrates, in a sense, the structures of its predecessors into a new unit. How can a growth model deal with this integration process? The answer is that, in a qualitative sense, it cannot. The growth model describes only growth levels and changes in them. It cannot account for structural properties other than the quantitative growth levels of the growers it refers to. On the other hand, the growth model can deal with predecessor or prerequisite connections between growers in a relatively simple way.

In a model I had been working on earlier, I had defined a precursor as any grower that prevented the dependent grower from growing, as long as the precursor threshold had not been reached. The understanding of addition and subtraction as separate operations is clearly a precursor to the understanding of how they are related. It is obvious that a child will make hardly any progress in learning to understand how addition and subtraction are related if he or she still lacks a minimal understanding of addition and subtraction as separate operations. In Chapter 7, I discussed the notion of precursor and suggested the term prerequisite to better capture its meaning in terms of a growth model. The prerequisite is the minimal level a grower should have reached in order to release the growth of the dependent grower. If only a little understanding of the addition and subtraction operations is required to get the understanding of their relationship off the ground, the prerequisite level can be set to any low value, for instance 20 per cent of the prerequisite's K or carrying capacity. Higher levels represent stricter prerequisite demands, and we may even demand, if there are any theoretical and empirical reasons to do so, a prerequisite level that is near to carrying capacity.

The simplest way to put a prerequisite relationship into a growth equation is to multiply the growth parameters of the dependent grower by a parameter p that takes the value 0 as long as the prerequisite threshold has not been passed and 1 in the other case. The dependent grower will then stay at its initial level as long as the prerequisite has not reached the minimal level necessary for the emergence of the dependent successor. For instance, to equation 8.1, I add a bimodal variable $prec$, which specifies the prerequisite relationship. This results in the following equation:

$$L_{n(t+1)} = L_{n(t)} + (r_n - r_n L_{n(t)}/K_n + sup\, L_{n+1(t)} - comp(L_{n+1(t)} - L_{n+1(t-1)})) \cdot p_t$$

Quadratic version: if $L_{n-1} > prec$, $p_t = 1 \cdot L_{n(t)}$, otherwise $p_t = 0$

Cubic version: if $L_{n-1} > prec$, $p_t = 1 \cdot L_{n(t)}^2/K$, otherwise $p_t = 0$ (8.3)

By the time we started to write down a simple version of the connected growers model, we discovered that we had to specify whether or not the support and competition were reciprocal. The understanding of the addition and subtraction operations (level 7) profits from the understanding of how they are related abstractly. Thus as soon as level 8 starts off, level 7 increases along with it.

Does the abstract understanding, in turn, profit from the increase in understanding them separately? And, similarly, is the competitive relationship reciprocal, in that an increase in understanding them separately negatively affects the growth of understanding how they are related? This is an example of the sort of question that typically comes up in the context of mathematical model building. While thinking about the equation specifying the growth of the successor, we asked ourselves whether we should make it symmetric to the equation of the predecessor, except that the prerequisite condition cannot apply from the successor to the predecessor. I think that I took an option for the 'aesthetic' solution, that is, for symmetry and argued for a reciprocal support and competition. Kurt and I had, as far as I can recall, no fundamental justifications for why it should be either one solution or the other.

Testing the behaviour of the model

At this point in the development of our model, we wanted to know how a simple version consisting of only two growers would behave, given the conditions of competition and support defined earlier.

Model 8.1 Testing the simple model of connected growers

Define a spreadsheet model with a grower A in the A column, grower B in the C column, and a prerequisite parameter in the D column. For convenience, start with cell $A11$ and use the following equation for the A grower:

$$A10*(1 + \$R\_A - \$R\_A*A10 - \$S(B > A)*C10 + \$C(B > A)*(C10 - C9)) \quad (8.4)$$

Since K is, by default, set to 1, it is omitted from the equation.

Cell C11 is the place for the equation of the B grower, whose prerequisite is the A grower. The equation is:

$$C10 + C10*(\$R\_B - \$R\_B*C10 - \$S(A > B)*A10 + \$C(A > B)*(A10 - A9))*$$
$$D11 \qquad\qquad\qquad (8.5)$$

In cell A10 write 'IN_A' and in C10 'IN_B'. IN_A and IN_B are the initial or starting levels of grower A and B, respectively. Cell D11 should contain the prerequisite formula, which is as follows:

$$@if (A10 < \$prec, 0, 1) \qquad\qquad\qquad (8.6)$$

Then copy A11..D11 to A12..D500 and define a graph that shows the values of the ranges A10..A500 and C10..C500, respectively.

The equations do not make sense unless you define a list of parameter values and names. The list of parameters can be inserted in range F1..F9. Range G1..G9 contains the list of parameter names. The following list shows the parameter names (right-hand side) with three possible sets of parameter values.

value set 1	value set 2	value set 3	parameters
0.2	0.2	0.2	r_a
0.2	0.2	0.2	r_b
2	2	2	c(B > A)
0	0.5	0	c(A > B)
0.1	0.1	0.1	s(B > A)
0	0	0	s(A > B)
0.5	0.5	0.99	prec
0.1	0.1	0.1	in_A
0.001	0.001	0.001	in_B

A parameter name such as c(B > A) means 'the competitive effect of B on A'. Note that I used a different sort of notation earlier, namely c(B → A). Unfortunately, the arrow symbol is not available in the spreadsheet.

Do not forget to define the parameter names for the spreadsheet. When, for instance, cell F1 contains the value 0.2 and G1 contains its name, r_A, define a parameter name 'r_A' whose value can be found in cell F1. Each column of values in the list above should be seen as a set of values that you can try in a single run of the model. Begin with the column at the left.

After having tried the three combinations of values, you may try any arbitrary set you want and see what sort of curves they produce.

The first thing we discovered in our simulations was that with a set of equations like this, we could obtain a growth pattern that was quite close to the empirical data. The magnitude of the dip could be manipulated by augmenting the value of the parameter C(B > A). Figure 8.4 shows the curves resulting from employing the parameters at the left (for the first 120 data points).

We learned at least two unexpected things from numerically testing the model. The first is that if competition and support are reciprocal – that is, if A competes with and supports B and *vice versa* – the trajectory soon becomes unstable. Try the list of values from the middle column, where only the competition has been made reciprocal. The result is an interesting but probably not very realistic chaotic oscillation of one grower around the other (see Figure 8.5). Maybe there are growth phenomena where the growers drag each other into chaos, but the empirical data that Fischer and his group have collected do not appear to show any. Maybe in reality the growth of the successor is indeed negatively influenced by the growth in the predecessor, but if that is the case the influence should be small and almost negligible.

The second unexpected effect we observed was that if we set the prerequisite value close to the carrying capacity level, that is, close to 1, we obtained turbulence in both the prerequisite grower A and the successor grower B (see Figure 8.6). Although there is no evidence for such turbulence in the data, there was no reason for us to discard this particular side-effect of the model. The data are cross-sectional group data and we treated the resulting age curve as a potential or characteristic individual growth curve applying to at least a significant number of subjects. But if a real subject showed anything like a turbulence, that is, a period of instability before taking the leap to a

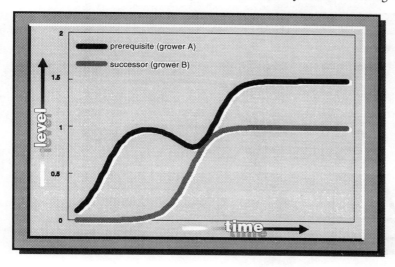

Figure 8.4 The prerequisite (e.g. stage 7 skills) shows a dip before it increases again, due to the increase in the successor (e.g. level 8 skills) by which the prerequisite is supported.

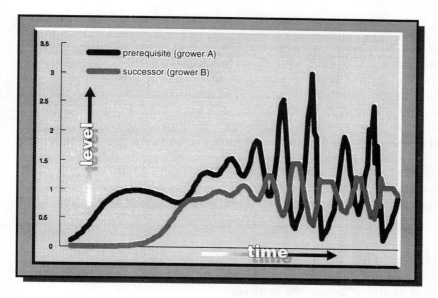

Figure 8.5 A reciprocal and symmetric competition-and-support relationship between a prerequisite and its successor produces instability and chaotic oscillations; in the model, prerequisite-successor relationships should be strongly asymmetric.

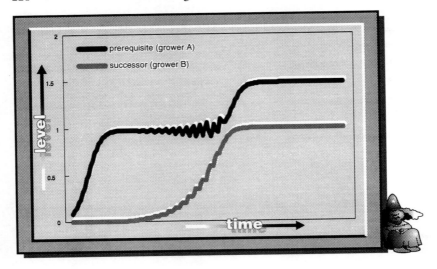

Figure 8.6 Turbulence in the prerequisite grower is caused by setting the prerequisite level of the successor high, for instance, close to the carrying capacity of the prerequisite B.

higher level, that phenomenon would not show up in our group data. In our discussion of conservation development, however, we have seen that instabilities may announce transitions to higher levels. A similar effect might occur in a variety of other areas, including the child's understanding of arithmetic operations that Kurt and I took as our modelling domain.

Another thing we found while experimenting with the simple model was that it would explode or crash if the parameters went beyond particular threshold values. Too much support or competition would result in unmanageable chaos. Crashes can sometimes be avoided by putting a constraint on the results computed in each cell, by preventing each cell from becoming smaller than an arbitrarily small number, which functions as the minimal growth level of the grower described in that cell.[2]

Building the model

The first model of connected growers

Even in a monastic place like the Center for Advanced Study, worldly duties keep knocking on your door and they often prevent you from reaching the spiritual heights that you dreamt of when you were packing your luggage. The usual writing obligations and overdue papers competed fiercely with the model-building work for the one resource that we thought would be abundantly available: time. So, after having worked on the basic model we did not make much progress for some time. That period might have functioned as a sort of incubation time, since the model building progressed rapidly once we actually got to the computer and started writing the sets of equations. The whole process was in a sense an illustration of S-shaped growth in the model builders themselves, if not of a transition.

One of our first working models had six different growers connected in the way described by the basic model. Each grower was conceived as a specific level in Kurt's structural model, applied to a specific domain of application. The first grower, for instance, could be the level of sensorimotor actions on collections of objects, the second would then be the level of sensorimotor mappings, the third that of sensorimotor systems and so on. Each grower (that is, each level in Kurt's model) would have its immediate predecessor as its prerequisite. For instance, we would set the prerequisite for the emergence of the second level to 50 per cent of the carrying capacity of the first. That is, once the first level had reached a score equal to 50 per cent of its carrying capacity, the second, dependent level was allowed to start growing. We did this for each set of successive growers in the row.

If you build a model of connected growers, there is a problem with the initial state. The initial state in the spreadsheet model is the value of the first cell of each column that represents a grower. In reality, it is the state of knowledge or mastery of each grower at the time you have chosen as the starting point for your modelling. Assume you take, for instance, *sensorimotor actions* as your starting point and want to continue up to the highest level, *principles*. At the age the child is coping with the problems of sensorimotor actions, the level of principles is still a non-existent realm. Technically, the initial state of principles at the age of sensorimotor actions should be equal to zero. Recall however that a grower with an initial state of zero will always remain zero. I had been confronted with this initial state problem before and I suggested the following solution. The initial state of each successor could be artificially set to one-tenth of the initial state of its predecessor. This low value, in addition to the prerequisite, would account for the spacing of the growth onset times.

Not only the initial state levels had to be decided on at the beginning, but also the carrying capacity levels of each grower. The default carrying capacity is set to 1 and this is what we used in the first model; each level of the developmental scale had the same equilibrium level, 1. This choice produced an undesirable result. We wanted each level to make a new leap when its more advanced successor emerged. Since the levels were connected in a chain of overlapping support relations, a level would make a leap each time a new level emerged, irrespective of whether it was directly connected with that new level or not. The model did what we wanted, but it did so in a very rigorous way. For instance, in the model the emergence of the level of principles, at the age of approximately 24 years, had a considerable effect on the mastery of sensorimotor actions, which develop around the age of 4 months. That such an effect occurs in reality is highly implausible. What we actually wanted was that the pay-off of every new and more advanced level for some earlier skill decreased as the distance to the newly emerging skill increased. Maybe the discovery of principles has some effect on sensorimotor actions in young adults, but if so, that effect must be very small and practically unobservable. The effect of emerging sensorimotor mappings on sensorimotor actions, on the other hand, is assumed to be considerable.

We solved this problem more or less by chance. We figured that it was not a good principle after all to set the carrying capacity of each grower to 1. The level of problem-solving complexity we can achieve with, for instance, abstractions, is considerably higher than the level we can achieve with single representations. This, we reasoned, should be reflected in the carrying capacities; lower levels should be given lower Ks. It can be doubted, however, whether this reasoning is correct. Each different grower operates on a different and independent scale, even if we put them together in one graph. Numbers on each of the grower scales have a meaning only in terms of that scale and what matters is how the numbers change, not their absolute level. If that reasoning is correct, we can attach any possible carrying capacity level to each grower and account for its relations with other growers in terms of the parameter settings. Anyway, we gave the growers carrying capacities that corresponded with their ordering in the model – later ones got higher Ks. By so doing, we obtained the result that we wanted, a decreasing pay-off of later growers on earlier ones. The emergence of principles did something to increase sensorimotor action levels, but that something was imperceptibly small.

It is easy to show by analytical means why this increasing pay-off effect occurs in the case of connected grower models. The effect of a grower E on an initial grower A, for instance, is equal to:

$$(K_A \cdot K_B \cdot K_C \cdot K_D) \cdot L_E \qquad\qquad (8.7)$$

and if the Ks are smaller than 1, that effect is only a fraction of the effect E has on its immediate predecessor D, namely:

$$K_D \cdot L_E > (K_A \cdot K_B \cdot K_C \cdot K_D) \cdot L_E \qquad\qquad (8.8)$$

As is often the case with model building, the analytical proof came after the more or less accidental discovery of the principle.

It turned out that there was a second way to avoid the problem of long-lasting effects of late growers on the earliest ones. This was again discovered by accident. Since we believed that the so-called cubic version of the model, the one I presented in Chapter 5, provided a good if not better alternative to the ordinary logistic one, we built a cubic version of the model of connected growers. One of the interesting side-effects of that model was that it greatly flattened the effect of later growers on much earlier ones. The sixth grower in the sequence had a considerable effect on the fifth, but only a very minor one on the first, for instance. This is an interesting example of the way in which dynamic models display a variety of emergent properties and effects that have not explicitly been built into the equations. The reason for adopting the cubic model was theoretical. As an unintended side-effect, it got rid of the undesirable late growth in the earliest growers.

Figure 8.7 shows the growth curve for a model of six connected growers, with different initial states, prerequisite relationships and carrying capacities of increasing magnitude.

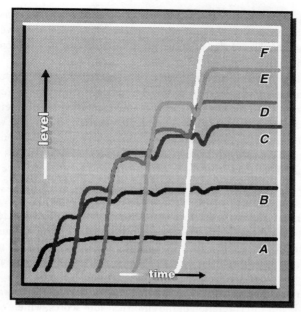

Figure 8.7 A model of six hierarchically connected growers: the overall pattern is one of step-wise increase, with temporary dips in prerequisite growers corresponding with a leap in the successor.

Within and between level growth

By this time Kurt and I were happy with the result of our model building. We had not made any attempts so far to fit the model to the actual empirical curves. What we had achieved, we thought, was a model that fitted the essential qualitative properties of the data. The growers would increase in a stepwise fashion, leaps towards a higher level would be preceded by regressions, the interval between any two successive growers would increase and the effect of later growers on earlier ones would decrease with distance between the growers. Kurt started to build a few models that accounted for connections between and also within levels.

A level, for instance, the level of single abstractions, is not some monolithic cognitive structure. Each level comprises a variety of different tasks, skills or task domains. For instance, the child's abstract understanding of arithmetic operations is different for the various operations – addition, subtraction, multiplication and division. The operations vary in difficulty and they are seldom if ever acquired at the same time, with the same speed or at the same level of mastery. Each of the arithmetic operations can be conceived of as a separate grower. This made the structure of the connections more complicated. For instance, the child's understanding of addition at the level of single abstractions would be connected to his later understanding of how addition and subtraction relate, in terms of an abstract mapping. We had modelled this connection in terms of simultaneous competition and support. But inside the level of single abstractions, the child's knowledge of addition would no doubt be connected with his knowledge of subtraction.

In the model of these within and between level connections, we employed the same connection principles for the within as for the between level links. For instance, addition would profit from the acquired level of understanding in subtraction, but be hampered by the actual increase of subtraction understanding. The result was a model that behaved pretty much like the previous one, in which we modelled only between level connections and considered the separate overall developmental levels as growers. This result supported our belief that the model produced a good qualitative fit with the data, irrespective of the level of aggregation of growers we chose.

Since some of the empirical data were based on a sort of sum scores of tasks on different developmental levels, Kurt wanted to know if the sum of growth levels would show the characteristic dips and jumps of the empirical data. For each simulated point in time, he summed the available levels. The result was a stepwise growth process, but there were no dips. Whenever the dips occurred, they were compensated by the increase of a higher level grower that actually caused the dips. We were quite concerned about this problem, although we would later find out the error was not in the model but rather in our interpretation of the empirical sum scores, which were not real sums but rather maximal levels. Nevertheless, this problem made us look out for several different solutions that would produce temporary fallbacks that would not be cancelled out by correlated increases in another grower.

Bumps or dips?

Meanwhile Robbie Case, with whom we met every week to discuss model building, had been working on his model of growth in a central conceptual structure. That structure was related with several task domains that grew independently of one another, although each grower affected each other one, via its contribution to the central conceptual structure. Robbie wanted the supportive effect of a grower on another one limited to the period of actual growth. He could have done this by making the support a function of the increase in the supporter, much as Kurt and I had done with competition. But Robbie chose a different solution. He multiplied the supporter's level, $L_{S(t)}$ by the unutilized capacity for growth in that supporter, namely:

$$L_{S(t)} \cdot (K_S - L_{S(t)})/K_S \tag{8.9}$$

This is consistent with the way in which growth is kept within limits by the logistic model, by multiplying the growth level by the unutilized capacity for growth, $(K - L)/K$. It is easy to see that as $L_{S(t)}$ approaches its carrying capacity K_S the value of the fraction $(K_S - L_{S(t)})/K_S$ approaches zero which then reduces the effect of $L_{S(t)}$ to zero. The effect is that sometimes the supported grower temporarily overshoots its carrying capacity. This overshooting lasts only as long as the supporting grower goes on growing. Whether or when this overshooting occurs is a function of initial state and

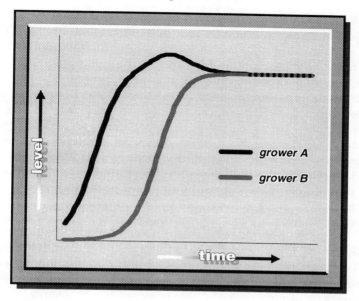

Figure 8.8 Support from a grower B during the growth period results in a 'bump' on the supported grower A.

parameter values, but the bump is a genuine effect of the dynamic principle from equation 8.9 (see Figure 8.8).

With the Case model in mind, the idea arose that what we had conceived of as a regression, introducing a leap towards a higher level, was not a regression in the sense of a dip, but a bump, a temporary overshoot above carrying capacity level, levelling off to carrying capacity as soon as the supporting grower ceased to increase.

In the hierarchical model that we had developed so far, we had made a distinction between growers on different levels (such as single representations and representational mappings) and growers at the same level (e.g. a single-representation understanding of addition and one of subtraction). We assumed, as Robbie Case did in his model of central conceptual structures, that growers within a level support each other only for the time they actually grow. Once they achieve their equilibrium level, the mutual support dies out.

It seems rather arbitrary to make a distinction between within and between level support, in that the between level support continues even after the growth of supporter and supported have stopped. The justification for this distinction, however, lies in the relationship between carrying capacity and supportive factors. Earlier I explained that if L is a grower and L_S is a grower supporting L, the carrying capacity of an L is $K \cdot (r + s \cdot L_S)/r$, for K the carrying capacity parameter (usually 1), r the growth rate, L_S the level of the supporting grower, and (lower case) s a parameter specifying the extent to which L_S actually supports L.

The difference between a supporter that goes on supporting and one that ceases to do so as soon as its growth has come to a standstill is that the first supporter contributes to the carrying capacity of the supported grower, but the second does not. It is plausible to assume that the emergence of a new form of understanding or a new skill level, for instance the discovery of the principle of representational mappings, contributes to the carrying capacity of the existing skills and understanding. This higher developmental level is a new source of information and understanding and will contribute to further mastery and understanding of the lower levels. That is, it enables those to rise to a level higher than the one they would have achieved without the new knowledge. Compare this with the relationship between different task domains at the same level. Opening a new task domain, where the same principles reign as in the task domains already explored and mastered, might certainly have a temporary positive effect on the already existing tasks of that same developmental level. But it will not have a lasting effect, since it adds nothing significantly new to the understanding at that level.

What happens if equation 8.9, causing the temporary bump, is built into the equations of hierarchically connected growers? It will produce a temporary overshoot of the carrying capacity of growers within the same developmental level. Growers within a level were identified as 'tasks', for instance as the task 'addition' and the task 'subtraction'. The overshoot occurs during the growth process itself. It will then regress to the normal carrying capacity level. Later, a grower at a higher level will emerge and will cause the earlier grower to increase its level. The whole pattern, from growth to overshoot to carrying capacity then to growth again, looks like a temporary regression or dip, announcing a leap. In the latter case, the dip will occur while the higher developmental level grows. When the two effects are added, the dip is cancelled out. The temporary overshoot, however, occurs in general before the jump (they are at least independent of one another). Thus if the level scores are added, the pseudo-regression is not cancelled out by the leap (Figure 8.9).

Compensating for changing carrying capacity

Recall that there are two meanings of the term 'carrying capacity' in the model. The first is the fixed carrying capacity parameter, usually set to 1, that figures as the K parameter in the logistic equation (and is left out if its value is 1). It would be more correct to call it the carrying capacity parameter, instead of just carrying capacity. The second meaning of carrying capacity is the equilibrium level of the grower. This equilibrium level is an expression of the resources available to promote and sustain growth in a growth environment. In the simple logistic equation, the equilibrium level is equal to the carrying capacity parameter (usually set to 1). In a connected growth model, however, growth is affected by additional variables, for instance a supporting grower, L_S:

$$K \cdot (r + s \cdot L_{S(t)})/r = K_t \tag{8.10a}$$

Since the only variable in the equation is the supporting grower L_S, the variation in the

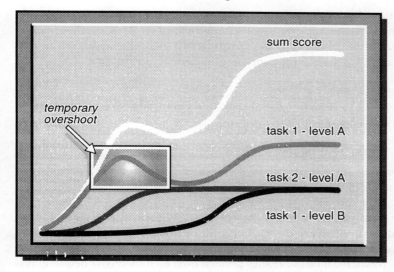

sum score

temporary
overshoot

task 1 - level A

task 2 - level A

task 1 - level B

Figure 8.9 A regression in the sum score of three tasks is caused by a temporary overshoot in one of the tasks.

equilibrium level is entirely determined by that variable. In our model, there was not just a single L_S and a support parameter s, but a sum of levels multiplied by support or competition parameters:

$$K \cdot (r + \underline{a \cdot L_{A(t)} + b \cdot L_{B(t)} - c \cdot L_{C(t)} + \ldots - \ldots + s \cdot L_{S(t)} + \ldots})/ r = K_t \qquad (8.10b)$$

It is much more convenient to write the underlined part of equation 8.10b in the form of a single variable, namely S_t. Thus, S_t is a compound variable consisting of the sum of all supporting and competing growth levels multiplied by their own support or competition parameter.

When I thought about these two meanings of carrying capacity, I realized that we were making a mistake using equation 8.9, which subtracted the growth level from K_S, then divided by K, $(K_S - L_S)/K_S$. If L_S's asymptote is equal to K_S, the value of the equation will approach zero, as we originally expected. We should have realized, however, that almost any variable in the connected growers model exceeds the level of its K_S parameter because of the effect of supporting growers. Thus as soon as L_S grows higher than its K_S parameter value (by default 1), it would turn the value of equation 8.9 into a negative variable. Its effect would no longer be to stop the growth of the grower that it modifies, but to make that grower go down and eventually disappear.

There is absolutely no reason to suspect that any grower would have a negative effect on another one as soon as it grew bigger than some predetermined carrying capacity value.[3] The solution to this problem is actually fairly simple; instead of using the value of the K parameter, we should use the value of the K variable, that is, the real carrying capacity. The carrying capacity variable is determined by the K parameter on the one hand and by the values of the supporting (or competing) variables on the other hand. Thus we changed equation 8.9 (the equation that confined the supportive relationship to the time span while the supporter was actually growing) by substituting the variable carrying capacity $K_{S(t)}$ for the constant carrying capacity parameter K_S:

$$L_{S(t)} \cdot (K_{S(t)} - L_{S(t)})/K_{S(t)} \tag{8.11}$$

The value of $K_{S(t)}$ was given by adapting equation 8.10a to the set of growers that in turn support the supporter L_S:

$$K_S \cdot (r_S + S_{S(t)})/r_S = K_{S(t)} \tag{8.12}$$

for K_S the carrying capacity parameter of supporter L_S, r_S the growth parameter of L_S, $S_{S(t)}$ the compound variable consisting of all the supporting and competing effects on L_S and $K_{S(t)}$ the carrying capacity variable at time t of the supporting grower L_S.

For some sets of parameter values, the curves would grow wild at the end of the trajectory and eventually make the whole system collapse. This happened primarily with the curves tracing the growth of the earliest levels. They were the levels whose magnitude increased the most, since they profited from each successive new level that emerged. The problems we have had with the behaviour of equation 8.9, especially the fact it related to an absolute carrying capacity, made me wonder whether the danger of an eventual collapse could not be countered by employing relative instead of absolute magnitudes. The idea is that it is not so much the absolute magnitude of a grower that determines to what extent it affects another grower, but its magnitude relative to its maximum. An easy way to introduce such a maximum value into the equation for connected growers is to work with the growth levels divided by the corresponding carrying capacities and not by the mere growth levels. Assume that we write the equation for a connected grower in an extremely simplified form, namely:

$$L_{t+1} = L_t \cdot p_t \tag{8.13}$$

p_t is a name for the function that we would put within the brackets in the complete form of the equation for connected growers. As L_t grows higher and higher, the effect of any constant parameters in p_t will increase accordingly and eventually drag the system into a chaotic oscillation. Instead of using the absolute value of L_t, we should use its value relative to its variable carrying capacity, K_t. Equations 8.10a and b specify the magnitude of that variable. Instead of the absolute form of equation 8.13, we should therefore work with relative magnitudes:

$$L_{t+1} = L_t/K_t \cdot p_t \tag{8.14}$$

Although each of the steps described here seems logical once it has been explained, it took Kurt and me a lot of trial and error before we arrived at these solutions. I am afraid that we did just try the model and experiment with it to see what it did. When you find out that it does funny things you did not anticipate, but that nevertheless resemble your empirical data or expectations, you are happy with the result. If something unwanted happens, you try to correct it by going over the equation and trying to understand what might have gone wrong. Of course, you should try to arrive at an analytical understanding of what the equation does irrespective of whether the results are anticipated or not, or wanted or not. But during the process of model building itself, often the excitement takes over. The pleasure of doing some sort of combination between a computer game and handicrafts often stands in the way of applying the rational analytical methods.

Finally, with all the elements ready, it is time to present our 'master' equation that we used to model the entire system of connected growers in development.

The equation for hierarchically connected growth

In an earlier stage of the work, Kurt and I had decided we would specify the model at the aggregation level of tasks. They constitute stronger psychological units than the levels or 'stages', which are more like abstract categorizations of task-specific skills. The minimal number of tasks per level we needed in order to make the structure of relations meaningful is two. In reality each level contains a multitude of tasks of very different kinds (social tasks, numeric tasks, emotional understanding, motor tasks and so forth). The strength of the relationship between any pair of tasks in such a set varies greatly, dependent on the nature of the tasks related. Some tasks bear significantly stronger relationships to one another, especially those that have a common general structure, or that can be integrated in an overarching structure at a higher developmental level. An example is the task addition and the task subtraction; the operations are logical inversions and they combine into a higher level structure. The most interesting connections between growers, therefore, exist between strongly related ones. Two such growers suffice to test the dynamics. We called them Task1 and Task2 and specified them on ten different levels. Just for terminological convenience, we called these levels stages and numbered them StA, StB and so forth (see Figure 8.10).

The Fischer developmental model counts thirteen developmental levels, which we now called stages to avoid confusion with the term growth level, divided into four different major tiers. We decided to exclude the first one, the reflex tier, from the model and confine ourselves to the ten levels that begin with the single sensorimotor action level. The tasks we had in mind when we built the model were things like reflective judgement or arithmetic operations. We felt that the developments at the reflex level would relate to those tasks only in a very weak way (although they would be indispensible as developmental prerequisites). Discarding them would make the resulting model a little bit more manageable.

In summary, the model we finally built consisted of two related tasks over ten successive developmental levels. Each task at each level was considered a separate grower, so that we had a model of twenty connected growers.

For each of the twenty growers we wrote a specific growth equation. The basis of that equation was the logistic form. We wanted to alternate between the ordinary (squared) version of the equation and the cubic form (the sharp transitional form) and used a *cubic parameter* to do this. In addition, we had to specify a *precursor parameter* that would cause the grower to change as soon as the precursor level of the prerequisite

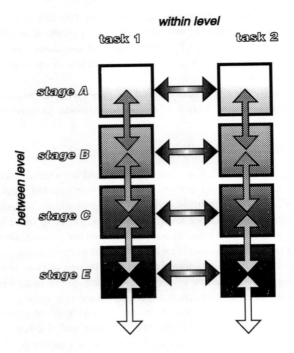

Figure 8.10 The structure of between- and within level relationships in the model of hierarchically connected growth.

grower was reached. The growth rate variable that caused the change in a grower was a combination of its own growth rate and of a set of influences from the other connected growers, which we called *joint factors*. Joint factors were based on two sources. The first are the influences from the grower at the next higher level – that is the between level factors. The second come from the grower at the same developmental level. They are the within level factors. Finally, we wanted all these growth factors to modify not the absolute magnitude of a grower, but the magnitude relative to the carrying capacity variable.

Instead of giving the usual equation with symbols, I shall present it in the form of the concept and variable names involved:[4]

Level now = Level_before + Precursor_value · (Level_before/
carrying_capacity) · (cubic_set_off_parameter · (growth_rate · Level_before/
carrying_capacity − growth_rate · (Level_before/carrying_capacity) ^2 +[5]
Joint_factors)

rate = *any number in normal growth rate range*

Joint_factors = joint_factor_rate_parameter · (Within_factors +

Between_factors)

 joint_factor_rate_parameter = *any number modifying the effect of within and between factors*

Within_factors = support_within_stage_parameter · level_of_supporter ·
(1 − level_of_supporter/carrying_capacity_variable_of_supporter)
− competition_within_stage_parameter · change_of_supporter

 support_within_stage_parameter = *any number*

 competition_within_stage_parameter = *any number*

 carrying_capacity_of_supporter = carrying_capacity_parameter_of_
supporter · (1 + level_of_supporter_of_supporter/
growth_rate_of_ supporter)

 change_of_supporting_task = Level_before_of_supporting_task − Level_
before_(level_before)_of_supporting task

 supporter_of_supporter = *grower supported*

Between_factors = between_stage_support_parameter ·
level_of_next_higher_level_of_task −
between_stage_competition_parameter ·
change_of_next_higher_level_of_task

 between_stage_support_parameter = *any number*

Precursor_value = 1 *if* level_of_prerequisite_grower >
precursor_parameter and Sum (all_preceding_precursor_values) >
precursor_set_on_parameter

  in all other cases precursor_value = 0

 precursor_parameter = *any number in growth range of prerequisite grower*
 precursor_set_on_parameter = *any number specifying a number of
times the value of the* prerequisite_grower > precursor_parameter (*if*
precursor_set_on_parameter = 1, the precursor_value = 1 *when the*
prerequisite_grower *has crossed the* precursor_parameter *once*)

cubic_set_off_parameter = 1 *if* cubic_parameter = 1
cubic_set_off_parameter = carrying_capacity/level_before
  if cubic_parameter = 0

 cubic_parameter = *0 or 1*

carrying_capacity = carrying_capacity_parameter · (growth_rate +
joint_factors)/growth_rate

 carrying_capacity_parameter = *any number, default = 1*

Finally, we experimented with several models. One consisted of seven levels (or stages) and two growers at each level, another combined ten levels and two growers. The most complicated model thus far contains five different growers per level.

Patterns of connected growth

The ultimate goal of model building is to obtain a good quantitative fit with the data, based on a theoretically justified model. Our data had the disadvantage of being group data, instead of the individual time series that a dynamic growth model ideally requires. Nevertheless, the group data enabled us to extract a number of qualitative properties which with sufficient plausibility also applied to eventual individual growth patterns. Those were the properties we hoped our model would simulate.

The first and most important of those properties is the stagewise character of growth. Fischer's data suggested stages in the form of separate skills that grow and change in a loosely connected way. A stage is introduced by a massive growth spurt in all the growers. Although time delays exist between the spurts, there is a clearly observable distinction between periods in which the spurts occur and periods of relative stability. On average, the periods of stability become longer as the (cognitive) complexity of the developing control systems increases. The simulated growth curves show this particular stage pattern very clearly. The pattern of spurts and plateaux is a bit fuzzy, though, in that growers within a stage are not strictly synchronized. Sometimes the spurts occur at about the same time; sometimes there is a marked delay. The overall image is one of a succession of periods where spurts and changes dominate and periods where the majority of the growers remain more or less stable. This fuzzy image of stages and spurts corresponds with the current view on stages as loose collections of separate skills or growers instead of the tight structures of the Piagetian universe (see Figure 8.11).

A second important property of the data is the stepwise growth pattern of the individual growers. Each time a new grower emerges at a higher developmental level, the existing growers receive a boost in the form of a new growth spurt. As the distance between a new grower and the benefiting grower increases, the support effect decreases. This property is salient in the simulated growth curves; each individual curve takes the form of a stair, the steps of which decrease in size as the distance from the growth onset time increases.

A third characteristic property is the performance dip that occurs after a spurt. In the model, those dips are caused by within-stage support on the one hand and between-stage competition on the other.

In summary, the model of connected growers shows the characteristic patterns that appeared in the empirical data and that are supported by theoretical considerations. Furthermore, the model allows for a large variety of patterns within this general stage scheme, dependent on the exact parameter values. Finally, the model shows that dynamic processes of connected growth occur only within (broad) parameter constraints. Once such constraints are violated they turn into 'pathological' deviations, in that they become unstable, show wild fluctuations or simply collapse. One of the

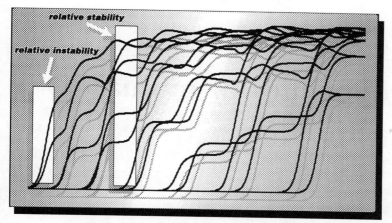

Figure 8.11 A model of two growers and seven different levels displays basic properties of stage-wise development: stepwise growth in each individual grower, and an alternation of periods of relative rest (horizontal growth levels) and periods of rapid change.

advantages of this type of model building is that it allows for a form of experimental theoretical psychology. That is, you can experiment with parameter values and various dynamic relationships and investigate the effects on the resulting growth patterns. Such numeric experiments may serve as a heuristic means to achieve a better understanding of the conditions and forms of quantitative aspects of development.

Notes

1. I realize that the use of the word *level* can lead to some confusion here. I usually refer to the *growth level* of a grower, for instance the grower 'use of single representations'. In Fischer's theory, however, *level* means a stage in a *tier*. For instance, the *representational tier* has a *level of single representations*, that is, a stage where the child works with single representations.
2. Did you notice I left the B column blank in Model 8.1? You can now use that column to define a minimal growth level.
3. Unless, of course, that predetermined value is an optimum. I discussed optimum models earlier and presented the example of self-esteem. If self-esteem grows far beyond an optimum value, its effect may become harmful and negative instead of supportive.
4. Kurt Fischer used the new Lotus-Improv program to build the model. It is based on the usual spreadsheet logic but works with equations that look more like verbal descriptions than the symbol strings you would get with Lotus 1-2-3. The actual form of the equation used in his program was quite similar to the one presented here.
5. The circumflex symbol ˆ means 'to the power of'; ˆ2 therefore means 'to the second power'.

9

The dynamics of mutual interaction

Development as a social process

The game of growth

When you are appointed a Professor at the University of Groningen you are also solemnly installed as a member of the University's Senate, which, in addition to being very old and dignified, is unfortunately a completely useless and obsolete administrative body whose only function is to install members and keep them busy until it is time to proceed to the next part of the festivities, the new Professor's inaugural Public Lecture. In times when the University was paid for by the hardworking town and country folk and a new Professor was appointed, the public had the right to see for themselves whether or not the new man was worth their money. Knowing the Groninger people a bit better by now, I can imagine this must have been a serious test in former days, particularly as far as the financial investment was concerned. Traditionally, the Public Lecture was a display of the new Professor's learnedness and erudition. Since it was meant for the public, however, it had to be accessible to and understandable by what was broadly referred to as the interested layman. Nowadays, the Public Lecture is a gathering of colleagues, family, friends and children, eagerly waiting for the moment the lecture is concluded by a solemn phrase, which is also the sign for a massive run to the place where the reception is held.

I decided that I would take the requirement of accessibility seriously and based my lecture on the metaphor of a popular board game. I explained to my audience that developmental processes were hardly predictable and hardly guidable because, in a sense, they take care of themselves. Development, I said, is like one of those traditional Dutch board games that combines the luck of dice with insight and strategy. The course of the game is a metaphor for the developmental process. The players are, for instance, a child and a parent. Both players try to win; that is, they try to achieve their personal and temporary goals, which are usually short-term, since neither has a real long-term overview of the future.

The parents, being adult and experienced, may think they have set their long-term plans with their children, but they will soon find that they have to readjust them

242

continuously because the game of development is likely to take a course they had not really foreseen. The metaphor represented development as a process governed by short-term goals and plans. They are acted out by players who are on the one hand autonomous and free to choose their own path and on the other hand dependent on the other player; they need to adjust their actions to what the other player has done. Despite the short-term structure, though, the long-term effect of the developmental game is stable in that it almost always leads to a mature, cultivated and educated being, even if it is impossible to tell how exactly the maturity, cultivation and education will take shape. The metaphor combined two important aspects, that of chance on the one hand, and that of co-construction or co-regulation on the other. In the first part of this chapter, I shall present a short overview of the idea of interaction dynamics between people. The rest of the chapter is devoted to three models: an elementary mutual interaction model, a model in which the carrying capacity is managed and, finally, a dynamic systems interpretation of Vygotsky's model of the Zone of Proximal Development.

Development as co-construction

If one looks at development in a longer time frame, that of successive generations, and a bigger spatial frame, that of social structure instead of the individual, development becomes the process in which culture is transmitted and transformed. The mature members are bearers of their culture. They know how to act within their cultural institutions; they possess skills and knowledge developed over the course of cultural history, such as reading and writing and scientific knowledge. There is a lot of division of labour in the way individuals carry their culture to new generations, but as a whole, culture reproduces and changes itself in the process of generational succession. A newborn child has virtually no culture at all. It is an empty vessel, as far as culture is concerned, that has to be filled. The metaphor of pouring the contents of a full vessel into an empty one is an obvious choice to describe the process of cultural transmission. If you want to continue that metaphor, you could say that the empty vessel has got only a little hole in it through which culture can be poured and so it takes quite a long time, on average, to fill it.

The vessel metaphor, though probably not aesthetically pleasing, corresponds with a standard view in sociology, anthropology and psychology of how culture is transmitted. Valsiner (1991) called this the 'unidirectional view': cultural information carries cultural messages one way, from the outside world into individuals. The unidirectional view is incompatible with the fact that development is a process of construction by the developing person itself. Basic concepts and skills are constructed by the person, given the information and guidance of the environment. A cultural message, sent in some encoded form or another to a child, is by necessity decoded and recoded by that child as a function of the codes and understanding that child has already developed. The recoded message is again decoded and recoded by the mature, cultivated person who then replies in the form of another message. Valsiner (1991) calls this a bidirectional process of cultural transmission.

Valsiner (1991), and several others, such as Barbara Rogoff and Alan Fogel, use the term 'co-construction' to refer to a process that has both the aspect of construction and the aspect of communality. The constructing environment and the constructing child act as a higher order unit.

A floating cat (or: the dynamics of co-regulation)

A couple of summers ago I drove from the Grand Canyon to Salt Lake City, Utah, to pay a visit to the Fogel family and to discuss the peculiarities of dynamic systems models with Alan Fogel. We spent a considerable amount of time in the Fogel swimming pool, in a company consisting of our wives, Brian Hopkins – whom we had accidentally met in the weirdest desert places and whose interest lies in early motor development – and finally the Fogel family cat who used to join the swimming party floating on an airbed. How can you get a cat on an airbed, floating on the lukewarm water of a swimming pool? The answer is by a process that Alan Fogel calls *co-regulation* and that is central to development. We had no definite plans to get the cat on the inflatable mattress at first, but the animal showed some interest for the people swimming. I guess Alan slowly pushed the airbed towards the rim of the pool, and out of typical feline curiosity, the cat approached. Alan pushed the bed a little nearer, meanwhile addressing the animal in the sort of voice cats find irresistible. And since the airbed's surface was dry and warm and formed a sort of extension of the ground, the cat jumped, and found itself soon in the middle of the pool. In his recent book *Developing Through Relationships* (Fogel, 1993), Alan Fogel defines co-regulation as a process that '. . . occurs whenever individuals' joint actions blend together to achieve a unique and mutually created set of social actions' (p. 6). Alan sees it as a basic process in the creation of communication, self and culture.

Children are not taught or instructed in the form of unidirectional input processes. The instructional activities take place within consensual frames, that is, within co-regulated consensual agreements about the scope and topic of the communicative process they are engaged in. Co-regulation leads to new patterns of action and communication via self-organization; there is no causal primacy, as Fogel calls it, neither in the parent, nor in the child. The self-organizing follows the principles of dynamic systems, which converge onto attractor states. There is no preliminary plan for the attractor state. The state just emerges from the way the components interact. I have given many examples of how different attractor states emerge from similar mechanisms, provided some of the control parameters have different critical values. The same holds for the emergence of developmental patterns.

Alan Fogel's own research focuses on the way early parent–infant co-regulated action plays a role in the emergence of 'elementary' and allegedly culture-free acquisitions such as grasping or posture control. By studying videotaped interactions in great detail, we can show how patterns such as holding a baby in our arms, or feeding a baby, come about by the same process that later on creates a social self and higher cognitive skills (Fogel, 1992; 1993).

Although co-regulation is a prime example of the working of a dynamic system, the system of mother–infant cultural environment, for instance, there is at present no way in which we can model the emergence of the qualitative patterns of communication, action and skills (Fogel, 1993). The dynamic systems models I presented in this book describe only macroscopic, quantitatve aspects of development; they cannot explain the emergence of a pattern of grasping, for instance, or a child's understanding of object properties. What I intend to do, however, is to show that even those macroscopic quantitative aspects of the co-regulation process are worth studying. They can reveal at least some of the general properties of those processes, for instance, how and why they converge towards their attractor states.

A simple dynamic model of co-construction and co-regulation

Co-construction and co-regulation are good examples of iterative dynamic processes. To illustrate the nature of the dynamics, I shall take a behaviour protocol from one of Piaget's famous investigations of formal thinking.

In one of his experiments, Piaget gave his subjects four similar flasks containing colourless and odourless liquids. There was no way to tell the difference perceptually, so each of the containers bore a number, 1 to 4. He then added a bottle with a different chemical substance, g, and a dropper. The subjects were shown that adding a drop of that substance to a particular combination from the four flasks produced a yellow colour. They did not know the secret combination that produced the colour, and had to find out for themselves, by making all possible combinations of the four liquids. One of the protocols, with a 7-year-old subject, shows the following interaction:

R (the child) tries $4 + g$, then $2 + g$ and $3 + g$
R: I think I did everything, I tried them all.
E (experimenter): What else could you have done?
R: I don't know.
E gives him the glasses again.
R repeats the sequence of adding drops.
E: You took each bottle separately, what else could you have done?
R: Take two bottles at the same time.
R tries $1 + 4 + g$, $2 + 3 + g$, thus failing to cross over between the two sets of bottles, for example $1 + 2 + g$, $1 + 3 + g$, etc.
When E suggests that he add others R puts $1 + g$ in the glass already containing $2 + 3$ which results in the appearance of the color.
E: Try to make the color again.
R: Do I put in two or three? R tries $2 + 4 + g$, then adds 3, then tries it with $1 + 4 + 2 + g$
R: No, I don't remember any more. (Inhelder and Piaget, 1958, p. 111)

The experimenter could have told the subject how to make a full combinatorial diagram given four elements, 1, 2, 3, 4, $1 + 2$, $1 + 3$, $1 + 4$, $2 + 3$, $2 + 4$, $3 + 4$, $1 + 2 + 3$, $1 + 2 + 4$, $1 + 3 + 4$, $2 + 3 + 4$, $1 + 2 + 3$, $1 + 2 + 3 + 4$. That would not have made much difference, since the 7-year-old would not have understood the logic behind that series anyway. The only way to tell him how to do it right would probably invoke a sort of learning and teaching sequence very similar to the one in the

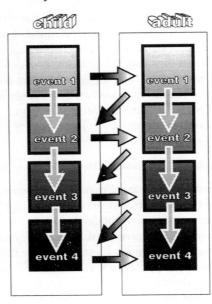

Figure 9.1 A communicative process takes the form of vertically and horizontally connected events; the vertical axis represents time, the horizontal axis the relationship between the contributors (e.g. a pupil and a teacher).

example. Assume that every action or communication by one of the interacting partners is a single event. We number them, beginning with R's first attempt and explanation and divide them over a column for R's actions and statements and one for E's. How would each of the events relate to one another? Each event is directly related to two others. The first is its own predecessor. For instance, if E suggests R to add other glasses, that suggestion takes the earlier suggestion into account. The new suggestion, for instance, is a little more explicit, or it extends the possibilities suggested in the previous suggestion. The second event to which it is related is the preceding action from the child. The child makes a highly specific combination of liquids and the experimenter tries to make clear that more combinations should be tried. If I represent a conditional link between two events by an arrow and an event by a block, the structure of the interaction could take the form represented in Figure 9.1.

It probably does not require too much imagination to view the entire communicative event as a couple of connected iterative processes. The iterator at the left-hand side is the child; the iterator at the right-hand side is the adult. In the dynamic models I described earlier, we knew exactly what the nature of the iterator was: a growth equation of some particular type. In this case we do not know exactly what the child's or adult's mind is doing, but we do know that they take their previous output and the output of the other party as their input and produce an output, which can then be taken as input again and so forth for as long as their communication lasts.

Formally, a model of co-construction or co-regulation processes does not differ from the models of connected growers. The challenge, however, is to find a form for the iterator, that is, the equation that specifies exactly what each of the partners is doing in the communicative process. When I say exactly, however, I do not mean completely. We have not the faintest idea of all the thoughts, processes and activities that go on in the child's and adult's minds when they are involved in a communicative process like the one described above. What we should do, therefore, is to isolate one relevant factor from the stream of internal events, then try to specify how that factor behaves and changes over the successive events.

Since we are primarily interested in the process of developmental growth and learning, we should take the growth level of a skill or cognitive principle in the child as our relevant factor. For instance, in the example from Piaget's research protocols, we could simply pretend that each action of the child represents a level of understanding of the combinatorial principle. Over the short span of this experimental session, we should not expect too much change in that level to occur, especially since the child still has little knowledge of the relevant principle. But if each event is a teaching session, spread out over a time-scale of, say, a few years, the relevant variable – understanding of the combinatorial principle by the child – might show a significant increase and eventual transient drops. The next question is: What is the relevant factor in the other partner, the adult? Is it the level of formal knowledge of combinatorial principles, since we may expect the adult to understand them fully. In the coming sections, I shall discuss a few different ways of conceptualizing what it is that changes dynamically in the adult partner, provided it is a level of skill or knowledge that changes in the child partner.

The unexpected complexity of a simple mutualist dynamics

A short sketch of an utterly simple and too elementary theory of learning

When you teach, you have a goal in mind that you want a child to reach. That goal is some level of understanding of mastery of a skill. The child has not yet achieved that goal and would probably never achieve it on its own. Teaching amounts to confronting a child with something that is closer to the intended goal than the child's actual level of understanding or mastery. Learning is a way of profiting from that confrontation by decreasing the gap between your current level of mastery and understanding and the goal state. (So far this looks more like an entry for 'Education' in a Martian encyclopedia than a serious explanation of what learning and teaching is, but in the title I promised that what followed would be utterly simple and elementary. Allow me to go on with our utterly simple and too elementary theory of learning.)

It is completely unclear what teaching and learning entail if conceived at the level of specific activities and processes. There seem to be so many forms of teaching and learning that I would not dare to present a generalized account. But whatever they are in particular, in general they amount to a sequence of more or less separate events. The teacher does something, the child does something, the teacher again, the child, etc. Sometimes these events overlap, but that does not seem to be essential to the process.

Let me assume that a child is learning about some property of the world – where babies come from, the meaning of the square root of a number, the different ways of combining four liquids – and a teacher is teaching. The teacher, of course, knows where babies come from and what a square root is. This is the knowledge or the understanding he/she wants to teach the child. Let me represent this goal state of knowledge by the letter K. The child's current knowledge level of that property is the state L. Teaching takes place in the form of encounters where the teacher presents to the child something that relates to K. The encounter may consist of a story, a task, an explanation and so forth. With each discrete cognitive encounter with the intended property K, the child has some experience of K. It is an experience presenting the property in a form close but not similar to the child's current level of understanding of that property. Let us call that experience E.

What determines the nature of E? It is, first, determined by the teacher's choice of how to present K to the child. In the olden days people told their children that babies were brought by the stork and they only gradually worked their way towards revealing the real process. Nowadays parents tell their children that babies grow in their mother's belly. Second, E is determined by the child's own understanding. Even when the parents tell the mummy and belly story, the child makes his or her own interpretation that has probably only very little to do with the biological facts that the adult intended to convey.

The goal K and and current learning state L differ from one another in many respects. In Chapter 1, I introduced the notion of a descriptive space that would contain as many descriptive dimensions as needed to specify the distinction between an initial and a final developmental state. The initial and the final developmental state are two distinct points in that descriptive state. It is trivial, then, that there is some distance line between L and K in that space. Since we do not know exactly which descriptive dimensions are used in the space and what their properties are, we represent this distance in some general abstract form. For instance, we set the initial level for L at some arbitrarily small value and give K the value of 1.

I claimed that the experience E is a sort of local temporary representation of K in a form that the child can grasp. It is based on the child's own understanding and the teacher's estimation of what he/she should do to bring the child closer to the goal K. E has all sorts of varying properties, but it has one formal property we should be interested in, its distance to L and K, respectively. E can be closer to K than L, further from K, or at the same distance from K as L. I assume that learning proceeds as a function of the learning and teaching experiences (at least in this simple model, and probably also in a considerable part of reality). Since learning, in this simple theory, amounts to reducing the distance between L and K, preferably to a zero distance at the end, E must have the function of dragging L somewhat closer to K. It is E, not K, that functions as an attractor point for L, since K is represented in the form of E. Therefore the position of E is crucial.

The verbal description of the model allows us to infer the following set of equations that will describe the changes in the respective distances between L, K and E. The model prescribes that E should be at a small distance from L and ahead of L:

$$E = L + L \cdot d'$$
(9.1)

for d' a parameter that determines how far E is from L. For example, if the experience is a helping instruction from a teacher, and d' is very small, then the help is very close to what the child already knows. If d' is large, then the help is way ahead of the child's current understanding.

The model further claims that as a result of the occurrence of E, L will make a jump towards E. Let us say that this jump is some fraction c of the distance between E and L (if $c = 1$, L bridges the distance between L and E in one jump):

$$\text{jump } (L) = (E - L) \cdot c$$
(9.2)

Recall that d' is a parameter that causes E to move. Since K is the goal state, E should gradually move towards K and if it arrives at K, it should stay there; this is just an alternative way of saying that teaching is a goal-directed activity. In determining the level of the child's next learning experience, the teacher wants to shorten the gap between the previous learning experience and the goal state:

$$(\text{teacher's increase of E}) = (K - E) \cdot d$$
(9.3)

The actual learning experience, however, is a function both of what the teacher does and how the child understands this, given the current knowledge level. The jump in experience level is therefore a function of the teacher's choice and the child's level:

$$\text{jump } (E) = L \cdot (K - E) \cdot d$$
(9.4)

Since the experiences and learning encounters are discrete events, we may write down the relation between L and E in the form of a set of coupled difference equations over time intervals t, $t + 1$, $t + 2$ and so forth. The first is the equation specifying the progress that L will make, given a teaching experience E:

$$L_{t+1} = L_t + \text{jump } (L_t) = L_t \cdot (1 + (E_t - L_t) \cdot c)$$
(9.5)

Now we need a second equation that specifies the level of the next learning experience. Equation 9.1 says it is the sum of the learning level and an increase variable. This increase has been specified in equation 9.4, so that our equation describing the level of the next learning experience is a combination of equations 9.1 and 9.4:

$$E_{t+1} = L_{t+1} \cdot (1 + (K - E_t) \cdot d)$$
(9.6)

Model 9.1 describes the spreadsheet format of this simple model, whose far from simple outcomes we will investigate in the next section.

Model 9.1 A simple learning and teaching model with complex patterns

The model combines two versions of the learning and teaching model. One is the standard version, from equations 9.5 and 9.6, the other is an alternative model based on the idea of a random walk. It will be explained later. Define the following set of range names and values:

value	parameter
9	K
200	in_divisor
0.2145	c
0.18	d
0	rand_L
0	rand_K
0	rand_E

The most important parameters are c and d. The parameters K and In_divisor are used to set the initial state level as a ratio of the goal state.

The A column, starting with cell A10 will contain the values of the L variable, B will contain the values of the E variable, and column C the value of the goal state K, which will vary only if the value of the parameter Rand_K differs from zero. In cell A10, type:

$$+\$K/\$IN\_DIVISOR \qquad (9.7)$$

and in cell B10, type '+ A10'. It is not necessary for the initial E to differ from the initial L.

Cell C10 contains the initial value of K, $K (which remains constant under the non-randomization condition).

Write the equation for L in cell A11. Its first part is the basic equation as explained earlier, the random part is needed if you want to study the effect of a random walk on the growth process:

$$+A10*(1 + (B10 - A10)*\$c) + \$rand\_L*(@rand - @rand)*(C10 - A10) \qquad (9.8)$$

Cell B11 has the equation for the E variable, namely:

$$+A11*(1 + (\$K - B10)*\$d) + \$rand\_E*(@rand - @rand) \qquad (9.9)$$

Note that the random factors take effect only if the value of rand_E is not zero. Finally, cell C11 describes an eventual random walk for the value of K, which occurs only if rand_K is not zero:

$$+C10 + \$rand\_K*(@rand - @rand)*(C10 - A10) \qquad (9.10)$$

Copy the range A11..C11 to A12..c500. Define four graphs. One, Timeseries_1 is a line graph of columns A10..A500 and B10..B500. Timeseries_2 plots only the first 100 steps, namely A10..A110 and B10..B110. The third graph, Phaseplot, is an xy graph. Take the column B100..B500 as its x-axis, and A100..A500 as the y-axis. The first 100 steps are omitted from the phaseplot. The fourth graph can be called K_L_plot. It takes A10..A500 as

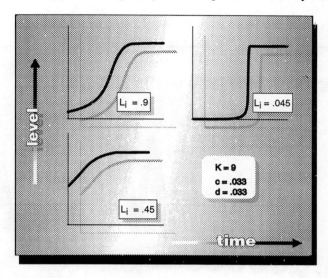

Figure 9.2 Three different curves resulting from low c- and d-values and different initial state values; if the initial state value is very low (in comparison with K), the resulting growth is a sudden jump (note that the time scales are very different for the curves at the left on the one hand, and the curve at the right on the other; the sudden jump requires a much longer time span).

its x-axis and C10..C500 as y-axis and is defined as an xy graph. It is useful for showing the endpoint of the process in terms of both K and L values in the case of the random walk version of the model. You can experiment with values described further in the text.

The complex properties of a mutualist dynamics

If the ratio between K (arbitrarily set at value 9) and the initial level L_i is about one-tenth of K and the growth parameters c and d are low (0.033 for both), a curve results that has the classical ogive or S-form (see Figure 9.2, top left-hand side) that we also found with the standard logistic equation.

With an initial L about 1/200 of the K level the S-curve takes a different slope. We now find a long platform which stays close to the initial level, then a very sharp increase and a rather abrupt levelling-off at the K level (see Figure 9.2, bottom left-hand side). This is the sort of curve found with the transition version of the logistic equation, the cubic equation.

Finally, with an initial learning level about one-half of the K level, we find a curve that resembles classical learning curves. It is important to note that considerable random perturbations imposed on c and d do not change the overall qualitative pattern (e.g. for random variations of $0 < c < 2c$ and $0 < d < 2d$).

The fact that this model produces curves qualitatively similar to the logistic and transition models can be interpreted in different ways. You could argue that, since

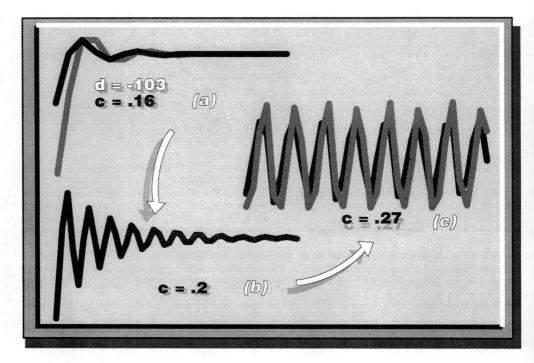

Figure 9.3 With increasing parameter values, the mutualist model evolves from oscillatory to chaotic fluctuations.

those curves are produced by simpler models, the present one should be considered superfluous. On the other hand, you could defend the position that the present model has been based on an elementary theory of teaching and learning and as such forms the dynamic expression of that theory. The finding that an entirely different type of model based on learning and teaching yields the same type of growth curves could be seen as a further justification for the claim that such growth forms are universal and robust, in that they are produced by dynamic models based on different principles.

Given that the mutualist model produces curves similar to the logistic model, we may expect that it should resemble that model also in its oscillatory and chaotic patterns. Experimenting with increasing parameter values for c and d shows the expected resemblance. For instance, with an arbitrarily determined fixed d value of 0.103, increasing c values produce qualitatively different evolutions (see Figure 9.3a). For $c = 0.16$, a mismatch between E and L occurs around K, but it is easily compensated, and E and L quickly settle down at the attractor point K. For $c = 0.23$, the oscillation towards the attractor is more complicated (Figure 9.3b). For convenience, only the iterated points of L have been drawn. They show a pattern of

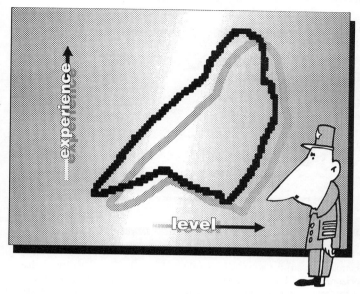

Figure 9.4 State space plot for a chaotic oscillation: the vertical dimension represents the level of experiences, the horizontal dimension the growth level of the knowledge variable whose growth is dependent on those experiences; note that the points are not connected by a time line (a time line connects a point to its successor in time); strangely enough, the state-space representation is highly reminiscent of an important figure in recent French history.

waves of oscillations towards K. For $c = 0.27$, E and L no longer evolve towards K but settle into what seems to be an infinite mutual chase without L and E ever catching each other in an equilibrium state (Figure 9.3c). In psychological developmental terms, this means that for increasing values of c and d a mismatch between learning and experience may emerge resulting in the impossibility of reaching the goal state. Phenomenally this may take the form of oscillations between under- and overgeneralizations of a learned principle or rule, a perpetuating conflict between a parent and an adolescent about which norms to follow and how, the impossibility of finding a solution for a problem and so forth. It is likely, however, that if this were to happen in real life, attempts would be made to relax whatever psychological properties correspond with the c and d parameters.

For still higher values of c and d, the model settles into the infinite oscillation already seen in the previous example. Figure 9.4 represents a state space plot for such chaotic oscillation in the plane consisting of the values of E and L. It is just one of the many possible plots, showing that the chaotic oscillations are not random but have their own intrinsic order.

Earlier I described a technique for showing the number and magnitude of the attractor points of a process for different parameter values. This bifurcation diagram is

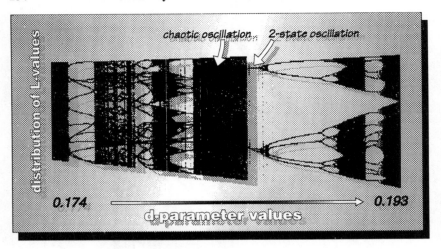

Figure 9.5 A bifurcation diagram for a range of d-values shows the non-linearity of chaos in the model: the horizontal axis shows the range of increasing d-parameter values; the vertical axis specifies the sets of final growth levels that correspond with the d-parameter values; sets of d-values corresponding with heavy, chaotic oscillation alternate with highly regular patterns in a complex, unpredictable fashion.

an alternative way of showing the order underlying the chaos of time series. It is particularly suited for showing the non-linearity of the model; increasing parameter values correspond with increasing chaos, punctuated by highly orderly intermediate states. Figure 9.5 shows a bifurcation diagram for a range of parameter values of d, between 0.174 and 0.193, with a constant value of c, 0.18. Black bands represent chaotic oscillations occurring with the corresponding d values. The chaotic regions, however, jump suddenly towards simplicity, for instance, towards a two-state oscillation. In turn, the simple states gradually evolve towards chaos again.

The simple model described in this section is but one of a large family. A description of the alternative versions and their equations can be found elsewhere (van Geert, 1992a).

Random walks in a mutualist dynamics

The model discussed in the previous section incorporates an extremely simplified but, I hope, basically correct, vision on the nature of a co-construction or co-regulation process. It shows how a learning state in a learner evolves towards a goal state via experiences that are functions both of the goal state and the learning state. If the crucial parameters c and d stay under a threshold value, the process leads to a point attractor, K. If not, chaos sets in. In the 'normal' case, the learning and teaching process reaches its goal state. This somewhat boring conclusion is misleading, though, in that the model shows only the distance between goal and learning state. It is a distance defined over an arbitrarily complex space of variables and properties. In that space, the goal state and the learning state may shift randomly (or systematically) during the process of learning and teaching, for instance, because both learner and teacher redefine their goals. This wandering process of goal and learning state is not shown in the model; it says only that the distance between the two is bridged after a while, but it does not specify to which points in the space the distance measure applies.

In order to introduce the notion of continuous goal and learning state redefinition in the simple, one-dimensional growth model of the mutualist dynamics, we can add a random walk aspect to it. The assumption behind this is that each step in the process of the L, K and E variable is the result of a systematic factor on the one hand and a coincidental factor on the other. The systematic factor is the dynamic model of L and E adaptation described in the previous section. The coincidental factor is simply a random number added to or subtracted from the number computed on the basis of the dynamics. This random number varies between an arbitrarily chosen negative lower and a positive upper boundary. I assume that it should be a function of the distance between the learning and the goal state; the further away the goal state from the learning state, the easier it is to take a deviating road, for the learner as well as for the teacher. This is, of course, just an assumption, but it is based on the idea that a long distance between goal and learning state corresponds with less information for both the learner and the teacher about what the goal state and learning state entail. The equation for the goal state K is as follows:

$$K_{t+1} = K_t + \text{rand} \cdot (K_t - L_t)$$
$$\text{for } -b < \text{rand} < +b \tag{9.11}$$

With values for the rand parameters of 0.1, the process shows an interesting variety of final state points, that is, points where both the wandering K and the wandering L lock each other up into some attractor region. The stable end states line up in a somewhat skewed unimodal distribution (Figure 9.6).

Social interaction and the management of the carrying capacity

Carrying capacity as the educational model

The interactions between more experienced and mature members of a culture and the less experienced, less mature ones can take any of a vast variety of forms. They range from strictly organized, formal teaching and learning practices to highly informal imitative processes where neither the imitator nor the imitated person have any conscious intention to either teach or learn something. In the previous section, I discussed a simple model explaining how educational goal states are achieved in a process of mutual adaptation.

But how does this variety of cultural transmission and appropriation processes relate

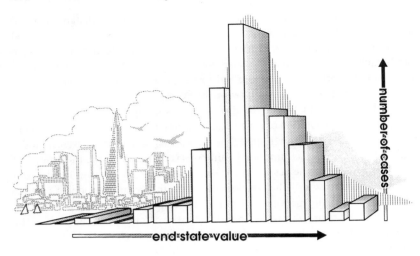

Figure 9.6 The distribution of final states after 200 runs of the random walk mutualist dynamics: the pattern resembles the 'normal' bell shape of the Gaussian distribution of random events (the picture in the background represents the skyline of the city where this simulation was run).

to the logistic growth model? It contains only two parameters, the growth rate and the carrying capacity. The growth rate is more or less confined to the learning person itself and represents an abstract property relating to the person's speed of learning, changing, inferencing, etc. The carrying capacity has been defined as the asymptote of the growth process, or more precisely, as its equilibrium level. A very important step in the construction of the logistic growth model was the assumption that this equilibrium level forms the expression in terms of the growth level of all the resources available to the grower. These resources were of various kinds: spatial, informational, energetic, temporal, etc. They could come from the subject itself, for instance the subject's knowledge or skills that support the learning or achieving of some new knowledge or skill, or from the environment, for instance, the information and help given to a child in the form of instruction and guidance by a more experienced person.

Whatever we call education, teaching or guidance actually amounts to monitoring part of the environmental component of the carrying capacity. For instance, when children are taught addition at school, the curriculum is carefully sequentialized. The teacher begins with elementary concepts and very simple forms of addition. Gradually, the tasks become more complex and the requirements increase, following the increasing competence of the children. It is almost trivial that, if the the teacher did not adapt the level of teaching to the increasing learning level and remained at the low initial level, hardly any learning would take place. If you never taught more than just elementary addition of numbers below ten, most of the children would never get any further than that. That is, their addition growth level would reach an asymptote at the level of skill embodied in this very rudimentary teaching. As a general rule, we may state that the maximal level of learning a child may achieve is proportional to the level embodied in the teaching.

For the sake of simplicity, we set the individual's contribution to the carrying capacity of one of its growers, such as addition, to a constant. The level of that constant will greatly differ between individuals, but that need not concern us here. The environmental part of the carrying capacity will fluctuate and will do so in function of the information, tasks, demands and guidance given by a teacher, a parent or any other mature member of the culture. It is an almost trivial observation that, on average, the level of information, demands, or task complexity increases during an educational or teaching process, or, to put it differently, this is at least the intended course of events. Since that information or demand level is a measure for the carrying capacity at each moment, it follows that an educational process basically amounts to increasing the carrying capacity level. The increase will level-off and come to a standstill as soon as some goal state has been reached. It also stops when the person for whom the educational efforts are meant is no longer making any progress (again, this is the ideal case).

The basic model of carrying capacity increase

We can now write an equation that describes the growth of the carrying capacity level as a function of the increase of mastery in the learner. Let L_t be the learner's level, for instance of addition and K_t the carrying capacity level embodied in the teaching. Assume further that the goal state level of the teaching is set to 1; in practice, the teaching goal could be reaching the end of the handbook, or successfully finishing a curriculum. The equation for the growth of the carrying capacity is:

$$K_{t+1} = K_t \cdot (1 + d \cdot (L_t - L_{t-1}) \cdot (1 - K_t)) \tag{9.12}$$

(the meaning of the parameter d will be explained later).

Since the growth of the learning level is a function of the carrying capacity, the equation for that growth is:

$$L_{t+1} = L_t \cdot (1 + r - r \cdot L_t/K_t) \tag{9.13}$$

In this model, K grows as a function of the absolute increase in the learner's level. We may expect this when the learner's level is measured with some sort of objective scale. An example is addition and other arithmetic operations for that matter, which are described in handbooks and explicitly formulated curricula. But if you deal with less formal skills or forms of knowledge, there is hardly any absolute yardstick. In that particular case, the instructor has probably an idea of the relative increase. A mathematically simple way to describe relative increase in the equation for the growth of K is as follows:

$$K_{t+1} = K_t \cdot (1 + d \cdot (L_t - L_{t-1})/L_t \cdot (1 - K_t)) \tag{9.14}$$

What is the psychological meaning of the parameter d in equation 9.12? Mathematically, it is a parameter that determines to what extent the increase of the learner's level contributes to the increase in the teaching level that embodies K. Some instructors will tend to increase the demands much more than others, given they react to the same increase in a learner's capacity. Some will react to any increase, others only every now and then. The extensive literature on the developmental effects of interactions between parents and babies has produced a concept that applies to this issue, *sensitivity*.

Sensitivity is a property of a parent that relates to the extent to which the parent's reactions to the baby's activities are developmentally adequate, that is, contribute to the child's growth. The concept entails two aspects, namely the adequacy of the reaction and its contingency, the extent to which the reaction is direct and consequent. Apply this, for instance, to teaching arithmetic to a single child. A sensitive instructor will provide an adequate increase of information and demands, in response to the child's learning progress. The instructor will also be consequent, in that any progress in the learner is followed by some adaptation of the teaching level. The parameter d is assumed to specify the instructor's sensitivity, in the broadest sense of that word. In the following spreadsheet model, I shall divide that parameter into a component that corresponds with an ordinary parameter and a component that specifies a probability.

Model 9.2 Increasing the carrying capacity in response to growth

In this model you will have to define the following list of parameters:

value	parameter
0.1	K_in
0.01	L_in
0.7	K_d
0.2	L_R
0.02	d_start
1.1	d_stop
0.02	step
1	K_rand
1	rel_model

K_in is the initial state of the changing carrying capacity K. L_in the initial state of the learning level. K_d is the d parameter in equations 9.12 and 9.14 that modifies the effect of the increase of L on K. L_R is the growth rate of the learning level L. The following three parameters, d_start, d_stop and step are needed in a macro that will simulate an arbitrarily chosen number of runs of the model. K_rand is the parameter that determines the probability that K will actually react to an increase in L. If K_rand is 1, that probability is 100 per cent, if K_rand is, for instance, 0.7, the probability is 70 per cent. The last parameter, rel_model, lets you switch between a model based on equation 9.12 and one based on equation 9.14 (the relative increase model). If rel_model is 1, the chosen model is that from equation 9.14.

In cell A10 write K_in; in cell C10 write L_in. They are the cells containing the initial values for K and L. Cell B10 contains a random parameter determining whether or not K will actually change in a cell. Write the following equation in cell B10 and copy it to B11:

$$@IF @RAND < \$K\_RAND,1,0) \tag{9.15}$$

It says that if a random number, which is different for each cell, is smaller than the value chosen for the parameter K_rand, the value of the corresponding B cell is 1, but 0 in any other case. The function of this cell becomes clear from the formula that goes into cell A11:

$$+ A10 * (1 + B10 * ((C10 - C9)/@if(\$rel\_model = 1,C10,1)) * \$K\_d * (1 - A10)) \tag{9.16}$$

If B10 is zero, there is no growth in K, that is, the value of A11 is the same as that of A10.

The function of the @if statement in the equation is to turn the equation 9.14 model on and off. If the value of the parameter rel_model is 1, (C10 − C9) is divided by C10. That is, the growth of K is affected by the relative increase in the learning level, found in the C column. If the parameter is 0, (C10 − C9) is divided by 1.

The C column contains the equations for the growth level. It is a straightforward logistic equation. Given that you have put L_in in cell C10, cell C11 takes the following equation:

$$+ C10 * (1 + L\_R - L\_R * C10/A10) \tag{9.17}$$

Copy the range A11..C11 to A12..C400.

Remember that the A column contains the values of the carrying capacity. Try some values of K_d and observe the effect on the final state level.

Now it is time to write two simple macros that will allow you to vary the value of K_d systematically and study its effect on the final state value. Go to cell L1 (or any other cell that you prefer) and write the following:

$$\{for \ K\_d,d\_start,d\_stop,step,test\} \tag{9.18}$$

This macro will specify a value for the cell you named K_d. The first value will be the value you have specified in the cell named d_start. It will then perform the action described by the macro 'test', which you will define in a minute. Then it will add the value specified in the cell 'step' to K_d, and again perform 'test'. It will continue to do so until the value that goes in cell K_d is equal to the value you defined in d_stop. Thus d_start is the minimal value of K_d and d_stop is the maximal value of K_d. The number of times the macro 'test' will run is equal to (d_stop − d_start)/(step). Before you go on, you must specify a name for the macro under cell L1. This can be done by defining a range name, a procedure you should now be familiar with. Define the name 'Go' and attach it to the cell L1.

Since spreadsheets differ in their menu structures, it is better to compose the following macro by executing and recording the commands. Recording can be done via a Transcript option contained in the spreadsheet menu. Turn it on, and perform the following actions: Go to K8 (via the GoTo command; F5 in Lotus); press End; press Down twice; copy the Range Value of the cell name K_R_damp to the current cell (the first empty cell under K8); go to J8; press End; press Down twice; calculate (F9 in Lotus and Quattro Pro); copy the Range Value of cell C400 to the current cell (the first empty cell under J8). When you have performed all these actions correctly, you will find a transcript of them in the Transcript window. Copy the description and paste it into cell L10. Define the range name 'test' for cell L10.

In cell K9 type 'Parameter Value', in cell J9 'Final State'. Type an 'x' in cells K8 and J8. For each run, the macro will type the corresponding parameter value of K_d in column K and the final state value associated with that value in column J. It will add new values at the end of the column of values. In order to run the macro, hit Tools/Macro/Run from the main menu.

You can graph the results of the repeated runs by assigning the column of parameter values (column K) to the x-axis and the column of final state values to the y-axis.

You can also assess the effect of randomly distributed K growth. Recall that if K_rand is equal to 1, K responds to the increasing growth of L in every cell. That is, the growth of K is completely contingent on the growth of L. If K_rand is smaller than L, say 0.5, K remains constant in every cell for which the value of a random number is smaller than K_rand. In order to study the effect of a random increase pattern, you need to define a macro that repeats the calculation of K and L with different columns of random numbers. Go to cell L40 (provided you chose column L as your macro column) and define cell L40 with the range name 'loop'. The macro Loop consists of the following actions which can be recorded and pasted into cell L40 via the Transcript command: Go to K8; End; Down twice; copy the range value of cell K_d to the current cell (the first empty cell under K8); go to J8; End; Down twice; calculate (F9); copy the range value of cell C400 to the current cell (the first empty cell under J8). Copy the set of instructions from the Transcript window and paste it into L40. At the end of this set of copied instructions add the string:

$$\{\text{loop}\} \tag{9.19}$$

The macro will add the value of K_d to the K column, then calculate the value of the resulting end state and copy that to the end of the L column. It will then repeat itself and continue to do so until you hit Ctrl-Break to stop the loop.

The qualitative behaviour of a K grower

If you run the program from Model 9.2 with a few different parameter values of K_d, the K adaptation parameter, you will have noticed a characteristic property of the model. The carrying capacity as well as the dependent growth level evolves towards a stable level that can be anywhere between the initial state level of K and the maximal level of K, which is 1. The smaller K_d, the closer the equilibrium level is to the initial level of K, that is, the less growth in L. This is very different from the effect of a low growth rate on the growth level. With a low growth rate, it takes a longer time to reach the equilibrium level, but the asymptote of that level is always the maximal value of K. With a low adaptation rate of K, the system settles into an equilibrium state that can be much lower than the maximum. Figure 9.7 shows the distribution of final state values for a K_d parameter ranging between 0.02 and 1.42. The increase in the values is an S-shaped function of the linear increase in K_d. This means, among other things, that any increase in K_d is more effective in the middle range of K_d values than in the extremes.

A second characteristic property of the present dynamics is what happens if the random parameter affects the growth of K. With K_rand set to 0.5, the probability for K to change in reaction to a change in L is 50 per cent for each step of the computation (that is, for each cell). With K_d = 0.7 and K_rand = 0.5, I obtained a distribution of end states that differs rather considerably from a normal bell-shaped distribution

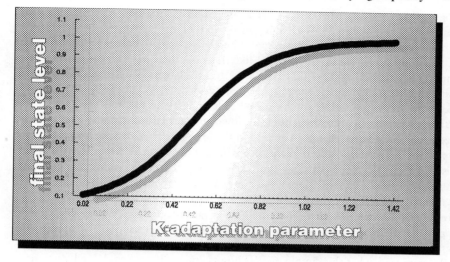

Figure 9.7 The final state values differ with different K_d values: the final states corresponding with the set of linearly increasing K-adaptation parameters follow an S-shaped pattern (note the difference with the ordinary logistic S-curve, which is a pattern of levels over time).

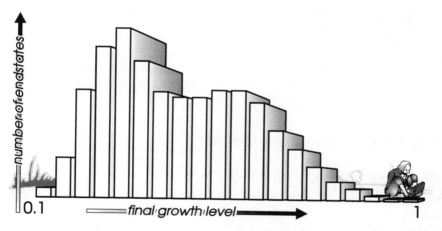

Figure 9.8 The distribution of 4,500 endstates with K_d = 0.7 and K_rand = 0.5; the horizontal axis represents the level of the final state of each individual case (growth process) ranging from 0.1 to 1; the vertical axis specifies the relative number of cases with final states grouping around similar averages; there is a characteristic maximum in the number of final states which are around the value 0.25, and another concentration of values around 0.6; only very few runs reach the maximal level (value 1).

(Figure 9.8). The figure looks more like a bimodal distribution with one characteristic peak around the value 0.25. With different versions of this model (two are described in van Geert, 1991), I obtained sharper bimodality. What explains this particular distribution of end states? In a model like this one, the earlier steps have a greater impact on determining the equilibrium level than the later ones. This is an unintended consequence of the way carrying capacity and growth level influence each other over the course of the process. If you have the bad luck that your first five to six steps show little or no growth because the random numbers just turned out that way, you will have a considerably greater chance to end up in the low end of the distribution than if the first steps drew better tickets from the lottery. This effect is reminiscent of a folk wisdom about development, that your earliest experiences determine much of what you will become in later life. I make no claims about the potential truth or falsehood of that belief. What matters here is that there is at least one formal growth model, the one presented in this section, that shows this kind of early stage effect. Wherever the model applies in the real world, we may expect that earlier experiences – whatever their nature may be – will have a bigger impact on development than later ones.

In summary, what this simple model shows is that if growth and K adaptation are linked, as is most probably the case in a variety of educational practices, the speed with which the instructor adapts to growth in the learner determines the final state level. This level can be well below the level achievable, given a better adaptation process. In the current model, better adaptation simply means a higher K adaptation parameter. In reality, however, we may expect a more subtle relationship between the learner's level and the level embodied in the teaching. More precisely, if the teaching level deviates from an optimal distance with the learning level, either above or below that optimum, the learner will profit less from the teaching. In the next section I shall discuss a classic developmental model, Vygotsky's, in which instruction plays a major role. We shall see that the notion of an optimum distance is of crucial importance.

Vygotsky's dynamic systems

From potential to actual development via help

The model that I shall discuss in this section is the famous *proximal development* model, which tries to answer how learning emerges out of the activity of an instructor and a learner who cooperates in a particular fashion. The Zone of Proximal Development is defined as the distance between the actual development and the developmental level that can be reached from the latter, given adequate help by more competent adults or peers. It expresses several thoughts at once: first, that the actual developmental level is an unstable state, continuously changing and drifting towards a state yet to be actualized; second, that the change is a function of two parameters, namely the child's own capacity and the help given by others. But why does the help provided by other more competent people turn into a competence of the subject helped? The answer lies in a major mechanism, interiorization: activities carried out at the social intersubjective

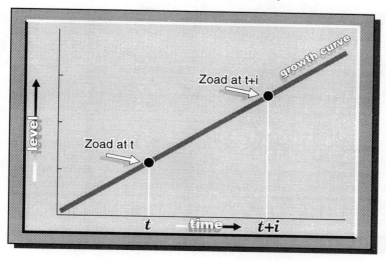

Figure 9.9 The growth curve of a developing competence consists of a sequence of levels of actual development (*Zoad*); in this figure, the sequence is a highly idealized linear progression of *Zoad*-levels.

level will gradually move onto the intersubjective personal level and become part of the person's own competencies.

But the definition of the Zone of Proximal Development immediately poses a fundamental problem. How much help is the help that gets internalized? It is not difficult for an experienced painter to 'help' a blind child paint a realistic and colourful landscape, but this help will of course not be internalized. Let me try to get a better grasp on this rather elusive concept of 'help' by making a number of simplifications.

I shall start with an arbitrary developing skill, such as the ability to solve addition problems. The child's actual skill level, i.e. the level at time t, is his/her Zone of Actual Development (Zoad). Let me pretend I also know the Zoad at some later time $t + 1$ (see Figure 9.9). According to the definition of the Zone of Proximal Development (Zoped), we know that this later Zoad at time $t + 1$ is the Zoped at time t (actually, we have defined the time difference between t and $t + 1$ in such a way that it allows for a given Zoped to become a Zoad). By convention, we project the later Zoad at time $t + 1$ into the current Zoped at time t by drawing a horizontal line (Figure 9.10).

We can perform this projection for each point on the time-scale. This results in a curve that actually parallels the growth curve of the skill itself. This second curve is the growth curve of the proximal (or potential) development, whereas the original curve refers to the actual development. Apart from representing the proximal development, the second curve also represents another important aspect of the developmental process. According to the definition, the Zoped turns into a Zoad as a function of help given to the child.

It follows then that from a purely formal point of view, the help given on the one

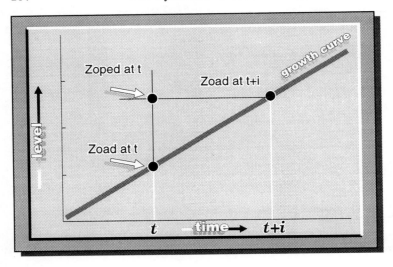

Figure 9.10 A current *Zoped* represents a later zone of actual development (*Zoad*).

hand and later developmental effect of that help, in the form of a later level of actual development, are interchangeable. That is, the curve representing the later Zoad levels instantiated in the present Zoped levels, is formally similar to the curve representing the level of help given. Put differently, we can define the level of help as the level of the Zoad that will result out of it after a given amount of time has elapsed.

The curve representing the growing Zoped must be similar to the curve representing the optimal help – the help that turns the Zoped into the Zoad at time $t + 1$. We do not know what this help is and it will fully depend on the actual circumstances in which the help is given, but we know that the second curve must represent that particular form of help, since Zoped and optimal help are equivalent as far as the transformation into a new Zoad is concerned (see Figure 9.11).

Since we express the help given in terms of the skill level that will be reached later, we can ask ourselves what would happen if that help lay below or above the ideal point corresponding with the Zoped. In the first case, the help is too close to the child's actual level and will add hardly anything significant to what the child already knows or masters. In the second case, the help is too far from the child's actual level and it will not be understood or assimilated. In both cases, such help will project onto a later competence level at time $t + 1$ that lies significantly below the level produced by optimal help (Figure 9.12).

The dynamics of Zoped

How can this model be translated into a mathematical form? First, there is a state the learner will achieve as an outcome of the learning and instruction process (e.g. mastery

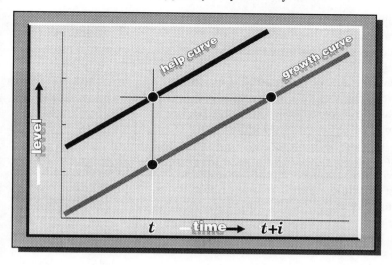

Figure 9.11 The growth curve of the levels instantiated in the help given to the learner corresponds with the growth curve of the *Zopeds*, that is, of the sequence of proximal development levels of the learner who receives that help.

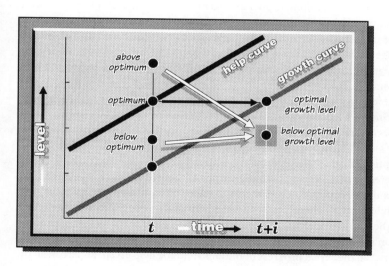

Figure 9.12 Help above or below the optimum will project onto a lower future *Zoad*, whereas optimal help produces optimal growth of the actual developmental level.

of writing skill). In formal instruction contexts, such as schools, the end state is explicitly represented, in the form of an educational goal, for instance. But consciousness of the end state is in no way essential to reaching that state. We have seen that in the simple logistic model – as in any dynamic model – the end state is a dynamic process. It is either a stable state that gets maintained over time, or a cyclical attractor, or a chaotic oscillation and so on. Whatever the end state, it is always a function of the whole of resources available. The conscious goal representation of an educator may be part of that complex of resources and in that way play a role in the process, but it is certainly not necessary.

The learner is put in a situation where the learning of the skill is made possible. The learner's activities represent some point along the line leading from complete lack to full mastery of the skill (e.g. a child making scribbles is close to the minimal level). The 'helper' or tutor is able to provide help in that a joint activity is created that is closer to the goal state than the child's solitary activity would be. In this sense, the helper is always a little bit ahead of the learner, in the direction of the goal state. If the help is optimal, the child will be able to interiorize it and so reach a higher level, the competence level as represented by the current joint activity of helper and learner. This means that the child is continuously approaching the level instantiated in the help given. The present model is very similar to the dynamics based on the experience component (Model 9.1 in this chapter).

The dynamics is highly reminiscent of the apocryphal story of the farmer and the donkey. The donkey was unwilling to go home, so the farmer tied a carrot to a stick and held it in front of the donkey. As the donkey went forward to reach out for the carrot, it made the carrot move forward too. The donkey's fruitless chase continued until they both reached the farm.

The mathematical simulation of this model is based on two components and two basic assumptions. The components are the level of the learner on the one hand, and the level as instantiated by the help given, on the other hand. The model deals only with the quantitative aspect of the skill or competence growth.

The assumptions are as follows. First, the increase in both the learner's competence and the helper's level of help given is described by the logistic growth model. The second assumption is that the growth rate (the speed with which the skill or competence increases over time) of both the learner's competence and the helper's help level will depend on an optimum. If the instructor can keep an optimum distance between the child's actual competence and the help given, the child will maximally profit from the help and proceed faster than if the help is above or below that optimum.

The optimum not only holds for the learner, but also for the helper. For instance, if the distance between the actual progress of the child and the help given, as perceived by the helper, is beyond or below a certain optimum, the helper will tend to stay closer to the learner's actual competence level than if the perceived distance were optimal. So the model allows for conflicts between optima that hold for the learner and optima that hold for the helper. Imagine the case of a very bright child and a tutor who is used to teaching much slower children. The bright child will profit most from a large gap between actual competence and help given. The tutor, on the other hand, is used to keeping a much smaller gap between the learner's competence and the help given and this will eventually be to the disadvantage of the bright fast learner. For instance, assume that the tutor keeps giving detailed and concrete instructions, forcing the child to stop and check every single step. A bright child might profit much more from a teacher explaining general principles of the task. A mentally retarded child, on the other hand, will profit more from the first form of instruction and learn virtually nothing from abstract rules that are given verbally.

The mathematical model is very similar to the one from the preceding section. It contains two coupled equations, one for the learner's level and one for the help (for more details, see van Geert, 1992b, 1994b; for a somewhat different form of the model, see van Geert, 1992a). The help is equivalent to the carrying capacity that the level feeds on. One major difference with the preceding model, however, is that the growth rates in both equations are multiplied by an optimal distance variable. That variable is maximal if the distance between level and help is optimal. The optimal distance is given by an optimality parameter, which is different for the learner and the helper. This optimality parameter is a function of the so-called unutilized capacity for growth, which, given that the carrying capacity is 1, amounts to the function $(1 - P_i)$. The whole model amounts to a combination of four coupled equations: one for the learner's level, one for the help level and two for the growth rate variable for the learner and help, respectively:

$$A_{i+1} = A_i(1 + R\_A_i - R\_A_i \cdot A_i/P_i)$$
$$P_{i+1} = P_i(1 + R\_P_i - R\_P_i \cdot P_i)$$
$$R\_P_{i+1} = r\_P - (P_i/A_i - O\_P) \cdot b\_A \cdot (1 - P_i) \tag{9.20}$$
$$R\_A_{i+1} = r\_A - |(P_i/A_i - O\_A)| \cdot b\_P \cdot (1 - P_i)$$

The variables used in this model are the following: A and P are the growth levels of the actual and potential developmental level, respectively. R_A and R_P are their respective variable growth rates. The growth rates are determined by a constant growth rate (r_A and r_P, respectively) and an optimality function, which depends on optimality parameters (O_A and O_P) and damping parameters (b_A and b_P). The vertical lines in the fourth equation mean that the absolute value of the enclosed function has to be taken.

Figure 9.13 shows five different patterns, resulting from different parameter constellations (see Table 9.1). The ideal pattern – as far as the speed and of growth is concerned – is the S-shaped curve from Figure 9.13a. It is somewhat flatter in the beginning than the S-shaped curve that would result from a singular logistic equation. The S-shaped curve evolves towards a clear stepwise curve or sudden jump, with increasing O_P parameter values (which means that the potential level tries to stay ahead of the actual developmental level, but with a bigger distance between A and P than in the previous case). Figure 9.13c shows that potential and actual developmental level sometimes get trapped in a deadlock (note that the scale of representation of Figures 9.13c and d is different from the other curves; the point where the virtual standstill occurs is close to the initial state level). Sometimes P and A drag each other towards a zero level, to a complete disappearance. With still other parameter values,

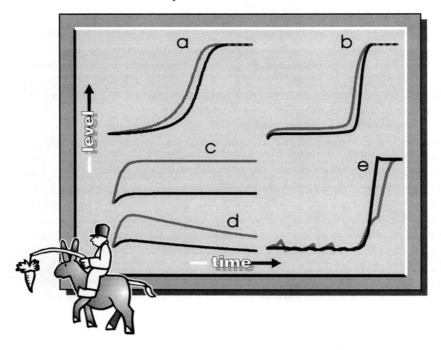

Figure 9.13 Qualitatively different growth curves result from a continuous change in the *optimal distance* parameter; ideal, S-shaped increase (a), a sudden jump in both the help and the actual developmental level (b); a process where both help and actual developmental level reach a maximum which is far below the potential maximum (c), one in which both levels drop back to almost zero after an initial period of increase (d), and an irregular oscillation followed by a sudden jump to the maximum level (e).

the pattern shows a chaotic fluctuation in the beginning, but sometimes manages to escape and achieve the maximum attainable level (Figure 9.13e).

As the critical parameter value increases, the qualitative nature of the resulting learning or growth curves changes, as Figure 9.13 clearly shows. In the vicinity of these changing points, the resulting curve could be either of the form typical of lower parameter values or of the form typical of the higher value. Which of these two actually

Table 9.1 Parameter values for growth trajectories in Figure 9.13

	in_A	in_P	r_A	r_P	b_A	b_P	O_A	O_P
a	0.01	0.011	0.1	0.1	0.1	0.1	0.2	0
b	0.1	0.101	0.1	0.229	0.1	0.229	0.2	0.2
c	0.01	0.0101	0.1	0.1	0.1	0.1	0.1	0.1
d	0.01	0.0101	0.1	0.1	0.1	0.1	0.1	0.12
e	0.01	0.0101	1	0.9	1	0.9	2.68	2

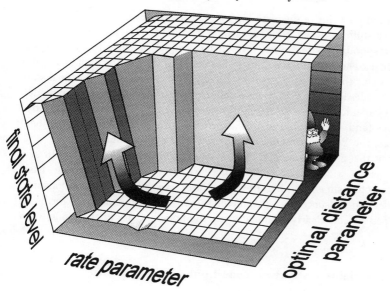

Figure 9.14 A final state space for the control variables *rate* and *optimal distance* as applied to the help component in the Vygotsky model; the space is divided in a region with final states close to K, and final states close to 0; there exists a sharp discontinuity and an irregular boundary between both regions.

emerges depends on small fluctuations in the starting points. Put differently, in the vicinity of qualitative switch points, the actual outcome is very sensitive to minor random influences. Small normally irrelevant differences in starting point, for instance, could lead to major long-term differences in the resulting developmental trajectory. Beyond such switch points, the resulting trajectory is not sensitive to minor perturbations, and thus very predictable (if we know the parameter values, that is).

Finally, it is interesting to note that the model does not always create the ideal developmental outcome. The parameters can be seen as dimensions in a control space, and only part of that control space (only part of the possible combinations of parameter values) leads to an optimal learning or developmental outcome. Take for instance Figure 9.14.

The vertical axis represents the average final growth level (the last 500 iterations of a simulation consisting of 2000 iterative steps). The horizontal axis corresponds with a range of values of the r_P parameter (see equation 9.20), which refers to the growth rate of the help level. The depth axis shows a range of values for O_P (the parameter defining the optimal distance between the pupil's level and the tutor's help level). Both parameters, r_P and O_P, are control parameters for the tutorial aspect in the Vygotsky model. It is easy to see that each point on the horizontal plane corresponds with a combination of a specific r_p with a specific O_P value. For each of those pairs of values there is a unique value of the resulting average growth level. Figure 9.14 clearly shows the sudden shifts between values for which the final growth level is about zero, and values corresponding with a final growth level equal or close to the carrying capacity level. It also shows that the boundary between the low and the high final states is quite irregular (for this part of the r_P/O_P control space, that is). This final state control space provides a good illustration of the non-linearity of the Vygotsky model: the model shows a sudden jump in the equilibrium level for a specific set of control parameter values (and, if the jump is also associated with hysteresis and additional catastrophe flags, the Vygotsky model is an example of a cusp-catastrophe).

It is important that a developmental model can explain not only success, but also failure (for instance a zero outcome), since we may assume that the basic developmental mechanism is not different in both cases (see van der Veer and Valsiner, 1992). The collection of 'successful' parameter values in the control space forms an irregularly shaped object, clearly demonstrating the non-linearity of the model (van Geert, 1994b).

Growth under variable instruction conditions

The models I described in this chapter differ in a number of assumptions. They are similar, however, in the basic assumption that instruction, teaching, help or support by a more competent person amounts to an increase in the carrying capacity of the skill that grows with the learning subject. The carrying capacity embodied in the instructional practice grows in response to growth in the dependent skill. Carrying capacity and the skill level in the learner are mutually dependent growers.

An interesting aspect of these models is that they show that processes of instruction or help are not necessarily beneficial to the learner. The dynamics determining the help level are governed by a set of parameters, whose values may differ over individuals. Some value ranges could drag the whole process into chaotic oscillation. Others result in stable state endpoints well below the value that could have been reached if the parameter values would have been different. Still others result in upward and downward movements of a learning level that will never reach the goal state. In general, however, the different models show how a mutualist dynamics can lead to a predefined goal state as a consequence of a true interaction between an instructor and a learner. In this type of process, both participants are equally important.

In this chapter, my standard model involved the interaction between a tutee or novice and an expert, or tutor. This is of course only one of the many forms that a co-construction process can take. For instance, co-construction and co-regulation may occur in an interaction between two novices, or between children at different levels of mastery or knowledge of a co-constructed skill. Interaction between equals involves the problem of the goal representation in the system. In the cases described in this chapter, the goal was represented in the form of an expert, adult or teacher, but if two (or more) novices are concerned, the goal – or should I say, the set of potential goals – is represented in an entirely different way. Models of interacting equals are the subject of further research.

Epilogue
Towards an experimental theoretical developmental psychology

Unsolved problems abound

Problems with empirical research

The dynamic growth approach that I presented in this book is a new and exciting approach to development (or, to put it more modestly, I think it is sufficiently new to be interesting and I am excited each time I try an equation that simulates some developmental interaction pattern and discover that it does what I expected; if it does not, I am sometimes even more excited). In order to really understand why somebody would spend day after day building mathematical models of development instead of going to the beach, sunbathing or playing volleyball, it is necessary to do the model building exercises and see the computer do its conjuring tricks. But all the modelling exercises explained here and the multitude of dynamic building blocks and models presented cannot conceal that the unexplained problems largely outnumber the explained ones.

The first is the empirical problem. In principle, the dynamic growth model produces curves that describe potential individual growth patterns. An individual is characterized by a set of parameter values and a history of external events that shape his or her particular growth trajectory. Unfortunately, there is still only little longitudinal research, especially of the kind that a dynamic model requires, namely data with a high sampling frequency. It is possible, though, to use cross-sectional data, especially if they are based on good developmental scales. In our attempt at building a model of hierarchically connected growers, Fischer and I used group data we pretended would characterize at least a significant subset of individuals. In some cases, it will be practically impossible to obtain the ideal longitudinal data, for instance, when the process of development lasts much longer than the average research project. Cognitive development between birth and 25 years of age is a good example. This does not mean that we should not try to set up longitudinal research that spans this long period. But in the meantime, we have to rely on data that cover much less than the time span covered by the models. I see several partial solutions to the empirical data problem. First, we could concentrate more on major developmental processes that take only a short time. A good example is language development. One child, two years of daily observation and a lot of little notebooks is all you need to carry out an interesting longitudinal study that describes the growth of a complex phenomenon, language, between its onset and a stage that is rather close to maturity on a number of criteria. Infancy is a particularly good age range, because it comprises many major changes over short periods. Second, we could perform longitudinal studies of learning processes, for instance, learning in the classroom or computer-based instruction. Such learning processes can be observed non-obtrusively, since the testing and observation is usually part of the learning and teaching itself and does not intervene with that process in a distortive way. Third, we could focus more on microgenetic studies, which involve processes that recapitulate, in a sense, long-term changes over a short time span. Nira Granott's studies (Granott, 1993) on how adults try to understand the principles behind the behaviour of small but complicated electronic robots is a good example of how fruitful such studies can be, but also a good example of how much is required to arrive at a really interesting measurement. The justification for microgenetic studies lies for a good deal in the expected scale invariance of developmental processes. That is, we may assume that the really interesting phenomena repeat themselves over any different time-scale, ranging from a couple of hours to a lifetime (and even beyond that range). Fourth, as far as long-term developments are concerned, we could try to focus on the moments where the real changes take place, provided such changes are indeed unevenly distributed over the time-scale. The study of transitions requires individual longitudinal designs. We have seen earlier that transitions are characterized by increased variance, by considerable changes over short intervals and by fluctuations that approach chaos and turbulence. As a matter of principle, such processes cannot be studied in group designs. Finally, we should try to bring our cross-sectional methods more in line with the need for longitudinal data. It is very important, for instance, to have good, theoretically justified developmental scales that apply to many different contexts. A good example of such scales are those developed on the basis of Fischer's model of developmental levels. They combine a strong logical ordering with contextual flexibility. Another way of improving longitudinal methods is to apply mixed designs, that is, overlapping sets of repeated measures in different age groups. Instead of focusing on measures that capitalize in one way or another on averages or means, we should make more explicit use of changes in variance and other measures that relate to individual differences.

The basic adaptation, probably, should lie in changing our expectations of how development takes place. As long as we go on trying to reduce irregularity, turbulence, dips and bumps, acceleration and deceleration to error variation imposed upon a basically smooth, gradual and straight underlying process, we will miss the basic insight that it is the irregularity rather than the smoothness that is essential to the process we want to understand.

Problems with statistics

Fortunately, psychology can now rely on a truly impressive arsenal of statistical weapons useful for silencing anyone who dares say that the study of the soul is not real science. Unfortunately, however, most of the statistical tools are aimed at a different goal than the one pursued by developmentalists. They are very well suited for describing and analyzing differences among populations but considerably less adapted to the problem of change in individuals. There is a vast literature on time-series analysis and the growing interest in non-linear dynamics has boosted the development and distribution of statistical techniques uniquely designed for capturing the parameters and forms of change. In order to yield interesting results, however, such techniques usually require a great number of repeated measurements, often much more than is possible with even the most ideal repeated measurement designs in psychology.

How can one test whether the growth curves a model has produced really fit the available data? The simplest test makes use of an old and small instrument that many people use primarily to watch TV, the eye. In general, you can easily see whether or not a curve follows the available data, or whether one curve produces a better fit than the other. If you can see that things are similar, it is not necessary to deploy an army of statistical forces that comes up with a bunch of numbers which, at best, correspond with the judgement of the naked eye. In the models I built of early language development, I relied almost exclusively on the power of the visual sense. It was possible to make the claims I made more impressive by using a least-squares method or something else that tells you to what extent, on average, two curves are similar, but that would not have made the conclusions more reliable or valid. Another easy way to check data against a mathematically obtained collection of curves is to test for the presence of distinctive qualitative features. For instance, in building the model of hierarchically connected growers, Kurt Fischer and I used the data to argue for a number of qualitative properties, such as growth spurts, temporary regressions and fluctuation. We then checked the mathematical curves to see whether these distinctive properties occurred, and if they did, under which combinations of parameters.

This does not mean we should not bother to look for strict and formal statistical testing procedures. Our quest for such methods should be based on the model of change that we believe in, instead of the other way around. At this moment, Han van der Maas and Peter Molenaar are working on statistical procedures testing for transitions in the strong sense, that is, patterns of change that follow the cusp catastrophe. When Kurt Fischer and I were working on our dynamic model at the Stanford Center for Advanced Study, we were fortunate to have some money to pay for the travel expenses of consultants to the project. One week we brainstormed with John Willett from Harvard University, who has done a lot of work on statistics for behavioural growth and change. Although his models and ours were rather different, John came with a brilliant idea after seeing a time-delay state space diagram (recall that such diagrams are very easy to draw in a spreadsheet program). He explained that our growth equations contained variables that were linear in the parameters, that is, parameters simply added or multiplied values of variables. The only thing our growth equations did was describe a relationship between a previous state and a next state. That relationship is fully specified by the equation. Given a sufficient (but not astronomical) number of repeated measurements, you could take the preceding states as predictors for succeeding states. The parameters relating pairs of states could be estimated by a statistical technique which is usually employed only with group data, LISREL. Since the nature of the relationships has been fixed by the dynamic equation, LISREL would be capable of making quite reliable estimations of the parameters. Once estimated, the parameters could be fed into the equations again, and you could then test whether or not they produced the required growth curves. At the time of writing, it is not known to me if this suggestion will be worth the excitement we felt when we first heard it. But for whatever it is worth, it is a nice illustration of the fact that with a good deal of creativity you could adapt existing methods to the needs and requirements of the study of growth and change.

Problems about time and coincidence

When I look at the neat rows of numbers lining up in the spreadsheet as little soldiers ready to fight the enemy of ignorance, I cannot help feeling that they are all too neat and regular. The cells in the spreadsheet correspond with single loops of the iterative equation and each iteration is supposed to take its own time. The iteration time is the feedback delay of the system. It has no temporal interpretation in the difference model (and the spreadsheet model for that matter) in that it is not known how much time it takes to go from one iteration to the next (or from one cell to the next). If I draw a diagram of the successive points of a growth curve, I usually call the horizontal axis the time axis and I almost automatically assume that the time intervals between any two points are equal. But they need not be. If the time between one iteration and the next depends on some environmental event, such as the child being confronted with a problem, the length of the intervals will differ greatly over the growth curve. Just imagine the growth curve is printed on a rubber sheet and the sheet is stretched unevenly between any two points. The series of cells (or iterations) in the model is not a time series, but an event series. Each cell is a learning or growth event, triggered either by some internal factor or by an environmental and contextual event. A row of cells in the model represents a single point in time, but given the previous argument, it should actually represent an event. In the model, a variable changes over each new cell. In reality, however, a variable changes only if it is involved in some sort of event that causes it to change. The distribution of such events can be very different for different growers and the speadsheet model does not account for that; it makes all variables change in unison, at each tick of its internal clock that makes the system proceed one row of cells. It is possible, however, to treat inter-event time as a separate variable which is determined by the grower to which it applies. The transition model of logistic growth, for instance, can be simulated by making the interval between successive learning events depend on the growth level (higher levels, shorter intervals). The cumulative curve of event times can be employed as the x-axis in an x-y graph, with the growth level as y-axis.

The problem of variable inter-event time is related to that of coincidental influences and eventual unreliability of information as it travels through the developmental dynamics. In the spreadsheet model (and in the mathematical model), each succeeding cell knows the exact value of the preceding cell and the exact value of the parameters. A constant parameter remains literally constant. But how does this work out in reality? How does the vocabulary system knows how many words it contains? How does the representational level know how many problems it can solve? In some way or another, those systems 'know' about their quantitative properties in that a model that mimics the knowledge can produce quite realistic growth curves. But this does not mean that the quantitative information in real systems is transmitted without considerable error. Part of the error is probably due to environmentally triggered coincidental events. Fortunately, however, it is not too difficult to account for both the random variation in event intervals and in reliability of the information available to the system. You can add any form of random variation to each of the steps in the computation of a growth curve and study if, where and when such random perturbation makes a major difference. In some dynamics, the random factors add up linearly to the growth pattern. Such is the case with the logistic growth equation. Just add a random perturbation to each of the variables and parameters in the cells and you will see that the results are not very different for different random runs of the model. In other dynamic models, random perturbations may have non-linear effects. For instance, in Chapter 9 we saw that the learning model that made use of the carrying capacity adaptation principle suffered much more if a random perturbation occurred at the beginning than at the end. I am currently experimenting with growth models which compute growth as a function of a 'fuzzy', randomized representation of an average growth level in the near past. These models produce interesting oscillatory patterns that are very similar to longitudinal data sets on the growth of syntax in individual children (Ruhland, unpublished paper). Models working with 'fuzzy' growth states are probably very appropriate for describing growth patterns that are (partly) based on the person's mental representation of his or her skill or knowledge level.

The haunted house of problems

In San José, California, there is a place called the Haunted House. In comparison to Scotland, sunny California is a lousy place for ghosts, but this particular house carries an interesting metaphor. It belonged to a lady who believed she would never die as long as she went on building, adding rooms, staircases leading into blind walls and whatever else her imagination suggested. In the end she died, of course, like everybody else, when the time has come. In scientific model building, theorists often behave like the San José lady, thinking that they can chase basic problems away by doing more research and adding more aspects to their models. In the house of the dynamic growth models, one problem keeps haunting me and even though I think I can conjure it by continuing to add new parts to the building, I know the day will come when it will overtake me and that I shall have to face it anyway. The problem is that of novelty, the construction of new developmental forms out of existing ones. One of the more fundamental limitations of a growth model is that it does not explain where the growers come from. What is it that turns a non-verbal act of communication into a word, a pre-operational concept into an operational one? More than a century ago, Darwin showed that new species can be created when small random variations on the building plan of an existing species are selected by differential survival. Maybe something along these lines would prove to be the solution for the creation of novelty in development. In Chapter 5, I have demonstrated how a principle of minor gradual change may nevertheless produce a jump to a different level, suggesting that gradual local mechanisms may in principle produce sudden qualitative change. But in order to develop a theory of novelty creation, a model is needed of a dynamics applying to detailed structural models of the skills, competences or abilities in question.

A very good example of a field in which the explanation of how novel patterns come about as a result of non-linear dynamic processes is motor development. Ground-breaking work in this developmental area has been done by Esther Thelen and colleagues (see Thelen, 1989, for an overview). The dynamic models apply to a well-developed structural model, namely that of the physical body: a structure of joint, stiff levers (the bones) moved and connected by muscles and coordinated neural components. This particular structure is the domain of study of a discipline called biodynamics, which explains actual motor patterns, such as walking, reaching and grasping. My Dutch colleague Peter Beek even managed to describe and explain juggling in terms of a dynamic systems model of biodynamics (Beek, 1989; I heard he had to practise juggling himself before he could do this research; psychology indeed asks for many different talents). In a recent special issue of the journal *Child Development*, fourteen papers appeared discussing several aspects of how motor patterns emerge during development as a consequence of self-organizing principles that apply to the neural and physical structures of the body. Thelen and colleagues studied the emergence of reaching in terms of the infants' ongoing intrinsic movement dynamics (Thelen *et al.*, 1993). A comparable dynamic systems analysis has been applied to the development of walking (Clark and Phillips, 1993). In their commentary on the papers, Turvey and Fitzpatrick (1993) note that several of the authors emphasize the importance of spontaneous movements as exploratory and formative mechanisms, leading to new motor patterns. The dynamic explanation of qualitatively new patterns of action has been very successful in the motor domain. Smith and Thelen (1993) conclude their discussion of the question whether dynamic systems theory can be usefully applied in areas other than motor development by saying that 'this hammer is well worth trying out'.

Another phantom haunting the house of dynamic models is the problem of different time-scales, their proper dynamics and how they relate. I have some ideas about how this problem may be specified further and eventually solved (van Geert, 1992c), but those ideas have hardly left the cradle. How can a dynamic system determine its own goal state, or construct its own attractor? This is a problem associated with a model of co-construction involving two novices. It is, obviously, related but not similar with the problem of novelty construction.

These are only a few of the many theoretical problems that still hide somewhere in the many rooms, closets, halls or doorways of the house of dynamic systems of development. They have managed to escape from being exorcized, so far, and they will continue to do so as long as we do not find a way to fomulate those problems in explicit terms.

Towards an experimental theoretical developmental psychology

This book was primarily about theory, not so much about a new theory of development as about a new way to reformulate the old ones. There is a lot of dynamic systems theory behind the models of our founding fathers, Piaget, Vygotsky, Werner and several others. There is a lot of dynamics behind simple theories of learning and teaching. The point is, however, that the dynamics remained implicit. It required a simple method of mathematical model building to peel them out of the verbal, philosophical form in which they had been caught. Once we managed to translate those models and theories into a genuine dynamic form, we found out that they contained a number of unexpected properties. We discovered the regularity and robustness of some and the turbulence and chaos of others. We saw how a model showed simple stepwise increase under some circumstances and temporal regressions under others. The dynamic models defeated the possibility of simple, linear extrapolation. This notion implies that a local process can be extended and projected into the future and that the magnitude of the effect is proportional to the magnitude of the time interval. We are inclined to think that a little progress over a little time interval, corresponds with roughly five times as much progress over a time interval five times greater. The non-linearity of many dynamic processes, however, stands in the way of this simple extrapolation principle. The only way to know what a dynamic model is doing is to simply try it out under as many conditions as possible. The Latin origin of the word *experiment* is 'the act of trying', and it is in this sense that the study of the behaviour of dynamic models, in itself a part of theoretical developmental psychology, is a form of *experimental theoretical psychology*. When your models and theories have a dynamic character, you cannot suffice with a mere verbal form, preceding the inference and testing of hypotheses. An intermediate stage is required, where a formal procedure is used to investigate the set of potential hypotheses the model offers. The growth concept and the dynamic modelling presented in this book is one particular approach to experimental theorizing that developmental psychologists might apply in their attempts to come to a better understanding of that most elusive of all phenomena, change. At the end of the day, we may find out that these models are not any better than the concrete wooden shoes my grandfather made, but it is better to use concrete wooden shoes than to wear no shoes at all, because if you hurt your feet, you will get nowhere.

References

Apter, M. (1982). *The Experience of Motivation: A Theory of Psychological Reversals*. New York: Academic Press.

Baddeley, A. (1990). *Human Memory: Theory and Practice*. Hillsdale, NJ: Erlbaum.

Bak, P. and Chen, K. (1991). Self-organizing criticality. *Scientific American*, **265**(1), 46–53.

Bee, H. (1989). *The Developing Child* (5th edn). New York: Harper and Row.

Beek, P. (1989). Timing and Phase Locking in cascade juggling. *Ecological Psychology*, **1**, 55–96.

Bentler, P.M. (1970). Evidence regarding stages in the development of conservation. *Perceptual and Motor Skills*, **31**, 855–69.

Bever, Th.G. (1982). *Regressions in Mental Development: Basic Phenomena and Theories*. Hillsdale, NJ: Erlbaum.

Bidell, T.R. and Fischer, K.W. (1993). Developmental transitions in children's early on-line planning. In M.M. Haith, J.B. Benson, R.J. Roberts Jr. and B.F. Pennington (eds), *Development of Future-oriented Processes*. Chicago: University of Chicago Press.

Bijstra, J. (1989). *To be or to look . . . that's the question. A comparative study on social-cognitive development*. University of Groningen: Doctoral dissertation.

Bleiker, C. (1991). Validating a common-ceiling model of short-term memory growth: consonant spans in young children. In R. Case (ed.), *The Role of Central Conceptual Structures in the Development of Children's Numerical, Literary and Spatial Thought*. Year 2. Report submitted to the Spencer Foundation.

Boulding, K. (1978). *Ecodynamics: A new Theory of Societal Evolution*. Beverly Hills: Sage.

Boyd, R. and Richerson, P.J. (1985). *Culture and the Evolutionary Process*. Chicago: University of Chicago Press.

Brainerd, C.J. (1973). Neo-Piagetian experiments revisited: is there any support for the cognitive-developmental stage hypothesis? *Cognition*, **2/3**, 349–70.

Brown, R. (1973). *A First Language: The Early Stages*. London: Allen and Unwin.

Bryant, P. (1982). Theories about the causes of cognitive development. In P. van Geert (ed.), *Theory Building in Developmental Psychology*. Amsterdam: North Holland.

Case, R., Marini, Z., McKeough, A., Dennis, S. and Goldberg, J. (1986). Horizontal structure in middle childhood: cross-domain parallels in the course of cognitive growth. In I. Levin (ed.), *Stage and Structure. Reopening the Debate*. Norwood, NJ: Ablex.

Case, R. (1992a). The role of the frontal lobes in the regulation of human development. *Brain and Cognition*, **20**, 51–73.

Case, R. (1992b). *The Mind's Staircase: Exploring the Conceptual Underpinnings of Children's Thought and Knowledge*. Hillsdale, NJ: Erlbaum.

278

Clark, J.E. and Phillips, S.J. (1993). A longitudinal study of intralimb coordination in the first year of independent walking: a dynamical systems analysis. *Child Development*, **64**, 1143–57.

Corrigan, R. (1983). The development of representational skills. In K.W. Fischer (ed.), *Levels and Transitions in Children's Development* (Vol. 21, pp. 51–64). San Francisco: Jossey-Bass.

Costa, P.T. and McCrae, R. (1976). Age differences in personality structure: A cluster analytic approach. *Journal of Gerontology*, **31**, 564–70.

Costa, P.T., Jr. and McCrae, R. (1980). Still stable after all these years: Personality as a key to some issues in adulthood and old age. In P. Baltes and O. Brim (eds), *Lifespan Development and Behavior* (Vol. 3, pp. 65–102). New York: Academic Press.

Dawkins, R. (1976). *The Selfish Gene*. Oxford: Oxford University Press.

De Sapio, R. (1978). *Calculus for the Life Sciences*. San Francisco: Freeman.

Dromi, E. (1987). *Early Lexical Development*. New York: Cambridge University Press.

Dromi, E. (1986). The one word period as a stage in language development: Quantitative and qualitative accounts. In I. Levin (ed.), *Stage and structure*. Norwood, NJ: Ablex.

Ehrlich, P.R. (1986). *The Machinery of Nature*. New York: Simon and Schuster.

Eichorn, D.H., Clausen, J.A., Haan, N., Honzik, M.P. and Mussen, P.H. (1981). *Present and Past in Middle Life*. New York: Academic Press.

Eldredge, N. and Gould, S.J. (1972). Punctuated equilibria: an alternative to phyletic gradualism. In T.J.M. Schopf (ed.), *Models in Paleobiology*. San Francisco: Freeman.

Eldredge, N. and Tattersall, I. (1982). *The Myths of Human Evolution*. New York: Columbia University Press.

Fischer, K.W. (1980). A theory of cognitive development: The control and construction of hierarchies of skills. *Psychological Review*, **87**, 477–531.

Fischer, K.W. and Lazerson, A. (1984). *Human Development from Conception to Adolescence*. New York: Freeman.

Fischer, K.W. and Pipp, S.L. (1984). Processes of cognitive development: Optimal level and skill acquisition. In R.J. Sternberg (ed.), *Mechanisms of Cognitive Development* (pp. 45–80). New York: W.H. Freeman.

Fischer, K.W. and Rose, S.P. (1993). Development of coordination of components in brain and behavior: A framework for theory and research. In G. Dawson and K.W. Fischer (eds), *Human Behavior and the Developing Brain*. New York: Guilford.

Fischer, K.W., Kenny, S.L. and Pipp, S.L. (1990). How cognitive processes and environmental conditions organize discontinuities in the development of abstractions. In C.N. Alexander, E.J. Langer and R.M. Oetzel (eds), *Higher Stages of Development* (pp. 162–87). New York: Oxford University Press.

Flavell, J.H. (1963). *The Developmental Psychology of Jean Piaget*. New York: Van Nostrand.

Flavell, J.H., Green, F.L. and Flavell, E.R. (1986). *Development of Knowledge about the Appearance–Reality Distinction*. Chicago: University of Chicago Press.

Fodor, J.A. (1980). Methodological solipsism considered as a research strategy in cognitive psychology. *Behavioral and Brain Sciences*, **3**, 63–109.

Fogel, A. and Thelen, E. (1987). Development of early expressive and communicative action: Reinterpreting the evidence from a dynamic systems perspective. *Developmental Psychology*, **23**(6), 747–61.

Fogel, A. (1992). Movement and communication in infancy: The social dynamics of development. *Human Movement Science*, **11**, 387–423.

Fogel, A. (1993). *Developing Through Relationships: Origins of Communication, Self and Culture*. Hemel Hempstead: Harvester Wheatsheaf.

Gann, L.H. and Duignan, P. (1979). *The Rulers of Belgian Africa, 1884–1914*. Princeton, NJ: Princeton University Press.

Gleick, J. (1987). *Chaos*. New York: Penguin Books.

Globerson, T. (1983). Mental capacity and cognitive functioning: developmental and social class differences. *Developmental Psychology*, **19**, 225–30.

Gottlieb, G. (1984). Evolutionary trends and evolutionary origins: relevance to theory in comparative psychology. *Psychological Review*, 91, 448–56.

Gould, S.J. (1992). *Bully for Brontosaurus*. New York: Norton.

Granott, N. (1993). Play, puzzles, and a dilemma: Patterns of interaction in the co-construction of knowledge. In R. Wozniak and K. Fischer (eds), *Specific environments: Thinking in contexts*. Hillsdale, NJ: Erlbaum.

Hamilton, E. and Cairns, H. (eds) (1963). *The Collected Dialogues of Plato*. Princeton, NJ: Princeton University Press.

Harter, S. (1978). Effectance motivation reconsidered: Toward a developmental model. *Human Development*, 21, 34–64.

Harter, S. (1983). Competence as a dimension of self-evaluation: Toward a comprehensive model of self-worth. In R. Leahy (eds), *The Development of the Self*. New York: Academic Press.

Ho, M.W. and Saunders, P. (1984). *Beyond Neo-Darwinism: An Introduction to the New Evolutionary Paradigm*. London: Academic Press.

Honzik, M.P., MacFarlane, J.W. and Allen, L. (1948). The stability of mental test performance between two and eighteen years. *Journal of Experimental Education*, 4, 309–24.

Hylan, J.P. (1898). *The fluctuation of attention*. Monograph Supplements to the *Psychological Review*, 2(6), March 1898.

Inhelder, B. and Piaget, J. (1958). *The Growth of Logical Thinking from Childhood to Adolescence*. New York: Basic Books.

Jakobson, R. (1959). Why 'mama' and 'papa'? In B. Kaplan and S. Wagner (eds), *Perspectives in Psychological Theory*. New York: BALR.

Kagan, J. and Moss, H.A. (1962). *Birth to Maturity*. New York: Wiley.

Kahneman, D. (1973). *Attention and Effort*. Englewood Cliffs, NJ: Prentice Hall.

Kitchener, K.S., Lynch, C.L., Fischer, K.W. and Wood, P.K. (1993). Developmental range of reflective judgment. The effect of contextual support and practice on developmental stage. *Developmental Psychology*.

Klausmeier, H.J. and Allen, P.S. (1978). *Cognitive Development of Children and Youth: a Longitudinal Study*. New York: Academic Press.

Kohlberg, L. (1969). Stage and sequence: The cognitive developmental approach to socialization. In D.A. Goslin (ed.), *Handbook of Socialization Theory and Research* (pp. 347–480). Chicago: Rand, McNally.

Kunnen, S. (1992). *Mastering (with) a Handicap: The Development of Task-attitudes in Physically Handicapped Children*. University of Groningen: Doctoral Dissertation.

Labov, W. and Labov, T. (1978). Learning the syntax of questions. In R.N. Campbell and P.T. Smith (eds), *Recent Advances in the Psychology of Language: Language Development and Mother–Child Interaction*. London: Plenum Press.

Leontew, A.N. (1973). *Probleme der Entwicklung des Psychischen*. Frankfurt am Main: Athenaum Fischer.

Lumsden, C.J. and Wilson, E.O. (1981). *Genes, Mind and Culture: The Co-evolutionary Process*. Cambridge, MA: Harvard University Press.

Mandelbrot, B.B. (1982). *The Fractal Geometry of Nature*. New York: Freeman.

Mandler, J. (1992). How to build a baby: II. Conceptual primitives. *Psychological Review*, 99(4), 587–604.

Matousek, M. and Petersén, I. (1973). Frequency analysis of the EEG in normal children and adolescents. In P. Kellaway and I. Petersén (eds), *Automation of Clinical Electroencephalography* (pp. 75–102). New York: Raven Press.

May, R.M. (1976). Simple mathematical models with very complicated dynamics. *Nature*, 261, 459–67.

Mayr, E. (1976). *Evolution and the Diversity of Life: Selected Essays*. Cambridge, MA: Harvard University Press.

References

McCall, R.B. (1983). Exploring developmental transitions in mental performance. In K.W. Fischer (ed.), *Levels and Transitions in Children's Development* (Vol. 21, pp. 65–80). San Francisco: Jossey-Bass.

McCall, R.B., Appelbaum, M.I. and Hogarty, P.S. (1973). *Developmental Changes in Mental Performance*. In Monographs of the Society for Research in Child Development, 38 (3); serial number 150.

Miller, G.A. (1956). The magical number seven plus or minus two. Some limits on our capacity for processing information. *Psychological Review*, 63, 81–97.

Nagel, E. (1957). Determinism and development. In D.B. Harris (ed.), *The Concept of Development*. Minneapolis: University of Minnesota Press.

Nelson, K. (1985). *Making Sense: The Acquisition of Shared Meaning*. New York: Academic Press.

Neugarten, B.L. (1964). *Personality in Middle and Late Life*. New York: Atherton Press.

Newport, E.L. (1982). Task specificity in language learning? Evidence from speech perception and American Sign Language. In E. Wanner and L.R. Gleitman (eds), *Language Acquisition: The State of the Art*. Cambridge: Cambridge University Press.

Nunnally, J.C. (1970). *Introduction to Psychological Measurement*. New York: McGraw-Hill.

Olson, J.M. and Sherman, T. (1983). Attention, learning and memory in infants. In M.M. Haith and J.J. Campos (eds), *Handbook of Child Psychology* (Vol. 2: *Infancy and Developmental Psychobiology*). New York: Wiley.

Oyama, S. (1989). Ontogeny and the central dogma: Do we need the concept of genetic programming in order to have an evolutionary perspective? In M. Gunnar and E. Thelen (eds), *Systems and Development. The Minnesota Symposia in Child Psychology*. Hillsdale, NJ: Erlbaum.

Pascual-Leone, J. (1970). A mathematical model for the transition rule in Piaget's developmental stages. *Acta Psychologica*, 32, 301–45.

Peitgen, H.-O., Jürgens, H. and Saupe, D. (1992). *Fractals for the Classroom. Part two: Complex systems and the Mandelbrot set*. New York: Springer.

Piaget, J. (1929). *The Child's Conception of the World*. New York: Harcourt, Brace Jovanovich.

Piaget, J. (1957). Logique et équilibre dans le comportement du sujet. In L. Apostel, B. Mandelbrot and J. Piaget (eds), *Logique et Equilibre. Etudes d'Epistémologie Génétique* (vol. 2). Paris: Presses Universitaires de France.

Piaget, J. (1975). *L'Equilibration des Structures Cognitives: Problème central du développement*. Paris: Presses Universitaires de France.

Rogoff, B. (1990). *Apprenticeship in Thinking: Cognitive Development in Social Context*. New York: Oxford University Press.

Ruhland, R. (unpublished). Transitions in early language development. University of Groningen.

Sanders, A.F. (1983). Towards a model of stress and human performance. *Acta Psychologica*, 53, 61–97.

Saunders, P.T. (1984). Development and Evolution. In M.W. Ho and P. Saunders (eds), *Beyond Neo-Darwinism: An Introduction to the New Evolutionary Paradigm*. London: Academic Press.

Schroeder, M. (1991). *Fractals, Chaos and Power Laws*. New York: Freeman.

Sena, R. and Smith, L. (1990). New evidence on the development of the word 'big'. *Child Development*, 61, 1034–54.

Siegler, R.S. (1983). Information processing approaches to development. In W. Kessen (ed.), *History, Theory, and Methods* (pp. 129–211). New York: Wiley.

Siegler, R.S. (1984). Mechanisms of cognitive growth: variation and selection. In R.J. Sternberg (ed.), *Mechanisms of cognitive development*. New York: Freeman.

Siegler, R.S. and Crowley, K. (1991). The micro-genetic method: A direct means for studying cognitive development. *American Psychologist*, 46(6), 606–20.

282 References

Simpson, G.G. (1983). *Fossils and the History of Life*. New York: Freeman.

Smith, L. B. and Thelen, E. (1993). Can dynamic systems theory be usefully applied in areas other than motor development? In L.B. Smith and E. Thelen (eds), *A Dynamic Systems Approach to Development: Applications*. Cambridge, MA: MIT Press.

Strauss, S. and Stavy, R. (1982). U-shaped behavioral growth: Implications for theories of development. In W.W. Hartup (ed.), *Review of Child Development Research*. Chicago: University of Chicago Press.

Strauss, S. (1982). *U-shaped Behavioral Growth*. New York: Academic Press.

Ta'eed, L.K., Ta'eed, O. and Wright, J.E. (1988). Determinants involved in the perception of the Necker cube: an application of catastrophe theory. *Behavioral Science*, 33, 97–115.

Thatcher, R.W. (1992). Cyclic cortical reorganization during early childhood development. *Brain and Cognition*, 20, 24–50.

Thatcher, R.W., Walker, R.A. and Giudice, S. (1987). Human cerebral hemispheres develop at different rates and ages. *Science*, 236, 1110–13.

Thelen, E. (1989). Self-organization in developmental processes: Can systems approaches work? In M. Gunnar and E. Thelen (eds), *Systems and Development: The Minnesota Symposia in Child Psychology*. Hillsdale, NJ: Erlbaum.

Thelen, E., Corbetta, D., Kamm, K, Spencer, J.P., Schneider, K. and Zernicke, R.F. (1993). The transition to reaching: Mapping intention and intrinsic dynamics. *Child Development*, 64, 1058–98.

Thomas, A. and Chess, S. (1986). The New York Longitudinal Study: From infancy to early adult life. In R. Plomin and J. Dunn (eds), *The Study of Temperament: Changes, Continuities and Challenges*. Hillsdale, NJ: Erlbaum.

Tomlinson-Keasey, C., Eisert, D.C., Kahle, L.R., Hardy-Brown, K. and Keasey, B. (1978). The structure of concrete operational thought. *Child Development*, 50, 1153–63.

Turvey, M.T. and Fitzpatrick, P. (1993). Commentary: Development of perception–action systems and general principles of pattern formation. *Child Development*, 64, 1175–90.

Valsiner, J. (1987). *Culture and the Development of Children's Action: A Cultural–Historical Theory of Developmental Psychology*. New York: Wiley.

Valsiner, J. (1991) Introduction: Social co-construction of psychological development from a comparative-cultural perspective. In J. Valsiner (ed.), *Child Development within Culturally Structured Environments. Volume III: Comparative-cultural and Constructivist Perspectives*. Norwood, NJ: Ablex.

van der Maas, H. and Molenaar, P. (1992). A catastrophe-theoretical approach to cognitive development. *Psychological Review*, 99, 395–417.

van der Maas, H. (1993). *Catastrophe Analysis of Stage-wise Cognitive Development: Model, Method and Applications*. University of Amsterdam: Doctoral dissertation.

van der Veer, R. and Valsiner, J. (1992). Voices at play: Understanding van der Veer and Valsiner. *Comenius*, 48, 423–9.

van Geert, P. (1985). Sociocultural reproduction and individual mental development. *Cognitive Systems*, 1(3), 207–31.

van Geert, P. (1986). The structure of developmental theories. In P. van Geert (ed.), *Theory Building in Developmental Psychology*. Amsterdam: North Holland.

van Geert, P. (1986a). The concept of development. In P. van Geert (ed.), *Theory Building in Developmental Psychology*. Amsterdam: North Holland.

van Geert, P. (1986b). The structure of developmental theories. In P. van Geert (ed.), *Theory Building in Developmental Psychology*. Amsterdam: North Holland.

van Geert, P. (1987a). The structure of developmental theories: A generative approach. *Human Development*, 30(3), 160–77.

van Geert, P. (1987b). The structure of Erikson's model of the Eight Ages of Man: A generative approach. *Human Development*, 30(5), 236–54.

van Geert, P. (1987c). The structure of Gal'perin's theory of the formation of mental acts: A generative approach. *Human Development*, **30**(6), 355–81.

van Geert, P. (1988). A graph theoretical approach to the structure of developmental models. *Human Development*, **31**(2), 107–35.

van Geert, P. (1990). Theoretical problems in developmental psychology. In P. van Geert and L. Mos (eds), *Annals of Theoretical Psychology: Developmental Psychology*. New York: Plenum.

van Geert, P. (1991). A dynamic systems model of cognitive and language growth. *Psychological Review*, **98**, 3–53.

van Geert, P. (1992a). The complicated dynamics of a simple interaction model. Unpublished paper.

van Geert, P. (1992b). Vygotsky's dynamic systems. *Comenius*, **48**, 383–401.

van Geert, P. (1992c). The dynamics of developmental sequences: Towards a calculus for developmental theory. Unpublished paper.

van Geert, P. (1993). A dynamic systems model of cognitive growth: competition and support under limited resource conditions. In L.B. Smith and E. Thelen (eds), *A Dynamic Systems Approach to Development: Applications*. Cambridge, MA: MIT Press.

van Geert, P. (1994a). Dynamics of development. In R. Port and T. van Gelder (ed.), *Mind as Motion*. Cambridge, MA: MIT Press.

van Geert, P. (1994b). Vygotskyan Dynamics of Development. *Human Development*, **37**.

Vygotsky, L.S. (1978). *Mind in Society: The Development of Higher Psychological Processes*. Cambridge, MA: Harvard University Press.

Waddington, C.H. (1957). *The Strategy of the Genes: A Discussion of Some Aspects of Theoretical Biology*. London: Allen and Unwin.

Werner, H. (1948). *Comparative Psychology of Mental Development*. New York: Science Editions.

Winfree, A.T. (1987). *The Timing of Biological Clocks*. New York: Scientific American Library.

Zajonc, R.B. and Markus, G.B. (1975). Birth order and intellectual development. *Psychological Review*, **82**, 74–88.

Zeeman, E.C. (1976). Catastrophe theory. *Scientific American*, **234**, 65–83.

Index

Index